The Four Gospels and the Jesus Tradition

John F. O'Grady

PAULIST PRESS
New York/Mahwah, N.J.

Library of Congress Cataloging-in-Publication Data

O'Grady, John F.
    The four gospels and the Jesus tradition/John F. O'Grady.
        p.   cm.
    Bibliography: p.
    ISBN 0-8091-3085-8
    1. Bible. N.T. Gospels—Criticism, interpretation, etc.
    2. Jesus Christ—History of doctrines—Early church, ca. 30-600.
    I. Title.
    BS2555.2.04   1989
    226'.06—dc20   89-33659
                                                                        CIP

Published by Paulist Press
997 Macarthur Boulevard
Mahwah, New Jersey 07430

Printed and bound in the
United States of America

Contents

V. THE JESUS TRADITION AND MERCY: LUKE

■ Dedication ■

*A friend loves at all times,
and a brother is born for adversity.*
Proverbs 17:17

For Dean Albert Palamides
and
The Rev. Daniel Stanley Siwek

Preface

*T*he Jesus tradition fascinates me. After more than fifteen years of studying and teaching I think that I have some grasp of what Jesus meant to some members of the early Christian community. I realize, however, that what I understand is only part of the Jesus tradition, for it continues, as people of faith respond to him and accept him into their lives.

This work is limited. It deals only with the four gospels. Thus, it leaves out the whole understanding of Jesus for Paul and the later works of the New Testament. One could even say it is necessary to distinguish the early Paul and the later Paul and how he understood Jesus and grew in that understanding. The scope is narrow. I am concerned only with the gospels.

Development surely took place. Any reading of the New Testament shows that. But just how much and when the development occurred remains problematic. We can compare the gospels and see the development, but it is not always clear why the development took place. I hope in this cursory approach to the four gospels to show some reasons for the development. I propose not just to see what happened in the past but to help Christians to continue to remain open to development in the present and in the future. If the Jesus tradition continues, then it will change as people change.

I anticipate a college level audience: those who are taking a course in Jesus or the gospels. I also envision this book being helpful for people who want to read and think and pray about Jesus and their faith in him. The work is not exhaustive but rather serves as an introduction to the general themes that run throughout the gospels. I have been selective with the hope that my choice will encourage further study. I have also tried to avoid long lists of biblical references and long footnotes. As an introductory text in the gospels, I have

1

attempted to incorporate the best of contemporary New Testament scholarship. Such, I hope, will encourage people to do further reading of the bibliography provided.

The reader need not read the gospel text along with the chapters. Once you have completed the section on a gospel I would suggest that you read the gospel in question from beginning to end. I would also suggest that you write down, after each chapter in the gospel, anything that in particular impressed you. When you read the gospel, again in its entirety, continue the same practice. Note how at different times and at different moments in life the gospel will speak differently to you. Save your reflections, and perhaps years later you will rediscover them and again the gospel will continue its task of bearing testimony.

The material on the gospel of Mark as well as the second chapter of the first section has largely been published earlier in my book: *Mark: The Sorrowful Gospel.* I have revised it completely, but anyone who has read the earlier book will find the material familiar.

Some may wonder about the order of treatment. I present the gospel of John after the gospel of Mark rather than the usual approach of the three synoptics and then John. I wanted the reader to experience the unusual approach of the author of John immediately after studying Mark. In this way, I believe, the reader will better appreciate the differences in the four gospels.

Years ago, Rev. Joseph P. McClain, C.M., a professor of systematics, chided me: "You will learn much faster if you learn willingly from others." I recall the context of the remark. Evidently I was not too willing to learn too much from others. Years later I know that I have learned much from the scholars of the gospels. I had the good pleasure to be a student of Rev. Raymond Brown, S.S., an expert on John; I was at the Biblical Institute with Rev. John Meier when he was working on his study of Matthew. Over the years I have learned much from Rev. Jerome Kodell, O.S.B., and Rev. Robert O'Toole, S.J., both experts on Luke/Acts, and recall with fondness the years I was a colleague of Rev. Theodore Weeden, an expert on Mark. I have learned from them all, as well as from students in Albany, Rochester, Pittsburgh, and Miami. I learned faster as I willingly learned from others.

I hope that this work will contribute to the understanding of the faith of the early Christian community and strengthen the love that binds all followers of Jesus together. Since all believers share in the common pursuit of the reign of God and the experience of salvation, these efforts to unfold the Jesus tradition in the early church may be of assistance to others.

Since coming to Barry University I have been supported and encouraged by many people, but especially Dr. J. Patrick Lee, Academic Vice-President and Dr. Eileen McDonough, Dean of Arts and Sciences. To them I offer gratitude. Dr. Mary Ann Jungbauer offered me immeasurable service in proofreading the text. I offer her my gratitude as well. Finally Linda Marcus put up with my frenetic pace as I neared completion of the manuscript. I am also grateful to my graduate assistant, Karen O'Neill, who not only assisted in the typing of this manuscript but also performed many other services that have made this a better book.

The sunshine of south Florida has made me conscious of the goodness of creation. I hope that some of that sunshine is visible in this work as people seek in their own way to understand the Jesus tradition.

Miami, 1988

■ PART I ■

The Jesus Tradition

1.

The Early Faith Formulation

*T*he phrase "Jesus tradition" may sound unfamiliar to many Christians, but in fact the meaning of this phrase is the foundation of Christianity. Who was Jesus and how was he understood by the early church? How do Christians understand him today? What has been handed on from generation to generation? How has this meaning of Jesus been understood and what development took place?

Over the past two thousand years Christians have been handing on the meaning of Jesus, or the tradition of Jesus. People have come to understand who he was for others before them, and in learning his meaning for those who preceded in faith, Christians have discovered what Jesus means today. The phrase is apt. It portrays in a few words that a person and his meaning have been handed on. The understanding of Jesus has progressed from century to century, culture to culture, individual to individual.

This book deals with the Jesus tradition—not how Jesus was understood over the two thousand years of Christianity (that would require a library) but rather how Jesus was understood by the writers of the four gospels. The reader will quickly learn that precisely because we are involved with a tradition, development took place even among the earliest Christian communities. They knew that they were being faithful to Jesus but also recognized that they were passing on a tradition that would be affected by the faith of those who accepted the tradition and in turn passed it on.

Beginnings are a good place to start, and so this work starts not with the gospels but with the earliest faith formulae of the early church: those short and succinct expressions of faith that attempted to capture the meaning of Jesus for his first followers. What elements of the understanding of Jesus, of christology, were primordial and most ancient in the early church?

Since we are involved with a tradition, an evolution in understanding would naturally follow from the time of the apostles to the formation of the New Testament, and then, in the succeeding centuries, in the development of christological doctrine. The period of development, however, in the time of the formation of the New Testament, differs from the development in the earliest centuries of Christianity. In the former, the church first identified certain formulas as expressing its faith in Jesus. The later development was further unfolding of this earliest understanding of Jesus.

Raymond Brown presents an historical progression working backward from the resurrection of Jesus to his pre-existence. The Acts of the Apostles proclaims Jesus as Lord and messiah in his resurrection (Acts 2:36). Mark has Jesus proclaimed Son of God in his baptism (Mk 1:11); Matthew proclaims Jesus as God's Son in his conception (Mt 1:18–25) as does Luke (Lk 1:31–35), and finally the last written gospel, John, proclaims Jesus as the incarnation of the eternal Word of God (Jn 1:1–14). Such a progression helps us understand the development that took place as the early church struggled to understand Jesus and formulate his meaning in a tradition that could be passed on to future generations. We are accustomed to accept the most recent of formulations: Jesus is the incarnation of the pre-existent Word of God. Such has been part of every generation of Christians for centuries. But what was the earliest formulation of faith? What were some of the primitive creeds that helped establish this Jesus tradition?

Let me begin by saying that we do not know the most ancient formula of faith and probably never will. The evidence from the New Testament gives several possibilities, with scholars divided on all sides. The writings of the New Testament are collections of pericopes which have been theologically elaborated over a long period of time, and thus we cannot easily detect in these writings the earliest formulas of Christian faith in Jesus. We can, however, come to some general conclusions.

Some see certain formulae in Acts as most ancient:

God exalted him at his right hand as leader and savior, to give repentance to Israel and forgiveness of sins (Acts 5:31).

God has made him both Lord and Christ, this Jesus whom you crucified (Acts 2:36).

But these and other formulae in Acts are already theologically elaborated. Even the very ancient "Maranatha," "Come Lord Jesus," which seems most primitive, will not find acceptance as the earliest formulation among all scholars.

Some will attempt to construct the most primitive formula of faith from Matthew 25:31–46, the scene of the final judgment, or Mark 14:61, when the high priest asked Jesus: "Are you the Christ, the son of the Blessed?" or from Luke 12:8, when Jesus speaks of acceptance and denial of the Son of man. These last three probably have a Palestinian and Jewish Christian origin and would be older than any formula that would be associated with Gentile Christians. As much as this may help, it does not solve the question of the earliest formula in the Jesus tradition.

The general theory that Hellenistic christology is more recent and more developed than Palestinian and Jewish Christian christology makes sense. While I cannot hope to solve all of the scholarly problems I believe we can discover some basic tendencies and come to some plausible conclusions before we become involved in the development of early preaching and finally into the gospels.

Jewish Christian christology presented Jesus as raised by God after crucifixion. God justified him, and now Jesus lives with God. I do not think the earliest belief in Jesus expected another coming of Jesus, or a parousia. The eschatological time of salvation is now present, and the power of the Spirit proves this presence of salvation. Jesus has already been exalted by his resurrection and has experienced justification by God and now sits at the right hand of God in glory. People are called to respond in faith to him so that they will experience his Spirit.

In such a formulation of faith, no one was initially concerned with the origin of Jesus nor with his pre-existence nor with any future coming. He came; he preached; he died and was raised and exalted in his resurrection. The rest depends on people responding to him as Lord and Savior and accepting his Spirit.

But since Christian faith arose from Judaism and since Jesus was crucified, a death most scandalous to Jewish faith, soon Jewish Christians included in their faith formula a public manifestation of his exaltation. This gave birth to the inclusion of a parousia, or second coming, in early Christianity. He will appear before the universe as exalted Lord. "He may send the Christ appointed for you, Jesus, whom heaven must receive until the time for establishing all that God has spoken . . ." (Acts 3:30) and "you will see the Son of Man sitting at the right hand of Power, and coming with the clouds of heaven" (Mk 14:62) are theological formulations with the notion of a second coming. These formulas might have been early, but the inclusion of a ng points to a further development. Such development ... ken place in the early Jewish Christian community pre- ...y because of the need for Jewish Christians to overcome the unbecoming death by crucifixion. The earliest formulation of the Jesus tradition affirmed that Jesus had been exalted in his resurrection. Then the idea of a second coming or parousia was added.

The meaning of exaltation needs further study. In his resurrection Jesus received power and glory. He sits at the right hand of God. Perhaps the oldest formulation with exaltation is Acts 2:32–36: Jesus is raised (v. 32) and exalted (v. 33), and pours forth his Spirit (v. 33). Jesus became the messiah in power, able to communicate his Spirit when he was raised by God in resurrection. The early church understood the resurrection as the messianic exaltation of which Psalm 2 and Psalm 110 speak. God the Father constituted Jesus as messiah and Lord and Son of God in the resurrection. Exaltation means messiah in power and Lord of all.

Once the early community had recognized this new mode of life for Jesus, naturally they began to think of his life on earth. Several New Testament texts juxtapose the earthly life of Jesus with his heavenly life. Romans 1:3 refers to Jesus as descended "from David according to the flesh and designated Son of God in power according to the Spirit of holiness by his resurrection." 1 Peter 3:18 refers to Jesus as "put to death in the flesh but made alive in the spirit." 1 Timothy 3:16 states: "He was manifested in the flesh, vindicated in the Spirit."

In each of these citations writers in the church attempted to deal with the two modes of Jesus' life without any effort at ontology or metaphysics. Nor is there any notion of two natures in one person. Jesus once lived an earthly life and now he lives a heavenly life. That is all. The authors make no effort to deal with a pre-existence nor with a second coming. Later in the New Testament we will have the highly developed christology of John, and also of Paul. In this earliest stage Christians believed that Jesus once lived an earthly life and through the power of God he was raised from the dead. Now he lives a heavenly life capable of communicating his Spirit to anyone who will respond to him in faith. This, I believe, was the earliest formula of the Jesus tradition. With the passage of time, evolution took place and some development happened quickly, especially the notion of the second coming in glory. With this simple formulation we have the foundation for the development of christology not only in the New Testament but in the later centuries of the church.

In the task of preaching and collecting and handing on, the early

Christians always had in their hearts the ancient christological formula: "God has made him both Lord and Christ" (Acts 2:36). From this grew the diversity, but never the contradiction, that would give us the four gospels as well as the other writings of the New Testament and the formula of the councils of the church. Ultimately, they all speak of the meaning of Jesus: what he meant to those who preceded us in faith and what he means now and for future generations. Jesus is exalted now through his resurrection; previously he lived an earthly life, and now through his resurrection and exaltation he brings salvation. Here begins the Jesus tradition.

2.

The Earliest Preaching

When God the Father raised Jesus from the dead, he gave a clear affirmation to the teachings, life and death of the Christ. As a result, people could have their faith based on a sure foundation. Jesus was alive and exalted. Gradually these people who believed in Jesus gathered material about him. They should not be considered as the greatest of theologians nor even as the greatest writers. They were ordinary believers not only limited in their understanding but also circumscribed by the confines of first century Palestine. What they eventually produced for future generations were documents of faith.

■ Collections ■

The early followers of Jesus were Jews. "Man of Israel, hear these words" (Acts 2:22); "you know the word which he sent to Israel, preaching the good news of peace by Jesus Christ" (Acts 10:36). The early Jewish Christians began by public preaching. Gradually they experienced some need to preserve his teachings in writings. In all probability early in the history of Christianity they gathered collections of his miracles as well as groupings of some of his ethical teaching such as found in Matthew 13:31–33:

> *"The kingdom of heaven is like a grain of mustard seed which a man took and sowed in his field; it is the smallest of seeds, but when it has grown it is the greatest of shrubs and becomes a tree so that the birds of the air come and make nests in its branches."*
> *He told them another parable: "The kingdom of heaven*

12

*is like leaven which a woman took and hid in three measures
of meal until it was all leavened."*

Similar collections are found in the same chapter, verses 44–48:

*"The kingdom of heaven is like treasure hidden in a field
which a man found and covered up; then in his joy he goes
and sells all that he has and buys that field.*

*"Again the kingdom of heaven is like a merchant in
search of fine pearls who, on finding one pearl of great value,
went and sold all that he had and bought it.*

*"Again the kingdom of heaven is like a net which was
thrown into the sea and gathered fish of every sort; when it
was filled men drew it ashore and sat down and sorted the
good into vessels but threw away the bad."*

A similar collection of ethical sayings is found in Mark 9:37–50.
With these, the early community could preserve some of the traditions
about Jesus and begin to use them in their understanding of the
contemporary life of the community.

We also know that soon the Jesus tradition included an expectation of a second coming of a glorious messiah. Jewish Christians joined
the hope that Jesus would return and manifest himself to the acceptance of a suffering messiah. When he returns he will fulfill the expectations of Israel. Such thoughts caused an emphasis in the early
christology on the theology of exaltation, joined with a hope for a
parousia or second coming in glory.

■ **Gospel** ■

In the early groupings of writings about Jesus a community of
people, affected by his life and teachings, joined the meaning of Jesus,
his cross and resurrection, to his teaching message. They gathered
material for the sake of those who believe and will come to believe.
The result of all of this energy is a gospel.

The word gospel (*euaggelion*) is the reward for the transmission of
good news, or the good news itself. In the Hebrew of Isaiah 40:9, 52:7
and 61:1 the verb *bissar* means to proclaim the good news of salvation.
This will influence the New Testament.

The Old Testament tradition, as recorded in Second Isaiah, affirms a close link between the messenger of God who proclaimed the eschatological message of the inbreaking of God's royal rule and the message itself.

> *The Spirit of the Lord God is upon me because the Lord has anointed me to bring good tidings (bissar) to the afflicted (Is 61:1).*

> *How beautiful upon the mountains are the feet of him who brings good tidings (Is 52:7).*

The good tidings is the final living word of God preached, and not a document. In the New Testament the gospel is not a biography of Jesus, nor a chronicle of his life and activities, but a proclamation of the good news of salvation in Christ.

We can actually examine the four "gospels" as we have them now and discover that they are joined fragments, each with its own purpose and particular theological approach to the Jesus tradition. Born of the faith experience of Jesus by the early church each one gives a deeper understanding of the saving presence of God in Jesus. We can even speak of several layers in the gospels: the foundation which is proclaimed by Jesus himself, the oral tradition that passed from one generation to the next, preserving the meaning of Jesus for new converts, and, finally, the written traditions that were needed to preserve for all generations the Jesus tradition and which we call the gospels.

■ The Task of Interpretation ■

All of these layers and divisions, however, do not mean that the early church was not interested in the facts of Jesus' life. They clearly proclaimed "how God anointed Jesus of Nazareth with the Holy Spirit and with power, how he went about doing good and healing all that were oppressed by the devil, for God was with him" (Acts 10:38). The early community of believers, however, were never content to merely recount the facts. The good news then needed to be interpreted so that the meaning was evident to the world. The preachers of the good news were prophets, not reporters. They heard the word of God in Jesus and interpreted the religious dimension present or absent in life as a result of hearing that word. They explained the meaning of the events much as Moses acted the prophet and gave the meaning to the experience of the exodus and Mount Sinai to the early Jews.

Readers should be conscious of this interpretive task of the evangelists. None of the gospel writers, for example, present an objective account of the multiplication of the loaves. They told the story in a way that the listener could understand the meaning of the event. Compare Mark 6:34–44, wherein Jesus feeds his flock like a good shepherd, with Exodus 16 and Psalm 23. Just as God fed the people with manna in the desert, so will Jesus. Compare also John 6:4–14, with its clear eucharistic tones, with the last supper narratives in Matthew, Mark and Luke.

Each gospel contains both fact and interpretation, both history and theological reflection. In the gospels we see Jesus through the eyes of the faith of the early church. Surely the disciples had been eye-witnesses of what Jesus had said and done during his public ministry but they had often been unable to understand the meaning of the events:

"Who then is this that even the wind and sea obey him?"
(Mk 4:41).

But he said to them, "I have food to eat of which you do not know." So the disciples said to one another: "Has anyone brought him food?" (Jn 4:33).

The disciples began to clearly understand only after the resurrection. The Holy Spirit, given by Jesus, opened up their minds to know the meaning of what they had experienced with Jesus. Each gospel proclaims this Easter faith.

Those who preached the good news about Jesus carefully selected the traditions about Jesus which best revealed the meaning of his mission and the mystery of his person. The long process of the formation of the gospel traditions revealed the effort to unfold the meaning of Jesus. They interpreted in the selection of narratives and sayings. Not everything about Jesus had been included in the gospels: "Now Jesus did many other signs in the presence of his disciples which are not written in this book" (Jn 20:30), but only those things were recorded which the church understood to be important for itself and then for succeeding generations.

■ Events Changed in Context ■

Even the particular form used in the narratives about Jesus was carefully selected. The wording chosen also suggests some deeper meaning such as we have noted in the multiplication of the loaves. One evangelist will present a miracle of Jesus and relate the story to the power of Jesus, while another will take the same event and relate it to the problems of the early church. A change in context and the sequence of events can bring out more clearly the theological intent of the author. Matthew, for example, places the stilling of the storm in 8:18 in the context of the following of Jesus. Three times before he narrates the event he uses the word "to follow." He arranges the order of events and has a liturgical formula used by the disciples in their fear: "Save, Lord." Mark presents the same story in the context of the power of Jesus over evil and instead of the liturgical formula of Matthew has: "Teacher, do you not care if we are perishing?" (Mk 4:38). Matthew knew Mark. We can see how context and sequences can alter the meaning when we make the comparison.

Many such examples explain why modern scholars will not accept the gospels as histories in the sense of contemporary biography. The gospels are documents of faith coming from a community of faith attempting to proclaim the good news of salvation in Jesus to themselves and to others. The gospels contain history with specific theological interpretations.

Since we have spoken so frequently of the proclamation and have noted that the authors selected from a vast amount of material what was to be proclaimed, one might ask: What was the primitive organized preaching (kerygma) that the early community proclaimed and preserved for us? To discover the answer to this question we turn to the Acts of the Apostles and discover in some of the speeches recorded there the proclamation of the early church.

■   **The Primitive Preaching (Kerygma)**   ■

The speeches of the Acts of the Apostles attributed to Peter (2:14–36; 3:12–26; 4:8–12; 5:29–32; 10:34–43) are compositions by Luke, the author of Acts, and contain certain Lucan editorial adaptations. Scholars agree that these sermons, while the work of Luke, are not composed in their entirety. According to Dodd and others, they contain genuine reminiscences of a very primitive preaching about Jesus. These memories go back to the early days of the church's reflection upon the events which formed the formal point of its faith, even if they are not identified with the earliest faith formulae. They are memories theologically elaborated. The early apostolic preaching was the result of the recollection of the apostles of the ministry of Jesus, as well as the result of the experience of the risen Lord and the gift of the Spirit. This combination forms the fundamental unity for the entire New Testament and is discovered in the accounts in Acts.

■ Content of the Preaching ■

At the heart of the gospel message stands the crucified and risen Lord: "You crucified and killed him by the hands of lawless men. But God raised him up . . ." (Acts 2:23–24). This same proclamation is found in Acts 3:13–15; 4:10; 5:30; 10:39–40; 13:27–30.

Note the choice of words used to describe the crime committed by people and the response of God the Father:

> *"do away with" (2:23; 10:39; 13:28)*
> *"nail up" (2:33)*
> *"crucify" (2:36; 4:10)*
> *"kill" (3:15)*
> *"murder" (5:30)*
> *"hang up" (5:30; 10:39)*
>
> *"God raised him up" (2:32; 3:26; 5:30; 13:33, 37)*
> *"glorified" (3:13)*
> *"exalted" (2:32; 5:32)*

The early church preached a crucified and risen Lord. This created the heart of the kerygma and forms an inner circle that will be surrounded by other aspects of the meaning of Jesus.

The next element in the primitive preaching is the recollection of the ministry of Jesus: "Jesus of Nazareth, a man attested to you by God with mighty works and wonders and signs which God did through him in your midst . . ." (Acts 2:22), or, more simply put: "He went about doing good" (Acts 10:38). This forms part of the first outer circle to be completed by the sending of the Spirit by Jesus: "Having received from the Father the promise of the Holy Spirit he has poured out this which you see and hear" (Acts 2:33).

Finally, the second outer circle contains the preaching that Jesus was the fulfillment of Old Testament expectations and he will come again as judge: "He is the one ordained by God to be the judge of the living and the dead" (Acts 10:42). The Jesus tradition as recorded in these sermons in Acts includes in this outer circle the second coming, even if originally this was not part of the earliest faith formula of Jesus. The early Jewish Christians preached Jesus as the fulfillment of the Old Testament as well as one who would come again. They reflected on their own Jewish traditions. Later, for Gentile Christians the fulfillment of the Old Testament will not seem so necessary, and even the second coming will lessen in importance, as we shall see in the Johannine tradition.

This preaching effected a religious experience in the listener, a call to repentance, a change in the way of living. Believers turned over a new leaf by making an act of faith, sealed by the acceptance of baptism: "Repent and be baptized, every one of you, in the name of Jesus Christ for the forgiveness of your sins" (Acts 2:38).

From this brief summary of the content of the early preaching the primitive character of the church's appreciation of Jesus becomes evident. The early preaching expressed no concern about the origin of Jesus, nor of his pre-existence. No explicit statement as to the peculiar relationship between God and Jesus as his only divine Son forms part of this earliest preaching. Nor do we find any explicit statement (such as 1 Corinthians 15:3: "Christ died for our sins") of the redemptive purpose of the death of Jesus. Finally, they do not allude to the love of God or of Jesus as motivation in effecting this good news of salvation. God offered salvation to all through Jesus. The explanation of motivation will come later.

My comments do not imply that the early preachers did not have a profound understanding of Jesus. They understood his meaning and emphasized what was essential for faith. Readers today must see the preaching as it was and not read back into it what we have learned from later New Testament writings as well as two thousand years of Christian tradition. Perhaps we can better appreciate this preaching if we pay close attention to the titles used in these texts.

■   Titles for Jesus: Servant   ■

Jesus is God's servant (Mk 3:13). The apostolic church very early in its reflection found in the theme of the suffering and glorified servant of God a most congenial vehicle for expressing something of the personal attitude of Jesus. We shall see later how this combination becomes particularly dear to Mark and his gospel. The glorified servant suffered and now is present to the Christian community; "God having raised up his servant sent him to you first, to bless you in turning every one of you from your wickedness" (Acts 3:26).

■ Messiah ■

Jesus is also called the anointed, the messiah, the Christ. This use in the primitive preaching testifies that Jesus fulfilled the divinely given messianic hopes of Israel. "Let the house of Israel therefore know assuredly that God has made him both Lord and Christ . . ." (Acts 2:36; see also 3:18; 10:36). At the second coming the exalted Jesus would enter into his full messianic function: "He may send the Christ appointed for you, Jesus, whom heaven must receive until the time for establishing all that God spoke by the mouth of his holy prophets from of old" (Acts 3:20–21). Jewish Christians would emphasize this title.

■ Prophet ■

The archaic designation of Jesus as prophet in Acts 3:22 probably took its origin from Deuteronomy 18:15 where Moses predicts the coming of another prophet like himself. This title seems to have fallen from use quickly, with only John 1:45 preserving the title for Jesus, while the other evangelists tended to identify the Baptizer with the prophet of the end times (Mk 9:12–13). Certainly Jesus was a prophet in the Old Testament tradition of one who spoke the word of God and who interpreted the present scene in the light of the presence of God. But for the early church he was more than just a prophet. This would account for the short-lived use of this designation.

■ Lord ■

Lord seems to imply divinity. In its Aramaic form (*Mari*) it seems to have been used as an honorific title for Jesus during his ministry. More significant is the liturgical use of the phrase: *Maran atha,* "Come, our Lord," which was probably an eucharistic acclamation expressing faith in the divine character of Jesus (1 Cor 16:22; Rev 22:21).

Modern scholars are divided as to whether the title "Lord" actually expressed the Christian belief in the divinity of Jesus. It should be recalled that the Greek translation of the Old Testament, the Septuagint (LXX), rendered the sacred name of YHWH as *Kyrios,* Lord. Since the preaching spoke of Jesus as exalted, it could be that his unique relationship to the Father accounted for the evolution of the title "Lord" as a divine title for the exalted Christ.

■ **Judge** ■

We have noted that Jesus is the judge of the living and dead (Acts 10:42; 17:30–31). In Israel God alone judges (Gen 18:25). Now Jesus in the primitive preaching shares in that prerogative.

■ **Savior** ■

Finally, Jesus is the savior (Acts 5:31; 13:23). He will save his people from evil and from the sense of despair that often seems to accompany human life. His saving presence will be felt in the exultant shout: "What shall we do to be saved?" This preaching was directed to outsiders to call them to conversion. The same testimony is given within the heart of the community when the apostles bear witness to Jesus:

> *Now the company of those who believed were of one heart and soul and no one said any of the things he possessed was his own but they had everything in common. With great power the apostles gave their testimony to the resurrection of the Lord Jesus (Acts 4:32–33).*

The members of the community "devoted themselves to the apostles' teaching" (Acts 2:42). Thus this preaching will be the unity not only of the gospels but also of the epistles and the whole New Testament. Jesus is preached as Lord and savior. It is his person and his word and his work enshrined in the primitive preaching which unifies not only the New Testament but all of Christianity.

When we look at the gospels we can see that they are the fourfold articulation of the early preaching, the kerygma. Each one has its own genius, born more of the creative dynamism of the Spirit than a mere result of words and deeds. The gospels are the good news springing

from the living witness of Christian faith by four privileged representatives of the apostolic church. Each author interpreted to serve the
divine purpose of preaching the saving truth of the word of salvation.

> *Brethren, sons of the family of Abraham, and those among
> you that fear God, to us has been sent the message of salva-
> tion (Acts 13:26).*

Further Study

C. H. Dodd, *The Apostolic Preaching and Its Development.*
J. Rohde, *Rediscovering the Teachings of the Evangelists.*

■ PART II ■

The Jesus Tradition and the Cross: Mark

1.

Mark:
The Need for a Gospel

---

*T*he early preachers of Jesus challenged listeners to change their way of living and become part of God's kingdom. From what we have already seen, very soon the early followers of Jesus believed in an imminent return of Jesus in glory, even if this was not the most primitive understanding of exaltation. When he returned God's reign would be evident visibly and would do away with the then-known political structures. With such a purview the attention was centered not on the past, the beginning of the kingdom in Jesus, but on the immediate future which would break into the present time. Their concern for the present was seen as preparation for the fullness of the kingdom about to come.

In this context, an elaborative effort to preserve in detail past events would seem unnecessary. If Christ were coming quickly there was no need to be greatly concerned about the future generations nor was there a felt need to systematize the life and teaching of Jesus. All this seems evident in a close reading of the earliest writings of the New Testament.

Such a preoccupation with the future, however, does not mean that they were disinterested in the historical Jesus. If Jesus inaugurated the kingdom of God and did so as an itinerant preacher in Palestine, then those who experienced him as the risen Lord, through the preaching of the apostles, developed a great interest in his teaching as well as the events associated with his life. It was only natural that anecdotes would be preserved and orally transmitted. People would remember incidents in their experience of the earthly Jesus and tell others. Bultmann's study of the synoptic tradition shows that sayings of Jesus, his miracles, his parables, were circulated throughout the Mediterranean world by Christian missionaries. Specific sayings of the Lord would be used to settle new problems of the early community such as in 1 Corinthians 7:10: "To the married I give charge, not I but the Lord, that the wife should not separate from her husband . . ."; or in the same epistle, 9:14: "In the same way the Lord commanded that those who proclaim the gospel should get their living by the gospel." The problem of apostasy and poorly grounded faith would give rise to the interpretation of the parable of the sower recorded, for example in Mark 4:14–20.

■ Freedom of the Evangelists ■

Early in the history of Christianity individuals collected sayings of Jesus, parables, miracle stories, collections of quotations which might refer to him from the Old Testament. They also seemed to exercise a great sense of freedom in using these materials. We have already seen how Matthew and Mark present the stilling of the storm at sea. Theological intent looms more important than the particular details. The parable of the sower could become an allegory with each example of the fallen seed assigned to a group of people actually existing in the early church. The multiplication of the loaves could be modified to suit the purpose of John as well as Mark. Even Paul, who did not know the early Jesus, felt free to amplify the sayings of the Lord to suit his purpose. How could this be?

The early church believed that Jesus himself is God's Word. If he was present in his community, they need have no great concern about the exact words of the earthly Jesus. The risen Lord, as God's Word, lives, still guiding the church. Luke makes this explicit as he recounts the meeting on the road to Emmaus: "And beginning with Moses and all the prophets he interpreted to them in all the scriptures the things concerning himself" (Lk 24:27). Jesus continues to teach his church as the risen Lord.

John continues the same thought through the presence of the Spirit: "But the counselor, the Holy Spirit, whom the Father will send in my name, he will teach you all things" (Jn 14:26). "When the Spirit of truth comes he will guide you into all the truth" (Jn 16:13). The early Church experienced the presence of the risen Lord and thus, with the presence of Jesus, what he had done as the earthly master was reshaped to meet the new conditions of the times. Jesus would continue to speak to his followers, but now through the church.

Remembering isolated events in the life of Jesus or even collecting some of his sayings and using them to respond to the needs of the times makes eminent sense. But to combine these units into a literary form, which we call gospel, still raises some unanswered questions. What caused the early church to develop this literary form?

■ Why Write a Gospel? ■

Some crisis, some problem or turning point, some new understanding, had to have occurred which made it imperative for the early church to gather carefully the traditions about Jesus and combine them into an orderly sequence. During this period, however, the church did have literary activity. The letters of Paul predate the gospels by anywhere from fifteen to thirty years. This literary form, the letters, met the missionary and theological need for the initial period of preaching, but then another form of literary activity arose which culminated in the four gospels.

In some sense we can never adequately answer why the gospels were written. Luke informs us that he wrote his gospel for Theophilus to help him:

> It seemed good to me also, having followed all things closely for some time past, to write an orderly account for you, most excellent Theophilus, that you may know the truth concerning the things of which you have been informed (Lk 1:3–4).

John tells us that he wrote his gospel so that we may believe:

> These are written that you may believe that Jesus is the Christ, the Son of God, and that believing you may have life in his name (Jn 20:31).

No doubt these are partial answers since no gospel is the work of an isolated individual. If gospels arose they met the need not of a literary author alone, but the needs of a Christian community. As each gospel is different, so the particular needs of the individual communities must have been different.

We also know that as the church grew, questions continued to arise. People wanted to know more about Jesus. As the parousia was delayed a sense of pain was experienced as people awaited the return in glory. A concern for preserving accurately the material about Jesus would have developed, especially as those who knew him personally experienced death. Even as they awaited a coming in glory, now delayed, people would have been interested in how he lived as a man.

Some historical crisis could also have precipitated the writing of a gospel. We know that there were conflicts between Jewish Christians and the Gentile converts. Did one have to become a Jew first in order to be a follower of Jesus? A gospel could help solve some of these tensions and begin to move toward a final resolution. A gospel that could give an opening for a Gentile community could give a direction in which the church could move. For some authors today, the crisis between synagogue and church is evident in the fourth gospel and helped the coming into being of that gospel.

All such crises, as well as the natural tendency to preserve traditions, were involved in the origin of the gospels. We cannot, however, understand the gospels together without seeing that each one has its own peculiar characteristics. We have to speak not only of the origins of the gospels but the origin of the individual gospel, and we begin with the origin of the gospel of Mark.

■   Mark: The First Gospel   ■

Scholars are not completely in agreement, but in general we can say that the majority of New Testament scholarship favors the viewpoint that the gospel of Mark was the first written gospel. (W. Farmer holds to the priority of Matthew, as do many of his followers.) Then Luke and Matthew used Mark as one of their sources for their own gospels, along with a collection of sayings of Jesus called "Q" and certain other material proper to each evangelist.

If Mark was the first, and if Matthew and Luke used Mark, we can understand Matthew and Luke by examining how they react to Mark. Unfortunately, for Mark we have no prior means of comparison. If we hope to understand the meaning of Mark as he arranged the traditions of Jesus we have to read Mark himself and read most carefully.

In the past Mark was often thought to be the simplest of the gospels and the one more closely related to the historical ministry of Jesus without any great theological reflection. More recent work on Mark by Marxsen, Trocme, Kee, Weeden, and others, however, shows the gospel to be like the other efforts to preserve the Jesus tradition. The gospel has its own theological perspective and should not be judged more historically accurate nor less historically accurate than the other three gospels. The days of thinking of Mark as somewhat simplistic with absurd transitions and unresolved conflicts are over. The author writes with subtlety, with a sophisticated theological mind as he faced the problem of ordering a vast amount of material into an orderly fashion. His genius was recognized by no less authorities than the authors of Matthew and Luke who trust his basic framework and rework their own interpretation of the meaning of the Jesus tradition in light of his approach.

Mark may not have the depth of John or Paul, but when people study this gospel they learn the insights of Mark. Scholars today continue to probe into the origin and meaning of the first of the gospels with a fresh approach. Mark saw the need to create a gospel. If we are to understand the gospel he offered us, and the early church, we have to discover the need that Mark himself experienced as well as the need of the early followers of the Lord for a written record of the Jesus tradition.

■ History in Mark ■

On first reading it might seem that Mark constructed his gospel on the actual historical event of Jesus. Jesus is presented in the gospel as preaching to the masses of people (chapters 1-8), but when faced with opposition he turns to the small band of followers and speaks only to them (chapters 9-13). He does this, for he knows that he must die and they must eventually be prepared for his passing and carry on his preaching (chapters 14-16).

The historical analysis, however, contains many flaws upon closer examination. Upon reading Mark one might get the impression that he preached in the north, went south to Jerusalem and died, all in one year with one visit to the holy city. John, however, has many visits to Jerusalem and has at least a three year public ministry, unlike the one year of Mark. Which gospel is historically accurate? Some might be tempted to construct an historical account of Jesus by combining the details of all four gospels. Such was attempted in the nineteenth century but with the conclusion that the gospels cannot be considered historically accurate accounts of the life of Jesus. The same statement must be true for any individual gospel. Accurate history is not the concern of Mark.

Mark, Achtemeier shows us, also seems to get quite confused when he tries to deal with chronology. In Mark 4:35 we learn that evening had come, but before we have any reference to time again in Mark 6:2, Jesus crossed the sea, stilled the storm, healed the Gerasene

demoniac, made another trip across the sea, healed the woman with a
flow of blood, went to the house of Jairus, and returned to his own
country. Evidently chronology is not important for Mark. Nor can we
say the geography was his concern. He frequently becomes confused
as to location. The Sea of Galilee, for example, is not in the midst of
the decapolis (ten cities).

Perhaps we could look at the same material and construct the
gospel theologically. The opposition in Galilee encouraged Jesus to
turn to the heart of Judaism—Jerusalem. He desired to help people to
understand the good news which began in his preaching and would
conclude in his death. Mark expressed this theological approach in his
gospel.

■ Theology, Not History ■

Needless to say, Mark has arranged his testimony to Jesus not
because of history, nor with attention to detail of time and place, but
for a purpose that can only be explained through a particular theology.
If we can understand the theological purpose of Mark we are well on
the way to understanding the gospel. Such a process, however, is not
an easy adventure. We have already noted that Mark used sources, the
collections of sayings, stories, about Jesus. We can actually sift out
some of these. This process is known as form criticism. This shows us
that the material had circulated long enough orally to be refined and
made into a set pattern. Such an effort would in itself involve some
theological purpose which would have been different from the theological purpose of Mark. The compilers of these traditions, those
members of the early church communities who wished to preserve the
sayings or anecdotes of Jesus, would have their own reasons. They
expressed these reasons in the material they collected and how they
arranged it. Such material would reflect the level of theological development of the church in which it first circulated.

■ Levels in the Gospel ■

We have also noted that some of this material goes back to Jesus
himself, which is the first of the three levels found in any gospel: (1)
Jesus, (2) the collected traditions of the community which preserved
their understanding of Jesus, and, finally, (3) the gospels as actually
written by the evangelists. To try to reach through the authors of the

gospels, and to continue through the early community to grasp something of the historical Jesus, offers only limited possibility. We are too far removed in time and circumstance from the ministry of Jesus to construct a clearly delineated portrait of the Jesus of history. Thus, we need to be most cautious in making statements about the historical events in the career of Jesus or attestations about the exact words of Jesus. Very often these events and choice of words cannot be disentangled from the other levels of the gospel. The Jesus tradition is a tradition and not a verbatim record of what Jesus said and did.

■ The Purpose of Mark ■

All of this brings us back to the purpose of the gospel of Mark. Why did he gather the material together? How did he arrange things to suit his purpose? What was the need in his community to which his gospel could give a response?

As early as 1890 Kahler suggested that the gospel of Mark was a passion story with an extended introduction. This can be accepted as accurate with certain modifications. Since the passion and death of Jesus stands as the center of Markan theology, the gospel emphasizes the final destiny of Jesus, but Mark also deals with what Jesus taught and did.

A good example of the power of the passion is the way in which Mark treats John the Baptist. The tradition contained in Mark 1:2–8 portrays John as a forerunner of Jesus. Mark also makes him a forerunner of the passion of the Lord. This is the reason for the thematic synchronism in Mark 1:14: the catchword "to be handed over" points to Jesus being handed over during the passion. The association of the Pharisees and Herodians in Mark 3:6 is understood in the same way: there is a relationship between the people who have John executed and those who destroy Jesus.

The mention of the legend concerning the beheading of John the Baptist in Mark 6:14–29, between the sending out of the disciples and their return, may rest on similar grounds. Mark hardly needs this insertion (which disappoints the most elementary chronological expectation) in order to fill up the time between the sending out and the return of the disciples, as older exegetes supposed. This characteristically Markan technique of composing by inserting one story in the midst of another connects the Christian mission indirectly with the death of Jesus. According to Mark 1:1–14 and 3:6, the death of John the Baptist proleptically points to the death of Jesus. All of these passages conflate the fate of John the Baptist with Jesus. This relates the fate of Jesus to his passion at the outset of his ministry and thus illuminates the activity of Jesus from the perspective of the cross. Then the mission of the disciples is joined to the same context of the dying Lord. John comes, preaches, is handed over and dies; Jesus comes, preaches, is handed over and dies. The followers will preach, will be handed over, and they too will die, seems the logical conclusion.

■ Messianic Secret ■

Two other Marcan themes can be mentioned briefly. Often Jesus forbids any speaking of who he is. We face what has been called the "messianic secret in Mark." For years since Wrede first wrote his book on the messianic secret, scholars have tried to study the meaning of this tendency without any complete consensus. Can it be that the need for silence is due to the lack of an understanding of a suffering messiah?

■ Disciples' Misunderstanding ■

A second Marcan theme is the apparent lack of understanding of Jesus on the part of the apostles. Can we say the same thing with regard to the followers of Jesus in the time of Mark—that their lack of understanding was their failure to see the meaning of the suffering and death of their Lord?

To return to the purpose of this chapter: to understand the meaning of the gospel of Mark demands a clear appreciation of how he ordered the traditions about Jesus to suit the needs of his community. The key to understanding Mark is to know the meaning of the death of Jesus and how his ministry prepared for this death. This perspective colors the writing of Mark, and within this perspective we have to read the final product, the gospel. Mark chose to write an orderly account of the meaning of Jesus by concentrating on his cross and death. As we study the passion in Mark we will receive further insights into the community for which he wrote, which will in turn add to our awareness of his purpose in writing.

Further Study

W. Kelber, *The Kingdom in Mark.*
W. Marxsen, *Mark the Evangelist.*
P. Achtemeier, *Mark.*

2.

The Passion

Since the advent of biblical criticism scholars have studied the synoptic gospels to discover the teachings and deeds of Jesus. They examined the way in which the early church transmitted and altered these traditions and the theological concerns of the individual evangelists. Although the passion narratives form the climax of the gospels and occupy about fifteen percent of the tradition, the research had been directed more to the pre-passion parts of the gospels. Several reasons account for this tendency to overlook the passion account. Some thought that this material was the most traditional and most historical and thus offered the least amount of theological research. Also, since it was so closely related to the historical Jesus, there would be little influence coming from the early church and even less from the individual evangelists.

In contrast to the earlier stages of study, the last decade has witnessed an explosion in studies on the passion accounts. Each passion narrative arises as much a result of theological reflections as any other part of the gospels. This is especially true for Mark. In the passion narrative, we not only have the climax of the gospel, but the climax of the theology of Mark. The recent collection of articles on the passion edited by Kelber gives an excellent survey of the material involved.

We have already noted that for Mark, Jesus is himself the model for discipleship. Just as Jesus was given up, as was John, so will the disciples. Mark sees Jesus as the obedient and righteous Son of man who suffers. We can learn the meaning of the passion by studying the predictions of the passion in Mark 8:22–10:52.

■ Cures of Blind Men ■

Surrounding this section, the central section of the gospel, Mark placed the healing of the blind men in 8:22–26 and 10:46–52. Throughout the gospel Mark seems to wish to give a catalogue of all of Jesus' cures. Out of the nine stories of healing, only one illness is shown occurring in more than one time—blindness—and these miracles surround the central section of the gospel. It cannot be by accident that the author chooses to situate his teaching on the meaning of the death of Jesus in this framework. When someone discovers the significance of the passion of the Lord, that person "sees"; the blindness is removed.

Throughout the gospel Jesus attempts to give sight to his disciples. He tries to teach them the meaning of his impending passion and death. Continually he fails to penetrate their understanding. The Jesus who could give sight to the physically blind could not give sight and understanding to his apostles. For Mark, this is one of the great tragic motifs of the gospel. As he tells his story, he also constantly reaches out beyond the disciples to his own listeners, attempting to help them to understand what the disciples had so significantly failed to understand: following a crucified Lord means accepting suffering.

Mark accomplishes this by three blocks of carefully constructed prediction units:

Predictions of the Passion

> *And he began to teach them that the Son of man must suffer many things and be rejected by the elders and the chief priests and the scribes and be killed, and after three days rise again (8:31).*

> *For he was teaching his disciples, saying to them, "The Son of man will be delivered into the hands of men and they will kill him; and when he is killed, after three days he will rise" (9:31).*

> *"Behold we are going up to Jerusalem; and the Son of man will be delivered to the chief priests and the scribes, and they will condemn him to death, and deliver him to the Gentiles; and they will mock him and spit upon him and scourge him and kill him; and after three days he will rise" (10:33–34).*

Misunderstanding of the Disciples

> And he said this plainly. And Peter took him and began to rebuke him, but turning and seeing his disciples he rebuked Peter and said, "Get behind me, Satan. For you are not on the side of God, but of men" (8:32–33).

> But they did not understand the saying and they were afraid to ask him (9:32).

> And James and John, the sons of Zebedee, came forward and said to him: "Teacher, we want you to do for us whatever we ask of you." And he said to them, "What do you want me to do for you?" And they said to him, "Grant us to sit one at your right hand and one at your left in your glory." But Jesus said to them, "You do not know what you are asking. Are you able to drink the cup that I drink or to be baptized with the baptism with which I am baptized?" And they said to him, "We are able." And Jesus said to them, "The cup that I drink you will drink, and the baptism with which I am baptized you will be baptized, but to sit at my right hand or at my left is not mine to grant, but it is for those for whom it has been prepared" (10:35–41).

Teaching by Jesus To Correct Misunderstanding

> And he called to him the multitude with his disciples and said to them, "If any man would come after me, let him deny himself and take up his cross and follow me. For whoever would save his life for my sake will lose it; and whoever loses his life for my sake and the gospel's will save it. For what does it profit a man to gain the whole world and forfeit his life? For what can a man give in return for his life? For whoever is ashamed of me and of my words in this adulterous and sinful generation, of him will the Son of man be ashamed, when he comes in the glory of his Father with the holy angels (8:34–9:1).

> And they came to Capernaum, and when he was in the house he asked them, "What were you discussing on the way?" But they were silent, for on the way they had discussed with one another who was the greatest. And he sat down and called the

twelve; and he said to them, "If anyone would be first he must be last of all and servant of all." And he took a child and put him in the midst of them, and taking him in his arms he said to them, "Whoever receives one such child in my name receives me; and whoever receives me receives not me but him who sent me" (9:33–37).

And Jesus called them and said to them, "You know that those who are supposed to rule over the Gentiles lord it over them, and their great men exercise authority over them. But it shall not be so among you; but whoever would be great among you must be your servant, and whoever would be first among you must be slave of all. For the Son of man also came not to be served but to serve and to give his life as a ransom for many" (10:42–45).

■ **The One Who Serves** ■

This final section closes with the climactic interpretation of the meaning of Jesus: he has come to serve and to give his life. The disciples do not understand. They are concerned with the Jesus of glory who will establish his kingdom and offer them a share. Jesus teaches them that the way of self-giving and suffering is his way, and it is also the way of his followers. As one studies these three predictions two things become evident: the variety in the references to the passion and the lack of variety in the references to the resurrection.

The references to the passion vary between the two distinctive ways of speaking of the passion of Jesus in the New Testament. The first uses the Greek work *dei* (must) which is often used to designate divine necessity, especially the divine necessity revealed in scripture ("Why do the scribes say that first Elijah *must* come?"—Mk 9:11; "Brethren, the scripture *had to be* fulfilled"—Acts 1:16). The second and third references use the word *paradidomai* (to deliver up) which is a technical term in the New Testament to describe the passion of Jesus ("For I received from the Lord what I also delivered to you, that the Lord Jesus on the night he was *delivered up* . . .—1 Cor 11:23). We have already seen that the same word is used in reference to John the Baptist (1:14), and it is used in Mark in connection with the potential fate of Christian martyrs in 13:9 ("For they will deliver you up to councils"). All are delivered up: John, Jesus and the disciples; each suffers a passion. One prediction speaks of divine necessity; the others speak of the passion common to all followers of the one true God.

■ Comparisons of the Predictions ■

The variations in the predictions go beyond the use of the above words. The first and third offer considerable details concerning the passion itself. The third almost summarizes the events in chapters 14–15. The second prediction is more terse to the point of bluntness. Such variations tend to highlight the sterotyped nature of the reference to the resurrection: "After three days rise again . . . after three days he will rise . . . after three days he will rise." Clearly, as Perrin shows in his study of the resurrection, Mark is not nearly so interested in the details of the resurrection as in the passion. He is interested in the resurrection, but he emphasized the passion to suit his theological purpose. This central section of the gospel merits a more careful analysis of the other material contained in this section.

■ Discipleship ■

Between the second and third block of material, Mark has inserted a teaching on the meaning of discipleship. Singlemindedness, divorce, acceptance of children and riches are discussed. Each involves the following of Jesus; his followers are of one mind; they honor their marital commitments; they accept children and live as God's children; they deal with riches carefully. The section ends with a pericope of hope and expectation of the age to come:

> Peter began to say to him, "Lo we have left everything and followed you." Jesus said, "Truly I say to you there is no one who has left house or brothers or sisters or mother or father or children or lands for my sake and for the gospel who will not receive a hundredfold now in this time, houses and brothers and sisters and mothers and children and lands with persecutions and in the age to come eternal life. But many that are first will be last and the last first" (10:28–31).

■ Transfiguration ■

The story of the transfiguration in this section (9:2–8) also functions as a message of hope and symbolizes the post-resurrection situation. Since Moses and Elijah were thought to be in heaven, when Jesus is transfigured, speaking with Moses and Elijah, Mark sees Jesus proleptically in the post-resurrection state and situation. This makes particular sense since Mark has no resurrection appearances of Jesus. Jesus lives in heaven with God, and with the ancient prophets. He will return to earth as the powerful and glorified Son of man.

The disciples within the story of the transfiguration are urged to obey the words of Jesus. In this context, the content of obedience concerns the true meaning of discipleship. The reference to Elijah in v. 13: "But I tell you that Elijah has come and they did to him whatever they pleased, as it is written of him," shows that the suffering of John the Baptist, Elijah returned, was also a way of suffering parallel to that of the Son of man and then of the disciples. Jesus specifically refers to John the Baptist, which, as we have seen, Mark identifies with the fate of Jesus. The healing of the boy after the transfiguration could also have some reference to the resurrection. The boy looked like a corpse so that the crowd judged him to be dead. When Jesus healed him, Mark may have been symbolizing that Jesus will enable others to rise from the dead and to be with God just as he would and be with God. The only condition is faith. Since Mark uses the healing of the blind men for symbolic purposes, he may be attempting the same thing in this pericope with the healing of the boy.

■ Anthropology, Not Christology ■

The motif and movement of the entire section is not so much on christology (although that is part of the meaning) but on anthropology: Mark wishes to speak about true discipleship. Jesus is the suffering Son of man and he is the model for all disciples. In writing, Mark is concerned not solely with the death of Jesus, but with his mode of living as well. The author wishes to present his way of suffering and his rejection, and finally in Mark 10:45 he climaxes his thinking in the servanthood of Jesus. Mark writes about the cross, but not the cross as making atonement for sins as much as the theology of the cross that involves suffering in obedience. God decided that his Son must suffer, and so the Son willingly accepts his fate. It must be. Thus God wills it. Mark patterns Jesus after the righteous sufferer in Psalm 22:

> *My God, my God why hast thou forsaken me. . . . Yet thou art holy, enthroned on the praises of Israel. . . . Yet thou art he who took me from the womb; thou didst keep me safe upon my mother's breast. Be not far from me, for trouble is near, and there is none to help (Ps 22:1, 3, 9, 11).*

Since Jesus exemplifies godly living in his ministry and in his dying, in his death we see the deepest meaning of the cross in Mark's theology. The death of Jesus lays open a quality of life which patterns and gives an example of what true life means for all. The true follower of Christ must take up his cross daily and follow the Lord; no optional road, no substitute and no other means exists by which a person can be a disciple. Jesus extends the offer only to the brave of heart. To find life is to live as Jesus did, which involves a share in his sufferings. The true believer will walk like Jesus:

> *For whoever is ashamed of me and of my word in this evil and adulterous generation, of him will the Son of man be ashamed when he comes in the glory of the Father with the holy angels (Mk 8:38–9:1).*

To be ashamed of Jesus means to reject his suffering. "My words" is the expectation on the part of Jesus that his disciples will follow him even if this entails the road to suffering. Mark brings his christology into the closest contact with the church and believer. He reveals the incarnational christology of power and depth that will pervade this gospel. Mark presents in his gospel an apocalyptic drama in which Mark and his community are self-consciously caught up in events they view as the end of history. The gospel portrays this drama in three acts.

■ Delivered Up ■

First John preaches and is delivered (Mk 1:14). Then Jesus preaches and he is delivered up (Mk 9:31; 10:33; 14:41). Finally the Christian preaches and is delivered up (Mk 13:9–13) with the hope directed toward the return of Jesus as the glorious Son of man: "And then they will see the Son of man coming in clouds in great power and glory" (Mk 13:26); ". . . and you will see the Son of man sitting at the right hand of power, and coming with the clouds of heaven" (Mk 14:62).

For Mark the cross and suffering are always in the foreground, but in the background, as the foundation for hope, looms the resurrection. The glorified Lord will bring his faithful followers to share in that same glory.

Further Study

W. Kelber, *The Passion in Mark.*
N. Perrin, *The Resurrection According to Matthew, Mark, and Luke.*
T. Weeden, *Mark: Traditions in Conflict.*

3.

The Son of Man

We have already seen that a principal aim of the gospel of Mark is his christology which carries with it an anthropology. The understanding of Jesus implies equally an understanding of what it means to be human. The evangelist presents the religious dimension of human life in the words of Jesus. The author leads the reader into a deeper understanding of Jesus himself as well as an appreciation of what it means to be a disciple.

■ A False Christology ■

T. Weeden believes that Mark emphasizes the christology of one who suffers before he is to enter into glory to counteract an appreciation of the glorious Christ without the willingness to accept the suffering, obedient Christ. A false christology of glory had affected some of the community, and thus Mark sought to correct this inadequate view of the Christian life with his insistence on the suffering Son of man. We shall return to this point later. For the present the reader should be aware that Mark carefully teaches that the messiah must suffer before he enters into his glory.

In spite of the classical work by Todt on *The Son of Man in the Synoptic Tradition,* no scholarly consensus exists concerning the precise meaning and importance of the title in pre-Christian tradition. The title surely means much for Mark, and it would be helpful to appreciate the origin and the meaning of the title in Judaism.

The phrase can mean simply "man" in a generic sense as found in Psalm 8:4:

*What is man that thou are mindful of him, or the Son of man
that thou dost care for him?*

This also may have been the meaning in the pre-Markan tradition as
found in Mark 2:28:

So the Son of man is Lord even of the sabbath.

The original meaning may have been that every man makes decisions
with regard to the rightful observance of the sabbath, since the sabbath was made for man and not vice versa. The uses of "man" and
"son of man" stand in parallelism. The original meaning of the story
of the disciples going through the fields of standing grain may have
been an effort on the part of Jesus to give "man," simply as a human
being, authority over the sabbath. No doubt, however, that in Mark
this meaning underlies the more important thought that Jesus as the
"Son of man" is actually "Lord" of the sabbath.

■ Old Testament Meaning ■

The Old Testament usage can be found in Daniel 7:13 in which
the title describes the heavenly figure in the fifth vision of Daniel.
Here the figure stands for the faithful remnant of Israel. The title is
also found in 1 Enoch and carries with it the theme of judgment
(chapters 46–53). In this usage the Son of man is also called the
anointed one, and the elect one. This joins the image of the Son of man
to the eschatological figure of the messiah of Israel.

These varied uses, joined with the meaning in Ezekiel, makes it
difficult to draw any definite conclusions as to the precise meaning of
the title in Judaism. By the time of Mark, however, the title had been
firmly attached to Jesus even if Jesus himself never actually used the
phrase.

■ Son of Man in Mark ■

N. Perrin has devoted much study to the meaning of the Son of
man in Mark. His conclusions are generally accepted. We can note
with Perrin that in Mark, Jesus himself alone used the title and always
in the presence of his disciples or the inner circle of Peter, James and
John. Certainly we can question whether Jesus ever actually used the

title himself and associated it with dying and rising. Mark alone among the synoptics used the title in this context. If Jesus actually used the title thusly, one would expect to find it in the other gospels. The use of the title in the gospel of John carries another nuance with the theme of suffering eliminated.

■ Two Levels of Meaning ■

In the use by Jesus two levels, or phases, can be distinguished. Five occurrences derive from traditional material at Mark's disposal and appear to have been left untouched by the evangelist:

. . . and how is it written of the Son of man that he should suffer many things and be treated with contempt (Mk 9:12).

And then they will see the Son of man coming in great power and glory (Mk 13:26).

For the Son of man goes as it is written of him but woe to that man by whom the Son of man is betrayed (Mk 14:21).

The hour has come; the Son of man is betrayed into the hands of sinners (Mk 14:41).

And you will see the Son of man sitting at the right hand of power and coming with the clouds of heaven (Mk 14:62).

Since these references seem to have been left untouched by Mark they must have been consistent with the peculiar Marcan emphasis in their original form, but tell us little about the originality of Marcan use.

Throughout the gospel the title refers to Jesus as the one who was betrayed (Mk 14:21) and arrested (Mk 14:41), who suffered (Mk 9:12) and died (Mk 10:45), who was raised from the dead (Mk 9:9) and was seated at God's right hand in heaven (Mk 14:26), and who would come at the end of the age to collect the faithful into the kingdom of God (Mk 13:26). The various uses of the title in Mark is important, but the use by Mark between 2:10 and 10:45 (excluding 9:12) are characteristically Marcan.

■ Power ■

In 2:10 and 2:28 Mark introduces the concept of the authority of the Son of man, his *exousia* (power) to forgive sins and to deal in an unorthodox way with the sabbath law. The primary element in Mark's christology connects the power (*exousia*) of Jesus with the work of his earthly life. The other synoptics make a similar connection but only when they have a clear dependence on the Marcan material. Even if the pre-Marcan tradition had hinted at the authority of the earthly Jesus, it was never definitely or explicitly stated. Mark added the emphasis on the power of the earthly Jesus.

■ Suffering ■

Suffering becomes a theme in the christology in the crucial Caesarea Philippi pericope. Mark has moved from a statement of the Son of man's authority in chapter 2 to the necessity of his suffering in 8:31 and to the apocalyptic authority in 8:38. With the passion prediction in 8:31 the evangelist binds together the Son of man's earthly and apocalyptic authority.

Mark's passion introduction (Mk 8:27–10:52), as previously noted, includes in each block a prediction of the passion followed by misunderstanding and a teaching about disciplehood. This central section of the gospel constitutes Mark's concept of discipleship and culminates in 10:45 with the theme of the servant for all. This treatment also climaxes the treatment by Mark of the Son of man.

A clear progression exists in the use peculiar to Mark from an understanding of the earthly authority of the Son of man, to the necessity of the suffering of the Son of man, and finally, to the apocalyptic authority with the final dramatization of the soteriological significance of the passion of Jesus. Mark unites all of these themes in his choice of title "Son of man."

■ Son of Man—Son of God ■

Mark used the title Son of man in a clear pattern in his gospel. He also juxtaposed it with the title Son of God to give a corrected understanding of belief in Jesus. He joined the earthly authority of Jesus as the Son of man to Jesus as the Son of God. In 3:11 a Marcan summary emphasizes that Jesus exercises his authority on earth as Son of God. In 2:10 and 2:28 Mark stresses the authority of Jesus as Son of man. In chapter 8:38 the tone is the apocalyptic authority of the Son of man, carefully linked by a time reference seven verses later to the voice of the transfiguration that addresses Jesus as "my beloved Son." The high priest asks Jesus if he is the Son of the Blessed, and Jesus replies by using the title Son of man (14:61–62). Mark relates the meaning of Son of God to the meaning of the Son of man.

Mark unites the various themes of suffering and apocalyptic authority and, finally, the soteriological significance by using the title Son of man in each case. The title was used before him in reference to the earthly ministry of Jesus. To this Mark joined the emphasis on "power." We have noted the use of the title in the apocalyptic literature in the Old Testament. Mark could take that title and adapt it easily to his own perspective. The title was also used in connection with the passion. Mark developed the passion predictions with the teaching about discipleship. Finally, the saying about service became soteriological in the affirmation that Jesus as Son of man came to serve others.

■ Threefold Purpose in Mark ■

A threefold purpose exists in the Marcan use of Son of man: Mark counteracted an emphasis on the glorious Christ by including the notion of the suffering Son of man. Secondly, this suffering forms part of the ministry and experience of the disciples. Finally, this suffering was actually the way to the experience of the saving presence of God for Jesus and will be the same for all of his followers. Mark binds all of these ideas together in the title Son of man.

Further Study

N. Perrin, *A Modern Pilgrim in New Testament Christology.*
H. Todt, *The Son of Man in the Synoptic Tradition.*

4.

The Power of Jesus in Word and Miracle

The preaching and teaching of Jesus, as well as his power to work miracles, form the foundation for the whole meaning of Jesus in the gospel of Mark. He wrote more than just a passion account with an introduction. The heart of the gospel may be the suffering Son of man, but the activity of the Son of man must also be understood if we are to enter into the fuller meaning of the good news according to Mark.

■ Preacher and Teacher ■

Achtemeier divides the activities of Jesus as preacher and teacher mainly because Mark included in his vocabulary both words and seems to have a slightly different nuance with his choice of the different words in individual contexts. Rather than complicate the issue unduly, I will treat both activities under the notion of the power of Jesus in word.

The Son of man also performs miracles, and more than any of the other gospels, Mark fills his account of Jesus with references to his miracles. In fact, in comparing the four gospels the interest in the miraculous activity of Jesus declines as we progress from Mark to Matthew to Luke and finally to John. For Mark, more than the other gospels, Jesus' ministry included great acts of power. Jesus preached with power and worked miraculous deeds.

The gospel almost begins with a reference to preaching: "The gospel of God is at hand" (Mk 1:14–15). This opening chapter ends with a sense of compulsion. Jesus had to go about the land preaching (Mk 1:38).

■ Little Interest in Content ■

Mark does not dwell, however, on the actual content of the preaching of Jesus. Even when Jesus sent out his disciples to preach he does not mention precisely what they were to preach (Mk 6:12). He speaks only of repentance, which repeats the actual preaching of Jesus in 1:15 and the very content of the preaching of John the Baptist in 1:4.

The apparent lack of interest in the actual content of the preaching can be explained by the way Mark identified Jesus with the kingdom of God. For Mark, Jesus is the beginning of God's final and glorious rule. What Jesus said was important, but also how he lived and how he died. All form part of the gospel, and all are part of the preaching, and all are involved with the inbreaking of the reign of God.

Mark also speaks about preaching in 13:10 and 14:9:

And the gospel must first be preached to all nations (Mk 13:10).

Wherever the gospel is preached in the world, what she has done will be told in memory of her (Mk 14:9).

With these we have seen all of the references in the gospel that deal with preaching. There are, however, other activities which deal with the same reality, although the word "preaching" is not used. To "speak the word" can be seen as a parallel to preaching (Mk 1:15; 1:45; cf 14:9) and can also be seen as a parallel to teaching (Mk 4:33; 8:32; cf 9:31). Evidently Mark was not overly careful, or greatly concerned, with his particular choice of vocabulary. Jesus was the presence of the reign of God and he himself was the gospel. For this reason Mark could interchange vocabulary since all of the words and ideas would help fill out the fuller meaning of Jesus. One such choice of vocabulary that seems to have had great import to the author of the second gospel, however, is the word "teaching" or "teacher."

■ Teacher ■

Jesus often functions as a teacher of the law, a "rabbi." In Mark 10:17 a man asks Jesus about eternal life, and Jesus reacts out of the tradition of the law just as a rabbi or scribe might react. People also address Jesus as a teacher, whether friend or foe (Mk 12:14, 19, 32; 9:38; 10:35; 13:1). He taught in the synagogue, beside the sea, or wherever crowds would gather. Also, Jesus identifies his ministry with teaching:

> *Day by day I was with you in the temple teaching . . . (Mk 14:49).*

He also used the title "teacher" when he instructed his disciples to prepare the passover:

> *The teacher says: "Where is my guest room, where I am to eat the passover with my disciples?" (Mk 14:14).*

Mark saw teaching as a regular activity of Jesus, and when the disciples return from their preaching journey they narrate not only what they had done but also what they had taught (Mk 6:30), even though they were not instructed to teach (Mk 6:7, 12–13). For Mark, if Jesus taught, then his disciple had to teach just as his church would teach. The combination of the teaching activity of Jesus and of the church appears clearly in the parables. Mark saw the parables as a principal way in which Jesus taught, and then the church could use the parables in its own teaching.

■ **The Parables** ■

Modern scholars see the parables as the most characteristic element in the teaching of Jesus as recorded in the gospels. They have the stamp of a highly individualistic mind and carry a strong ring of authenticity. But while most agree on the close connection between Jesus and the parables, complete agreement cannot always be found among scholars on the interpretation of the parables. I will present more ideas on the parables later in this work and will limit the comments here to some general ideas on parables and their presence in Mark's gospel.

The word parable (Hebrew: *mashal*) means a simple comparison or a similitude: the eye is like the light of the body (Lk 11:34). But when these simple comparisons become elaborated into stories we have parables proper, a peculiar figure of speech which carries power in its very use of words. Even when scholars such as Perrin, Via, Funk and Crossan become involved in the careful study of the parables as literary teaching devices, we should not lose sight of the original sense of comparison. Parables are not carefully constructed allegories in which every detail has some hidden meaning. The situation narrated in the story presents the lesson, with no great interest in trying to discover symbolic elements in every aspect of the story.

■ Symbolic Elements ■

In some parables, however, some of the characters can be identified. In the parable of the prodigal son the father is clearly God, the young man is a sinner (perhaps even a Gentile), and the older brother represents the righteous who practice obligation piety. But the parable involves the situation constituted by the interplay of the characters: God freely offers love to all who seek it. The main point of the story could be lost if we became too involved with allegorical interpretations.

Parables were the chief teaching device of Jesus, and Mark saw that the church must continue the teaching function of the Lord. As a result, many of the parables were embellished by the early church as they sought new meaning in the teachings of Jesus and as they tried to apply the parables to the present situation of the followers of Jesus.

To understand the teaching of Jesus and of the church, we have to follow the concern of J. Jeremias and try to reconstruct the life-situation in which the parables were first used by Jesus and the situation of the apostolic church within which the parable traditions took their final form.

■ Reinterpretation of the Parables ■

The church and the writers of the gospels were not so much concerned with the actual words of Jesus as with his prolonged presence as teacher in the community. The church would never merely hand on what Jesus had actually said to a particular group or just repeat a parable. The early community applied the parable and made sense of it for themselves in their situation. The most obvious reason for this reinterpretation of the parables was the change in audience. It would seem that very few of the parables were originally addressed to the circle of disciples but rather to those outside (Mk 4:11) to the multitude of people gathered to listen to Jesus or even to his opponents.

The parable of the laborers in the vineyard (Mt 20:1–16) was originally addressed to those Pharisees who criticized the good news of Jesus. The Lord attempted to show them a parable to demonstrate how unjustified and loveless and unmerciful was their opposition. In the gospel of Matthew, the audience has changed and the same parable is addressed to the followers of Jesus who have to be willing to allow all people into the kingdom and rejoice that many share in the same good fortune. A study of the parable of the sower will make these points more evident.

■ Parable of the Sower ■

The parable of the sower combines the teachings of Jesus with the teaching of the early church. Most contemporary scholars believe that Mark 4:13–20 represents a homiletic commentary on the parable of Jesus by the early church. Scholars reached this conclusion because verses 13–20, in contrast to the actual parable, is un-Hebraic in style and contains a whole series of words which appear nowhere else in the sayings of Jesus, but which are very characteristic of the later epistles in the New Testament. These verses result from the church's efforts to draw the meaning from the parable and apply it to the situation of the times of the community. Thus, a reader can easily miss the precise meaning of the parable as intended by Jesus and concentrate on the meaning as taught by the early church. A reader need not prefer one to the other. Rather, both situations, that of the ministry of Jesus and that of the church, give us a fuller appreciation of the parable.

In light of the further development of parable studies by Perrin, Via, and Crossan, which we shall study in greater detail when we examine the gospel of Matthew, we can also say that it is possible to prescind from both situations. We can allow the parable as metaphor to affect us in understanding the teaching of Jesus even as it is overlaid by the experience of the early church. The parables as the principal means of teaching by Jesus give opportunities for all of his followers to increase their self-understanding as believers.

■ The Meaning of the Parable ■

To return to the parable of the sower, the main point in the teaching of Jesus is the wonderful power of the seed to bring forth a marvelous harvest, no matter what the obstacles. When a person sows a lawn he is not concerned that some seed falls on the driveway, or some falls in the flower beds or some falls on the road or some falls on the edge of the property to be lost forever as far as growth. He knows that with care there will be a lawn.

In spite of the problems and even the failures in his ministry, Jesus knew that in him God the Father had made a marvelous beginning and in the end there would be a great harvest; there would be a lawn; God would reign on earth. The harvest had been a traditional image to describe the final fulfillment. We find the image in the Old Testament to describe the fruitfulness of the messianic times (Am 9:13–15). The psalmist also used it:

> *May those who sow in tears reap with shouts of joy. He that goes forth weeping bearing the seed for sowing shall come home with shouts of joy bringing his sheaves with him (Ps 126:5–6).*

To human eyes, the preaching and labors of the whole line of prophets culminating in the ministry of Jesus must have seemed in large measure a failure, but Jesus knew otherwise. In the parables he teaches that in spite of indifference, opposition and unwillingness to understand, the seed which Jesus had implanted in people would bear fruit. The glorious harvest would take place.

Originally the formulation of the parable showed little or no interest in the specific nature of the obstacles to the reception of the seed. The beaten path, the birds, the stony ground, and the thorns are simply typical obstacles taken from the experience of farming. No obstacle can hinder the power of the word of God. As the main meaning of the parable, it continues to have meaning to the church in every age. The scandal, however, of the apparent failure of the power of God's word remains. The marvelous seed of new life, the word of God, will always experience obstacles, but when received the results are a transformation and a fruitfulness in love which signifies God's activity in the world, and in the end the word will be powerfully effective. No obstacle, nor power, nor force can imprison the word of the Lord.

■ Application by the Church ■

In the apostolic church, however, the preachers chose to bring out an aspect of the parable which had been secondary. What precisely were the obstacles which sometimes prevented the fulfillment of God's saving plan with regard to particular individuals? The question which the preacher addressed to the listeners in recounting the parable was: "Are you perhaps one of those who for whatever reasons refuse to accept the word of God?" In this perspective the preacher could easily find in the agricultural obstacles a counterpart to the potential problems in the lives of the listeners. The situation of the community of Mark, which witnessed some who belonged only for a time, gave the preacher the opportunity to tie the situation of the church to the actual words in the ministry of Jesus.

This allegorical interpretation, found in Mark 4:13–20, brought out the present obstacles in the church. Compared to the original meaning, the allegorical interpretation seems ponderous. It does not, however, destroy the parable. Such a development continues the teaching of Jesus in the actual church of the apostles by applying the parable to the situation in which the early believers found themselves. Mark 4:13–20 bears witness to the church's fidelity in attempting to draw all the meaning possible from the teaching of Jesus and make it fully relevant to the church's contemporary situation.

■ Miracle Worker ■

Another example of how the author of the second gospel preserved traditions about Jesus and added to them is his account of Jesus as a miracle worker. The ancient world teemed with magicians and wonder workers. Both Jews and Greeks had their share of those people associated with marvelous deeds. Rabbis healed the sick, conquered evil spirits, and even made ugly women beautiful. The Greek world had its magicians and devotees of gods who made the lame walk and the blind see. Jesus' deeds as a miracle worker do not set him apart from many of his contemporaries. A contemporary New Testament scholar, Morton Smith, even presents Jesus as a magician. To perform a miracle does not in itself attest to the identity of the presence of God's envoy or that the miracle worker was the one who would inaugurate the kingdom of God. Even the miracles themselves, as performed by Jesus, are open to various interpretations. We can read the miracles of Jesus from our own perspective and they appear to be signs of the presence of God with him. To his opponents, however, they were proof that he must be destroyed because he was involved with the power of evil:

*He is possessed by Beelzebul, and by the prince of demons he
casts out demons (Mk 3:22).*

Even his family thought he was mad after they witnessed his deeds of
power:

*And when his own heard it, they went out to seize him, for
they said, "He is mad" (Mk 3:21).*

With such a mixed background, we might marvel that the miracle
stories survived in the early tradition. Concentration on what Jesus
taught and avoidance of the ambiguity of the miraculous was in fact
the path followed by some of the fathers of the church.

But for Mark, this was not the solution. Evidently Jesus did
perform miracles, and if they could be ambiguous, Mark decided to
preserve the stories and give them his own interpretation or at least
the interpretation of his community.

■ Structure of the Miracles ■

The miracles themselves have a distinctive structure. First, the
author states the problem; then he recounts a solution; finally, some
proof confirms that the solution did in fact solve the problem. Further
details can be added to the stories but the structure remains virtually
unchanged. When we encounter a theological interpretation we can
strip off the added elements and always come back to the basic structure. In the gospel of John the interpretation occupies more attention
than the miracle itself.

■ Theological Interpretation ■

Mark joined his theological interpretation by actually adding additional meaning to the miracle through his inclusion of other material
or by giving the story a new framework that would alter its meaning.
The healing of the paralytic is a good example of the insertion of
theological issues.

Mark presents the problem in 2:2-4: friends brought the paralytic
but they could not reach Jesus. The solution is found in 2:4-5, 11: they

take off the tiles from the roof, and Jesus tells him to take up his pallet and walk; 2:12 contains the proof: the paralytic rose and walked, and all marveled.

In the midst of this story occurs the theological discussion on the power of Jesus to forgive sins. Notice how verses 5a and 10 repeat: "He said to the paralytic . . ." This is a clear sign of an interruption. Also, the theological issue is more important than the miracle both for us and for the community of Mark.

The Jews always associated sin with physical illness. This gave Mark the possibility for his theological interpretation. The man is obviously worthy of being cured, as is evident in the care and concern shown by his friends. Notice that the man himself says nothing but Jesus forgives him his sins. The church of Mark, as well as the church of today, needs the forgiving presence of Jesus even though his physical presence can no longer heal us of our physical infirmities. Mark carefully situated his theological meaning to enhance the miracle of Jesus in his ministry and thus gave to his community a sense of the continuing presence of Jesus to forgive sins. We can recall the miracle of the ministry of Jesus but grow in understanding of his presence to his community as one who heals believers of their sins.

■   The Fig Tree   ■

The destruction of the fig tree (Mk 11:12–35), a minor miracle story, has always caused confusion to readers of the gospel. Mark joined this miracle to another account which also causes problems for readers: the cleansing of the temple. The combination of these miracles is a Marcan literary characteristic. The first story seems to place Jesus in a bad light since he seems to take out his frustrations on a fruit tree that was not bearing fruit even though it is clearly stated that it was not the season for figs (Mk 11:13). Why curse a tree for not bearing fruit out of season?

■   Cleansing of the Temple   ■

The story of the cleansing of the temple also seems out of character. Jesus was not the type to become so angered. In many circumstances he faced evil but always dealt with the problem in a gentle way. To us it may seem out of character, but for Mark the story is more than the anger of Jesus at some activities within the temple precincts.

By his action Jesus demonstrated that the practices necessary for the normal functioning of the temple had ended. Sacrifice required animals: no animals, no sacrifice. If no shekels were available, the support of the temple and priesthood must end. If no vessels could be carried through the temple, then all activity relating to cultic celebration must end. The temple cleansing represents Jesus' prophetic and symbolic act of ending temple worship. To this, Mark has joined the destruction of the fig tree. The fate of the fig tree will be the fate of the temple. Both will be destroyed. Mark has preserved the story of the fig tree and placed it in the context of the cleansing of the temple to tie a theological interpretation to both incidents.

Previously we have seen how Mark and Matthew preserved the miracle of the calming of the storm on the lake and each gave it a theological interpretation to suit his own purpose. We could examine the miracle stories in all four gospels and draw similar conclusions. Each evangelist was concerned with preserving these authentic traditions of Jesus but would do so in his own way with his own purpose in view.

Mark continued the process of adapting and interpreting miracle stories as he had adapted and interpreted the teaching of Jesus to suit the needs of the early church. Both were sharpened to show that Jesus was powerful in word and in miracle in his public ministry. Jesus still lived in the church; he was equally powerful in word and deed for those who, through their faith in him, joined themselves into a fellowship of people whose Lord he would always remain. The power of Jesus works in his church which alone would be sufficient reason for Mark to write a gospel.

Further Study

P. Achtemeier, *Mark.*
J. Jeremias, *The Parables of Jesus.*
N. Perrin, *Jesus and the Language of the Kingdom.*

5.

The Disciples Before
the Word of the Lord

As the gospel unfolds, the followers of Jesus seem to grow not in understanding but in misunderstanding. The twelve appear as ignorant, ambitious, insensitive and, in general, failures. In the other gospels the twelve do not fare so poorly since Matthew and Luke modify the extreme position as found in Mark. They both present the closest followers of Jesus in a positive light.

One might ask if such a picture painted by Mark can be historically accurate. The response to that question is two-sided. Certainly the disciples were failures since they did not follow the Lord to the cross. But they could not have been complete failures, since out of their faith came the Easter faith that was the source of the Jesus tradition. Secondly, as we mentioned previously, the picture painted by Mark seems to be a deliberate extreme. Could this be due to the set purpose of his gospel?

■ *Theios Aner* ■

Theodore Weeden holds that the disciples symbolize the heresy of those who held that Christ was a *theios aner* (a divine man), a miracle worker, and were overly concerned with the theology of glory rather than that of the cross of the Lord. This view, however, seems in itself to be an extreme, since it is hard to imagine that Mark would portray those closest to Jesus as representatives of a heterodox christology. Nevertheless it should be admitted that Mark does present an unusual portrait of the disciples, and there must be some explanation.

Although Mark does have a tendency to portray the disciples in a less than favorable light, a careful reading of the gospel shows that this is not always the case. In some instances Mark is more sensitive and positive with regard to the closest followers of Jesus. In the calling of the disciples in Mark 1:16–20, Jesus calls and they immediately follow him. The same attitude is present in Mark 10:28 in which Jesus assures them that since they have left all to follow him, they will receive a reward here as well as in the afterlife.

■ Followers and the Twelve ■

Mark also distinguished between the followers of Jesus and the twelve. Women followed Jesus and remained faithful to the end. In 14:50 all of the closest followers flee from the garden while in 15:40–57 the faithful women follow Jesus to the cross and prepare him for burial. These same women seem to be the first to learn of the empty tomb and are called to proclaim the resurrection to the twelve. Thus it is not accurate to speak of all of the followers of Jesus in the same way or to see them in the same light all of the time. Evidently Mark was careful in his portrayal of the followers of Jesus, and we must pay attention to his proper perspective.

Previously we noted the relationship between christology and anthropology in Mark. Perhaps the clue to understanding the role of the disciples in Mark, like that of the gospel of John, lies in relationship to the christology of Mark. The suffering Son of man expects his disciples to live a life that will also lead to suffering. The disciples in the gospel account of Mark will have two roles to play: they are important for the public ministry of Jesus and they will mirror the problems that anyone who chooses to be a follower of Christ will experience. This will be more evident if we examine the material on discipleship as contained in chapters 8–10.

We have already seen that in these chapters we have the three predictions of the passion (Mk 8:31; 9:30–32; 10:33–34). We have also seen that Mark always joins a saying about discipleship to those predictions of the passion, making it quite explicit that a similar fate awaits those who follow a suffering leader. Even when he spoke of the reward of discipleship he includes the phrase "with persecutions" (Mk 10:29–30), making it clear that the follower can expect a similar fate to that of the master. As the glory of the resurrection was preceded by the cross, so the path that leads to the kingdom of God will be strewn with pain and suffering. Jesus gives his life for others (Mk 10:45), and thus the disciple must follow along the same path.

Also in this section we have the account of the transfiguration. During this religious moment the Father tells the chosen disciples to "listen to him" (Mk 9:7b). As Jesus moves from the mountain of the transfiguration back through Galilee (Mk 9:30–58), and on toward Jerusalem (Mk 10:1–45), Mark, through a series of detached sayings and dialogues, presents the meaning of discipleship and the necessity of renunciation. Jesus, following the divine injunction to the disciples: "Listen to him," speaks the words of renunciation and discipleship.

■ Following the Lord ■

The disciples must take up their cross and follow him (Mk 8:34), renounce all honors and ambitions, and seek to be the servant of all (Mk 9:35); they must sell all and give to the poor (Mk 10:21), and finally they should give up their very self (Mk 8:35). The disciple must risk all in an act of loving confidence in the God who had given them Jesus and who had raised Jesus from the dead.

Because Jesus followed the road of humility and suffering in service, emptying himself (Phil 2:7–8), the disciple makes himself or herself least among the brethren: "Whoever would be first among you must be slave of all" (Mk 10:44). The lowly people, the little ones, are the models and the signs of the presence of Jesus, for it is to the children, those who are unassuming and dependent on God, that the kingdom belongs:

Let the children come to me; do not hinder them, for to such belongs the kingdom of God (Mk 10:14).

In spite of all these clear teachings throughout this section the twelve still seem to be blind and narrow-minded, seeking status and power for themselves in the future kingdom of God. Their experience on the mountain left them confused. Why such talk about suffering and death concerning God's chosen one? Was not Elijah to come first and restore all things and usher in a reign of glory? Jesus answered that Elijah had indeed come, but the restoration did not mean an end to suffering for Elijah himself (John the Baptist), nor for the Son of man, Jesus, and thus not for the disciples of the Son of man (Mk 9:13–19).

■ Disciples as Servants ■

In Mark 9:31–37, as they proceed to Jerusalem and the cross, the followers continue to be preoccupied with petty matters such as procedure in the kingdom of God. In this context Jesus speaks: "If anyone wishes to be first he must be least of all and servant of all" (Mk 9:35). Mark joins this to the saying of Jesus concerning receiving a "child in his name" (Mk 9:36–37). Rather than seek honor and riches and power the disciples must seek to make themselves the least of all if they hope to be part of the kingdom of God.

In the story of the man casting out demons in the name of Jesus who was not one of the followers of Jesus (Mk 9:38–41), Mark presents the same idea. The disciples must do away with petty jealousy and their own prerogatives and recognize that they do not have an exclusive claim over the saving presence of God. If someone does good in the name of Jesus, then he or she becomes part of the entourage even if he or she has not been identified or approved by the twelve.

■ Authority ■

Mark 10:35–45 contains some of the most important texts on the nature of discipleship and brings this section to a close. It also contains the classical text on the nature of authority in the church. The text begins by placing the twelve in a most unfavorable light. They are guilty of the fault of self-seeking and jealousy. When the sons of Zebedee sought a place of preference in the kingdom the rest of the twelve become indignant with the two brothers. Jesus replies by stating that they are not to exercise authority over the brethren in the same way that secular rulers exercise control. They should not "lord it over," should not act like the "high and mighty," but should model themselves after Jesus and how he exercised his authority. The Lord of all had striven to be servant of all. His followers should do nothing less.

■ Peter ■

Of all the disciples Peter seems to stand out the most in Mark. Some have thought of Mark as a disciple of Peter. Jesus calls Peter first (Mk 1:16); Jesus changes his name (Mk 3:11), and his name appears first in the list of disciples. Peter is the first of the inner circle (Mk 5:37; 9:2; 13:3; 14:33) and he functions as a spokesman for the group (Mk 1:36; 8:29; 9:5–6; 10:28; 11:21). Jesus foretold his denial explicitly (Mk 14:29–31) and it is later narrated in detail (Mk 14:66–72). Jesus also tells the women to announce his resurrection to Peter and to the other disciples (Mk 16:7). Peter seems to have remained with Jesus the longest during his passion, and Mark attests to Peter's repentance for his sin (Mk 14:72).

The examination of these passages in detail shows that Mark presented Peter in a favorable light and an unfavorable light. He expresses the best of being a disciple: "You are the Christ" (Mk 8:29), and the worst: "And Jesus took him and began to rebuke him, 'Get behind me, Satan' " (Mk 8:32–33). The first one called, Peter is also the one who repeatedly denies the Lord even after he had professed to be faithful to the end. He is the faithful lover and the unfaithful lover; the one who understood and the dullest of heart. Such a portrayal does not necessarily mean that Mark wants to denigrate Peter and then rehabilitate him and place him in a position of authority. Rather, the successes of Peter and his failures are the successes and failures of the twelve, and, we might add, of all the followers of the Lord. If the disciples in Mark depict the kind of problems any follower of Jesus might experience in the course of following the master, then Peter shows us that the career of a single disciple knows the heights of faith as well as the dregs of despair. The disciple must drink of the heady wine of enthusiasm and commitment as well as the sobering water of personal failure. The disciple has the experience of Tabor as well as the pits of the Gehenna of rejection, denial, and despair.

■ Suffering ■

No doubt, discipleship is important in the gospel of Mark, but, as we have seen, no understanding of discipleship exists without knowing the meaning of Jesus. Mark understood Jesus as the suffering Son of man. Suffering explains Markan christology as well as unlocks the key to understanding the meaning of discipleship. The fate of Jesus looms ever present throughout the gospel and seems to hang over the entire account of the ministry of Jesus like a pall. From the beginning the master experiences opposition and misunderstanding, and the climax of the gospel is his sad and cruel death. From beginning to end the Jesus of Mark's gospel is the suffering Son of man, and unless the followers clearly understand the pain of Jesus, they miss the meaning of Jesus. The disciples fail to understand during the public ministry because to understand Jesus is to see him as the one who suffered and died. Only the light of the cross illuminates the life of Jesus. The disciples could not know the real Jesus until he had suffered and died. Their failure to understand during the ministry is grounded in the christology that permeates the account of Mark. I write "permeates" since it is a sad gospel of pain and suffering.

The inability of the twelve to understand is not dependent on their own psychology. During the ministry they had yet to see him suffer and die; they had yet to come to grips with their own sharing in this suffering; they were too concerned about the wonders of the kingdom without seeing the price that would be paid to inaugurate the reign of God. When they saw him suffer and die, then they could understand him and begin to understand their own calling and destiny. Jesus "had to suffer" (Mk 8:31), as it was written of him (Mk 8:14–21), and thus there existed no possibility of ever understanding the meaning of Jesus until he had died his death on the cross.

Mark saw value in presenting Jesus as powerful in word and miracle, but no one will discover the meaning of the Lord here. We may be encouraged to follow him because of his power, but will become his disciples in truth only when we have accepted him as one who suffered. Just as the disciples could not understand him apart from his final destiny, the same is true for believers of all times. Mark says to succeeding generations of believers: to know Jesus and to love him and to follow him is to willingly embrace the folly of his cross.

Further Study

P. Achtemeier, *Mark.*
T. Weeden, *Mark: Tradition in Conflict.*

6.

Faith and the Community in Mark

The gospel of Mark, as should be evident at this point, is not an account of historical fact but a testimony of faith. He expresses his understanding of faith not in theological statements but in narrative forms. In the events of ministry, in the course of action, in details of time and place, Mark plants the hidden expressions of faith and not just in the spoken word. Mark comments on what people actually say in the course of action in which they are involved.

■ Faith ■

Peter attests to his faith that Jesus is the Christ in Mark 8:29, but also in the various actions that portray his relationship to the Lord. No explicit expressed faith comes to us from the paralytic nor from his companions in chapter 2, but their actions give evidence of its presence. The individual becomes a believer when he or she repents and accepts the gospel and then in faith joins the community that shares that faith. We have already treated many aspects of faith throughout these pages, but the final element in the understanding of faith in the gospel of Mark involves the role of the community. Howard C. Kee has contributed much to this aspect of Markan theology and to him the writer is much indebted.

■ Community ■

The grouping of people in Mark is a voluntary association of individuals who have actually listened to the preaching of the good news and have changed their way of living as a result of their commitment to Jesus. This choice involves them in a relationship with other believers. The corporate nature of faith appears in the meaning of the reign of God (Mk 1:14). For Mark this is a future reality:

> *There are some standing here who will not taste death until they see the kingdom of God come with power (Mk 9:1),*

but also a reality that has drawn near:

> *The kingdom of God is at hand; repent and believe in the gospel (Mk 1:15).*

The reign of God involves growth and conflict, and it must be entered and received (Mk 4:26–30; 3:24; 13:8; 9:44; 10:23–25; 12:34). The demonic forces that seem to erupt frequently in the gospel cause the conflict. Jesus explains to his own that his presence destroys the rule of Satan. The exorcisms of Jesus actually bind the "strong man" and presage his demise.

■ Kingdom as Gift ■

The notion of receiving and entering are Mark's way of showing that no one can merit the kingdom but must receive it as a gift. Still, the gift calls for personal involvement and the actual reception. God freely offers but the individual must also freely accept. This reception concerns not only the future, but the present as well. People enter the kingdom, having accepted it as a gift, now.

A key to understanding the entrance of the kingdom is expressed in the story of the man who sees the commandments summed up in the law of love. He is described as "not far from the kingdom" (Mk 12:34), and thus very close to entering it. At the same time the one who enters must acknowledge the demands. The follower abandons all worldly security, and all riches are given over to the poor. A community results from the joining together of those who have entered the kingdom. The reign of God involves a present age of discipline and renunciation in which a new type of community living is accomplished with a promise of an eternal communal life with God and other believers.

■ Community as Family ■

Mark offers an additional image in his gospel: the community of believers as a family. In Mark 3:31–35 the real family of Jesus is those who do the will of God (Mk 3:35). Bonds of blood no longer matter, nor is there any sex distinction in this new family of Jesus. Anyone who believes, who does the will of God, belongs to the family of Jesus, and all are on an equal footing. This new family implies a split with the old family, as seen in the actual experience of Jesus. Jesus' mother and brothers come to take him away (Mk 3:31); Mark also states that this actually took place at his home (Mk 3:19); Jesus makes the break from the former bond in a family to create a new bond of faith. As Jesus himself had to set the pattern for being part of a new group, so his followers must do likewise.

■ Future Rewards ■

The rewards of this new life are set out in exaggerated form in chapter 10: one hundred times as many homes, and brothers, and sisters and children and lands. The acceptance of Jesus in faith does not imply a deprivation but actually brings about a fellowship superior to anything that had preceded it. The reward finds completion in the future age which will be nothing less than eternal life.

Mark continues his theme of a community of faith when he presents Jesus as the shepherd to his flock of believers. He uses the image twice: Mark 6:34 and 14:27. In each case he makes explicit the interrelationship between leader and group. The latter reference occurs on the night before the crucifixion. The shepherd will be struck and the sheep will be scattered. But Mark will not leave his listeners disheartened. Jesus will be raised up and gather them together in Galilee (Mk 14:28).

The reference in the sixth chapter demonstrates the compassion of Jesus for the crowds who are like sheep without a shepherd. Jesus must respond to their needs, and so he teaches them (Mk 6:34). His concern continues when they are hungry, and so he feeds them (Mk 6:35–44). As once God called his people out of Egypt and cared for them in the desert, so Jesus will sustain his people until they enter the promised land of fulfillment. He will not forget them but will care for them as a shepherd cares for his sheep.

■ Covenant People ■

Mark explains, as a final image, the community of faith as a covenant people. He mentions it directly only once in the last supper scene:

This is my blood of the new covenant which is poured out for many (Mk 14:24).

The reference to the blood of Jesus refers presumably to the sacrifice of Jesus. The sacrifice will ratify the covenant, and will accomplish a new covenantal relationship with his people: "which is poured out for many." In the following verse the ultimate outcome of this new covenant is the consummation of the kingdom of God:

I shall not drink again of the fruit of the vine until that day when I drink it new in the kingdom of God (Mk 14:25).

The prophet Jeremiah presents the classical presentation on the new covenant in chapter 31. He emphasizes two components: forgiveness and the worldwide scope of the covenant community. Both features are present in the gospel of Mark. We have already seen how Mark joins the notion of forgiveness to the power of Jesus in the cure of the paralytic in chapter 2. We have also noted that the cursing of the fig tree (Mk 11:12–14) is an allegory on the end of temple worship. The lesson to be drawn, however, is less a polemic against Israel than a warning to the new covenant people (Mk 11:20–25) which culminates in an appeal to exercise forgiveness toward one's fellow human being:

And when you stand praying, forgive, if you have anything against anyone, so that your Father who is in heaven may forgive you your trespasses (Mk 11:25).

Mark also explains the all-encompassing nature of this covenant community. The angels will "gather his elect from the four winds, from the ends of the earth to the ends of the heavens" (Mk 13:27). Even more telling is the reference in Isaiah that speaks of the coming gathering by God:

Everyone . . . who holds fast to my covenant, these I will bring to my holy mountain and make them joyful in my house . . . for my house shall be called a house of prayer for all

*peoples. Thus says the Lord God, who gathers the outcasts of
Israel. I will gather yet others to him besides those already
gathered (Is 56:6–8).*

Mark quotes the central portion of this quotation in the quotation in
the cleansing of the temple (Mk 11:17) as he demonstrates that the old
limitations on the access to God are over. Now people have free access.
Those of Jewish background are welcome as are those of non-Jewish
background. The only criteria for entrance is faith, the hearing of the
word of God and the repentance that will change a person's life. The
result is a community of people who trust in the Lord and live a shared
life of faith together as they await the final outcome and the consummation of the reign of God.

Further Study

H. Kee, *Community of the New Age: Studies in Mark's Gospel.*
E. Trocme, *The Formation of the Gospel According to Mark.*

7.

The Origin of Mark

Most works on a gospel will begin by responding to some of the curious questions associated with the origin of the gospels: Who actually wrote the gospel? Where was it written? When was it written? These questions are of particular interest today, since by now many people have heard that the names we associate with the gospels may not be the names of the actual authors. I have chosen to wait until this point to deal with some of these curious questions with the hope that a study of the gospel will be of some assistance in understanding the tentative nature of my response to the above questions.

■ **The Author** ■

The gospel itself never states anything about its author, its origin, or the time of composition. For us to respond to these questions we will have to deal with inference within the gospel as well as conjecture and seek some evidence in other historical works. At the end we may still be no closer to any conclusive answers than we are at the outset. At least we will have tried to respond to some questions that often pique the curious.

Evidently the church felt no great interest in the authors of the gospels. As we have already noted, the communities were more aware of the continual abiding presence of the Lord with them and thus need not have been concerned with his actual words. This same conviction would have allayed any fears about the authenticity of the gospel accounts. But when the gospels began to multiply and a greater time distance developed between the historical Jesus and the church, many became concerned about the reliability of the gospels. If many were in existence how can one judge those that were in close continuity with

Jesus and his disciples? One such criteria could be the author. Establishing the reliability of an author would guarantee the authenticity of the gospel. If we could ascribe the gospels to apostles, or those associated with apostles, then this would give greater credence to the Jesus tradition as expressed in a gospel.

■ Anonymous Evangelists ■

Who wrote Mark? First, recall that nowhere does the author identify himself. The same is true for all of the gospels. Matthew does not identify himself, nor does Luke, and in the gospel of John the author seems to identify himself with the beloved disciple, but this cannot be equated with the apostle John (Jn 21:24).

In the past we have assumed that the authors were male—with emphasis on the word "assumed." Both in Luke and in Mark women figure rather prominently and, in general, seem to be more faithful followers of the Lord. Could this imply that the author of Mark or Luke was a woman? All we can say is that the gender of the author also is uncertain.

Obviously, the author saw no need to identify himself or herself, and the early church was content to deal with anonymity. We have seen that gospels were composed of available tradition about Jesus which the different evangelists arranged to their own purpose. If these traditions were generally known to the communities, there would be no great concern about preserving the identity of the one person or persons who arranged the material to suit the peculiar needs of the community. We have noted that the work of editing gave a peculiar stamp to the material, but editing was not a question of composing new material.

■ Efforts To Discover the Identity ■

Some people will turn to unusual details in the gospel and seek the identity of its author. Some will say that the only reason that the fleeing of the naked young man in Mark 14:51–52 was preserved was due to the fact that the young man was the author of the gospel. Such conclusions seem ill-founded.

The earliest reference we have to the author of the second gospel is found in the writing of Eusebius, bishop of Caeserea in the fourth century. This author attempted to write a history of the church from its inception and used as one of his sources the writings of an earlier historian from the second century called Papias. Papias claimed to have known some of the apostles and thus would have been a third generation believer. He deals with the origins of the gospels and claims that from Aristion and John the elder he had learned that the author of the second gospel was Mark, who had been Peter's interpreter. The traditions then would be coming from Peter. Eusebius made his own commentary on the matter by emphasizing that Mark was not a follower of the historical Jesus but merely tried to preserve the recollections of Peter without trying to make an arrangement of them. This tradition lies at the foundation of our ascribing the authorship of this gospel to Mark, the companion of Peter. From the same author we learn of the origin of the gospel of Matthew, an apostle who wrote first in Aramaic, and the origin of the fourth gospel as the account of John the apostle. We also learn that Luke was the traveling companion of Paul, and so his gospel becomes reliable because of his association with Paul. We will discuss these theories in greater detail when we study each gospel.

In various books of the New Testament we find reference to people named Mark. On the assumption that only one Mark was prominent in the early church, all of these references may be seen to be related to the author of the second gospel. John Mark was a companion of Paul and Barnabas on missionary journeys; he then had a disagreement with Paul, after which Paul would have nothing to do with him (Acts 12:12; 13:13; 15:37–40). He in turn is identified with the Mark mentioned in Philemon 24 as the fellow worker of Paul. Mark is again mentioned in Colossians 4:10 and in 2 Timothy 4:11 and 1 Peter 5:13. With so many references to Mark in the New Testament we can easily flesh out something of the identity of the author of the gospel. The only flaw in the construct is the assumption that there could be only one Mark among the early converts to Christianity. As a fact, we know that Mark was one of the most common and popular names in the Roman empire. Who is to say that each reference to Mark referred to the same person? Would it not be more likely that it referred to different persons?

We do, however, end up with the name Mark. If the concern was with authenticity, would it not have been smarter to ascribe the gospel to Peter instead of his companion? Maybe the author of the second gospel was named Mark, but that is about all we can say about him. We do have the reference in Eusebius, but from other studies we are aware of the tentative nature of the historical accuracy of this early historian, and he in turn relies on another historian who is not always the most accurate.

■ Conclusion ■

Our conclusion as to the author of the gospel of Mark is tentative and unsatisfying. Perhaps we need not ask the question. We have an account of the Jesus tradition that the early church accepted as reflecting the authentic faith of the community. Who wrote it is not as important as its contents. The gospel expresses faith and can aid faith, and so who actually wrote the gospel matters little. As documents of faith, the gospels transcend a need for authenticity of authorship.

■ Geographical Origin ■

With regard to its geographical origin, we have even less to guide us. Eusebius says nothing. The early traditions that associated Mark with Peter placed Mark in Rome at the time of the death of Peter and thus held that the origin of the gospel was Rome. This also would seem to be in accord with the general tone of the gospel which seems to be Gentile-oriented as well as Jewish-oriented. In the cryptic greeting from "Babylon" sent by the author of 1 Peter to "my son Mark" (1 Pet 5:13), if Babylon is interpreted as Rome, then some will find further evidence for Rome as the origin of the gospel. This also presupposes that Peter is the author of 1 Peter which is more than questionable. Some find further evidence for a Roman origin in the use of Latinisms in the gospel. Such, however, is not a clear argument since mixed cultures often borrowed words from various languages, just as English is filled with French words.

The question of suffering in the gospel has helped people to associate the gospel with the persecution of Christians under Nero. We know from ancient historians that Nero laid the blame for the burning of Rome on Christians and that they were actually persecuted and that the persecution did not extend far beyond the confines of Rome. If the community was persecuted and persecution was associated with Rome, then this would give some support to the origin of the gospel in Rome. To counteract this argument we also know that Christians were persecuted by Jews.

Other possible places of origin for the gospel are Palestine or Syria. Since the author associates chapter 13 with the destruction of the temple in the year 70 A.D., some would argue that the gospel came from a region affected by the events of 66–70 and the Roman conquest. The problem with this hypothesis is that the author seems to presume that his readers do not understand Aramaic phrases, and so he translates them into Greek, and he is greatly confused as to Palestinian geography.

Today more and more scholars are locating the origins of all of the gospels in Syria or Asia Minor. We know that this area had the strongest mixture of Jewish and Gentile Christians. We can presume that these groups would have early developed a need for written gospels. But to group all of the gospels in the same geographical area does not deal sufficiently with the circumstantial origin of the gospels.

■ Conclusion ■

As with the case of authorship, so with the question of origin, we remain in the dark. Tradition has associated Mark's gospel with Rome, and that has as much foundation as any other possible place. Once again we may be asking the wrong question. It matters little exactly where the gospel had its origin. We should recognize some of the circumstances in the gospel as depicting environmental conditions rather than try to discover the environment and use the environment to explain the gospel. The former approach is essential for a fuller understanding of the gospel; the latter is dangerous since it is founded on such weak evidence.

■ Date of Composition ■

We finally come to the question of date. In some sense we have more evidence here than in the two previous questions, but once again can not avoid the shadows. Since the majority of scholars believe that Matthew and Luke used Mark as a source, as we have previously noted, then Mark has to pre-date these two gospels. Since we have evidence in Matthew and Luke for a developed church, we can set limits for the earliest point in time in which they could have been written. Also, since we can conclude from these gospels that the temple has already been destroyed, we have additional information as to the terminus a quo of Matthew and Luke. They could not have been written before the year 70. We also have learned from our study that the gospel of Mark presupposed the existence of material that circulated in separate units. We would have to allow enough time for the traditions of Jesus to develop into literary units, as well as enough time for the question of the parousia to be discussed. Most scholars will place the origin of Mark in the decade between 60 and 70 A.D. Some might be happy with this conclusion, since it is the most definite answer yet made as to the origin of the gospel. While this is the general conclusion of scholars, that does not mean that it is without its problems.

While we can find reasons for stating that Matthew and Luke were written after the destruction of Jerusalem, there are counter-reasons as well. We might like to feel secure that Mark 13 refers to the conditions during the Jewish war of 66–70 before the actual outcome with the destruction of the temple. But the same conditions would have been present when Herod the Great waged war in Palestine seeking to impose his rule on the Jews in 37 A.D. We can even jump into another century, for the same conditions would have prevailed in 135 A.D. when Hadrian destroyed the city of Jerusalem. I do not intend to suppose that Mark was written in the second century by including this war, but just to demonstrate how the same facts can fit different circumstances.

We are forced to conclude with as much darkness as when we began. Repeatedly I have stated that the early church was concerned with the presence of Jesus in their midst. They were not overly concerned with his actual historical words and seemed to freely develop and alter historical circumstances. If they were so little concerned with these important aspects of the historical Jesus, we should not be surprised if they were not concerned with the time, place and authors of the gospels. Provided the gospels were an authentic expression of the faith of the church, they were accepted and used as a means of bolstering that faith. With the passage of time, a concern for authenticity developed as the early community receded to the background of history and new believers were asked to carry on the Jesus tradition. At this period we have the birth of concern for authorship.

For the church today, we have accepted the gospels as documents of faith; they have proven over two thousand years that they express and bolster faith. If their authors chose anonymity, they are part of that great throng of believers who have preceded us in faith and whose contribution was the passing on of the Jesus tradition from one generation to another. As we have been blessed with their expression of faith, we can recall their memory, whoever they were, and hold them in benediction.

Further Study

P. Achtemeier, *Mark.*
A. Jones, *The Gospel According to Mark.*

8.

The Meaning of Mark

Biblical scholars can often be accused of dealing with esoteric knowledge divorced from the reality of the Christian life or, at least, so far separated from the ordinary life of believers that it seems unrelated to faith. A study of the gospel of Mark, as is true for a study of any book in the New Testament, must make the bridge from the text to the life of the believer. If the Bible is, in truth, the word of God and if the word of God is alive and effective, then there must be means by which knowledge can be turned to the service of faith.

Old documents do not easily speak to the contemporary mind even if those old documents are taken from the Bible. To understand how we can move beyond the expression of faith in the New Testament to discover the ever present reality demands people who read and think and sometimes pray.

■ The Sad Jesus ■

Mark gives believers the opportunity to think after they have read and can be a catalyst that prompts prayer. The gospel is not often happy. Often life is not very happy. Jesus is sad. He comes to offer a sense of liberation and freedom and experiences shackled people who seem to be content in their misery. He thinks that people will change their hearts but gradually realizes that a change in heart is too much to ask for on their own. Only when he has lived his life and experienced the pain and suffering of everyone can the Son of man help people turn from their sense of pain and seek resurrection in faith. Glory exists with the Jesus tradition but not without the cost of human suffering, just as in every truly valuable experience in life some price is paid.

■ Suffering Today ■

To someone who lives in the final quarter of the twentieth century, pain and suffering are most real—perhaps no more real than in any other moment in history, but, after all, we have to live in this period and no other, and thus the pain and suffering needs no comparison. It might be easy to settle into the sadness and allow the pain to engulf a person, but the gospel of Mark says no. Pain hurts, all too much, but glory also abounds and even anticipated eternal glory.

The passion of Jesus hangs over his ministry like a veil as more and more people reject him. But some do say yes to the will of God (Mk 3:35) and become his mother and brothers and sisters. The resurrection is predicted as well as the passion (Mk 8:31; 9:31; 10:34). No pain exists beyond the influence of goodness and the Spirit of Jesus. Jesus could experience the suffering of the Son of man, know rejection and misunderstanding even on the part of his closest friends, and still believe in a resurrection. Jesus promised the same for his followers. All peoples of all times can take comfort in the suffering Son of man who lived and died and rose in glory. Life is sad; the gospel of Mark is sad. Life has its moments of glory; the gospel of Mark has its glory. Living in isolation has never brought much comfort. Joining with others who share a common vision makes the vision more clear and gives courage to the pursuit.

■ Hopeful Vision ■

Jesus offered people a vision. Better to bless than to curse, to forgive than to refuse the offer of peace. Love is the better alternative and makes a person close to the kingdom of God. To enter into such a vision demands a support as well as an invitation. Jesus challenged his followers to join with him but only after he made it evident that he loved them. A rich young man comes to seek this vision. Jesus looked upon him and loved him and then challenged him (Mk 10:21). Jesus promised him a share with himself and his followers. He would not be alone as he sought the vision of eternal life but first he would have to make his commitment in faith. No one could be forced, but the invitation must be freely accepted as it was freely offered. The young man walked away sad. He sought the vision, but could not accept the demands.

To his own, Jesus turned and reminded them what price a person has to pay in pursuing a vision. The cost is steep but the company is grand. With hyperbole, Jesus claims to grant hundreds of brothers and sisters and friends and homes, if only his listeners will cast their lot with him.

■ Cost of Discipleship ■

Faith is not throwing something away; faith is not losing what a person has; faith is the perfecting of what is already there. Faith does not isolate but joins people together in a common goal with a common means to attain that goal: the good news of Jesus, the kingdom of God present.

Mark will not forget the cost but will teach clearly the gains and promise a sense of belonging. Jesus will be the shepherd who cares for his flock; Jesus will be the guide who continues to teach and unravel the mystery of the meaning of life. All a person has to do is to turn in faith, to repent and believe the good news.

As a believer, Mark gives guidance by preserving the teachings of Jesus and adapting them to his own church. The parables of Jesus have a powerful effect on listeners. They give assurance of a future as well as the instruction for the present. There will be a marvelous harvest because God has so decreed. Already the growth takes place in spite of all obstacles. No one can imprison the word of the Lord. No power, no force, no person, no regime, no law, can prohibit the growth that God has so ordained. "Let him who has ears to hear him hear" (Mk 4:9).

■ Evil ■

Miracles happen. The ship of Peter may experience troubled waters; dark forces of evil can surround the community. Jesus may appear to be sleeping, but no believer should lose faith. Calm will be restored by the presence of the Lord. Demons can afflict individuals as well as groups. Whole institutions can be infected with evil forces, but the reign of God has begun in Jesus. He has bound up the "strong man" and now evil makes its final assault, knowing that its reign has come to an end.

People in the last quarter of the twentieth century may find it hard to accept that evil is bound. Mark says it is. Mark deals with the reality of evil all around him and remains convinced that Jesus and his power for goodness will ultimately bring the victory. Believers today have to experience the same assurance in their faith. Evil will lose.

The disciples in Mark are often failures. They are ambitious and lack understanding. They are insensitive to the needs of Jesus. Their leader and spokesman, Peter, epitomizes the best and the worst. He is smart enough to recognize the presence of God in Jesus but too blind to know its meaning. He believes, but often fails in that belief and needs assurance and acceptance. He recognizes his sins and weeps (14:72) and eventually becomes the rock for his fellow believers.

■ Faith: A Continual Acceptance ■

Faith is not a once and for all acceptance of the Lord. Faith is a daily effort to perdure in a commitment in spite of failure and sin. Mark knows no plastic saints in his gospel, only people who struggle between the wholehearted commitment that comes only in death and the selfish opportuneness that keeps Christianity as insurance. The believer knows the failure of despair, the tragedy of sin, even as the follower of the Lord delights in his enticing presence.

For the contemporary believer, tempted to see Christianity as leisure activity, Mark recognizes the failure and reminds those who listen that faith can live with sin provided that Christianity is living in the heart and not on the sleeve.

The gospel of Mark, as any gospel, remains so many printed words unless someone opens its pages and reads and thinks and prays. If scholarship can help in the thinking, then it can be a surer foundation for the prayer.

Christians need to have their faith nourished as they are surrounded by forces, at least indifferent to the gospel, if not hostile. Mark will not give answers but rather will unfold the responses that already exist in the human heart. Mark took the Jesus tradition and applied its meaning to a persecuted community, troubled in faith. He tried to assure them, as his gospel will do for all generations: The sadness will be turned to joy, for the "time is fulfilled, and the kingdom of God is at hand; repent and believe in the gospel (Mk 2:15) of Jesus Christ, the Son of God" (Mk 1:1).

Further Study

S. Blanch, *The Christian Militant: Lent with St. Mark's Gospel.*

PART III

The Heart of
the Tradition: John

1.

The Milieu of the Fourth Gospel

*T*he Jesus tradition expressed in the gospel of Mark differs from its expression in the gospel of John. I treat this gospel second because of the great difference between the synoptic tradition of Jesus and the Johannine tradition. Each evangelist responds to the needs of a particular community and each offers an understanding of the Jesus tradition.

The gospels, as we know, do not come to us from isolated individuals. We understand the gospel of Mark only when we can appreciate the community that was experiencing suffering. We understand John only when we realize that the gospel bears witness as the work of not just an individual, but an individual who founded, guided, and lived within a specific community of believers.

Today some people tend to talk about a "Johannine school." From a group of early Christians we have followers of a man called the "beloved disciple." From this school we have the legacy of the gospel of John, the letters of John and possibly the book of Revelation. In the ancient world students tended to flock around a distinguished teacher, and through their research they continued the work of their master. Often enough these students would record the teachings of the master and prolong his effect through their writings. Something similar happens today. Law students, for example, might choose to study under a distinguished professor, and often enough the results of that study will find expression in legal briefs for generations.

Whether such a Johannine school ever existed or not, we can be sure that such an individual, the beloved disciple, did exist as a eyewitness of the Jesus tradition. He also had a profound influence on a group of early believers. Later we shall try to unravel some of the

79

unknowns surrounding the origin of the gospel. For the present, I am more interested in offering to the reader some perspectives through which we can gain an entrance into the milieu of this gospel.

■ A Sectarian Community ■

The gospel shows a community narrow and sectarian. The members do not love the world:

Do not love the world or the things in the world. If anyone loves the world, the love of the Father is not in him (1 Jn 2:15).

Jesus does not pray for the world (Jn 17:9), but rather that his followers may live in the world and not be part of it (Jn 17:14–16). Only those who recognize the voice of the good shepherd can follow him (Jn 10:3). Other sheep belong to the shepherd but they must learn to hear the voice of the Lord and join those who already belong (Jn 10:16). The sense of belonging to the community binds each individual to the Lord as it binds the members to each other in love. If individuals choose to leave the community, clearly they never belonged:

They went out from us but they were not of us; for if they had been of us, they would have continued with us; but they went out that it might be plain that they all are not of us (1 Jn 2:19).

Even the great commandment of love: "Love one another as I have loved you" (Jn 13:34), seems sectarian. The followers of the Lord are not commanded to love their enemies. First and foremost, they must love the brethren, those who belong to the community. The author has evidently experienced a close-knit group of believers who emphasized the need for a commitment to the Lord, and a profound love of the brethren that binds people together as one flock under one shepherd.

A sect is a body of persons distinguished by peculiarities of faith and practice from other bodies adhering to the same general system. The Johannine community was a sect within the larger Christian church at the end of the first century. They shared the same general belief but separated themselves from other followers of the Lord through their own interpretation of the Jesus tradition. As a community they chose to emphasize the essentials: faith and love. Only then would they permit other Christian practices to exist.

■ A Community with Diversity ■

Mideast society at the end of the first century offered something for everyone. Judaism was strong; mystery religions with strange rituals attracted many with their promise of salvation. Early Gnosticism, the heresy that promised salvation through the communication of secret knowledge, had many adherents within both Judaism and Christianity. Greek philosophy offered everything from the delight of Epicureanism to the rigidity of Stoicism. Commerce flourished with the ever-present Roman might. Since no person can flee from societal influences but must pick and choose those which are helpful and avoid those which are harmful, the Johannine community had to learn to live in a diverse society and carve out its own sphere of influence. The community was composed of individuals. Thus, many of the above influences would be present in the community. Some people joined the community and later left, which further contributed to the sectarian nature of the group.

■ Groups of People in the Community ■

The gospel text gives evidence of several groups of people that formed part of the milieu of the Johannine community. Raymond Brown discovers five such groupings. The first group was the opposition. Some individuals belonged to the "world" just as the members of the community did not belong to the "world." We might characterize these people as those who deliberately chose to remain in the darkness. They are under the influence of Satan, the prince of darkness and the prince of this world. Their presence in the milieu would have further contributed to the feeling on the part of the Johannine community of being strangers in the midst of those who chose darkness.

A second group, associated with the former, but distinct because of tradition and opportunity, is the Jews. These Jews never accepted Jesus and persecuted any Jew who professed belief in Jesus. From this group we have the decision, sometime around the year 85, to exclude from the synagogue anyone who acknowledged Jesus as messiah. The Johannine Christian teaching that Jesus was one with the Father, as well as their teaching that he had replaced the temple, and thus its sacrifice, pointed a blow toward the heart of Judaism which had to be resisted.

At this period we also have those who believed that John the Baptist, and not Jesus, was the messiah. The Johannine Christians reduce the importance of John; he becomes a witness to Jesus who acknowledges that he must decrease while Jesus increases.

Others were "crypto-Christians." They chose to remain in the synagogue but privately believed in Jesus. They tried to live in both camps. Eventually, especially with the decision of the Jews to include in their prayers accusations against the followers of Jesus, these crypto-Christians would have to make a decision to publicly profess faith in Jesus or return to a full participation in the faith of the synagogue.

The divergent views on christology uncover yet another group. These Jewish Christians accepted Jesus as a miracle worker sent by God but did not acknowledge the high christology advocated by the author of the gospel. For the evangelist, these individuals could not be seen to be true believers even if they could trace their acceptance of Jesus to the community in Jerusalem. Initially it would be acceptable to view Jesus as a miracle worker, but such a faith had to develop into the acceptance of Jesus as the eternal Son of God.

The final group that appears within the Johannine tradition are Christians of other apostolic churches. These believers traced their origin to Peter and the twelve. They had developed a moderately high christology emphasizing the origin of Jesus as the miraculous intervention of God in human history but without explaining his precise relationship to God. Their ecclesiology also was a slight variance with the Johannine approach. Too often, for the Johannine community, they were occupied with corrolaries to Christianity instead of emphasizing the essentials of faith and love.

■   **Problems in the Community**   ■

The existence of these distinct groups helps us to appreciate some of the problems faced by the Johannine community. In John 9:22 the reference to expulsion from the synagogue comes not from the time of the ministry of Jesus but from the period of the Johannine community. Eventually Christians had to make a decisive break with the synagogue. This decisive step on the part of Judaism forced the crypto-Christians to make a decision for or against the new way of Jesus.

The presence of followers of John the Baptist, still claiming that he was the messiah and not Jesus, prompted the Johannine community to downplay the importance of John and depict him not as the Baptizer (the term is not used) but as a Christian witness who bears testimony to Jesus.

Docetism, an early Christian heresy, held that the body of Jesus was not really a human body. The Johannine gospel attempted to counteract this problem by emphasizing the reality of the body of Jesus in his ministry. Jesus thirsts; he is hungry and becomes tired. Even after the resurrection he eats with his disciples.

Previously I made mention of Gnosticism, that strange system of beliefs that created an intellectual elite promising salvation through the communication of secret knowledge. We can accept the presence of gnostic influences on this gospel. "The truth will make you free" (Jn 8:32) seems gnostic. Jesus teaches what he has learned from his Father, for he is the light of the world. This seems esoteric. Moreover, he tells us in this gospel that "I am the way, the truth, and the life" (Jn 14:5). Since the community lived in such a diverse environment we should expect some of these influences to find their way into the gospel, but we also must pay attention to the basic thrust of the author's understanding of salvation: salvation, through the communication of the Spirit, comes only through love and the death on the cross. "When I am lifted up, I will draw all men to myself" (Jn 12:32).

The community also faced problems with other Christian communities. By the end of the first century the Christian church had sufficiently developed to institutionalize certain ecclesial offices. The more charismatic type of church order gave way to an established authority and hierarchy. Certain church leaders traced their office in the church to Peter and laid claim to a share in the authority of Jesus himself. The Johannine community, sectarian to begin with, came into conflict with these interpretations of Christianity and attempted to offer its own formula for church order. The third letter of John, verses 9–11, implies that other Christian communities had difficulties with the Johannine community. We shall see later how the interpretation of Christian faith by the community of the beloved disciple differed from other early communities, and thus, inevitably, disagreements and dissensions created a troubled existence.

■ Johannine Dualism ■

The dualistic language of the fourth gospel invites further analysis. Light and darkness, truth and falsehood, above and below, good and evil, life and death, God and the world: do these concepts come from a gnostic background or are they rooted in Judaism? Some scholars have presented arguments in favor of the gnostic origin for this dualism while others have argued for the essential Jewish origin, especially through the influence of Qumran. The same concepts existed in Gnosticism as well as Qumran, and since the Johannine community flourished in a mixed social order, we can expect that no one answer can be found to this question of origin. The gnostic concept of life may very well have influenced the gospel. The general agreement in terminology in both the Qumran scrolls and the fourth gospel also shows a familiarity by the Johannine community of the thought present in the writings of the Qumran community even if we cannot discover a direct literary dependence.

The relationship between Gnosticism and the thought of Qumran has not been studied at great length. The discussion on the possible origin of Johannine dualism in one or the other milieus overlooks the gnostic elements that are part of the Qumran experience. We might even say that the experience of the Essenes at Qumran is an early form of Jewish Gnosticism which would have contributed significantly to the emergence of the later Christian Gnosticism. The eclectic and sectarian form of heterodox Judaism of Qumran best represents the intellectual environment from which the author of the fourth gospel discovered some of the language and concepts that he used to articulate his unusual formulation of the Christian message.

When contemporary students of John read of the struggle between light and darkness, good and evil, the world below and the world above, they must see these ideas coming from a group of people who are removed from the mainstream of social life; they expect to discover salvation through a personal relationship with God's envoy. The Qumran community withdrew from the orthodox way of Jewish life to a desert community in which they were dependent upon a teacher and awaited expectantly for the coming of the messiah who would usher in the final relationship to God. The Johannine community also withdrew from the mainstream of developing Christianity and accepted a Christian faith that allowed for no compromise. They too awaited a fulfillment, but a fulfillment that had substantially begun through the coming of Jesus.

■ John and the Synoptics ■

Any appreciation of the milieu of the fourth gospel must also include some investigation of the relationship between this gospel and the other three. We know that Mark, Matthew and Luke were in existence at this period of history and were accepted as authentic expressions of the Jesus tradition. Did the Johannine community use these gospels in any way?

Often in the past people looked upon the fourth gospel as an effort by John to fill in what was missing in the synoptics. Today such a theory has been dismissed. A careful study of the gospel shows no literary dependence by John on the other three. The fourth gospel seems closer to Luke and Mark than Matthew, but even when we examine the common elements between John and Luke and Mark we can find no evidence for a direct literary dependence. The author of John most likely did not know the other three gospels. The similarities can be explained by a similar oral tradition that lies behind all of the gospels. The plan of the last gospel conforms to that of Mark: Galilee, Jerusalem, death and resurrection, the sending of the Spirit. But how the author presents this basic plan differs significantly.

■ Order of Events ■

The order of events change in this gospel. The cleansing of the temple, for example, takes place at the beginning of the ministry of Jesus rather than at the end, just before his death. John can situate this event here, for, unlike the synoptics, John has Jesus visiting Jerusalem several times. Thus he can locate the cleansing at one of several visits.

John also places the crucifixion on a different day. The fourth gospel sets the crucifixion on the day of preparation for the Passover, at the time the lambs would have been slain in the temple in preparation for the Passover meal. For the synoptics, Jesus celebrated the Passover meal with his disciples and then died the following day.

The author also presents the words of Jesus in a manner different from the synoptics. All of the evangelists adapted the actual words of Jesus to suit the needs of the individual communities, but the authors of the synoptic gospels had a more conservative approach in preserving the historical words of Jesus. In the fourth gospel half of the verses are discourses unknown to the synoptics. John also seems to arrange and alter the words of Jesus with greater freedom. He presented the teaching of Jesus, but the words are those of the evangelist or, perhaps, of the beloved disciple.

We should not conclude, however, that the beloved disciple or the evangelist created these discourses of Jesus. We do have the so-called "Johannine thunderbolt" in the synoptics:

> All things have been delivered to me by my Father, and no one knows the Son except the Father, and no one knows the Father except the Son and anyone to whom the Son chooses to reveal him (Mt 11:27).

The terminology is closer to that used in the gospel of John. This encourages us to recognize that the basic ideas in the gospel of John are also present in the synoptic tradition even if in a germinal or indirect fashion. We discover in the fourth gospel a creative remembering of the Jesus tradition which adapts the teaching of Jesus to the needs of a particular church community.

■ The Risen Lord Speaks ■

Throughout this gospel, in distinction to that of the other evangelists, the author presents Jesus as speaking from eternity. The risen Lord addresses his followers more so than does the historical Jesus. The teaching is rooted in the earthly Jesus but carries a greater development. When the author, for example, narrates for us the multiplication of the loaves in chapter 6, he presents the event in the context of Jesus as incarnate wisdom as well as Jesus present in the eucharist. This differs significantly from Mark's presentation of the same miracle in chapters 6 and 8 in which Mark presents Jesus as the shepherd who feeds his flock and offers the food of the eschatological banquet.

All of the miracles of Jesus take on a different nuance in this gospel. In the synoptics they cause wonder. In the fourth gospel they become signs, deeds of the earthly Jesus. They involve faith in him not as just another miracle worker but carry as well a pledge of the future outpouring of the Spirit.

The Jesus in this gospel differs significantly from the Jesus of the synoptics. He is never without his glory, and this his followers have seen: "And we have seen his glory, glory as of the only Son from the Father" (Jn 1:14). In the earlier gospels the authors offered no hint of pre-existence. In Philippians Paul hints at pre-existence (Phil 2:6) but for John the Word was with God from the beginning, and even when the Word became flesh, the Word remained in the bosom of the Father (Jn 1:18).

Since Jesus speaks from eternity, he knows everything. He knew Nathanael under the fig tree (Jn 1:48), knew the Samaritan woman's marital status (Jn 4:17–18), knew his betrayer (Jn 6:70–71), knew when his hour had come to depart from this world (Jn 13:1), was aware of all that would befall him as he was apprehended in the garden (Jn 18:4); finally, knowing that he had accomplished all, he uttered "I thirst" to fulfill the scriptures and handed over his Spirit (Jn 19:28). No wonder he caused misunderstanding for Nicodemus, the Samaritan woman and his disciples.

The author did not set out to correct or amplify the synoptics, but, accepting a common oral tradition, developed his own approach to the Jesus tradition which was suited to the needs of his particular Christian community.

■ Conclusion ■

This survey of the milieu of the fourth gospel should make it evident to the reader that we have a syncretistic background. The community was sectarian; it flourished within a Christian environment that experienced internal as well as external problems; it had its opponents and critics, borrowed ideas and terminology from the heterodox Judaism of the Qumran community as well as Old Testament theology, relied on an oral tradition that was similar to the synoptics, especially Luke and Mark, but in the end produced a document far different from any other gospel. The community's experience included current religious motifs but also had, of necessity, to deal with philosophical, political, sociological and psychological elements. Freedom, individuality, clustering around a charismatic teacher called the beloved disciple, the experience of separateness—all are involved with psychology as well as sociology, and each element will find some expression in this gospel.

The work of recent scholarship has focused these influences, and thus students can better understand the gospel if they keep the milieu in mind. Later, we shall deal specifically with a number of the issues described briefly in this introduction. As students read the gospel they will be able to detect the currents described herein and begin to appreciate the genius and the value of this authentic witness to the meaning of Jesus.

Further Study

R. Brown, *The Community of the Beloved Disciple.*
O. Cullmann, *The Johannine Circle: A Study in the Origin of the Gospel of John.*
R. Kysar, *The Fourth Evangelist and His Gospel.*
J. L. Martyn, *History and Theology in the Fourth Gospel.*

2.

Faith and Love: The Foundations of the Community

*T*he original ending of the fourth gospel expressly states its purpose:

> *Jesus performed many other signs as well, signs not recorded here, in the presence of his disciples. But these have been recorded to help you believe that Jesus is the messiah, the Son of God, so that through this faith you may have life in his name (Jn 20:30–31).*

On these verses alone, we cannot determine whether the gospel reflects a missionary purpose, an attempt to enkindle faith in those who do not yet believe, or a homiletic purpose: to strengthen and confirm that faith of an already constituted congregation. We can, however, recognize these verses as emphasizing the importance of faith to the author and inspirer of the gospel.

Faith in the fourth gospel is the human response to the revelation of Jesus. This faith consists of an active acceptance, seen in the author's choice of a verb "to believe" rather than just the noun "belief." Jesus demands a decision as he encounters individuals. The individual becomes aware of need and the reality of sin and darkness. When Jesus enters into the individual's life, the person loses all false illusions and accepts the salvation offered. The believer accepts Jesus not just as a miracle-worker but as the Son of God. Once accepted personally, the words of Jesus become revelatory and lead to the acceptance by the Father.

God the Father also plays a significant role in the birth of faith. The Father gives the disciples to Jesus; the Father then draws the disciples to faith in Jesus and actually teaches them through the words of Jesus. Faith in this gospel becomes a gift of God the Father:

> All that the Father gives to me will come to me; and him who comes to me I will not cast out (Jn 6:37).

The author knows of the close relationship between Jesus and God. The Father has sent him into the world. He knows also the need for a divine initiative if an individual can recognize the presence of God the Father through Jesus and his preaching:

> Philip said to him, "Lord show us the Father and we shall be satisfied." Jesus said to him, "Have I been with you so long, and yet you do not know me, Philip? He who has seen me has seen the Father" (Jn 14:8–9).

> He who believes in me, believes not in me but in him who sent me. And he who sees me sees him who sent me (Jn 12:44–45).

God the Father speaks to the heart of the person which enables the individual to accept Jesus as the personal revelation of God.

■ Believing and Knowing ■

The relationship between Jesus and the Father in the origin and content of faith becomes especially evident in a study of the word "believing" and the word "knowing." Nearly two hundred times the author used the word "to believe" or "to know." Often he used figurative references which at times say more, and other times say less, than the literal words. Coming to the light is a figurative expression of faith in Jesus; hearing the voice of the good shepherd and recognizing it is a figurative expression within a parable. Remaining close to the vine in the parable of the vine and the branches also expresses the relationship of faith. Believing and knowing, and coming to Jesus and staying with him, are personal activities that pervade the entire gospel. We can also examine the major and minor personages in the gospel and see how some believe and others do not; some know him and others fail to recognize him. Jesus' disciples appear under every possible heading: fluctuating, changing and making faltering advances, as they come to believe and to know Jesus as God's personal envoy and their personal Lord and savior.

The opening chapter of the gospel already presents the image of light coming into a dark world calling people to faith:

> In him was life, and the life was the light of men. The light shines in the darkness and the darkness has not overcome it (Jn 1:4–5).

> But to all who received him, who believed in his name, he gave power to become children of God (Jn 1:12).

This same chapter narrates the call of the first disciples. In each instance, immediately they made a profession of faith. Andrew told his brother Peter: "We have found the messiah" (Jn 1:41). Philip told Nathanael: "We have found him of whom Moses in the law and also the prophets wrote" (Jn 1:45). Nathanael declared: "Rabbi, you are the Son of God; you are the king of Israel" (Jn 1:49). This opening chapter also situated the role of John the Baptist. He simply bears testimony to Jesus as the lamb of God and encourages his own disciples to follow Jesus (Jn 1:29–34).

Nicodemus comes from the darkness troubled by Jesus. He knows Jesus represents more than just a miracle worker:

> No one can do these signs that you do unless God is with him (Jn 3:2).

But Nicodemus does not make his profession of faith. He appears again in John 7:50, at the meeting of the Sanhedren, and displays a concern for Jesus that he be treated according to the law. Finally, in John 19:39 he helps prepare the body of Jesus for burial. His interest and concern for Jesus could be contrasted with the Samaritan woman who is receptive to Jesus and ultimately not only makes her profession of faith, but also becomes an evangelist, inviting her townspeople to listen to Jesus:

> They said to the woman, "It is no longer because of your words that we believe, for we have heard for ourselves and we know that this is indeed the savior of the world" (Jn 4:42).

Judas, of course, receives every opportunity to believe, to come to the light, but he preferred the darkness. At the last supper he left the upper room, and the evangelist tells us: "And it was night"

(Jn 13:30). Jesus will not force anyone to believe in him. Faith is God's gift which must be accepted in personal freedom.

The Jews, the leaders of the people, also had their opportunity to believe. Jesus taught daily in the temple. When questioned by the high priest Jesus responded:

> *I have spoken openly to the world; I have always taught in*
> *synagogues and in the temple, where all Jews come together.*
> *I have said nothing secretly (Jn 18:20).*

But for this group, faith in Jesus became impossible. They could not recognize the presence of the God of Abraham, Isaac and Jacob in Jesus and ultimately denied their heritage at the trial of Jesus. When Pilate asked the Jews: "Shall I crucify your king?" (Jn 19:15), the leaders answered: "We have no king but Caesar" (Jn 19:15). In the history of Israel God alone was their true king, and even when they had an earthly king, his presence represented their true king, God. The Jews in the passion of the Lord not only fail to come to faith in Jesus, but actually reject their own faith as expressed in the Old Testament.

■ The Faithful Disciples ■

The disciples of the Lord, as they appear in his ministry, also exemplify the various conditions of faith. Later we shall study Peter, the mother of the Lord, Thomas, the beloved disciple Martha and Mary, and Mary Magdalene. In each episode in which they appear in the gospel they become symbolic figures, representing not just their own level of belief, but also offering to other Christian communities an example and help in understanding the origin, value and meaning of faith.

■ The Content of Faith ■

Once we have recognized those who believe in Jesus or come to know him, we should also ask the content of that faith and knowledge. The answer to these questions becomes evident in almost every chapter: the objects of faith and knowledge are Jesus and his mission.

The object of knowing, however, is different in this gospel from the object of believing. When the author uses the word "to know," he rarely uses simple nouns or pronouns. These are common, however, with the use of the word "to believe." "To believe in," with an accusative, in two instances has God as the object: "He who believes in me believes not in me but in him who sent me" (Jn 12:44); "Let not your hearts be troubled; believe in God, believe also in me" (Jn 14:1). In all other instances, individuals are asked to believe in Jesus.

When the author uses the verb "to believe" with a dative, the objects are transitional; they are testimonies, words of Jesus or signs. In each case the signs point to the meaning of the mission of Jesus: "They believed the scripture and the word Jesus had spoken" (Jn 2:22); "Even though you do not believe me, believe the works that you may know and understand that the Father is in me and I am in the Father" (Jn 10:38).

The results of believing and knowing Jesus are eternal life or the entering into eternal life: "And this is eternal life, that they know thee, the only true God, and Jesus Christ whom thou has sent" (Jn 17:3); "Whoever believes in him should not perish but have eternal life" (Jn 3:16). The individual believes in Jesus and his mission, comes to know him and who he is, and understands the mission of Jesus. Then the individual believes and possesses eternal life.

The author of John stressed the relationship between believer and Jesus; he writes about the growth of faith, the role of the Father in bringing people to faith, and he speaks of the content of that faith: Jesus and his mission. The established purpose of the gospel, as given in chapter 20:31, helps individuals "to believe that Jesus is the Christ, the Son of God, and that believing you may have life in his name." If no faith exists, then for the community of the beloved disciple no Christian community exists. The essential need for this faith relationship is particularly expressed in the parable of the good shepherd.

■ The Shepherd ■

The image of the shepherd and the flock appears frequently in near eastern literature. In the Old Testament the book of Numbers used the image of shepherd when Moses asked God for someone to share in his authority (Num 27:17). Zechariah used a similar image (Zech 11:4), and the prophet Ezekiel used the image of the shepherd not only for the leaders of Israel but also for God himself (Ez 34).

Each of the synoptics used the same image. Mark presented Jesus as the shepherd: "I will strike the shepherd and the sheep will be scattered" (Mk 14:27). Matthew recorded the parable of the lost sheep

(Mt 18:12–14), and finally, Luke used the image in two places: in 12:32 he referred to his disciples as a flock: "Fear not, little flock, for it is your Father's good pleasure to give you the kingdom"; and in chapter 15 Luke also records the parable of the lost sheep (Lk 15:3–7).

What characterizes the parable of the good shepherd in the gospel of John is the reciprocal relationship between Jesus and the individual sheep. The sheepfold is unified by Jesus alone. Jesus has a close and intimate relationship with each sheep, grounded on the union and relationship between Jesus and his Father. The chapter actually contains two parables, that of the shepherd and the sheep, and that of the door and the sheepfold. In each instance the author presents the parable and then explains its meaning:

> The sheep hear his voice as he calls his own by name and leads them out. When he has brought out (all) those that are his, he walks in front of them, and the sheep follow him because they recognize his voice. They will not follow a stranger; such a one they will flee, because they do not recognize a stranger's voice (Jn 10:3b–5).

This parable finds its explanation after the author has explained the meaning of the door and the sheepfold:

> I am the good shepherd; the good shepherd lays down his life for the sheep. The hired hand, who is no shepherd nor owner of the sheep, catches sight of the wolf coming and runs away, leaving the sheep to be scattered by the wolf. That is because he works for pay; he has no concern for the sheep. I am the good shepherd. I know my sheep and my sheep know me in the same way that the Father knows me and I know the Father; for these sheep I will give my life. I have other sheep that do not belong to this fold. I must lead them, too, and they shall hear my voice. There shall be one flock then, one shepherd (Jn 10:11–16).

In the presentation of the parable (Jn 10:3b–5) Jesus calls his sheep by name. They know his voice. He does not confuse them, and they feel secure with the sound of his voice. Calling by name has a long biblical tradition implying intimacy as well as power and influence. Jesus knows his sheep sufficiently well to call them personally by name. He unites the individual with himself and the individual feels secure in following the Lord.

In the interpretation of the parable (Jn 10:11–16) the intimate knowledge is again expressed. The Old Testament knew of the intimate knowledge that existed between God and his people: "He knows those who take refuge in him" (Nah 1:7). Jesus exemplifies this intimate knowledge, for through him God expressed his care for his flock. The mission of Jesus in this parable makes clear the intimacy that also exists between Jesus and his Father. Jesus is for God; he is nothing apart from what he is for God. Because of this, Jesus could claim to be the revealer of God. The full parable also brings out God being for Jesus. Because Jesus is united with his sheep, then God is also for the followers of the Lord.

■ Unity ■

Verse 16 stresses the purpose of this knowledge: to bring all to unity. A mutual knowledge exists between Jesus and God, and between Jesus and the flock. This mutual knowledge unites the flock to God. For the author of John, this union of God and his envoy, Jesus, and the believer, makes eternal life possible for humankind. The sheep know the shepherd; the believer knows the Father and the one sent by the Father, and thus the believer has eternal life: "And this is eternal life, that they know thee, the only true God, and Jesus Christ whom thou has sent" (Jn 17:3).

The unity that exists between Father and Son is also expressed by the phrase: the Son being in the Father and the Father being in the Son (Jn 10:38; 14:11; 17:21); the author also used the expression: "The Son knows the Father" (Jn 10:15; 17:25). Jesus as the good shepherd who knows his sheep implies a relationship that is similar to that of Jesus and the Father. As the Son knows the Father and receives life from him, so those who know the Son know the Father and receive eternal life. A stringent bond unites the individual believer with the Lord.

■ The Meaning of the Flock ■

Commentators interpret the flock in many different ways. It appears that some of the sheep in the sheepfold are not of the flock of Jesus; only those who hear his voice belong to him. The image of many flocks in one sheepfold, each belonging to a different shepherd, fits the conditions of the time. In the morning the different shepherds entered the fold, and the sheep who belonged to them followed them out to pasture. Such an interpretation of the parable could imply that the larger flock symbolized the Jews at the time of Jesus.

The reference to sheep who belong to other folds could further call to mind the Gentiles and their call to faith in Jesus. Still further, the flock may be interpreted as a pre-temporal community closely akin to the gnostic myth of the revealer who gathers together the dispersed sparks of light present in every individual and unites these sparks into the original unity. As knowledge was the means by which the gnostic redeemer united individuals and brought salvation, so it is the mutual knowledge of Jesus and his flock that brings salvation and eternal life.

Whatever the interpretation, the collectivity is evident even if some do not belong to the group. The flock is diversified, with some united (those who hear his voice) with Jesus. Others remain separated (those who do not respond to his voice). The flock also seems open to growth (other sheep outside). In the interpretation of the parable, Jesus is the sole principle of unity based upon his unity with the Father. The unity that exists among the sheep is only implicit. Since they have a personal relationship with the shepherd, they may also have a personal relationship among themselves, but this dimension remains in the background. The author chose to stress, in this parable, the faith relationship between Jesus and the individual without discussing the relationship that also exists between believers.

The parable might mirror the historical situation of the call of Jesus to the Jews. It also may mirror the historical situation of the troubled Johannine community, separated from the synagogue, experiencing divisions within itself as well as problems in relating to other Christian communities. The parable would recognize the divisions but would also offer hope for a final unity, both within the community and without, in the future.

Thus far I have stressed the importance of a personal relationship, a faith commitment to Jesus by the individual person. This parable insists on the need to remain with Jesus as the leader and guide and to continue to respond to his voice. At first glance the image of the shepherd and flock might appear to be an image of the church, but such a conclusion needs careful nuancing. The parable concerns a personal and individual relationship with Jesus. In that relationship, because of the image of a flock, we have some reference to a community but only implicitly. For John, we cannot begin to deal with a community unless we have individual believers united with Jesus in faith. The parable of the vine and the branches completes the author's call for the essentials, for in this parable the faith that unites the individual with Jesus finds its expression in the love that binds believers together.

■   The Love of the Brethren   ■

The synoptic gospels record the question put to Jesus by the inquiring scribe: "Which commandment is the first of all?" (Mk 12:28). Jesus responded with the well-known reply of the twofold commandment:

> The first is, "Hear O Israel: The Lord our God the Lord is one; and you shall love the Lord your God with all your heart, and with all your soul, and with all your mind, and with all your strength." The second is this, "You shall love your neighbor as yourself" (Mk 12:29–31; see also Mt 22:34–40; Lk 20:39–40; 10:25–28).

Jesus quotes from Deuteronomy 6:4, the reference to the first commandment, and then from Leviticus 19:18, the reference to the love of neighbor. Each of the synoptics recorded this incident in the life of the Lord, and from this teaching Christianity has developed its insistence on the close relationship between the love of God and the love of neighbor.

Matthew and Luke also enjoin the followers of the Lord to love their enemies: "Love your enemies and pray for those who persecute you" (Mt 5:44); "Love your enemies, do good to those who hate you, bless those who persecute you, pray for those who abuse you" (Lk 6:27–28). Luke continues his call to expand the commandment of love by expecting the believers to turn the other cheek; "Give your cloak and your coat to the one who takes; give to all who beg and do to others as you would wish others to do to you" (Lk 6:29–31).

Christianity has flourished as a religion that offers love to all and will not discriminate even when the Christian faces rejection or persecution. The love of God and love of neighbor are irrevocably joined together. Matthew exemplifies this relationship when he records the words of Jesus:

> So if you are offering your gift at the altar and there remember that your brother has something against you, leave

your gift there before the altar and go first to be reconciled to
your brother (Mt 5:23–24).

■   The One Commandment in John   ■

How strange that the author of John fails to record this twofold
commandment! The gospel of John emphasizes love but omits the two
great commandments. "For the Father loves the Son" (Jn 5:20), and
will love those who keep the commandments of the Lord, who respond
to his word, and together Jesus and his Father will come to those who
love him (Jn 14:21–24). The author joins together the love of God for
the Son and then completes the love relationship by including in that
love all who come to believe in the Son. The mission of Jesus itself
manifests the love of God for humankind: "For God so loved the world
that he gave his only Son" (Jn 3:16). And the Father loves the Son
precisely because the Son as the good shepherd will lay down his life to
take it up again (Jn 10:15). All of these sayings, however, do not deal
with the love that should exist among the disciples.

Instead of teaching two commandments, John tells his followers
that Jesus demands only one:

> *A new commandment I give to you, that you love one an-*
> *other; even as I have loved you, you also must love one an-*
> *other. By this all men will know that you are my disciples, if*
> *you have love for one another (Jn 13:34–35).*

To understand the meaning of this command we also must read
what the author of 1 John directs to his readers:

> *If anyone says "I love God" and hates his brother, he is a liar;*
> *for he who does not love his brother whom he has seen,*
> *cannot love God whom he has not seen (1 Jn 4:20).*

The author of John knows that the love of God and neighbor
belong together but will emphasize that it is through the love of the
brethren that we can have the love of God. The *new* commandment of
the Johannine community does not mean the love command itself, but
the criteria by which the community will judge that love. No longer
does the believer love the neighbor as oneself. The follower of Jesus
must love the brethren as Jesus loved them. Since Jesus was the good
shepherd who gave his life for the sheep, the follower of Jesus

must love the brethren to the point of dying for a single member of the community.

The author also omits any reference to the love of the enemy. The members of the Johannine community love the brethren, those who are members of the community. Unless the followers are joined together in a bond of love, flowing from the bond of faith that joins the individuals to Jesus, they will be unable to fulfill the further mission of Christianity to the world. The sectarian Johannine community banded together for mutual support and protection, and, following the example of the Lord, they would willingly give up their lives for the sake of the brethren. If the parable of the good shepherd exemplified the faith relationship between Jesus and the individual believer, the parable of the vine and the branches completes this faith dimension by teaching the followers to bear fruit, to love one another.

■ The Vine and the Branches ■

Commentators often compare these two parables. They have a similarity in structure and in theology. Both present a parable followed by an explanation, but the more significant comparison lies in the theology. Both parables manifest the close relationship between Jesus and the individual, but the first stresses the faith dimension. The parable of the vine and the branches emphasizes the conclusion of faith: the love of the brethren. This parable expands and explains the love of the brethren in chapter 13.

The chapter opens with a recognition formula, an identification of Jesus as the true vine, along with a reference to the activity of the Father. We have already noted the function of the Father in calling disciples to faith. Here the Father prunes and cuts the branches to make them more fruitful. The meaning of fruitfulness, however, does not become clear until verse 12. In the opening verses of the parable the chief participants are presented and interrelated: the Father who loves Jesus and who brings individuals to Jesus, the Son who loves the Father and his disciples, and finally the disciples themselves as the branches which bear fruit by loving one another.

Unlike the parable of the good shepherd, chapter 15 presupposes faith: "You are already made clean by the word I have spoken to you" (Jn 15:3). The disciples already are related to the Lord by their faith commitment. The Lord now reminds them to remain close to him. With faith as the presupposition, the author can concentrate on the result of faith: the love of the brethren.

■ **Love of the Brethren** ■

The interpretation of the parable from verse 7 to 17 clarifies the need for love as the fulfillment of the command of Jesus and makes evident the responsibility to give one's life for a member of the community. Faith becomes authentic only when it leads to love of Jesus (Jn 15:9–10) and the love of one for another (Jn 15:12–17). Only through the presence of love in the community can the mission of Jesus continue. The author juxtaposes faith and love and mission, implying that the internal life of the community and its mission to the world are inseparable. If the believer wishes to fulfill the call to discipleship, this will be possible only through an internal love for the brethren which will include a willingness to give one's life:

> *This is my commandment, that you love one another as I have loved you. Greater love has no man than this, that a man lay down his life for his friends. You are my friends if you do what I command you (Jn 15:12–14).*

The final verse of the interpretation of the parable culminates the discourse which sums up what Jesus has been saying. He returns to his simple command: "This I command you, to love one another" (Jn 15:17).

■ **Life Through Jesus** ■

The parable stresses first the individual relationship to Jesus. While the word "life" is not mentioned, the notion is understood. Jesus is the source of life for the branches and so they must remain in him. No apparent relationship exists between branches. All receive their life from Jesus, the vine, and then each glorifies God by bearing fruit. The parable also contains the warning that a branch can be cut off and burned. Such an event has no effect on the other branches which continue to remain united with Jesus. The individual must remain in Jesus.

The individual figures prominently in this parable, as well as in the good shepherd parable. The relationship of individuals within the community then becomes clearer. The command of Jesus to love one another binds the community together. The power of love moves from the Father to Jesus to the disciples, with the culmination in the mutual love of disciple for disciple. Faith finds its completion not only in the love of the Lord but also in the love of the brethren.

With these two parables we witness the testimony of the Johannine community to the essentials of Christianity: the community must have its foundation on a personal commitment of faith to Jesus, and this faith must bear fruit. Without the personal acceptance of Jesus and the fulfillment of the command of love, there can be no Christian church.

■ Johannine Mysticism ■

In chapter 15 I have noted that the author interplays the "abiding with" or "being with" of the disciples and Jesus, and Jesus and God, and the disciples and God. Some call this "Johannine mysticism." The same notion appears in the farewell discourses, especially in chapters 14 and 17. The author implies a mystical union between Jesus and the Father. We also can detect some sense of future union that will involve all three participants:

A little while now and the world will see me no more; but you will see me as one who has life, and you will have life (Jn 14:19).

Because this author was aware of the importance of the present moment, this union was not divorced from history. The abiding of God through Jesus culminates and completes the fellowship made possible through faith. The future union was present in the earthly relationship between Jesus and his disciples. The fellowship had begun but would be perfected in a more intimate union when Jesus had been glorified:

If a man loves me he will keep my word, and my Father will love him and we will come to him and make our home with him (Jn 14:23).

Those who responded in faith entered into a special type of knowledge and love with Jesus and with the Father. The union joined not just the revealer and those to whom he revealed, but the very source of the revelation and the revelation itself: God the Father.

■ **Farewell Discourses** ■

The need for a fruitful life of love on the part of the believers appears in other sections of the farewell discourses (chapters 13–17). Mystical union and interiority appear in the first section of these discourses (Jn 13:31–15:10), while exterior expression and witness characterize the second section (Jn 15:12–16–33).

In the first section the command of love figures prominently as we have seen previously in John 13:34. This follows the footwashing. It is not repeated again until John 15:12. The intervening verses stress mutual indwelling. Thirteen out of the fourteen times when the author used the word "to remain in" occur in this first section. The mutual indwelling of Father and Son, and Jesus and his disciples, occurs seven times.

Chapter 14 begins with the call to the disciples to believe in Jesus as they have believed in God and promises that the goal of the journey is the Father (Jn 14:12). Through Jesus the disciples also will reach the Father and be with him (Jn 14:6, 23).

Chapter 15 continues the theme of mutual indwelling in spite of its abrupt ending. The development comes from a change in perspective. The author introduces the bearing of fruit as a result of the abiding in Jesus. The section climaxes in verse 10:

You will live in my love if you keep my commandments, even as I have kept my Father's commandments, and live in his love (Jn 15:10).

The focus of union and indwelling is the love of Jesus for his disciples, rooted in the love of the Father.

Johannine mysticism does not conclude in a sterile union but an abiding presence which rests on responsible love directed outward to the brethren. The centrifugal force of love becomes centripetal. Finally, the author sees the love as the perfection and the completion of the union already present. Seeing and believing become knowing and loving and, ultimately, uniting and testifying.

■ **The Essentials of Christianity** ■

The church results from belief in Jesus which accomplishes a union of hearts and wills with the Father. The same love that binds Jesus to the Father binds the Father to the followers, and the followers to each other. The one commandment of the Johannine gospel is possible because in its observance the individual experiences the love of God. Johannine mysticism, the relationship and union with God, demands a union of love among the brethren. Interiority becomes externalized in the community of believers.

■ The World ■

The need for a united community becomes more evident in contrast to the world. The section on hatred of the world (Jn 15:18–16:4) follows immediately after the mutual love explanation of the vine and the branches. The juxtaposition of these themes relates the stance of the disciples to the world to that of Jesus himself. Jesus was rejected. The disciples will be rejected for the same reason: "They do not know the one who sent me" (Jn 16:3); the disciples will be expelled from the synagogue (Jn 16:2) and will be put to death (16:2b), "because they knew neither the Father nor me" (Jn 16:3b).

Jesus prepared his followers for rejection and persecution but only after he had made them secure in his love and the love of the Father. In the first section of the farewell discourses, Jesus asks his disciples to deepen their personal assimilation in faith to himself as the Son. The second half presents the disciples growing in their union with Jesus in his personal relationship to the Father and in his mission from the Father to the world. The love they bear one for another will be the sustaining power for them to continue this mission.

Previously the author presented the orientation in faith as the work of the Father. The same idea occurs in the first section of the farewell discourses recalling the earlier statement: "No one can come to me unless the Father who sent me draws him" (Jn 6:44). In these final words before Jesus departs, the love that the disciples have for each other also has its origin in the love of God as Father:

For the Father himself loves you from the fact that you have loved me and have believed that I have come forth from the side of God (Jn 16:28).

The disciples' knowledge of God, through love, leads them to recognize the nature of God. This also explains the presence of only one commandment in the gospel of John as well as the emphasis in 1 John on the need to love one another.

■ Conclusion ■

The union of Jesus with his disciples through faith and love, the command of love and the witness of the followers in the world interact. They make the Christian community different from any other type of religious community. For the author of this gospel, faith and love are essential. When they are present the Lord, his Spirit and the Father are present. When these qualities are absent, there can be no Christian church.

The role of faith, the command of love and the mystical union that the author emphasizes in his gospel are all elements of the church. The evangelist does not present a complete ecclesiology in this gospel. Rather, he chose to present to his readers those elements which he saw as foundational for the church. For the Christian community of all ages the Johannine community continues to bear testimony to the essentials of Christianity. Everything the church possesses, or operates or directs, must have its foundation in the personal commitment to the Lord and the love of the brethren. Only then can the church fulfill its mission to all.

Further Study

J. T. Forestell, *The Word of the Cross: Salvation as Revelation in the Fourth Gospel.*

E. Kasemann, *The Testament of Jesus: A Study of the Gospel of John in the Light of Chapter 17.*

R. Kysar, *The Fourth Evangelist and His Gospel.*

R. Kysar, *John: The Maverick Gospel.*

J. F. O'Grady, *Individual and Community in John.*

3.

Jesus in the Gospel of John

Scholars and readers have long recognized that the fourth gospel portrays a divine Jesus. It begins with a hymn celebrating the pre-existent Word of God, related to God with a closeness of persons: "The Word was with God and the Word was God" (Jn 1:1). The Word became flesh as Son but never left the bosom of the Father: "The only Son who is in the bosom of the Father has made him known" (Jn 1:18). As Jesus of Nazareth, the Word became flesh, possessed supernatural knowledge; he cured with a word (Jn 4:50), changed water into wine (Jn 2:7–9), gave life through his word to Lazarus (Jn 11:43). With a sereneness that astonished all, he controlled his passion from the moment of arrest to his final proclamation that it is finished.

The contrast to the synoptics makes evident the emphasis on the divinity of Jesus in this gospel. In the earlier gospels Jesus does not know everything. He grows in wisdom and grace (Lk 2:52); he appears to be ignorant of the final day (Mk 13:32); he suffers a painful agony (Lk 22:40–42) and cries from the cross: "My God, my God, why hast thou abandoned me?" (Mk 15:34). Jesus experiences temptation (Mt 4:1–11; Lk 4:1–13) and appears defeated by the power of evil in his death. Most people look to the synoptics to study the human Jesus and study the divine Jesus in the gospel of John. In fact, the fourth gospel portrays both the human and the divine Jesus.

■ Logos (Word) ■

The origin and meaning of the title *logos* in the prologue of this gospel has generated an immense amount of literature over the centuries. The author used the title only in the prologue, although the

105

theology of the "Word of God" dominates the gospel. John seized upon a term used in both Jewish and Hellenistic circles and used it as his instrument to set forth a part of the Jesus tradition.

The theology of the title is broader than its use in the first chapter. Jesus *is* the word of God, and thus when he speaks, he reveals God. The words of Jesus have been taught to him by God his Father (Jn 8:40; 14:10, 24). The content of this Word from the Father concerns the person of Jesus and his relationship to the Father and to the disciples. As Word, he reveals the Father and invites individuals to respond to this revelation.

The prologue itself emphasizes the divinity of Jesus. The Word pre-exists; functions in creation; gives light and life; reveals the glory of God through the manifestation of grace and truth; returns to the Father from whose side he has never left. We can easily picture a divine person with God, descending upon this earth to fulfill a mission and then returning. The Word is divine; Jesus is divine.

■ The Son of Man ■

The title "Son of man" appears in all four gospels. The use in this gospel, however, differs significantly from the synoptics. John emphasizes the pre-existence of the Son of man as well as his exaltation and glorification. The stress lies on the divine. The author uses the title as a characteristic self-designation. The idea in the background seems to be a figure who is archetype of the human race. The Johannine Son of man descended from heaven and will ascend again.

No one has ascended into heaven but he who descended from heaven, the Son of man (Jn 3:13).

Then what if you were to see the Son of man ascending where he was before? (Jn 6:62).

Jesus, as Son of man, continues his union with God and dwells with God. He is the perfect man, the archetype who epitomizes the true and ultimate relationship of individuals with God. His heavenly origin is the basis for his ultimate elevation and glorification as well as his salvific activity. The Father has already set his seal on the Son of man (Jn 6:27), and from the Father he has received his transcendent message (Jn 3:11–13). This becomes the guarantee of his future return (Jn

6:62). The title carries a sense of pre-existence, and when people encounter the Son of man on earth, they face a divine being.

■   The Son of God   ■

"Son of God" does not appear often in this gospel. The original conclusion to the gospel tells us that it was written to help individuals to believe that "Jesus is the Christ, the Son of God" (Jn 20:31); it appears in the opening chapter used by Nathanael, and, in the trial before Pilate (Jn 19:7). Jesus is the Son of God because God sanctified him and sent him into this world for a mission. Since the title can be used for other divine emissaries, it need not denote divinity. The close relationship between Jesus and God is better expressed in the use of "Son."

■   Jesus as Son   ■

Jesus is God's Son. For John, this designated the close relationship between Jesus and God. The Son does only what he sees the Father doing:

The Son can do nothing of his own accord, but only what he sees the Father doing, for whatever he does, that the Son does likewise (Jn 5:19).

Such examples stress the dependence of the Son upon the Father, but other texts also imply equality. The Son, like the Father, gives life (Jn 5:21); the Son makes us free (Jn 8:36); the Son gives eternal life (Jn 3:36; 6:40) and the Father has given judgment to the Son (Jn 5:22). The Son seems to stand in equality with God and often cannot be completely distinguished from the Father.

■   The Son Belongs to the Divine World   ■

The Son lives in the divine world and receives all from the Father (Jn 5:20; 8:47):

He who comes from above is above all; he who is of the earth belongs to the earth, and of the earth he speaks; he who

*comes from heaven is above all. He bears witness to what he
has seen and heard (Jn 3:31–32).*

All that the Son reveals depends on his previous participation in the
divine world.

■ The Son as Divine Being ■

For John, speaking about a pre-existence is not sufficient to understand the Son. He gives to the human Jesus divine prerogatives. As
he knows things supernaturally, he also prays differently:

*Father, I thank thee that thou hast heard me. I knew that you
hear me always but I have said this on account of the people
standing by (Jn 11:41–42).*

Instead of a fear of death, as seen in the synoptics, Jesus, when facing
death, offers a prayer glorifying the divine name (Jn 12:27–28). As
divine, even his captors fall down before him (Jn 18:6).

The title Son of God may not signify a divine being, but when this
title is joined to "Son," the readers learn the intention of the author to
teach belief in a divine being.

■ The Use of *Ego Eimi* (I Am) ■

The study of *ego eimi* has also generated a wealth of material. The
author used the expression nine times without a predicate. Each time,
Jesus is speaking, addressing a variety of audiences. The exception is
found in John 9:9. The blind man responds with the expression *ego
eimi* when the bystanders question his identity. This example differs
from all the other times the phrase appears and will help clarify the
meaning.

In the past some dismissed these sayings as of little consequence.
More recently scholars have viewed the expression as a theophonic
formula representing the divine name or presence. Certainly on the
lips of the blind man the expression can mean: "I am the one." But the
other uses of the expression opens up other possibilities.

■ Source for the Phrase ■

Several possibilities can explain the origin of the phrase. Some claim that it comes from Hellenism; others that it comes from the Jewish tradition in which *ego eimi* is the Greek translation for the Hebrew expression *'ani hu* found in Deutero Isaiah, as well as the Jewish practice to substitute *ani* for the sacred name YHWH. I will follow the latter opinion.

The phrase *ani hu* occurs six times in Isaiah 40–55. The translators of the Hebrew text into Greek (LXX of Septuagint) chose the Greek expression *ego eimi* to translate *'ani hu.* In Isaiah YHWH uses the phrase to signify that he alone is God. It presents YHWH as the Lord of history and creator of the world, closely related to other expressions of divine self-predication, especially the phrase, "I am YHWH."

In Jewish liturgical practice the words "I" and "he," by themselves, were sometimes used as surrogates for the sacred name. The expression *'ani hu* was used in the liturgy of the feast of Tabernacles, and the expression also appears in commentaries on the Passover service.

■ The Phrase in John ■

John seems to have selected this terminology to indicate the close relationship between Jesus and God as well as to indicate that a new age has dawned by his presence:

I tell you this now, before it takes place, so that when it takes place you may believe that ego eimi (Jn 13:19).

Jesus answered them: "I solemnly declare it, before Abraham came to be, ego eimi" (Jn 8:53).

These examples admit of no predicate understood in context. We can compare the first with Isaiah 43:10:

You are my witnesses, says the Lord, my servants whom I have chosen, to know and believe in me and understand that

*I am. Before me no god was formed and after me there shall
be none.*

The author underlines the solemnity of the statement by Jesus. Only
he could make it, and only those who believe in him could understand
its meaning.

The second example helps in the further disclosure of the meaning of the phrase. When the Jews heard, *ego eimi,* "they took up stones
to throw at him" (Jn 8:59). A similar reaction appears in Jn 10:22–39.
Jesus is in the temple and proclaims: "I and the Father are one." The
reaction is the same: he has blasphemed, and they seek to stone
him. The use of *ego eimi* stresses the unity of Father and Son, God
and Jesus.

■ **Implied Predicate** ■

Other examples of the use of this phrase admit of a predicate
understood. Of particular interest is the use in the garden of olives.
The soldiers, with Judas, approach Jesus and his band of disciples.
Jesus maintains complete control and asks:

*"Who is it you want?" "Jesus the Nazarean," they replied. "I
am he," he answered. Now Judas, the one who was to hand
him over, was there with them. As Jesus said to them, "I am
he," they retreated slightly and fell to the ground (Jn 18:5–6).*

*"I have told you, I am he," Jesus said. "If I am the one you
want, let these men go" (Jn 18:8).*

The translators chose to add the pronoun "he." The Greek phrase
is *ego eimi,* I am. From the context we can presume that it means "I
am the one." But when Jesus said *ego eimi,* they retreated and fell
down. In the presence of the divine, the only appropriate reaction is
adoration.

Only one example in the gospel of John finds a parallel in the
synoptics. When Jesus comes to his disciples walking on the sea he
announced: "It is I (*ego eimi*); do not be afraid" (Mk 6:50; Mt 14:27). In
Deutero Isaiah *ani hu* occurs sometimes in association with the power
of God over creation, especially his power over the sea. Earlier people
often looked upon the sea as an abode of evil spirits, anxious to destroy all who ventured out too far. This may underlie the usage in

Mark and Matthew. Perhaps this was the source of the theology used by John in his use of the phrase.

■ Conclusion ■

John used the phrase in an absolute sense in 8:58 and 13:19. The phrase centers on the divine presence in Jesus. People must recognize the unity between God and Jesus. When Jesus spoke: "Before Abraham came to be, *ego eimi*" (Jn 8:53), his listeners and readers today should retreat in awe in the presence of the divine.

■ Humanity of Jesus ■

The image of Jesus portrayed in the fourth gospel differs significantly from that in the other gospels. Jesus is the eternal Word of God, the heavenly Son of man, the Son of God. He alone represents the presence of the eternal God. He appears so divine in outlook that Christians for centuries have used this gospel to preach the divinity of Jesus and often overlooked the humanity of Jesus. No one can deny the emphasis on the divinity of Jesus in this gospel. But to fail to see how this same Jesus is also very human does an injustice to the genius of the Johannine community, its theology, and the individuals responsible for the gospel. The gospel of John portrays a human Jesus as well as the divine Jesus.

Although the Word existed for all eternity with the Father, no hint at a supernatural origin for Jesus appears in this gospel. Matthew and Luke offer us infancy stories about Jesus, and both imply that the origin of Jesus was unlike any other human origin: Jesus was virginally conceived. This gospel, in contrast, refers to Jesus as the son of Joseph:

> *We have found the one about whom Moses wrote in the law, and about whom the prophets spoke—I mean Jesus, the son of Joseph, the man from Nazareth (Jn 1:45).*

> *They kept saying, "Is this not Jesus, the son of Joseph, whose father and mother we know?" (Jn 6:42).*

Jesus belongs to a particular family and, unlike Mark who refers to Jesus as the son of Mary (Mk 6:3), John calls him the son of Joseph.

In chapter 8 we have some evidence that perhaps Joseph was not the father of Jesus. In fact, Jesus was illegitimate. While Jesus debates the Jews, he makes reference to God his Father, and they reply: "Where is your father?" (Jn 8:19). The accusation becomes clearer as the debate continues. In reply to Jesus' accusation that the Jews do the work of their father, the devil, they reply: "We were not born of an adulterous union" (Jn 8:41). Some saw Jesus as the son of Joseph and Mary; others conclude that somehow he was illegitimate. Perhaps Jesus was born within the first nine month period from the time Mary and Joseph began to live as husband and wife. Some followers concluded that Jesus' origin was divine intervention; others thought he was born out of wedlock. The author of John chose to record the impression of the latter while also maintaining that Jesus was the son of Joseph.

■ Jesus: His Friends and His Needs ■

Jesus needed human affection. One of his disciples intimately leans on his breast at the last supper; he enjoyed dinner with Martha and Mary and Lazarus; he spent time with his mother and brothers and even attended a marriage celebration. On his journey to Samaria he grew tired and thirsty. Like thousands before him and after him, he stopped at Jacob's well to rest and receive refreshment. He changed his mind. When the disciples ask him if he intends to go to Jerusalem for the feast of Tabernacles, he declines. Then he changes his mind and goes (Jn 7:8–10). He does not experience a painful agony in the garden in this gospel nor temptation in the desert, but the author preserved some hint at these aspects of his life when he remarks:

> When Jesus saw her weeping, and when he saw the Jews who had come with her weeping, he was deeply moved in spirit, so that an involuntary groan burst from him and he trembled with deep emotion (Jn 11:33).

> Jesus said to them: "Where have you laid him?" "Lord," they said to him, "come and see." . . . Jesus wept. . . . Again a groan was wrung from Jesus' inner being (Jn 11:34–38).

> "Now my soul is troubled" (Jn 12:27).

> When Jesus had said these things, he was troubled in spirit (Jn 13:21).

The first two examples display the emotion of Jesus as he encounters his friends after the death of Lazarus. The human Jesus sorrows at the death of a friend. The divine Jesus utters a word and Lazarus comes forth. The next examples contain fear and anxiety. He knows he will die, but instead of seeking release, he gladly accepts the will of God.

Jesus appears happy in the presence of good friends. He knows bodily needs and experiences sorrow at the death of a friend. He also knows fear and anxiety as he faces death and even experiences the depression of someone betrayed by a friend. Jesus is very human in this gospel.

■ Titles ■

Many of the titles used by this evangelist connote a divine being as we have seen. We can also see in some of these titles some subtle hints that the divinity of Jesus was never separated from his humanity. *Logos* emphasizes divinity, but *logos* becomes flesh. The climax of the hymn in the prologue is the relationship between *logos* and flesh. The *logos* entered into the human and earthly sphere. Before *logos* was in the glory of God; now *logos* has taken on the lowliness of human existence.

In Johannine terms flesh (*sarx*) means the earthbound as seen in 3:6; it connotes the transient and perishable as seen in 6:63. Flesh is the typical mode of being human in contrast to the divine and the spiritual. We need not insist on a reference by this word to the sacrifice of the Lord, "my flesh for the life of the world," (Jn 6:51) but it might be in the mind of the evangelist. The prologue seems to contain the principal themes of the gospel. We might then expect this central point of Johannine theology to figure here as well. If we can detect a reference to the death of Jesus, we have a further indication of the relationship between the *logos* and human existence, destined to death. The flesh assumed by the *logos* is the presupposition for the death on the cross. Once the *logos* becomes flesh, the author no longer used *logos* in the gospel, for in the humanity of Jesus we have contact with the divine.

The fourth gospel frequently contains double meaning words with various levels of thought. The title Son of man would translate the Hebrew *ben adam,* a variant of the Aramaic *bar e nas* or *bar a nasa.* Recent studies have shown that these expressions can mean everyman, or anyone. Son of man can designate the ideal person, the ordinary person. We have already seen this in Mark. Matthew knows this meaning, for he changed Mark's "sons of men" to just "men" (Mt 12:31). Matthew knew that sons of men is generic for men just as son of man is generic for man or everyman.

John surely knew the Aramaic idiom and was capable of linguistic subtlety. We also know he was fond of using "man" in reference to Jesus when other more honorific titles could have been used:

Who is the man who said to you, "Lift up your bed and walk"? (Jn 5:12).

You, a man, make yourself God (Jn 10:33).

It is better that one man should die for the people, rather than the whole nation should perish (Jn 11:15).

The maid servant who kept the door said to Peter: "Are you not this man's disciple?" (Jn 18:17).

So Pilate came out to them and said: "What accusation do you bring against this man?" (Jn 18:29).

Behold the man (Jn 19:5).

The Son of man has a heavenly origin; he possesses divine characteristics. He is also everyman, a man like anyone else. He epitomizes the best in human nature, and in him people discover the divine reality.

Jesus is Son of God like other faithful messengers with a divine mission. He is "Son" as well, implying a divine existence with God his Father. The human dimension of his sonship, however, appears evident in two passages.

He who believes in me, believes not in me but in him who sent me. And he who sees me sees him who sent me (Jn 12:45).

Have I been with you so long, Philip, and you do not know me? He who sees me sees the Father (Jn 14:9).

Jesus reveals the Father because he is the Son. We look upon the humanity of Jesus and see the God of all. The Son reveals the Father in human flesh. We humans learn only humanly. If God chooses to reveal himself, he must do so humanly. The Son revealed the Father by being a human Son.

The unusual use of *ego eimi* relates Jesus to the divine. The author of this gospel, however, also used this phrase to predicate. Jesus said that he was "the bread of life" (Jn 6:35), "the light of the world" (Jn 8:12), "the door" (Jn 10:7), "the good shepherd" (Jn 10:11), "the resurrection and the life" (Jn 11:25), "the way, the truth and the life" (Jn 14:6), "the true vine" (Jn 15:1). Such self-presentation appears in the Old Testament (Dt 32:2; Sir 24) as well as in other ancient near eastern texts. Often it connotes the care that the deity has for the created order. The author of John added qualifying adjectives: Jesus is the "good" shepherd, the "true" vine and light. All such predicates and adjectives relate Jesus to human life. As *ego eimi* Jesus is divine; he is also light to people; he is truth and the way, offering guidance and direction; Jesus is bread and the vine that sustains the branches, both offering life. He is the door through which people enter to find security; he is the shepherd who gives nourishment and protection from evil. Finally, Jesus is the resurrection which promises eternal life.

Again, the author moves from the divine level to the human level with his use of *ego eimi.* When Jesus proclaims: "Before Abraham came to be, *ego eimi*" (Jn 8:58), we face the divine; when he tells us he is bread and light and truth, we know the divine has come humanly.

Messiah or Christ refers primarily to the humanity of Jesus. The gospel opens with a confession that Jesus is the messiah: "We have found the messiah" (Jn 141). The set purpose of the gospel in John 20:31 includes belief in Jesus as messiah. Throughout the gospel, however, the title implies a spiritual reality rather than a political reality.

In several passages in the Old Testament Wisdom replaces the role of the messiah. In their zeal for the law, some scribes even began to identify the law with Wisdom. We have two parallel movements which converge on Jesus.

A prophetic tradition saw salvation and redemption as God's work through a messiah in history. Wisdom literature depicted salvation and redemption already implanted in creation by God. Individuals who live according to their consciences would discover Wisdom and experience the saving presence of God. The former movement centered on the external, the latter on the internal.

Both concepts are united in the fourth gospel. Jesus is incarnate Wisdom. We look at him and discover the Wisdom which God has implanted in the universe. Jesus fulfills the law and prophets and is Wisdom incarnate. The title Christ focuses on humanity which expresses divinity. Jesus as the incarnation of Wisdom bears the divine. He cannot be the messiah unless we see a human being who releases all of the possible energies implanted in our nature by a provident

God. When the evangelist claims that Jesus is the messiah, the Christ, he proclaims that the human Jesus can lead us to the divine both as fulfilling the prophets and as expressing Wisdom.

The fourth gospel has long been recognized as emphasizing the divinity of Jesus. It also preserves his humanity. He does not, however, resolve for us the relationship between the two. We know only that the Johannine community preserved a particular sensitivity to the divinity of Jesus but would not fall into the mistaken notion that the divinity eclipsed the humanity. With careful progression the author led us from humanity to divinity without losing anything in the process. The divine Jesus of the fourth gospel is the very human Jesus of Nazareth.

Further Study

P. Harner, *The "I Am" of the Fourth Gospel.*
R. Kysar, *The Fourth Evangelist and His Gospel.*
————, *John: The Maverick Gospel.*
F. Moloney, *The Johannine Son of Man.*
M. Taylor, *A Companion to John.*

4.

The Disciples of Jesus

The original source for this gospel was probably a document which narrated the various signs or miracles of Jesus. Some believed in him as a wonder-worker. The addition of the various titles, however, and the theology of the gospel direct the individual to respond to Jesus because of who he is, and not merely for what he has done. This development becomes clearer as we study some of the individual believers in this gospel.

■ Nathanael ■

Nathanael appears only in the fourth gospel: in the first chapter (Jn 1:43–51), and in the final chapter (Jn 21:2), where he, and the other disciples, meet Jesus on the shore of the Sea of Galilee. His first appearance seems to be a transformed vocation scene. The conversation between the Lord and the disciple seems contrived but leads to the great testimony of faith: "You are the Son of God; you are the king of Israel" (Jn 1:49).

Nathanael represents the true Israelite who comes to believe in Jesus. John describes him seated under a fig tree. To a perceptive reader, this recalls the Jewish tradition about the study of the scriptures under the fig tree. Jesus reveals God and perceives the quality of incipient faith in a man who bears an Old Testament name and is engaged in an activity most characteristic of God's people. Nathanael is the true Israelite in whom there is no guile.

117

■ **The Samaritan Woman** ■

The faith of the Samaritan woman, and her profession of Jesus as the messiah, sharply contrasts with the searchers of miracles narrated in chapter 2:

Now when he was in Jerusalem at the Passover feast, many believed in his name when they saw the signs which he did, but Jesus did not trust himself to them (Jn 2:23–24).

Jesus offered her living water, revealed the true worship of God, and promised her salvation. The Samaritan woman accepted his words even if she did not fully understand. She not only came to faith, but became a missionary, bringing others to Jesus.

As the narrative unfolds the woman moves from curiosity to a final acceptance in faith. Jesus took the initiative. She recognizes that he is a prophet, and after Jesus gives her the meaning of true worship, she recognizes him as the messiah. The episode closes with the townspeople coming to accept Jesus not on the testimony of the woman but through their own experience of Jesus.

The Samaritan woman exemplifies the active receptivity needed in one who will follow Jesus. She also fulfills her responsibility as a follower by leading others to Jesus. Her lack of understanding never prevents her from acceptance, and her continual probing leads her to full faith.

■ **Philip** ■

Philip in the fourth gospel seems rather complex. He appears in four places: Jn 1:43–51; 6:1–15; 12:20–36; 14:1–14. The interpretation of the last three appearances depends on the remembrance of Philip in chapter 1. In the opening chapter Philip appears as a believing disciple. He heard the call and accepted Jesus as "the one of whom Moses in the law and also the prophets wrote" (Jn 1:45).

Philip in chapter 6 seems like a believer who does not understand. Jesus is aware of the misunderstanding. Philip finds it hard to believe that anyone can feed such a large multitude but learns from the experience that Jesus has such power.

The third occurrence also presents Philip as the misunderstanding disciple. He wanted a manifestation of God, a theophany, such as

Moses received, but no such theophany would be given to Philip. Jesus revealed the face of God. The follower who looked at Jesus could see the human face of God.

The final appearance of Philip casts this disciple in yet another role. In chapter 12 the Greeks wish to see Jesus and ask Philip. He speaks to Andrew. Both disciples bear Greek names. Previously, Philip was identified as coming from Galilee, the land of the Gentiles in a Jewish tradition. The symbolism seems complete. Just as the Samaritan woman introduced her fellow Samaritans to Jesus, so the Greeks are introduced to Jesus by Philip, who represents the Greek disciples. He also was a missionary and could never be hindered from his acceptance of the Lord in spite of his lack of full understanding.

■ Martha and Mary ■

Throughout the narrative of the raising of Lazarus, Martha believes in Jesus but her faith needs further development. She addresses Jesus with lofty titles: Lord, Christ, the Son of God, he who is coming into the world (Jn 11:27). She does not, however, yet believe that he has power to give life. She sees Jesus as a divine intermediary but does not see him as the giver of life. Jesus aids her faith by showing the deeper truth behind the lofty titles. As he raises Lazarus from the dead, Martha can come to understand that his words give life.

Mary falls at the feet of Jesus, but like her sister does not demonstrate a particularly deep faith. She also uses the right words but without complete understanding. Mary will come to believe that Jesus is the messiah who will give life to all who believe in him. Jesus will demonstrate further the result of personal faith when he speaks his word and Lazarus comes out of the tomb.

■ Judas ■

No presentation of the followers of Jesus could neglect Judas. He appears as one of the twelve (Jn 6:67–71), at the anointing of Jesus (Jn 12:1–8), in the supper scene (Jn 13:2, 26–30), and in the passion account (Jn 18:2–5). Each scene has a parallel in the synoptic tradition, but in this gospel the author adds his own understanding of this follower. He is a thief (Jn 12:6; 13:27–30) who takes what is not his own. He is a figure of darkness (Jn 13:30). The devil has entered him (Jn 13:2) and as a result he allied himself with the enemies of the Lord.

Judas exemplifies the person to whom faith was offered and rejected. He could have walked in the light but chose the darkness. At the moment of the passion two worlds stand in conflict: the world of the Father and Jesus and faith and light, and the world of the devil and evil and darkness. Jesus represented one world; Judas the other.

■ Mary ■

The mother of Jesus appears in only two episodes in this gospel: Cana (Jn 2:1–11) and Calvary (Jn 19:25–27). The evangelist does not call her by name. She is the mother of Jesus or his mother. She makes no profession of faith, and when Jesus speaks to her, he uses the title "woman."

From earliest times the figure of the mother of Jesus in this gospel has been interpreted symbolically. She is the new Eve, the symbol of the church, or Jewish Christianity, but more than any other symbolism, she exemplifies a complete and total faith in her Son. She believes in him and with that firm trust awaits the fulfillment of her faith. Mary remains steadfast in her commitment. She does not need to have her faith explained nor do we have any reference to the genesis of her faith.

At Cana she believed that Jesus would never allow the wedding couple to be embarrassed. She believed that Jesus would respond to the need. At Calvary, she joined the beloved disciple in a common faith and a common expectation of the full revelation that would take place at the "hour" of Jesus, his glorification. Mary demonstrated both the need for fidelity and its reward.

■ Mary Magdalene ■

Mary Magdalene also appears in two passages: 20:1–2 and 20:11–18. The latter is a dramatic presentation of the faith response of Mary to the risen Lord. The former refers to her visit to the empty tomb.

The encounter between Mary and Jesus might have an apologetic undertone. The objection that the disciples have stolen the body of the Lord cannot be valid since the possibility of grave-robbing is raised by one of the followers of Jesus. The main purpose, however, of the evangelist seems to be the presentation of faith in the risen Lord. Jesus called Mary by name and she responded by calling him rabbi (teacher). Mary at first does not understand the meaning of the resurrection and wishes to cling to him (Jn 20:17). Jesus himself interprets its meaning. The risen Lord must ascend to the Father. Mary must not just believe that the Lord has risen—"I have seen the Lord" (Jn 20:18)—but must become an evangelist to announce his resurrection to others. Mary heralds this proclamation of faith.

■ **Thomas** ■

Thomas appears in this gospel as one of the twelve in 11:16 and in this episode joins the resurrection of Lazarus to the approaching death of Jesus. In 14:5 he is the unknowing disciple: "Lord, we do not know where you are going; how can we know the way?" Even before we meet Thomas in chapter 20 we have seen him as the disciple with bravado who will die with Jesus and the disciple who just does not know.

In chapter 20, Thomas believes in Jesus because he has experienced him. He doubted the testimony of the other disciples who had seen the Lord. He wanted to put his fingers into the wounds of the nails and his hand in the wound of the lance. Jesus appears and Thomas explicitly makes a profession of faith in the divinity of Jesus: "My Lord and my God" (Jn 20:28). The final verse discloses the situation of all later communities: individuals must believe in the risen Lord as Thomas did, but without the actual appearance of Jesus: "Blessed are those who have not seen and yet believe" (Jn 20:29).

■ **Peter** ■

Peter figures prominently in all four gospels. In the fourth gospel he appears frequently (Jn 1:41; 6:8, 68; 13:6, 9, 24, 36; 18:10, 15, 25; 20:2, 4, 6; 21:2, 3, 7, 11, 15). These passages have some similarity to the synoptic tradition but also present a peculiar Johannine nuance. Often Peter functions in a subordinate position to the beloved disciple.

Jesus changes the name of Simon in chapter 1, after he has been led to Jesus through Andrew his brother. In chapter 6 he speaks for the twelve in his profession of faith:

> You have the words of eternal life and we have believed and
> we have come to know that you are the holy one of God
> (Jn 6:68).

The synoptic tradition presented Peter as confessing belief in the messiahship of Jesus. The fourth gospel bases this messiahship on the presupposition that Jesus reveals God. To be messiah in the fourth gospel does not mean the same thing as the messiah in the Old Testament tradition.

A third passage that needs our attention is the scene at the empty tomb (Jn 20:3–10). The beloved disciple arrived at the tomb first and waited for Peter, who looked in and saw that it was empty but did not believe. The beloved disciple looked in "and he saw and believed" (Jn 20:8). Peter did not come to faith in the risen Lord because of the empty tomb but only through and experience of Jesus as risen. The beloved disciple saw and believed.

In the final chapter Peter is listed first among the disciples (Jn 21:2), described as a fisherman (Jn 21:3, 11), and one to whom the risen Lord has revealed himself (Jn 21:14). The focus of the chapter centers on the pastoral office of Peter. Peter had come to faith in the risen Lord, and once he has professed his love of Jesus, then he can lead the sheep.

■ **The Beloved Disciple** ■

The beloved disciple appears with Peter in the final chapter (Jn 21:2–7; 19–24), at the last supper (Jn 13:21–26), at the foot of the cross (Mt 19:25–27), and in the race to the tomb (Jn 20:2–10). In the latter he is also called "the other disciple," and for this reason we can identify him with "the other disciple" in 18:15–16. The beloved disciple is not just another believer among many but epitomizes the believer, the disciple, the beloved, and the one who gives witness.

As believer the beloved disciple contrasts with Peter at the tomb. Neither Mary Magdalene nor Peter comes to faith in the risen Lord at the tomb. For the man who represents the believer par excellence, the empty tomb is sufficient. He has not seen but he has believed. In the final chapter the beloved disciple proclaims to Peter: "It is the Lord" (Jn 21:7).

He is the disciple. He followed Jesus and believed in his word. In the gospel of John discipleship extends beyond the group known as the twelve, and so we need not identify the beloved disciple with one of the twelve. He probably became a follower of the Lord only in Jerusalem, which would explain how he was known to the group surrounding the high priest (Jn 18:15–16).

This disciple is also described as the one whom Jesus loved (Jn 13:23; 19:26; 20:2; 21:7, 10) and preeminently deserves to be called a friend of Jesus (Jn 15:15). At the last supper he reclined on the breast of Jesus (Jn 13:25) and shared a community of faith with the mother of the Lord (Jn 19:26–27).

Because of his relationship with Jesus he could give witness and testimony. The faith and love qualified the beloved disciple to lead others to believe and to have eternal life. He had witnessed:

> He who saw this has borne witness—his testimony is true and he knows that he tells the truth—that you also may believe (Jn 19:35).

In the final chapter the testimony of the beloved disciple continues in the church through his account of the life and death and resurrection of Jesus, the Johannine gospel.

The beloved disciple exemplifies all that faith in Jesus implies. He shows the fidelity of Mary, the acceptance of Nathanael, of Peter, of Mary Magdalene. He never doubts, never misunderstands, but always knows in whom he has placed his trust.

This analysis of disciples could continue. The man born blind, Nicodemus, and the royal official also have close relationships to Jesus. I have chosen just some of the individuals of the fourth gospel to show how the divine and human Jesus fulfills his mission only when people come to believe in him. Each follower can offer some appreciation of faith, but it is the mother of Jesus and the beloved disciple who best manifest the ideal believers. In these individuals we come to recognize the fundamental need for a personal commitment to the Lord. With this faith comes the possibility of the love that alone binds individuals to Jesus and to each other.

Further Study

R. Collins, "The Representative Figures in the Fourth Gospel."
J. F. O'Grady, *Individual and Community in John.*

5.

Johannine Ecclesiology and Eschatology

The meaning of the church connotes different images to various members of the Christian community. Some see it as an institution, others as a sacramental system or close fellowship. Still others see it as a prophetic voice or a servant community responding to the needs of the world. The gospel of John does not respond to every aspect of the Christian church. Even the gospel at the end of the first century does not give us a complete theology. We find, however, insights into certain aspects of the church's life that remain important for all generations.

■ The Johannine Community ■

The foundations for the church community, for John, are faith in Jesus and a profound love of the brethren. A specific group of people stand behind this gospel, a community that stressed faith and love as their hallmark. The two parables already studied, the good shepherd and the vine and the branches, implicitly point to a collectivity even if the point of each parable stressed the individuals in the collectivity. We also can find a sense of community in the epistles of John even if they considered themselves a sectarian group. With the presence of faith and love all aspects of the church's life could have meaning. On the presupposition of this faith and love, the gospel gives specific teachings on baptism, the eucharist, and church authority.

124

■ Sacraments in John ■

The debate on the presence or absence of sacraments in the gospel of John continues without abatement. Some find strong sacramental references throughout the gospel and even manage to find some reference to all seven sacraments. Others find a sacramental approach but fail to discover the references to the seven sacraments. Still others admit the presence of at least baptism and the eucharist but think that the author, or the community, present their own distinctive approach to the Christian sacramental system.

■ Baptism ■

Unlike the synoptics, the gospel of John does not treat the baptism of Jesus by John. The first chapter, as well as the final witness of John to Jesus (Jn 3:22–26), implies that John baptized Jesus, especially when we compare these references to the synoptics. Still, the gospel does not tell us specifically that John baptized Jesus. Also, the author never refers to John the Baptist or John the Baptizer. He is simply "John." The author of this gospel is more interested in the baptism of the Spirit.

> And John bore witness, "I saw the Spirit descend as a dove from heaven, and it remained on him. I myself did not know him; but he who sent me to baptize with water said to me, 'He on whom you see the Spirit descend and remain, this is he who baptizes with the Holy Spirit.' And I have seen and have borne witness that this is the Son of God" (Jn 1:32–34).

The text has baptismal overtones, but the author chose not to emphasize baptism by water but rather a new baptism of the Spirit which Jesus would confer.

■ Nicodemus and Baptism ■

The dialogue with Nicodemus contains some references to baptism. The burden of the remarks of Jesus, however, concerns the entering into the kingdom of God, being born again, or from above, through the Spirit. God must raise the individual from the natural level of life to the divine level since flesh begets flesh and spirit begets spirit. Just as God breathed his Spirit into the lifeless form in creation to give new life, so in the new creation the same Spirit gives life through Jesus.

The text refers essentially to baptism by the Spirit. This outpouring of the Spirit should have been recognized by Nicodemus since the Old Testament contains several such references (Is 4:4; Zech 12:10; 13:11; Ez 36:25–27). Nicodemus, however, missed the meaning that Jesus intended.

One verse does seem to imply baptism by water: "No one can enter the kingdom of God without being begotten of water and the Spirit" (Jn 3:15). We should compare this with: "No one can see the kingdom of God without being begotten from above" (Jn 3:3), and with the following:

> *The wind blows where it will. You hear the sound it makes but you do not know where it comes from, or where it goes. So it is with everyone begotten of the Spirit (Jn 3:8).*

The entire dialogue refers not to water but to the Spirit. We can easily drop out the words "water and" and the entire passage makes eminent sense. For this reason some see these two words as additions to the chapter, added by a later hand to bring the teaching of this gospel in accord with the practice of water baptism. The problem with this opinion is the lack of any manuscript evidence to support it. Even the most conservative exegete, however, will admit that the original meaning of this text refers not to baptism by water but to baptism by the Spirit. We might explain the text on the supposition that somewhere in the process of the Johannine tradition the rebirth of the Spirit, the chief teaching here, became associated with the act of water baptism. The earliest tradition emphasized the role of the Spirit and faith. Since this was primary, in the thought of the Johannine community, water baptism could never suffice.

■   The Feast of Tabernacles   ■

On the feast of Tabernacles Jesus stood up and cried:

> *If anyone thirst let him come and let him drink who believes in me. As the scripture says: "From within him shall flow rivers of living water" (Jn 7:37–38).*

Other versions choose a variant reading:

> *Let him come and let him drink. He who believes in me,*
> *as scripture has it, from within him shall flow rivers of liv-*
> *ing water.*

From whom does the living water flow: Jesus or the believer or both? No matter what conclusion we draw, the point of the verse is faith and the Spirit, and not water baptism. The following verse clarifies more:

> *Here he was referring to the Spirit whom those who came to*
> *believe in him were to receive. There was, of course, no Spirit*
> *yet, as Jesus had not yet been glorified (Jn 7:39).*

We also can compare this verse with the following:

> *One of the soldiers thrust a lance into his side and immedi-*
> *ately blood and water flowed out (Jn 19:34).*

And recall the death of Jesus: "Then he bowed his head and handed over his Spirit" (Jn 19:30). The two ideal believers, his mother and the beloved disciple stood at the cross of Jesus to receive his Spirit as he was glorified. The outpouring of the Spirit and the flow of water in chapter 19 fulfills the prediction in chapter 7. Water in chapter 7 refers to the Spirit which is the source of faith. The ideal believers were present to receive this Spirit.

■   The Blind Man   ■

The cure of the blind man in chapter 9 by washing in the pool of Siloam was interpreted by many of the fathers of the church to refer to baptism. Does the text allow for such an interpretation?

The author narrates the miracle in one verse. He describes the gestures of Jesus and tells us that the man sees only after he has washed. The man's physical blindness contrasts with the spiritual blindness of the Jews who refuse to believe in Jesus. The man washes and sees and then he believes in Jesus. The dominant reference is faith, but the water also plays a part.

We also learn the meaning of the pool: Siloam, a name which

means "one who has been sent" (Jn 9:23). Since in this gospel Jesus is the one who has been sent (Jn 3:17; 34; 5:36 etc), the author associates the pool with Jesus. Water from this same pool was used during the feast of Tabernacles when Jesus remarked that he was the source of living water.

The man born blind, born in sin according to the Jewish interpretation, must be washed in the pool. Here and only here does the evangelist afford power to the water, but not in a magical sense, since the name of the pool binds the water to Jesus himself. The man needed to wash to be healed. Jesus caused the healing but used water and then the man believed. The baptismal overtones are strong in this chapter, but once again the emphasis lies on the presence of faith and the power of Jesus.

■ Footwashing ■

The sacramental meaning of the footwashing comes not from the choice of word, nor the context, but rather from the importance given to the gesture by Jesus himself: "If I do not wash you, you shall have no share in my heritage" (Jn 13:8). We are not involved with a simple example to be imitated but with a salvific act by Jesus. If the footwashing can symbolize the saving death of Jesus, then the importance of participation in the action becomes intelligible. The evangelist in this passage makes reference to the humility of Jesus:

> You address me as teacher and Lord, and fittingly enough, for that is what I am. But if I wash your feet, I who am teacher and Lord, then you must wash each other's feet (Jn 13:13–14).

This forms part of the meaning of the gesture, but the reference to sharing in his heritage also sees the action as proleptic of the humiliating death of Jesus. The opening statement of passing to the Father and the conclusion of the footwashing with reference to the betrayal of Judas situates the incident in the context of the death of the Lord. Jesus provoked Peter to question him, which in turn gave Jesus the opportunity to explain the salvific meaning of his death. People will share in his heritage and would be cleansed of sin.

If the meaning of the footwashing is salvific, can we find any baptismal allusions? The only possibility that I see for some baptismal overtones comes not from the footwashing but from its relationship to the death of Jesus. Jesus gives his Spirit when he dies. Possibly we can relate this chapter to the giving of the Spirit when Jesus dies and then relate that to chapter 7. Such references, however, are secondary if they exist at all. Baptism appears far from the mind of the author, since he is more concerned with faith and the giving of the Spirit in the death of Jesus.

■ Eucharist ■

The eucharistic interpretation of chapter 6 creates a most heated debate in the study of the Johannine sacramentary. Some find eucharistic meaning throughout the chapter; others admit eucharistic teaching but not in a primary sense, or at least not throughout the chapter. Still others limit the eucharistic teaching to verses 51–58:

> Let me solemnly assure you, if you do not eat of the flesh of the Son of Man, and drink his blood, you have no life in you. He who feeds on my flesh and drinks my blood has eternal life and I will raise him up on the last day. For my flesh is real food and my blood real drink. The one who feeds on my flesh and drinks my blood remains in me and I in him (Jn 6:53–56).

The chapter opens with the narrative of the multiplication of the loaves. Some eucharistic overtones appear in this miracle, especially when we compare the words used with the account of the institution of the eucharist in the synoptics. (The gospel of John does not narrate for us the institution of the eucharist at the last supper although the author has the longest section devoted to the last supper among the evangelists.) "To give thanks" appears in the miracle and at the last supper account in the synoptics. Jesus himself distributes the loaves as he gave the bread at the last supper. The use of "gather up" and "fragments" find parallels in the eucharistic prayer of the Didache, an early church document.

The first section of the discourse refers not to the eucharist but to the bread come down from heaven which is the word Jesus offered. Jesus, like Wisdom, invites all to come and eat of his bread, his word, which gives life. Jesus himself remarks: "And they shall all be taught by God" (Jn 6:45). The chapter speaks clearly of the need to believe in Jesus to have life. The final section informs us that not only from responding in faith, but also by feeding on his flesh and drinking his blood, shall we have life. The vocabulary in this last section has also changed: eat, flesh, blood, drink. The stress on eating the flesh and drinking the blood cannot be a metaphor for accepting the revelation offered by Jesus. It must refer to the eucharist since in a Jewish tradition people were forbidden to eat the blood of anything. These words present to the attuned ear the same basic wording in the institution account in Matthew: "Take, eat, this is my body . . . drink . . . this is my blood" (Mt 26:26–28).

A second indication to support eucharistic interpretation is the formula in verse 51: "The bread which I shall give is my flesh for the life of the world" (Jn 6:51). This resembles the Lucan formula: "This is my body which is given for you" (Lk 22:29). Even the announcement of the treason of Judas, which follows (Jn 6:71), adds another link to the last supper of the synoptics.

These verses are eucharistic and the earlier section of this chapter has a wisdom motif emphasizing faith (Jn 6:31–50). The author chose not to include the institution account of the eucharist in his gospel. What might have prompted him to include eucharistic teaching within a discourse on Jesus as the bread of life?

Some scholars suggest that the second section with its eucharistic themes serves to bring out the implicit eucharistic meaning of the bread of life discourse. I believe the opposite to be true: the first gives meaning to the second. The meaning of the Christian life may be summed up and expressed in the eucharist, but the eucharist can never be separated from faith. Jesus the revealer is primary. To him, people must respond in faith if they are to be saved. Since the Father draws people to Jesus and leads them to accept him and his words, then all else must rest upon this initial faith commitment. The community cannot celebrate the eucharist unless they have previously made their individual commitment in faith. The eucharist interprets the coming of Jesus and not vice versa. The Son continues to give his life to those who believe and who eat his flesh and drink his blood. The eucharist takes its meaning as the memorial of the redeeming incarnation of the Word of God and, for the church, presupposes a commitment in faith to Jesus.

■ Conclusion ■

The author of this gospel has his own distinctive interpretation of the sacraments. He stressed the spiritual value and related the sacraments to faith. Baptism and the eucharist take their place within the community based upon faith. Just as belief in the Lord as a miracle worker never sufficed, so a water baptism will not suffice. If people go to the font to be healed of their blindness, their sin, the font is Jesus himself and the healing comes from faith. The meaning of the eucharist depends upon a previous commitment to Jesus and an acceptance of him as Wisdom. Only when we have accepted him as the bread which reveals God and calls for faith can we "eat his flesh and drink his blood."

Perhaps at this time the early church had fallen into the error of emphasizing ritual over meaning, the danger for any organized church. The gospel of John reminded the Johannine community of the meaning of the sacraments and bore testimony to other Christian communities. They must all take great care never to lose the essential: the personal commitment in faith to the Lord.

We shall study the question of church authority when we examine the role of the beloved disciple and deal with the meaning of the gospel of John in the final chapter.

■ Johannine Eschatology ■

Eschatology studies the last things: death, judgment, heaven and hell. The word comes from the Greek, meaning the last thing or the last things. To talk about eschatology in the fourth gospel might cause some confusion since the gospel seems to take the future and bring it into the present time. The last things have already taken place. Throughout the gospel Jesus brings salvation in the present. The individual either accepts the offer of salvation or experiences damnation; he walks from darkness into light or remains in the darkness. John shifts the focus from future to present:

> *I solemnly assure you, an hour is coming, has indeed come, when the dead shall hear the voice of the Son of God and those who have heard it will live (Jn 5:25).*

This present eschatology, however, is not the only approach to the last things. Some passages in the gospel refer to a future resurrection and judgment. In the same chapter, as quoted above, the author refers to a future time when those in the tombs shall hear the voice of the Lord and come forth (Jn 5:28–29). In chapter 6 we have four stereotyped sayings: "And I will raise him up on the last day" (Jn 6:39, 40, 44, 57).

Some find these references to a future eschatology additions coming from the same hand that added "water and" in chapter 3 to bring this gospel in conformity with the more traditional approach to eschatology. All will at least admit that the gospel emphasizes the present rather than the future.

■ Eternal Life ■

Salvation, eternal life—the believer already possesses these according to the fourth gospel. The believer has passed from the realm of darkness and death and has entered into the realm of light and eternal life. God has given life to his Son, and the Son gives life to all who believe in him. People search for salvation and life and discover it when they accept Jesus:

> And this is eternal life, that they may know you the only true
> God and Jesus Christ whom you have sent (Jn 17:3).

The mission entrusted to Jesus means eternal life for people who believe. Since salvation is the goal of human life, people will possess this goal when they know God and Jesus. To know God and Jesus implies a communion between the believer and God through Jesus. The promise of eternal life is *now* and not postponed for some distant future. Eternal life is lived on earth, *now*. Once a person knows God and Jesus, he or she possesses eternal life and expresses this life in a love of the brethren.

■ Judgment ■

Judgment belongs to God who has given this responsibility to the Son: "The Father himself judges no one but has assigned all judgment to the Son" (Jn 5:22). The Son, however, does not exercise his responsibility in a legal or forensic fashion. Jesus offers people an opportunity to decide for darkness or light. If people choose to remain in the darkness, they bring judgment upon themselves; if they move to the light, they have passed through judgment. A future judgment is a ratification of what has already taken place. If a person decides against faith, then the Son must accept the decision and ratify that choice. When a person physically dies, the decision made in life becomes ratified for eternity:

He who refuses to honor the Son refuses to honor the Father who sent him. . . . The man who hears my word and has faith in him who sent me possesses eternal life. He does not come under judgment but has passed from death to life (Jn 5:23–24).

■ Resurrection ■

In chapter 11, the raising of Lazarus, Martha introduces the expectation of the resurrection on the last day. Jesus offers another possibility: he himself is the resurrection and the life; here and now in the presence of Jesus, resurrection takes place. In this very hour the dead hear the voice of the Son of God, and those who hear in faith come to a resurrected life and can never die. The teaching culminates in the actual raising of Lazarus who comes from the tomb after hearing the voice of the Son of God.

The study of the gospel of John includes a present and a future eschatology. Jesus saves *now*. He judges but only by giving people an option to decide. The author chose to emphasize the importance of salvation as already possessed through the coming of Jesus into human history. In Jesus the hope for fulfillment in resurrection has taken place. Martha moves from a future eschatology to an acceptance of a resurrection dependent upon listening to the word of the Lord and responding. The author did not reject the more traditional sense of a future eschatology but concentrated on the present.

This gospel displays a keen interest in a faith response by the individual. A person confronts his or her meaning in life with the possibility of eternal salvation through faith. The gospel has a profound existential flavor. With such an approach, it shifts emphasis from future to the present. The actual coming of Jesus is the eschatological event. Eschatology functions as part of christology. The fullness of salvation exists in Jesus *now*, and he offers this to humankind definitively and permanently. The personal decision brings about judgment and salvation and includes in itself the totality of the future.

Perhaps even for the Johannine community such a firm conviction about the reality of salvation existing in the present began to wane. They looked to a future fulfillment to make evident what they believed to have already taken place. For Christians today, the present eschatology of this gospel forces us to contemplate the meaning of life and the search for a personal existence in faith. The future can be less important if we can focus on the present reality. Whatever the future has in store for humankind, or the individual, we can never fall completely from God's love. God sent his Son so that we might pass from death through judgment and experience eternal life.

Further Study

R. Brown, *The Community of the Beloved Disciple.*
R. Kysar, *The Fourth Evangelist and His Gospel.*
————, *John: The Maverick Gospel.*
M. Taylor, *A Companion to John.*

6.

The Role of the
Beloved Disciple

---

*T*he gospel of John comes from a community of people, in all likelihood, under the guidance and direction of the beloved disciple. He founded this community and offered a distinctive approach to Christianity. He should not be identified as one of the twelve. In fact, this gospel downplays the twelve. The author concerns himself more with the disciples of the Lord than with the twelve apostles. This gospel often presents the beloved disciple as one of the closest companions of Jesus who fulfilled the demands of discipleship: faith in Jesus and the love of the brethren. The beloved disciple can testify to Jesus because of his relationship with the Lord. The bond of intimacy qualifies the disciple to lead others to believe and have eternal life because of their commitment in faith.

Chapter 21 has long been considered an addition to the gospel. (We shall return to the reasons for this later.) The first twenty chapters present one picture of the beloved disciple to be further developed in the final chapter.

■ The Beloved Disciple in Chapter 21 ■

In the first twenty chapters of this gospel the beloved disciple is the ideal follower of Jesus. He was an historical figure, even if he has been idealized. His presence in the final chapter suggests a person who played a most significant role in the Johannine community and this person had recently died:

*This is how the report spread among the brethren that this
disciple was not going to die. Jesus never told him that the
disciple was not going to die (Jn 21:23).*

If the beloved disciple was not an historical figure the question of his
death would never have arisen. The context of this final chapter is the
death of the beloved disciple.

The beloved disciple was an intimate of the Lord (Jn 13:23, 30),
and he would authenticate the testimony of the gospel (Jn 21:24). As
such, he would have had authority in his own right and would not have
been subservient to any other authority in the early church. When the
author of this chapter juxtaposes the beloved disciple with Peter, the
relationship between these two leaders of the church rises to the
surface.

■   Peter in Chapter 21   ■

Peter receives a pastoral office in this final chapter; he shares in
the authority of the good shepherd. This appearance of Peter, although proper to John, has some relationship to other episodes in the
synoptic tradition. Peter becomes the foundation of the church in
Matthew (6:16–19); he speaks for the apostles in Mark in his profession of faith (Mk 8:29), and in Luke Jesus tells him he will be a fisher
of men (Lk 5:10). Peter is always listed first in the list of apostles, and
Paul tells us that the risen Lord appeared to him (1 Cor 15:5).

The editor responsible for the final chapter of John did not seek
to establish the legitimacy of the ministry of Peter in the church since
this was already well-accepted. The purpose of the inclusion of Peter
in this chapter was to give an interpretation to an existing ministry.
The circumstances which marked the investiture of the first pastor
would create for all times the conditions for this ministry.

Jesus questioned Peter three times: "Do you love me?" Each time
Peter responded affirmatively and Jesus commissioned him to feed his
sheep. The first condition for ministry is the love of Jesus. The triple
repetition of the question may have the triple denial of Peter in the
background, but the meaning of the question and the ordering in the
dialogue forms the message "Feed my sheep" that presupposes the
love of Jesus.

The dialogue which follows, including the presence of the beloved
disciple, further elaborates the conditions of the ministry of Peter.

Previously the Lord called his followers to give up their lives for the brethren:

> This is my commandment: love one another as I have loved you. There is no greater love than this: to lay down one's life for one's friends (Jn 15:12–13).

Now Jesus calls upon Peter to die for Jesus if Peter wishes to exercise a role of ministry in the community. To die for the Lord would be the same as dying for the brethren. Such is the second condition for Peter's ministry.

When writing this chapter the author also carefully acknowledges that this office held by Peter has its foundations in Jesus. The author does not invent a ministry for Peter. Jesus himself conferred upon the prince of the apostles a share in his own authority. The writer does not wish to polemically question the authority of Peter but rather wishes to preserve a remembrance of the conditions upon which this ministry rests. Jesus chose Peter to share in his authority, his task of guiding the sheep, but did not give Peter an absolute authority. Jesus remains always the model shepherd to whom the Father has entrusted the sheep and no one can take them away from him. As Jesus died for the sheep, so anyone who will share in this pastoral ministry must also be willing to die for the sheep.

We are unable to verify the historical accuracy of the event so described in this chapter. Whatever the historical basis, in the mind of the author the authority in the Christian community must rest upon the love of Jesus with a willingness to die for the brethren. A pastoral ministry, unknown in the body of this gospel, but evidently part of the early church experience, forms the heart of the final chapter of the gospel of John. Why? What would have prompted the editor to add such a chapter?

■   Testimony of the Beloved Disciple   ■

Peter receives a pastoral office in this chapter; the beloved disciple receives the office of testimony. I have already expressed the opinion that the beloved disciple was the founder of the community, the source of its traditions and the guide that performed similar functions to those of the Paraclete. The gospel of John does not call the leader of the community a shepherd, but an analysis of the gospel gives evidence to the primacy of this historical figure in the Johannine community as a shepherd.

The beloved disciple functions as an ideal believer, the epitome of what a follower of Jesus should be. In this chapter he also has an ecclesial function. Since he stands with Peter, he assumes a role that was important, not just for his own community, but also for the church.

Some contemporary Johannine scholars see the beloved disciple as the sign of the bond between the believer and the Lord, or a representative of the prophetic and charismatic role of the church. Whatever symbolic role he plays, he remains an historical figure in the early church, someone who could not be overlooked.

Chapter 21 concludes with a declaration that this disciple bears testimony to Jesus:

> *It is this same disciple who is the witness to these things; it is he who wrote them down, and his testimony, we know, is true (Jn 21:24).*

His testimony is authentic since he enjoyed a privileged position with Jesus. He was with the Lord at the last supper and stood beneath the cross on Calvary listening to the words of Jesus to his mother and to him. His presence at Calvary enabled him to testify that indeed Jesus had died, but his presence also made him the inheritor, with Mary, of the last most intimate tradition of Jesus.

The words spoken to Mary and the beloved disciple do more than express a concern of Jesus for his mother after his death. Since he began his ministry, Jesus had left family and home; thus the use of "son" has more theological significance than filial concern. The beloved disciple takes the place of Jesus for Mary. We understand something of this relationship if we return to the marriage feast of Cana in chapter 2.

■ Mary and Jesus at Cana ■

Jesus changed water into wine after he seemed to have refused this request of his mother. He explained: "My hour has not yet come" (Jn 2:4). Mary fails to understand, but confidently instructs the waiters to do as they are told. Mary believed in her Son, and thus the hour that would be completed in his glorification on Calvary has begun.

On Calvary, the beloved disciple assumes a role similar to that of Jesus. He will testify as Jesus himself testified. The beloved disciple inherited the testimony of Jesus and continues this testimony through his gospel. Mary represents not just herself but the church standing beneath the cross and accepts the testimony of the beloved disciple as he takes her into his home.

Peter received a pastoral ministry in this final chapter, and the beloved disciple received a ministry of testimony. The ecclesial function of the disciple brings his testimony to the revelation of Jesus. As the intimate of the Lord his witness has great value not only for his own community but also for the entire church community. The gospel of John continues this ministry of the beloved disciple.

■ Peter and the Beloved Disciple ■

In this last chapter Peter and the beloved disciple stand side by side, each with his own responsibility. We know that by the end of the first century the church was sufficiently organized to produce Luke/ Acts and the pastoral epistles. We also have the origins of a monarchial episcopacy, as witnessed by the letters of Ignatius of Antioch. The reference to Diotrophes in 3 John manifests some tension within the church, especially with regard to leadership. Perhaps some church leaders became too proud in their position and laid claim to an authority of Jesus that demanded obedience. The author of 1 Peter seems to know of this problem:

> God's flock is in your midst; give it a shepherd's care. Watch over it willingly as God would have you do, not under constraint and not for shameful profit either, but generously (1 Pet 5:2–3).

Perhaps some ministers forgot the context of the conferral of office upon Peter and lorded it over their charges. Such an abuse of authority contradicted the expressed intention of the Lord as well as the conditions laid upon Peter by Jesus. The editor did not oppose the office of pastoral ministry but was greatly disturbed when the church leaders laid claim to the authority of Peter, and thus of the Lord, and then failed in the exercise of that office. By recalling the context in which Peter received his commission the editor reminded the church community of how authority must be exercised in the Christian church. At the same time he fulfilled the office of testimony of the beloved disciple which he also described in this final chapter.

Further insights into the historical circumstances of the final chapter are found in the reference to the death of the beloved disciple. As long as the founder and guide of the community lived, the Johannine community felt secure in its authentic interpretation of the Jesus tradition. But now that the founder had died, they would have to re-examine their position vis-à-vis the other Christian communities. Since clearly established hierarchical communities existed at the end of the first century, how would the Johannine community relate to these other churches, and what contribution would the testimony of the beloved disciple make to the developing church?

■ The Johannine Community ■

At the beginning of this book I described the Johannine community as a sectarian group. However, they differ from other Christian communities: they still claimed that their tradition extended back to Jesus himself through the beloved disciple. Without the line of continuity, the community would suffer from a credibility gap. Once we have accepted the authenticity of the Johannine tradition, however, we need not claim that this gospel presents a completely historically accurate portrait of Jesus. We need not also claim that the gospel of John and only that gospel presents the authentic Jesus tradition.

The Johannine community saw itself in continuity with Jesus, not necessarily as a group of eye-witnesses, but as heirs to an historical tradition based upon the testimony of the beloved disciple. The only possible justification for such a self-acceptance was the firm conviction that at the beginning of this community, and at the origin of its traditions, stood someone who had known Jesus personally. With this self-acceptance we can understand why the author of the first epistle of John could claim a right to make theological and ethical judgments with reference to other Christian communities. We can also understand how this community, through the beloved disciple, could present itself to the larger church, and offer a written document that would espouse a different approach to the Jesus tradition than that found in Matthew, Mark and Luke.

■ The Gospel of John and Gnosticism ■

Once we have accepted the peculiar nature of this gospel and maintain its authenticity, we also can appreciate something of what happened to both community and gospel in the second century. We know that the gnostics accepted this gospel and used it as one of their own. We also know that the church of this century had great misgivings about the gospel of John and only much later was it accepted as an authentic gospel. A line of development existed between the final acceptance of the gospel by the church in the late second century, but we are unable to trace this line back to the demise of the community, and before that to the beloved disciple. The use of the gospel by gnostics and its final acceptance by church authorities leads us to think that with the death of the beloved disciple some members of the community fell completely into gnosticism. Others would have become part of the established church. If we follow the various groups of people that R. Brown finds in this gospel, we might also presume that some returned to the synagogue. Some even fell into other heresies based upon their low christology. If the gospel turns up in both orthodox and heretical communities, someone had to offer them to these communities. Since the Johannine community was sectarian, I presume that members of the historical community carried the testimony of the beloved disciple with them as they became affiliated with other orthodox or heretical communities.

■ The Beloved Disciple Bears Witness ■

The final chapter was prompted by the death of the beloved disciple. As long as he was alive the community felt secure in its approach to Christianity. They preserved an authentic Jesus tradition and were living according to the interpretation given by their founder, a follower of the Lord. Upon his death, the Johannine community could continue to maintain its existence separated from the other churches, or it could become part of the developing hierarchical church. The editor prepared for the assimilation into the broader church through the inclusion of the final chapter. He accepted the authority of Peter but would not allow the office of testimony of the beloved disciple to fall forgotten into history. The beloved disciple had his contribution to make to Christianity—faith and love—and they alone are the true basis of Christianity. These are possible through the communication of the Spirit.

The Johannine community ceased to exist by the early second century. Like many other charismatic communities, it could not long survive in an evil world. Once the gospel became accepted by the larger church, the function of the beloved disciple, and his community, could continue their role in the history of Christianity. The gospel of John bears testimony, gives witness to the church of all times, to the faith and love that so characterized the teachings of the beloved disciple, and thus of Jesus.

Christianity can never be a monolith as long as this gospel exists. Jesus gave to the beloved disciple the office of testimony. He continues this function in the gospel that bears the name of John.

Further Study

R. Brown, *The Community of the Beloved Disciple.*
R. Culpepper, *The Johannine School.*
R. Schnackenburg, *The Gospel According to St. John, Vol. III.*

7.

The Origin of the Gospel

The origin and early history of this gospel remains in shadows. Many have offered their theories, and many more have disagreed with the various opinions that preceded their own explanations for the origin of the fourth gospel. A growing consensus accepts a collection of miracle stories as the most elemental source for the gospel. This collection emphasized the miraculous aspect of the life of Jesus and may have even concluded with the final verse of chapter 20:

> *Now Jesus did many other signs in the presence of his disciples which are not written in this book, but these are written that you may believe that Jesus is the Christ . . . (Jn 20:30–31).*

I have deliberately omitted the final section of this verse, "the Son of God, and that believing, you may have life in his name," since I would propose that this was added as the gospel itself developed. This final phrase shifts the emphasis from Jesus as a miracle worker to one who gives life to those who believe, a more highly developed christology than Jesus as a miracle worker.

Some authors (Bultmann in particular) detect a written source behind the many speeches of Jesus. The general opinion today rejects such a hypothesis. In all probability the actual speeches of Jesus as found in this gospel have their origins in homilies delivered by the beloved disciple to his community. As the beloved disciple continued to instruct his congregation on the teachings of Jesus, these homilies became incorporated into a document that eventually became our gospel.

Several people offer theories of development. Raymond E. Brown, in particular, presents his theory of five stages of development in his classic commentary on the gospel: first: a collection of traditional material independent from the synoptic tradition; second: this material developed into Johannine patterns probably through preaching and teaching; third: the organization of this material into a consecutive gospel; fourth: a secondary edition or perhaps several editions; fifth: final editing by someone other than the evangelist.

The problem with any theory of origin is conjecture. Each scholar can attempt to base his or her theory on the facts as known, but those very facts are limited. Thus they can have several interpretations. The gospel shows signs of development and various stages of writing, but this does not mean that anyone can ever completely or accurately explain this development. For the purpose of this introduction, the reader should be aware that the gospel shows signs of being "put together" by one or several editors and writers over an extended period of time.

■ Relationship to the Synoptics ■

The author of John has produced a gospel, and so parallels will exist between John and the other three evangelists. Some may think that the early Christians produced a new literary form when they created the gospels. Actually, the book of Jeremiah in the Old Testament offers a parallel to the gospels: the book is a collection of material some of which was actual teachings of Jeremiah, including biographical material, but which eventually was edited by a disciple into a somewhat coherent book. This parallel in the Old Testament could possibly form a literary model for all four evangelists.

When we actually compare the four gospels we can detect the similarities and the differences. Matthew, Mark and Luke are closer to each other, and often John stands off by itself. Still the similarities remain: all have a ministry of John the Baptist; all narrate a multiplication of the loaves, the healing of an official's son. Jesus has a ministry in both Galilee and Jerusalem. All have a last supper, a passion and the crucifixion. Each one has some teachings on the risen Lord.

In the past, writers and readers of the gospel supposed that John wrote his gospel to supplement and complete the synoptics. They envisioned the author with the three other gospels before his eyes and then carefully he filled in what was missing. The careful examination of the gospel shows no evidence for such a theory. The differences are too clarion to believe that John knew the synoptics as written documents. The best we can conclude on the relationship between John and the synoptics is a similar oral tradition behind all of the gospels. The similarities between John and Luke and, to a lesser degree, Mark (John and Matthew have the least in common) can be attributed to a cross-over of traditions in the early oral Jesus tradition. No evidence exists that would imply that John wrote knowing all of the synoptics and attempted to complete, correct or supplement them.

■ Influences on the Gospel ■

From what has preceded, the reader has learned that this gospel came from a mixed milieu and thus the intellectual, religious and cultural environment had its effect. Gnosticism may have influenced some thought patterns and may have caused the evangelist to teach that salvation is not from knowledge but through love, the glorification of Jesus, which was his death. Jewish speculation on Wisdom can account for some of the ideas in the prologue as well as the discourse on the bread of life. We cannot easily detect direct influences from Greek philosophy, but surely the milieu affected the community, and thus, indirectly, the gospel was shaped by its environment. This period of history allowed a general exchange of Old Testament thought, rabbinic Judaism, and Qumran ideology as well as Greek philosophy and at least inchoate Gnosticism. Since the author, and the Johannine community, lived in such a diverse milieu, we would expect to discover such indirect influences on the gospel. No one should conclude, however, that the gospel was a result of any one of the above-mentioned thought currents. The gospel of John is a document of Christian faith. The basic source is Jesus of Nazareth and those who have come to believe that he is the Son of God and have received life through faith.

■ Time and Place ■

The gospel of John was used by the gnostics by the middle of the second century. The two papyri discovered in Egypt, Rylands Papyrus 457 (P52) and Egerton Papyrus 2, the first of which is part of the gospel, the second of which includes part of a gospel probably using John, can be dated no later than 150. Since we have to allow a period of time for dissemination of the Johannine tradition, we can push its origin closer to the year 100. We also have the reference to the expulsion from the synagogue of Christians in chapter 9:22 and 16:2. Sometime between 85 and 90 Rabbi Gamaliel introduced the benediction to exclude Jews who confessed Christ from the synagogue. This will place the lower limit for at least one edition of the gospel. Since we cannot pinpoint an actual date, especially if we accept the theory of various editions, we are left with an elastic period sometime between 85 and 100. Personally I am inclined to date it closer to 85 than to 100 to account for the divergent viewpoints in this gospel when compared to other New Testament literature.

With regard to place, in the history of the interpretation of the gospel several locations have been suggested: Ephesus, Alexandria and Antioch in Syria. The more traditional place of origin is Ephesus. Irenaeus, the bishop of Lyon (circa 175), associates the apostle John with the fourth gospel as well as with Ephesus. This tradition, however, lacks strong early support, and this city would not provide the diverse cultural milieu needed. The same can be said for Alexandria. I would personally ascribe to Antioch in Syria as the place of origin. My one reservation on such a theory is that contemporary writers associate Luke and Matthew with Syria (some also locate Mark in Syria). I am somewhat skeptical in accepting the origin of all of the gospels from the same general area.

■ The Evangelist ■

The author of each gospel has chosen to remain unknown. He or she fulfilled a need for the early Christian communities and then chose to remain anonymous. Only later did each gospel become associated with a particular person. In the later generations of Christians, some saw the need to associate the gospels with the apostles, and thus Luke became the disciple of Paul and Mark became the disciple of Peter. Irenaeus, through a tradition from Polycarp, associated the fourth gospel with John the apostle. Historically we know that this tradition cannot be uncritically accepted.

The more current opinion accepts the beloved disciple, not to be identified with John the son of Zebedee, nor with one of the twelve, as the founder of the Johannine community and the source of its tradition. We have already discussed this unknown figure. While source of the tradition, he need not be considered the evangelist. Perhaps he was responsible for the early stages of the gospel, but eventually one other hand, if not several, shaped the final document. The comparison of chapter 20 with chapter 21 shows two conclusions. We have evidence that a final editor added chapter 21, and perhaps also the prologue and several other insertions within the body of the gospel. The gospel, in the opinion of both evangelist and final editor, can be associated with the beloved disciple since he was the source of the teachings. Since he was a confidant of the Lord, his teachings can be accepted as true.

The gospel of John portrays a fascinating interpretation of Jesus. This gospel continues to give guidance to the Christian church of this generation as it has fulfilled the mission of the beloved disciple in the past. We need not worry about the identity of the beloved disciple; we need not worry about the place of origin nor the actual date. Whether the evangelist was in fact several people, or whether we have one or two editors, matters little when we read the fourth gospel as a document of faith. We look to it for testimony to the teaching tradition and can only be enriched as this unknown founder of a particular Christian community leads us into the ever-deepening mystery of the Jesus tradition.

Further Study

R. Brown, *The Community of the Beloved Disciple.*
B. Lindars, *The Gospel of John.*
R. Schnackenburg, *The Gospel According to St. John.*

8.

The Meaning of the Gospel of John

Society vacillates between individualism, and collectivism. In most periods of history the extremes are not so evident, as the pendulum continues its swing. Recently, however, the emphasis on individualism has waxed strong. People live their own lives, make their own decisions, often not based on any consideration of the needs of the community. This sense of individualism is present in every aspect of life: education, politics, the economy, the family and religion.

The recent interest in eastern religions is individualistic. The charismatic movement has encouraged an individual faith commitment to Jesus as personal savior. Individuals become aware of their need to relate to Jesus on a deeply personal level and grow in the awareness of salvation as personally experienced. They have been baptized in the spirit of Jesus and know that the Lord has a personal interest in their lives. Jesus knows them by name, calls them to himself and promises the joys that only a personal commitment can create. The believer then leads others to Jesus so that they too may experience this joy. A community exists in the process but based on the personal relationship to Jesus.

The reactions of individuals, both as members of society and as members of the church, surely, are due in no small part to the emphasis on the collectivity that had characterized both society and the church for a long period of time. The reaction should have been expected. Recall the education that characterized the schooling of most adults: the program was controlled, based solely on chronological age. Gradually people learned that such a system was detrimental to intellectual growth, and change set in.

In Christianity, especially Roman Catholicism, the community was fundamental. Theology was based upon a philosophy that promoted the common good. On that basis decisions could be made for individuals. Decrees, regulations, and directives were universal in scope and application. If a person wished to participate in the life of the community, the only choice was to accept what was imposed from above. The other alternative was to leave the community. Uniformity in doctrine imposed rigidity in thought and practice. The Roman church may never have been in theory a monolith, but in practice it was just that. The Caiaphas principle prevailed: the individual will be sacrificed for the sake of the community.

The results were unfortunate. Intellectual activity died; adults were treated like children; regulations did not take into consideration changes in society, or different cultures; opportunities for enrichment to the church were lost. Often people became aware of their personal needs and found it impossible to remain within the church community and left.

The church influences society and vice versa. If society was influenced by the control of the collectivity, so would the church. Often, however, the Roman Catholic Church itself encouraged such attitudes that were in the environment and increased their strength. The structure of the church, with its concentration on power in the hierarchy, heightened the tendency to control individuals and treat them as parts of the whole.

The causes and sources for the current unrest that erupted at the Vatican Council may be more numerous and more intangible than historians can count. Certainly part of the unrest comes from the undue emphasis on the collectivity. The church failed to deal with the needs, hopes and expectations of the individual. For too long the person was lost in the sea of bureaucracy. Finally, people decided to make their presence and their needs felt.

As might be expected, all the problems of society and the church were not resolved with the advent of individualism. Perhaps we have only shifted from one problem to another. The tension remains. Both society and church have to maintain a creative tension between individual and community.

■ Individual and Community in John ■

Certainly the Johannine community struggled with individualism and reacted against a strong collectivism. The gospel stressed the individual commitment to the Lord as fundamental. The author saw a need for the collectivity characterized not by authority and structure but by a mutual love of the brethren. The gospel places communal elements in their rightful perspective. Ritual, the celebration of baptism and the eucharist, will mean nothing unless it expresses the hearts of people committed to Jesus. Authority is necessary and possible but not the type that lords it over others. A common faith and a profound love of the brethren will bind the community together with bonds more powerful than established authority and hierarchical structure. The gospel contains a tension resolved in favor of neither the individual nor the community.

The gospel of John calls the church back to its roots. Christianity can never really function, if it is based on organization, order and control, a system of doctrine and a code of ethics. When a community settles for a formalized ritual and fails to encourage and accept personal involvement and commitment, the church teeters on its demise. When church authority fails to consider the needs, expectations, and hopes of the individual believers, the authority is suspect. The Johannine community knew the pitfalls other Christian communities experienced and tried to give its own testimony to the essentials of the Jesus tradition. Without the individual believers, the church loses its foundation. The gospel even admits differences in faith. Some doubted, some lacked full understanding, some were impetuous, and some even fell from faith. Jesus accepted them and the beloved disciple made room for them in the community.

The Johannine tradition did not oppose an organized and hierarchical church. Evidently some traced their authority to Peter. The final editor recognized the legitimacy of such claims but also pointed out the conditions under which the authority should be exercised. From the perspective of the twentieth century we know that Christianity could not have survived without order and organization. The author of the final chapter recognized this as well and knew that at times individuals must yield their rights in favor of the needs of the community—but not always.

Today, decrees, regulations and organization mean little unless they come from people with the faith commitment to the Lord with a willingness to die for one of the brethren. This must be especially visible in the leaders of the church, those who share in the authority of the good shepherd.

The contemporary world pays attention when the heart of Christianity is proclaimed and professed in church structures. The bond of love and the faith commitment builds up the community. At times, some will become so overwhelmed by the power of faith and love that they will overlook good order. They forget what the daily operation of a community of 750 million people entails. Yet, they too must be allowed their rightful place in the church so that the testimony of the Johannine community will continue. Such individuals stand as beacons to all members of the church, reminding, and chiding if necessary, that faith and love creates the Christian church.

Historically the enthusiasts, the charismatics, called the gospel of John their own. We also know that historically church leaders used Matthew, Luke/Acts and the pastoral epistles as their mandate. No Christian can choose one book of the New Testament to the exclusion of the others. The word of God comes to us expressed in many works that compose one Bible. If those inclined to organization studied the gospel of John, and if the enthusiasts studied Matthew and the pastorals, we might have the creative tension that produces much good.

The testimony of the beloved disciple lives as long as people read the fourth gospel. It remains until the Lord returns, for it has been written that you may believe and love and profess that "Jesus is the Christ the Son of God and that believing you may have life in his name" (Jn 20:31).

PART IV

The Jesus Tradition and the Church: Matthew

1.

The Ecclesial Gospel

Sometime between 70 and 80 C.E. a Christian community, composed of Jewish converts and Gentile converts, recorded for posterity the gospel we have come to call Matthew. This community, approaching the final quarter of the century, experienced various factions, each one calling for recognition. Under the influence of the Jewish Christians, many believed that Jesus would return quickly in triumph. With the passage of time and the death of many of the followers of the Lord, a rethinking had to take place. The number of Gentile converts also increased and Jewish converts decreased. Something drastic was happening to Christianity. It looked to a different future than many had anticipated. Matthew, the unknown author, presented himself as the

> scribe who had been trained for the kingdom of heaven . . .
> like a householder who brings out of his treasure what is new
> and what is old (Mt 13:52).

As the Matthean community looked to a delayed coming of Jesus and saw that the future was with the Gentiles, he would preserve the best of the old while being very open to the new.

The gospel is ecclesial. He alone among the evangelists used the word *ecclesia,* "church," and used it three times.

> If he refuses to listen to them, tell it to the church, and if he
> refuses to listen even to the church, let him be to you as a
> Gentile and tax collector (Mt 18:17).

> And I tell you, you are Peter, and on this rock I will build
> my church and the gates of hell shall not prevail against it
> (Mt 16:18).

Earlier in this work I compared the stilling of the storm in Mark 4 and Matthew 8. Recall that the context of Matthew is following Jesus. The disciples followed him into the boat. In early Christian symbolism, the boat was often used to signify the church and so the followers of Jesus joined him in the church. While in the boat, the storm develops and the disciples turn to the sleeping Jesus and pray, "Lord, save," not unlike our prayer, "Lord, have mercy." Jesus arises from sleep. First he assures his followers that he is with them and then calms the storm. The reaction is that "all marvel." This ecclesial gospel presents the stilling of the storm in the context of following Jesus, not just in the time of the Lord but for all times. Believers will have storms as members of the church but Jesus is with them; they should pray and feel assured of his presence. In the end, anyone who looks upon the church will marvel at its strength in bearing with adversity.

The gospel offered guidance to teachers and administrators in the church. The teachers would continue the teaching of Jesus and the administrators would insure the continuation of the community. All would be committed to the good news: God has visited his people offering salvation, revealed in and through Jesus, the Son of God, messiah and Lord of all. They proclaimed this gospel first to the Jews and now to the Gentiles, for the reign of God had drawn near to humankind. God offered a communion to all who would believe in Jesus. This Matthean community would continue this preaching with a keen recognition that the future lay with the Gentiles and with a desire to preserve those elements in Judaism which would benefit the nascent Christian church. The Jesus tradition underwent another development.

The author knew the liberal and conservative factions among both Jewish and Gentile Christians. He hoped to establish a centrist position which would maintain both the left and the right. He chose Peter to symbolize this centrist position. Peter was known in early Christianity as part of the earliest Jewish Christian community open to the Gentiles. His position in Acts is well known. He struggled to maintain acceptance and good relationships with the more conservative Jewish Christian community at Jerusalem and at the same time recognized with Paul the need for the opening to the Gentiles. The leader of the apostles preserved the Jewish roots and was open to the concerns of the Gentiles. Matthew knew that Christianity had to seek its own identity. It had to separate from the synagogue but in such a way as not to repudiate its origins. To record for future generations of church-goers this preservation of the old and the acceptance of the new, he composed the gospel. In an evil world, influenced by sin, this church had to become organized with an authority, with rules, teaching and ritual. Then it would survive.

Any group of people which hopes to survive eventually faces the question of organization. A college fraternity or sorority, a bridge club or poker club, a parish council or a labor union—each group will need some authority; someone has to be in charge. It also will need rules. Constitutions are established or procedures are accepted. Finally, the group has to meet.

I remember a story of a bishop of an east coast diocese who returned from the Vatican Council and established a liturgical committee for his diocese. He appointed members, asked the chair to draw up a set of procedures, and forbade the chair ever to call a meeting. The organization had authority and rules, but without meetings the organization never existed. Meetings without authority and procedures will destroy any organization. Authority and meeting without rules and procedures will dehumanize. All three are necessary: authority, rules and teachings, and meetings and ritual.

The author of Matthew knew the need for authority in this church and presented Peter as the leader, the great centrist who would appeal to both Jew and Gentile convert. He increased this circle of authority by concluding his gospel with the commissioning of the twelve:

All authority in heaven and on earth has been given to me. Go, therefore, and make disciples of all nations, baptizing them in the name of the Father and of the Son and of the Holy Spirit, teaching them to observe all that I have commanded you, and lo, I am with you always to the close of the age (Mt 28:18–20).

He also saw the need for rules and wrote his gospel filled with the teachings of Jesus presented almost in a catechetical format. The great sermon on the mount is the charter of the church, the way these followers would live. The stories of Jesus, the parables, each is related to the Christian community as it struggled to function in a world that was often opposed to its very tenets of belief. The combination of authority and teaching kept the community together as it gathered to express in ritual its belief that Jesus continued to be with them.

We have already seen the prayer of the community in the stilling of the storm: "Lord, save." The conclusion of the gospel records for us the ceremony of baptism:

*Go, therefore, make disciples of all nations, baptizing them in
the name of the Father and of the Son and of the Holy Spirit
(Mt 28:19).*

The gospel also recalls for us the celebration of the eucharist.
Matthew records for us the institution of the eucharist at the last
supper (Mt 22:26–29). This Matthean community was a worshiping
community. They met and proclaimed the presence of the Lord among
them. The combination of the three elements: authority, teachings
and rules, and ritual meeting would preserve the Christian church for
the future.

Some look upon the gospel of Matthew as too much "church." It
is too conscious of authority. After all, it alone has the commissioning
of Peter:

*Upon this rock I will build my church and the gates of hell
shall not prevail against it. And I will give you the keys of the
kingdom of heaven, and whatever you bind on earth shall be
bound in heaven, and whatever you loose on earth shall be
loosed in heaven (Mt 16:18–19).*

The Roman Catholic Church in particular has liked this gospel, and
until the reform of the Vatican Council used this gospel almost exclu-
sively in Sunday readings throughout the year. Compared to the more
charismatic gospel of John or the gentle gospel of Luke, this gospel of
Matthew seems too restrictive. This, however, is only true with a quick
reading. A more careful study of the gospel presents a different image
to this most ecclesial of gospels.

First the commissioning of Peter was meant more as a centrist
position rather than as an authoritarian leader of the church. It may
also be true that Matthew writes with irony here. Throughout the
gospel Peter is not presented as a rock. He is a vacillating figure who
misunderstands Jesus and is called Satan (Mt 16:23); he is a stumbling
block (Mt 16:23) who professes never to deny Jesus (Mt 26:33) and, in
fact, denies him thrice. We might say that Jesus calls him Peter but
says that he is no rock. In spite of this, Jesus will build his church upon
him because of the faith of Peter and the presence of Jesus in the
whole community. Peter will share this authority with the other apostles, for Matthew gives to the community the power to bind and loose
in chapter 18.

*Truly I say to you, whatever you bind on earth shall be bound
in heaven, and whatever you loose on earth shall be loosed in
heaven (Mt 18:18).*

The nuancing of the ecclesial gospel takes place in chapter 18.
The scene opens with Peter and Jesus. Then the other disciples, out of
jealousy, bring up the question of rank. Jesus responds with a teaching
on the true greatness in the kingdom.

*Truly I say to you, unless you turn and become like lit-
tle children, you will never enter the kingdom of heaven
(Mt 18:3).*

A child has no security; the child was considered property, lowly and
dependent. The true disciples, whether leader or follower, will be such.
The true greatness is lowly acceptance in the presence of God.

The second teaching involves scandal in the church. All, especially leaders, should help to prevent the little ones from falling. No
pride or hypocrisy should characterize this community. Even the individual can be a cause of sin for oneself, and so all should be careful lest
they lose themselves.

*Woe to the world for temptations to sin. . . . And if your
hand or your foot causes you to sin cut it off and throw it
from you (Mt 18:7–10).*

The third episode is also directed to the leaders. They are to seek
out the lost. The least significant are the most significant. If God takes
care of the neglected, how much more should the leaders of this community.

*So it is not the will of my Father who is in heaven that one of
these little ones should perish (Mt 18:10–14).*

The fourth episode involves church discipline and prayer. The
steps of fraternal correction begin with reserve and privacy and end
with the intervention of the whole church and not just the leader. The
leadership does not swallow up the authority of the assembly, for the
local church can also bind and loose (Mt 18:15–20).

Finally, this chapter closes with the last word on church authority and discipline: limitless mercy. Forgiveness is seventy times seven: "I do not say to you seven times, but seventy times seven" (Mt 18:21–35).

For Matthew, christology is ecclesiology. Jesus is humble and lowly; he suffers and gives his life for others. He goes after those in need, will not allow them to fall, and can forgive limitlessly. The church of Jesus, according to Matthew, must do likewise. And so this ecclesial gospel is very much like Jesus.

Setting the scene for the gospel of Matthew enables us to study in greater detail how the author responds to his task of preserving the old and being open to the new. Authority must exist but always within the context of the whole community; teaching must continue for Christianity to survive. The wisdom of Matthew continues among those who seek to understand his concern for the present and future church.

Further Study

R. Brown and J. Meier, *Antioch and Rome.*
J. Kingsbury, *Matthew.*
J. Meier, *Matthew.*
———, *The Vision of Matthew.*

2.

The Infancy Narratives

For centuries the infancy accounts of both Matthew and Luke were accepted as historical accounts of the origin of Jesus. In the minds of most believers the historicity of these events became ingrained in the memory. Each year Christian churches erected nativity scenes at Christmas time and each family told and retold the events surrounding the birth of the Lord. Three periods of scholarship and three periods of a mental attitude can be distinguished in the understanding of the infancy narratives.

In the history of scholarship, the first period of interest in the infancy narratives began to separate the birth material from the material narrating the ministry of Jesus. The latter dealt with the teachings of Jesus and the events of his life as an itinerant preacher. The material comes to us from people who were witnesses from the baptism in the Jordan to his crucifixion and resurrection (Acts 1:21–22). But who was responsible for the story of the birth? In the past some have suggested that the source was the testimony of Joseph or Mary. Such opinions are pure speculation.

Discovery of the testimony behind the stories became more difficult when the infancy narratives were subject to biblical criticism. This is the second stage in scholarship. Matthew and Luke actually tell two different stories of the origin of Jesus which agree in very few details and present many contradictions. In fact, both echo Old Testament stories, which causes more doubts about historicity. The final stage of scholarship concentrates not on the historicity of the narratives nor on their origin but on the theology that they present.

On a popular level, somewhat parallel to the above periods of scholarship, some believers have moved from accepting the historicity of the narratives to rejecting the entire story as fanciful (who can believe in a magic star, exotic characters from the east, etc.?), to the final point of asking what these stories might mean. Presently the

161

efforts at scholarship and the desire for the believer to know more about the meaning of the infancy narratives help us to see the good news of salvation truly proclaimed in the stories of the origin of Jesus.

We know that the infancy narratives represent the last part of the gospel tradition to develop. Mark does not offer us an account of the origin of Jesus. John has in its place the hymn to the pre-existence of the Word of God. We also know that compared with the third century *Proto Evangelium Jacob* and the *Infancy Story of Thomas the Israelite Philosopher,* the accounts of Matthew and Luke are only in the incipient stage of development. We also know that the infancy narratives are late in origin since no mention of the actual origin of Jesus appears in the primitive kerygma. The preaching in Acts speaks only of the ministry of Jesus from baptism to resurrection. Galatians 4:4 makes mention that Jesus was "born of woman," but this hardly can be seen as a story of origins. Paul refers to Jesus as being "descended from David according to the flesh" (Rom 1:3). This contrasts Jesus as Son with power according to the Spirit. These stories are not primarily historical. They are late in origin but still part of the proclamation that Jesus is the saving presence of God among his people.

The first two chapters of Matthew are more than charming stories. They are the overture to the gospel in which the evangelist gathers together various themes that will be played out as the gospel unfolds. Matthew tells us who Jesus is and the goal of his life. He is son of David and son of Abraham; he is in continuity with Old Testament salvation history (genealogy: Mt 1:1–17); he is born of Mary by the Holy Spirit and is called Jesus, savior, Emmanuel, God with us. His goal in life will be persecution unto death and he will be restored to life through the intervention of God his Father. The passion narrative in the body of the gospel with the death of Jesus by a cruel ruler is anticipated by the efforts of a cruel king to put him to death at his birth (Mt 2:16–18). The universalism of the command to proclaim the gospel to all nations is anticipated in the coming of the magi to worship the newborn infant (Mt 2:1–12).

■ Structure of the Matthean Infancy Account ■

The first two chapters of Matthew can be divided into six sections:

1. Genealogy (1:1–17)
2. Birth (1:18–25)
3. Adoration of the Magi (2:1–12)

4. Flight into Egypt (2:13–15)
5. Slaughter of the Children (2:16–18)
6. Return from Egypt (2:19–23)

These six sections can be further grouped together into two major units: the genealogy which has its own divisions and the birth sequence which contains five biblical citations. The first section (1:18–25) contains reference to Isaiah 7:14:

> Behold a young woman shall conceive and bear a son and shall call his name Emmanuel.

The adoration of the magi refers to Micah 5:1–3:

> But you, O Bethlehem, Ephrathah, who are little to be among the clans of Judah.

The flight into Egypt refers to Hosea 11:1:

> When Israel was a child I loved him and out of Egypt I called my own.

The slaughter of the children refers to Jeremiah 31:15:

> A voice is heard in Ramah, lamentation and bitter weeping. Rachel is weeping for her children; she refuses to be comforted for her children because they are not.

The final reference in the return from Egypt is: "He shall be called a Nazarene." Although Matthew says it was spoken by the prophets, we can find no such reference in the Old Testament. From the outset we can see that the infancy narrative of Matthew must be understood in light of the Old Testament.

■ Midrash ■

Once we see the relationship between Matthew and certain Old Testament stories or events, we face the question of the literary nature of the infancy narratives. "Midrash" means an interpretation and comes from the Hebrew word *darash* meaning to dig or to search. Today most scholars assume that Matthew used the midrash form in his infancy narratives. As early as 1907 the French exegete Alfred Loisy believed that Matthew composed his infancy narratives in a

spirit of haggadic commentaries on the Old Testament. The midrash
form developed in the synagogue when the rabbis realized that a gap
separated the experience of those about whom the scriptures spoke
and the people who listened to them. Midrash attempted to apply the
lessons and laws of the scriptures to the contemporary audience. *Hallakah* arose in the rabbinic schools and sought new explanations of
traditional laws. *Haggadah* arose in the synagogue service and frequently was the homily preached. The rabbis applied the narrative
material of the scriptures to the lives of the congregation. They instructed, offered edification and sometimes offered a literal exegesis of
the text (*peshat*). At other times, they presented a literary embellishment and application of the text (*derash*).

Matthew did something similar. He combined certain Old Testament texts with events in the life of any individual such as birth and
parents. He then interpreted these events in the light of the actual
ministry and ultimate fate of Jesus to create for us stories about the
origin of Jesus. The evangelist wrote theologically and not historically,
seeking meaning and not wishing to narrate specific events.

■   The Genealogy   ■

Genealogies establish continuity, legitimacy, relationship, and
historical frameworks. By beginning his gospel with a genealogy
Matthew established the continuity of Jesus with the Old Testament
tradition. He affirmed the legitimacy of Jesus as messiah from the line
of David. He explained the relationships among individuals who ultimately were under the provident control of God. Finally, by this genealogy he established the historical framework which reached its
completion in the coming of Emmanuel.

Much has been written on the Matthean genealogy trying to understand its significance for the evangelist. Primarily, Matthew wants
to emphasize the origin of Jesus in the people of God and sees him as
the fulfillment of Old Testament salvation history. He divides his
genealogy into three sets of fourteen generations. By joining sets of
generations he can construct an outline of history that culminates in
Jesus as the beginning of the seventh period, the period of perfection
and fulfillment. The imagery is apocalyptic, meant to emphasize that
God has carefully ordered the history of salvation so that all of Israel's
history moves purposefully toward the messiah. Jesus is that messiah.
He also may be playing with numbers. In Hebrew the first letter of the

alphabet is given the numerical value one, the second, two, and so on. The consonants in Hebrew (there are no vowels) in the name David (D W D) amount to 14: D = 4, the fourth letter of the alphabet; W = 6 the sixth letter in the alphabet, and thus D W D = fourteen. What this might have meant to Matthew remains beyond the scope of scholarship at the present time.

Since Matthew has a community of both Jewish Christians and Gentile Christians, he begins his story of Jesus by proclaiming that he is son of David and son of Abraham. As son of David he fulfills the Jewish expectations; as son of Abraham, in him all nations of the earth will be blessed (Gen 22:18). Matthew pleased both his Jewish Christians by linking Jesus to David and pleased his Gentile Christians by linking him to Abraham, the one in whom all nations would be blessed.

Of special interest are the four women named in the genealogy: Tamar, Rahab, Ruth, and indirectly Bathsheba (the wife of Uriah). Some see these women as sinners: Tamar was a seductress and pretended to be a prostitute (Gen 38); Rahab was a prostitute (Jos 6); Ruth may have sinned with Boaz (Ruth 3:6–9:14); Bathsheba was an adulteress (2 Sam 11–12). Others emphasize their Gentile connection. Perhaps the principal reason for their inclusion is their position in the history of salvation. They represent discontinuity. Something irregular or extraordinary was associated with the union with their partners. Yet, this union continued the blessed line of the messiah. They played a special role in the plan of God. God chose them as special instruments in the history of salvation. They may even foreshadow that special and extraordinary role of Mary recorded in this gospel. The genealogies have a specific purpose in Matthew's gospel. They unite Jew and Gentile in Jesus; they establish continuity with the history of Israel and proclaim that God in his providence controls history and makes use of the irregular and extraordinary to fulfill his purpose.

■ The Birth Story ■

Matthew explains the conception of Jesus through supernatural intervention. The primitive tradition affirmed that Jesus was born of a very young woman in the first state of her marriage. Matthew takes up this tradition and accentuates the divine activity in the birth of the Lord by alluding to his conception by the Holy Spirit. He gives a Christian formulation to the tradition and interprets the origin of Jesus by reference to Isaiah 7:14.

"Joseph, son of David, do not fear to take Mary as your wife, for that which is conceived in her is of the Holy Spirit; she will bear a son, and you shall call his name Jesus, for he will save his people from their sins." All this took place to fulfill what the Lord had spoken by the prophet: "Behold a virgin shall conceive and bear a son and his name shall be called Emmanuel, which means 'God with us' " (Mt 1:20–23).

The child to be born is the presence of God among us, Emmanuel. The emphasis is on the name Emmanuel rather than the question of the virginity of Mary. In 1:25, Matthew further expands his virginal conception tradition by affirming that Joseph "did not know his wife" until the birth of Jesus. This statement leaves open the question whether or not Joseph and Mary had subsequent sexual relationships and other children. In any case, this verse emphasizes the traditional belief in the virginal conception of Jesus. Further, we can say that this birth story affirms that Jesus is the Son of God because of his supernatural conception. Matthew knew this tradition from the ministry and resurrection experiences of the Lord and elaborated on this belief in his story of the origins of Jesus.

■ Adoration of the Infant Jesus (2:1–12) ■

The mention of the wise men from the east (no number is given) and the star emphasizes the importance of the birth of Jesus and the universality of his message. Matthew takes his framework from the testimony of Balaam, a magus from the east who is supposed to curse Israel and instead blesses it: "A star shall rise from Jacob and a scepter from Israel" (Num 24:17). We need not attempt to discover astrological phenomena at the time to explain what is theological and literary. Gentiles came from the east to worship the newborn king of Israel. Gentiles recognized the presence of God while the Jews failed to see in Jesus the fulfillment of their history and hopes.

■ The Flight into Egypt (2:13–15a) ■

This section focuses on two themes: the hostility of Herod and the affirmation that Jesus fulfills the prophecy of Hosea 11:1: "Out of Egypt I called my son." The story reminds us of the origin of Moses when Pharaoh attempted to destroy a rival. Like Israel, God's Son,

Jesus, will undergo an exodus from Egypt and return to the promised land. Innocent children will die to preserve the messiah but only so that later the innocent Jesus might die to save his people from their sins.

■ Slaughter of the Children (2:16–18) ■

The massacre of the children of Bethlehem, although not beyond the character of Herod, has no foundation in history. Herod, who killed his wife and at the time of his death ordered the execution of several hundred people to ensure that the land would be in mourning, might well have thought of a massacre of children. But if Josephus, the Jewish historian, and no great friend of Herod, makes no mention of such an event, we can presume that the story comes from the thought of Matthew. At the birth of every great person, according to ancient near east legends, evil forces or people seek to destroy that person before he can accomplish his destiny. It happened to Moses, and Matthew tells us that Jesus experienced the same fate. Even the citation from Jeremiah is somewhat problematical since originally it represents a lament over Israel. Matthew probably used it here because of the tradition that Rachel was buried near Bethlehem.

■ Return from Egypt (2:19–23) ■

In these verses Matthew, like Mark, links Jesus with Nazareth at the very beginning of the gospel with the citation: "He shall be called a Nazarene." Matthew knew the tradition that Jesus grew up in Nazareth and must somehow place Jesus in Nazareth as a child. He accomplished his task by using the above citation. The problem lies in the lack of any such passage in the Old Testament. A possible solution can be found if we recall that Nazareth reminds the reader of Nazarene which may not necessarily have the same meaning. Nazarene can be derived from *neser* in Hebrew which means root or branch. Thus, the reference is to Isaiah 11:1 where the offspring of David is called a *neser*, or branch or shoot from the stump of Jesse. It may also come from the Hebrew word *nazir* which means holy or consecrated. This is an illusion to the order of Nazarites, one of whom was Samson (Jgs 13:5-7), an ascetic who was set aside and consecrated to save Israel. Jesus is from Nazareth but is also the consecrated one sent to save. He is also the shoot from the root of Jesse.

■ Historicity of the Infancy Account ■

We can conclude from the analysis of the first two chapters of Matthew that Jesus was born toward the end of the reign of Herod. His mother was Mary, and people presumed that his father was Joseph. He was brought up in Nazareth. His Davidic descent and the virginal conception might be seen as theologoumena, i.e. aspects of the story that support faith but need not necessarily be considered as matters of faith, at least not according to the New Testament. The rest of the narrative comes from the use of the Old Testament to illuminate the fuller meaning of the origins of Jesus.

■ Christology of the Infancy Narratives ■

Matthew presents a rather sophisticated christology which centers on Jesus as son of David and Abraham, and king. He must be the legal son of Joseph since through Joseph he is related to David. Joseph gives Jesus his name. As the ideal David he will shepherd his people.

The birth of Jesus also fulfills the divine plan of salvation. Matthew incorporates into his account the wonderful story of the virginal conception, the great sign of God's intervention. Jesus comes to us as God's gift, not due to humanity in any way. The magi and star highlight the universality of the mission of Jesus and the plan of God: salvation for all, Jew and Gentile alike. Matthew further presents Jesus as the new Israel and the new Moses. All of these themes will become part of the fabric of the gospel as Matthew unfolds his understanding of the Jesus tradition. Old Testament stories of Israel and Moses and Balaam have been reworked into a unified anticipation of the passion and resurrection of Jesus. The cast of characters is the same: the secular ruler, the priests and scribes. All are against Jesus who has God with him. God saves Jesus at his birth and brings him back to life after his crucifixion. In the process those who should have recognized Jesus fail to see him as Emmanuel, while Gentiles come to adore. The Matthean infancy narrative is not only the gospel, the good news, but the good news in miniature. Perhaps this explains why this story is so well known and has such a powerful appeal. In the origin of Jesus, people have come to recognize the presence of God in the form of a child waiting to be recognized by people of faith.

Further Study

R. Brown, *The Birth of the Messiah.*
B. Nolan, *The Royal Son of God.*

3.

The Kingdom of God

Jesus preached a kingdom, a reign of God upon earth not limited to a geographical place, but related to an activity which would bring salvation. Matthew, more than Mark or Luke, insists on this kingdom. The other two evangelists use the expression kingdom of God. Matthew more often chooses to use kingdom of heaven. Scholars have questioned which was the more primitive expression and what difference exists between the two phrases. Since the Jews would refrain from using the divine name, one might assume that the Matthean expression is more primitive, but we also know that Jesus did not hesitate to speak of God directly. Today, however, most scholars see the expression of kingdom of God as more primitive. No matter what position one may take, the idea behind both expressions remains the same.

The term kingdom in English is somewhat ambiguous but usually suggests a territory or a place governed by a specific ruler. The Greek *basileia,* which is translated into English as kingdom, is also ambiguous. The Aramaic phrase *malkuth shemin,* well-established in Jewish usage, clearly means kingship, kingly rule, reign, or sovereignty. If Matthew refers to the kingdom of God he means that specific aspect, attribute, or activity by which God is revealed as king or sovereign of his people or of the universe.

■ History of the Meaning of Kingdom of God ■

God is king of Israel in the exodus experience as well as in the conquest of Canaan (Ex 15:11, 13, 18). God continues to be king of Israel in the period of the judges as well as in the monarchy. Even when Israel has earthly kings, they were considered more as vice-gerents, for God alone was the true king of Israel. The ark of the covenant, and later the temple, was the throne of God from which he rules his people. The vision of Isaiah (Is 6:3) presents the temple area, with the holy of holies, as the throne of God. God's court surrounds the throne, and they offer homage to him as sovereign. In the prophets we also have the notion that, in some way, the God of Israel is also the ruler over the Gentiles (Am 9:7; Jer 10:7–12).

When the people of Israel gathered in worship they proclaimed that God was king. The historical reign of God over his people was actualized and relived as the people expressed their homage and adoration:

> Sing praises to God, sing praises! Sing praises to our king, sing praises! For God is king of all the earth, sing praises with a psalm (Ps 47:6–7; see also Pss 93, 94, 97, 99).

The prophets looked to a future victory of God as king of all of the enemies of Israel. God will appear and take possession of the realm. Such a belief was expressed in various prophetic images: a new entrance into the promised land (Hosea), a new David and a new Sion (Isaiah), a new covenant (Jeremiah). Perhaps Deutero-Isaiah used the most encompassing image when he spoke of a new exodus in which the messiah becomes the vice-gerent of God and instrument of God's reign. This era will bring peace and a manifestation of the justice and holiness of God; Israel will be restored and the Gentiles will feel the effects of this holy reign.

In the intra-testamental period the idea of the reign of God took on various forms in rabbinic orthodoxy. It expressed nationalistic expectations and apocalyptic hopes. The rabbis believed that God will rule over all peoples as well as reign over Israel:

> It shall come to pass when he (the messiah) has brought low everything that is in the world, and has sat down in peace for the age on the throne of his kingdom, that joy shall then be revealed and rest shall appear (Apoc. Bar. 73).

They joined these ideas with the teaching that the observance of the law of Moses by Israel will hasten the day when God in truth will reign over all peoples. Rabbi Levi remarks: "If only Israel did one day of penance they would be redeemed immediately and the son of David would come immediately."

The more popular nationalistic notion of the reign of God identified this rule with the political restoration of Israel. God would send the messiah, the king, and through him the kingdom of Israel, with all of its ancient glory of reunited tribes, would conquer all enemies. Then the true service of God and fulfillment of the law of Moses would fill the land. The popular Jewish prayer, *Shemoneh 'Esre* states:

> *Be King over us, thou alone and root out this government of scoundrels and hasten to destroy them in our day.*

This popular belief became the foundation for the Zealots who sought to expel the Romans, and by human effort they would bring about the true reign of God.

In apocalyptic Judaism the final reign of God over all peoples will come about through the activity of God alone. The sovereign action will be a judgment which rewards the good and punishes the evil. The Jew can no longer claim an exclusive right to experience God's rule, although the Jew does have the advantage in knowing the will of God. God will rule over Israel and over all peoples in distinctive ways through a decisive intervention in history:

> *And then his kingdom shall appear throughout all his creation. And then Satan shall be no more and sorrow shall depart with him (Assumption of Moses 10:1).*

They shall experience the goodness of God:

> *Then he will raise up his kingdom for all ages over all men; he who once gave a holy rule to godly men, to all of whom he promised to open the earth and the world, and the portals of the blessed and all joys and everlasting sense and eternal gladness (Sibylline Oracles BK 3, #767).*

■ **The Kingdom of God in the New Testament** ■

Although the expression appears in Mark and Luke, Matthew presents the fullest teaching on the reign of God. We shall concentrate on the Matthean understanding and occasionally make reference to the other evangelists.

The two elements of the apocalyptic understanding of the kingdom—the definitive intervention of God in human history and the concern for the blessed—also figure in the teaching of Jesus. He rejects out of hand the popular nationalistic opinion and also rejects any human effort to accomplish this reign. God alone establishes his reign. All three evangelists present the reign of God as a definitive act by God alone:

> *The time is fulfilled and the reign of God is at hand; repent and believe in the gospel (Mk 1:15).*

> *The kingdom of God is not coming with signs to be observed, nor will they say, "Lo there it is!" or "There!" for behold the kingdom of God is in the midst of you (Lk 17:21).*

> *The kingdom of God is at hand (Mt 10:7).*

The beatitudes of Matthew and Luke both begin with a concern for the poor who will inherit the kingdom (Mt 5:3; Lk 6:20).

Jesus seems to hold this general apocalyptic understanding of the reign of God but he also adds his own content. His frequent use of the term emphasizes the urgency in responding to this intervention of God in history. By reign of God he also designates the fulfillment of all of human hopes and expectations. It is a feast, a celebration; it has begun slowly and secretly but bursts upon the scene with a force that shocks. Those who face this challenge of the reign of God must take sides and determine for themselves whether or not they shall be part of this reign. The kingdom comes and those who wish to participate must be ready. The urgency forestalls any effort at delay. The moment has arrived; the judgment is upon the land and the people must respond.

■   The Kingdom as Eschatological   ■

The final intervention by God will destroy the present course of the world with the evil forces and powers under which human society struggles. All pain and sorrow will be wiped away. God always reigned over the universe, but now his reign will be fully realized and activated in an irrevocable manner. Salvation for the people of God awaits as the promises of old are fulfilled. The never-to-be-repeated event has come and finds its fulfillment when God is all in all.

This final activity is the act of God alone which emerges onto the stage of history without any human effort. The event is "miraculous:"

Then the king will say to those at his right hand, "Come, blessed of my Father, inherit the kingdom prepared for you from the foundation of the world" (Mt 25:34).

The reign of God inaugurates a religious moment in history and not a political rebirth of Israel. In the ministry of Jesus the Zealots attempted to use the prophet from Galilee in their efforts to overthrow foreign domination, but Jesus always rejected their proposal. After the multiplication of the loaves some wanted to proclaim Jesus as king but he withdrew into the mountains by himself (Jn 6:15).

The rejection of a political kingdom appears in Matthew 26:52 when Jesus tells his followers to put the sword back in its place. The same refusal to accept the popular notion of kingdom occurs in the description of his triumphal entry into Jerusalem. Jesus enters not as a conquering king seated on a horse, the symbol of power and war, but upon a lowly donkey. He knows that the intervening of God into human history involves more than a gathering of earthly delights, for Jesus knows his own destiny. The reign of God does not involve the passing out of honors and positions of power (Mt 10:35–45), but the acceptance of suffering as the power of good struggles against the forces of evil.

The presence of suffering, however, never negates the essential positive aspect of the kingdom: the salvation offered to all. In Matthew John the Baptist proclaims a kingdom as a manifestation of judgment:

His winnowing fork is in his hand and he will clear his threshing floor and gather his wheat into the granary but the chaff he will burn with unquenchable fire (Mt 3:12).

In spite of the pain, the message of Jesus offers mercy and forgiveness. The parables of mercy, especially in Luke, manifest this compassion; the workers in the vineyard in Matthew (20:1–15) demonstrate not only the goodness of God, but the need for all followers to be merciful to each other and to rejoice in each other's good fortune. Jesus himself associates with sinners, with tax collectors, that despised segment of Jewish society, and with anyone else thought to be pushed to the outside and not belonging. What Jesus taught in his parables, he lived in his personal activity. When he teaches his disciples to pray, he assures them they will be forgiven, for they can pray to a God who is like a kind and loving parent for them.

Jesus insisted on salvation as the principal element in the final reign of God. In rabbinic thought the experience of salvation was the result of the reign of God but not the actual reign of God itself. For Jesus, the experience of the saving presence of God in history, and in the lives of individuals, becomes the marrow of the reign of God, giving the teachings of Jesus a unity beyond measure. He proclaimed God's salvific will for all and offered redeeming mercy as a present reality. The fullness of blessedness for believers will be accomplished when they enter into this reign of God through personal choice.

The moment has arrived. The special time of salvation is at hand. The beatitudes beckon to the individual. Jesus proclaims that God has definitively entered into human history through the advent of Jesus and his preaching. The final call is heard, demanding a urgent reply that will accomplish the hopes and expectations of forgotten generations.

> Many prophets and righteous men longed to see what you see and did not see it, and to hear what you hear and did not hear it (Mt 13:16).

Jesus offered the challenge and expected his listeners to respond and change their way of living.

The reign of God must enter into the deepest recesses of the heart. The person who becomes part of this rule lives in light of that kingdom and expresses the commitment to the will of God. The ethical dimension of the reign of God in the gospel of Matthew stands out prominently in the sermon on the mount, but before we examine this chapter of the kingdom in detail, some understanding of the portrait of Jesus as found in Matthew will facilitate the further study of the first gospel.

Further Study

W. Kummel, *The Theology of the New Testament.*
J. Kingsbury, *Matthew: Structure, Christology, Kingdom.*
A. Richardson, *An Introduction to the Theology of the New Testament.*

4.

Jesus in the Gospel of Matthew

The Jewish character of the gospel of Matthew shines forth in every chapter. Although the community was composed of Jews and Gentiles, the author anxiously preserved the old from Judaism and added the new from Christianity. The genealogy places him in the line of David, and the author finds parallels throughout the Old Testament even in places where no one else might see the relationship. Every word of the Old Testament that might have prophetic significance for Jesus, Matthew seems to discover and incorporates into his gospel. Perhaps an early member of the Jewish Christian community gathered together possible references to Jesus from Jewish writings and Matthew used this collection as a source for his gospel. The suffering servant of Isaiah is the servant of the Lord of the gospel who himself has borne our afflictions and carried our sorrows:

> *This was to fulfill what was spoken by the prophet Isaiah,*
> *"He took our infirmities and bore our diseases" (Mt 8:17).*

The proclamation of Hosea: "Out of Egypt I have called my son" (Hos 11:1), although referring to the exodus of the Israelites, becomes for Matthew a renewal of the ancient history of Israel in the Son of man.

The Jewish character is also evident in the attitude of Jesus toward the law of Moses. It almost seems as if the law remains in force without any modification. We have already seen that some Jewish Christians in the community of Matthew would be anxious to continue the observance of the law, and they would find sure foundation in the words of Jesus recorded by Matthew:

> *Think not that I have come to abolish the law and the prophets; I have come not to abolish them but to fulfill them (Mt 5:17).*

The statement added by Jewish Christians:

> *Whoever then relaxes one of the least of these commandments and teaches men so, shall be called least in the kingdom of heaven (Mt 5:19),*

further establishes for the readers of Matthew the understanding that Jesus fulfills the old covenant and does not abolish it. Possibly to respond to the needs of his Gentile Christians, Matthew also records the twofold commandment of love of God and neighbor and then adds:

> *On these two commandments depend all the law and the prophets (Mt 22:40).*

The Old Testament is the background for the christology of Matthew but not without a sense of an opening to the Gentiles. Jesus fulfills the Old Testament but the emphasis remains on the fulfillment.

Twelve times in the gospel, Matthew underlines the significance of an event in the life of Jesus by an explicit appeal to an Old Testament prophecy. Each is introduced by the phrase: "This took place to fulfill what the Lord said through the prophet . . ." The twelve incidents are important in the life of Jesus and establish a structure for Matthean christology:

1. The choice of his name (1:21) and virginal conception (1:23)
2. The place of birth in Bethlehem (2:5)
3. The exile in Egypt (2:16)
4. The threat by Herod (2:18)
5. The relocation to Nazareth (2:23)
6. Preaching in Galilee (4:15)
7. Healing ministry (8:17)
8. Mission to the Gentiles (12:18)
9. Preaching in parables (13:14, 35)
10. Entry into Jerusalem (21:4)
11. Betrayal and arrest (26:56)
12. Fate of Judas and the acceptance of responsibility for the death of Jesus by the Jewish leaders (27:9)

The power of the Old Testament tradition affects every major aspect of the life of Jesus. The Old Testament creates the history and milieu out of which Matthew creates his portrait of Jesus.

■ Exalted Son of God ■

In his first four chapters Matthew treats the person of Jesus and acknowledges that he is both son of David and son of Abraham, but that preeminently Jesus is the exalted Son of God. His origin is in God, for he is conceived by the power of God; he will shepherd God's people (Mt 2:6), and he proves himself in confrontation with Satan (Mt 4:3–10). But for Matthew Jesus is not Son of God in the manner of ancient kings, or angels, or even the just. Instead Jesus is the Son of God who will be raised and will reign with God with all authority in heaven and on earth:

> And Jesus came and said to them: "All authority in heaven and on earth has been given to me . . ." (Mt 28:18).

As Son of God, Jesus enjoys a unique relationship with the Father and has been chosen by God to be his exclusive representative among peoples. He shares in the divine authority and confronts his listeners and so reveals the Father to whomever he will. As Son of God, Jesus acknowledges his election by God by living in complete fellowship with God and relying upon God totally by being perfectly obedient to God's will. The so-called Johannine thunderbolt in Matthew expresses this relationship well:

> All things have been delivered to me by my Father, and no one knows the Father except the Son and anyone to whom the Son chooses to reveal him (Mt 11:27).

In the second part of his gospel (4:17–16:20), Matthew fills out the meaning of the Son of man by explaining his ministry of teaching and healing. In the third part of the gospel (16:21–28:30), Jesus as Son moves toward death and fulfillment in the resurrection. The Sanhedrin condemns Jesus for claiming divine sonship (Mt 26:63–66); he is ridiculed as the Son of God by the people (27:39–40), and dies upon the cross trusting completely in God his Father (Mt 27:38–54). But God will not allow his Son to experience eternal defeat. God raised him up:

He is not here; for he has risen, as he said. Come, see the
place where he lay. Then go quickly and tell his disciples that
he has risen from the dead, and behold, he is going before
you to Galilee; there you will see him. Lo, I have told you
(Mt 28:6–7).

God exalted him to absolute and universal authority in heaven and on
earth (Mt 28:18–20). Now others will be empowered by the Spirit of
God to make disciples of all nations, assured of the abiding presence of
the Son of God until the end of the age. The title Son of God appears
at his conception, birth and infancy, baptism and temptation, public
ministry, death, resurrection and exaltation. It expresses for Matthew
the mystery of the person of Jesus as messiah and represents an
exalted confession of the Matthean Christian community.

■ Messiah as Teacher and Healer ■

The ministry of Jesus in Matthew's gospel emphasizes his teaching and healing. He teaches the new covenant much as Moses was the
teacher of the old covenant. He has the boldness to proclaim: "You
have heard that it was said to the men of old . . . but I say to you" (Mt
5:21–22). In the eyes of the Jews Jesus blasphemed by such a claim to
authority. As the new teacher he claims an authority that intrinsically
requires no credentials other than the obvious rightness and truth of
his declarations. He truly speaks about God in a new way. Unlike the
scribes, he teaches with authority and the people recognize that a
prophet has risen in the land:

And when Jesus finished these sayings, the crowds were as-
tonished, for he taught them as one who has authority, and
not as their scribes (Mt 7:28–29).

Not only does he teach but he lives what he proclaims. The teacher of
new ideas remains relatively harmless unless these new ideas are put
into practice. Jesus lived what he taught. He has a devotion to the law
but interprets this law based on the criteria of love of God and love of
neighbor. The scribes and Pharisees offered interpretations of the law
but never in the radical way in which Jesus taught and lived. Whatever
helped in the fulfillment of the command of love of God and neighbor
must be practiced. Whatever hindered these commands, especially the
love of neighbor, must be ignored. Love is the foundation of all law,

and love alone is the principle by which the law of Moses must be interpreted and judged (22:34–39). For Jesus love meant an unlimited and unconditional willingness to serve. This command he lived personally and he called all of his followers to do likewise.

The great teacher proclaimed a new approach to God based upon love but not without its pain. The ancient law of Deuteronomy promised, for the most part, the material blessings of harvest, and fertility of cattle, and many children, and a long life. Jesus also proclaims a blessing to his followers but one which involves a commitment to an ideal, to the kingdom of God. They will renounce personal rights and privileges and willingly serve and endure persecution, even unto death, for the name of the Lord.

Matthew also presented Jesus as a healer. Jesus knew the need for physical healing. He does not just dispense wisdom like the oracle of Delphi. The exalted Son of God and great teacher touched people with compassion. He overpowers the forces of evil that threaten human society and brings wholeness. In four chapters Matthew gathers together the miracle stories about Jesus (chapters 8, 9, 12, 14). Most of these miraculous events appear also in Mark, but here in Matthew they are often abbreviated to emphasize the essential elements: the person in faith recognizes that Jesus makes manifest the saving power of God. Miracles result from faith; they reveal the healing effects of God's grace which has been given to the individual because of the person's faith in Jesus. Faith heals the woman with the hemorrhage (Mt 9:18–22); two blind men see because of their faith (Mt 9:27–31). The miracle collection in Matthew 14:13–15:39 parallels the miracles of Mark 6–8 with such important miracles as the multiplication of the loaves, the walking on the water and the healing of the daughter of the Canaanite woman. Here Matthew, unlike Mark, used the miracles to invite the people to follow Jesus in faith. In the narrative about the walking on the water in Matthew, the disciples fall down in worship (Mt 14:33). In Mark the disciples do not understand, for their hearts are hardened (Mk 6:53–56). Jesus bears God's message of compassion and healing, and those who believe, who recognize the saving presence of God in Jesus, are restored to life.

■ Other Christological Titles ■

Some of the other titles employed by Matthew relate to his fundamental title Son of God such as: Jesus, prophet, and *Kyrios* (Lord). Others such as Emmanuel, messiah, and son of David fill out the significance of the more essential titles. Jesus means savior and defines the mission of Emmanuel, God with us. Prophet is a title used more as a reaction of the crowds, while teacher is a role of Jesus in this gospel. This last title was used by Judas and the leaders of Israel and their cohorts attributing to Jesus a limited level of respect.

The title *Kyrios,* however, is significant in the first gospel. It occurs on the lips of persons who address Jesus in faith (the only exception is the accursed in the last judgment scene in 25:37) and has a confessional character. Most often Matthew used this title to attribute divine authority and an exalted station to Jesus (Mt 8:2, 6, 8, 25; 14:28 etc.). We probably should conclude, however, that the usage was more from the Matthean community than the actual time of the ministry of Jesus. We have already compared the use of the title in Matthew 8:25 with Mark 4:38. The disciples in the boat seek the help of the sleeping Jesus and call out: "Lord, save," in Matthew. The same scene in Mark has the title "teacher" (Mk 4:38). No doubt Matthew used this Greek expression to denote the exalted position of Jesus: someone close to God, for the title is also used to translate the sacred Hebrew name of God into Greek. *Kyrios* was used by the Matthean community in worship and prayer and was also the title used for the second coming of Jesus in glory. Matthew projects the use of the title backward to the ministry of Jesus, for he knows that Jesus now lives as exalted Lord of all.

When we combine all of the titles of Jesus, such as Son of God, son of David, son of Abraham, Emmanuel, messiah, Son of man, and *Kyrios,* they form an image of Jesus as the divine and exalted one from God who has returned to God and who has taught and healed as the manifestation of the loving God in human history. Jesus is the presence of the transcendent God and thus demands worship and adoration. He is also the sign of the closeness of a compassionate God through his power to heal.

Many times readers of Matthew note that he lacks the vigor and detail of Mark, but his gospel has a dignity which has made it the source for centuries of preaching on the person of Jesus. Nowhere is this more evident than in the conclusion. This ending of the gospel (Mt 28:16–20) may well be the Matthean summary of the resurrection proclamation rather than the actual words of Jesus. Any believer of the second or third generation also might have used those words to express what it means to be a Christian. Whatever the origin of the conclusion, the true believer knows that all authority and power had been given to Jesus. In his ministry Jesus had transformed the lives of men and women and had drawn them away from a life of sin and self-concern into the fellowship of a new creation. Where once people had been divided and separated, now they were united in a common faith. Only a person of extraordinary power could have accomplished such a task. Even the limitations on the relationship between God and people of the old dispensation has been done away with. In Jesus one of us has been exalted as Lord. Now the church, as the community of believers, could go out into the world and proclaim the sovereignty of Jesus as Lord of *all*. The resurrection and exaltation has made permanent and universally available the presence of the master. That presence in the church as exalted Lord and Son of God was the pledge of victory and of the ultimate fulfillment of the plan of God for *all*. The Jesus of Matthew's gospel inspires awe and worship and gives guidance and direction; he assures the presence of a kind and compassionate God who is ever willing to respond to the human world of suffering, conflict, and pain. Jesus is God with us.

Further Study

J. Kingsbury, *Matthew: Structure, Christology, Kingdom.*
S. Neil, *Jesus Though Many Eyes.*
D. Senior, *Matthew: A Gospel for the Church.*

5.

The Sermon on the Mount

*T*hus far I have attempted to quote in the text the relevant passages from the Bible to help the reader avoid going back and forth to the biblical text. Here, because of the length of the material, I would suggest you read through the sermon on the mount in Matthew 5:1-7:29 and the sermon on the plain in Luke 6:20-49.

The Sermon on the Mount may well be the charter of the kingdom for Matthew but for most Christians it seems too much. Even the very best have trouble being as perfect as God is perfect (Mt 5:48). Unfortunately, for many believers the problems associated with living up to all the demands of the sermon on the mount only encourage the reader to relegate this great teaching to the realm of the untried or the consciously forgotten. The meaning of the sermon on the mount, as understood in Matthew, is not that every individual lives up to the ideals all of the time. Every believer at some time, in his or her life, lives parts of this great sermon. We begin with the various interpretations found in the history of Christianity.

■ Perfectionist Interpretation ■

Jesus in the gospel of Matthew is the great teacher of the new law, as Moses was the great teacher of the law for Judaism. He came not to destroy but to fulfill. The sermon on the mount calls the follower to obey the teaching of Jesus and live. In reality it differs little from the demand of the Jewish law. Just as Moses gave the law after coming down from the mountain, so the new Moses, Jesus, gives the new law seated on the mountain. Surely the will of God makes hard demands but the individual believer must respond by personal exertion. The attempt must continue even if failure persists. To stand in the presence of God, to experience justification, demands works on the part of the believer.

The only problem with such an approach is that Jesus seems to go beyond the law of Moses. He is not interested in justification by works but proclaims how the kingdom of God is within the believer. God has entered into human history to bring his saving presence through Jesus, and, as savior, Jesus freely offers this salvation to anyone who will believe in him. Jesus may be the new Moses as teacher; however, he does not teach law but a gospel of salvation. Besides, who can really ever live up to this level of perfection?

■ Impossible Ideal ■

Closely related to this perfectionist interpretation is the theory of the impossible ideal. Everyone knows the old adage: aim high so that you may come closer to the target. Every teacher knows that students rise to the level of their expectations. Raise the requirements, and often students will achieve more. So, Jesus proposed the same. Who can live these demands of the sermon which call for: being meek, merciful, peacemakers, salt of the earth, light of the world, turning the cheek, and all the other demands? If the people of Israel could not live up to the law of Moses, this law outdoes Moses! But then when the believer comes close to despair, the belief in the presence of God enters in which one prepares for salvation. No one can do this without God, and so the impossible ideal helps the individual to rely upon God and gives a goal that one can strive to attain. The sermon on the mount helps the believer to move beyond self-reliance to the acceptance of the power of God and at the same time encourages continued effort.

However good this might seem, it does not fit the gospel of Matthew. It might be close to the teaching of Paul on the law, but Jesus in this gospel does not seem to want people to despair. Nor does he want to present to his listeners an ideal which is beyond them. If the kingdom is within, then somehow what Jesus teaches must be the real and not the ideal.

■ Interim Ethic ■

Finally, some have found a solution in the theory of an interim ethic. If Jesus is returning so quickly, then his followers are called upon to achieve heroic virtue, but only for a brief period, while they await his coming. This ethic makes sense only at the last hour. Somehow this last hour ethic has become part of the on-going understanding of the church. The nice thing about this approach is that Christians today really do not have to worry about the sermon on the mount. It applied only to those early Christians who thought that Jesus was about to return in triumph shortly.

The great problem with this interpretation, however, is that the text gives no foundation for such an approach. Jesus is not a fanatical enthusiast who calls for the impossible to be lived briefly. Moreover, if Matthew is preparing his church for a delayed coming of Jesus, the opinion accepted in this book, then an interim ethic just makes no sense. Why would he include this sermon if he was writing for a community that would continue in history? The sermon on the mount cannot be valid only for a brief period of time for a limited number of people but must make sense for all Christians for all times. Evidently the time has come to rethink the meaning of the sermon on the mount.

■ New Thought on the Sermon on the Mount ■

The sermon on the mount in Matthew should be compared to the sermon on the plain in Luke 6:20–49. A careful comparison of these two great discourses reported by the evangelists will allow the reader to conclude that much editorial activity is at work on the part of the writers. By this time the reader of this book knows that we cannot just accept the words and events as recorded by the evangelists as literally historically accurate. The individual writers had their set purpose in mind and freely used the Jesus tradition to respond to the particular needs of the early church communities. Whether there was a sermon on the mount or a sermon on the plain makes little difference. What matters is the use of the Jesus tradition.

■ Collections of Sayings ■

The careful analysis of the two great sermons reveals an underlying Aramaic tradition. No one doubts that the teaching contained goes back to Jesus, but instead of a sermon preached by Jesus at a particular time and place, we have a collection of sayings of Jesus that are linked together by the evangelists. One of the ways in which we can recognize this editorial phase is by noting the change in person in

Luke. Luke uses the second person; Matthew uses the more generic third person. Both Matthew and Luke joined together various teachings of Jesus to suit their individual purpose.

The original Christian preaching was a proclamation of the good news of salvation, as seen in Acts. Jesus died and rose from the dead; he fulfilled the Old Testament, went about doing good in his ministry, has sent the Spirit and will come again. The response to this proclamation was conversion. With the development of Christian commitment the kerygma (preaching) became didache (the kerygma plus ethical instruction). It was not just ethics, for it presupposed the response to the kerygma.

In Acts 2:42 we noted that the followers of Jesus devoted themselves to the teaching of the apostles, fellowship, the breaking of the bread, and prayers. The sermon on the mount will add to this experience of the Christian community the ethical response of faith. Matthew composed his sermon as pre-baptismal instruction for Jewish Christians and, in all probability, Luke composed his sermon as similar instruction for Gentile Christians. This becomes more evident when we compare Matthew 6:5–15 and Luke 11:1–13. Matthew is speaking to Jewish Christians who know how to pray but who should be conscious of the misuse of prayer. Luke is writing for Gentiles who, he presumes, do not know how to pray. Matthew places his words in the context of improper prayer, and Luke places his teaching in the context of encouraging prayer.

These individual sayings are preceded by proclamation and conversion. Because of what individuals have already experienced, they will be able to understand the teaching of the sermon on the mount. Three elements are involved: Jesus or God, the effect and response of the believer, and the result of the previous two elements. Jesus is the light of the world affecting people who come to the light and are changed. They in turn become a light to others (Mt 5:14); God has forgiven sins and trespasses; this has brought the believer close to God; they should forgive others (Mt 6:15; compare with Mt 18:35, preceded by the parable of the great debt cancellation). God has loved all people, loved the followers of Jesus even in their sins; they are to love their enemies (Mt 5:44–45).

One troubling teaching of the sermon on the mount, for me, concerns the turning of the other cheek. Does Jesus really teach me to be a pacifist and allow others to physically abuse me? The striking on the cheek in the ancient mideast was an insult, much as the striking of the cheek by a glove was considered an insult in the days of chivalry. In this context, the striking of the cheek means the insulting of disciples by non-believers. When the follower of Jesus is dishonored, the disciple bears with the insult and injustice. He or she overcomes the evil of the injustice and demonstrates the commitment to the Lord. Just as Jesus was reviled and did not strike back in kind, so the disciple will do likewise.

The meaning of the sermon on the mount is not that the follower of Jesus will always live these demands but that, because the individual has committed to Jesus, sometimes in life these will be actual experiences. The follower has been forgiven, and so the follower can sometimes forgive or be a peacemaker, or pure in heart, or poor in spirit. Sometimes the believer will be able to bear with insult and not strike back, actually be the light of the world for others and the salt of the earth, and love enemies. The sermon on the mount is not a new set of laws but a proclamation of the gospel. God has entered into the believer's life, and now he or she can live life based on that good news. The sermon is not just ethics or morality but a lived faith which is actually experienced, at least sometimes, in life. We are not concerned with a perfectionist demand nor with an impossible ideal nor with an interim ethic. Out of a sense of thankfulness to God for what God has done, the individual believer attempts to live a new life and actually does so, at least at intervals in life.

The sermon on the mount encourages people and does not make impossible demands. Because a follower of Jesus has once been a peacemaker, he or she can be a peacemaker again. Because the disciple has experienced giving light to others once, the experience can be repeated. Because bearing with insult was present in the past, it can be present again in the future. How marvelous for Christians to know and experience the sermon on the mount! They know that this great teaching of Jesus is possible in their lives even if that possibility is only intermittently present. The new life has begun with the commitment, and now human life can never again be the same.

With this interpretation the sermon on the mount takes on new meaning. Instead of something that seemed beyond Christians, it becomes an encouragement for the present and the future. The believer need not be condemned to just repeat the mistakes and failures of the past but can look back and know that being a peacemaker did happen, or at least that once an enemy was forgiven. Such an awareness helps the same follower of Jesus to feel assured of what can be again. No one can ever live up to all of the teachings of Jesus all of the time, but everyone can live up to some of the teachings some of the time. That alone gives encouragement and a sense of self-worth. The sermon on the mount is indeed the charter of the kingdom because it is lived in the Christian community. At any one moment Christians around the world are functioning as peacemakers, forgiving enemies, bringing light to others, suffering injustice without responding in kind. The teaching of Jesus and this great sermon live on in the lives of his followers.

> *Blessed are the poor in spirit . . .*
> *Blessed are those who mourn . . .*
> *Blessed are the meek . . .*
> *Blessed are those who hunger and thirst for righteousness . . .*
> *Blessed are the pure in heart . . .*
> *Blessed are the peacemakers . . .*
>
> *You are the salt of the earth . . .*
> *You are the light of the world . . . (Mt 5:3–16).*

Further Study

J. Jeremias, *The Sermon on the Mount.*
J. Lambrecht, *The Sermon on the Mount.*

6.

Parables

Parables occur in all four gospels, and each evangelist has his own approach. We have seen how Mark used the parable of the sower and how John used the parables of the good shepherd and the vine and the branches. Since Matthew seems to have the more developed use of parables in his gospel, we will study this usual mode of teaching by Jesus principally in Matthew and make reference to the other synoptics where helpful.

Already the reader knows that a parable is a type of figurative speech. The Hebrew word *mashal* in the ordinary language of post-biblical Judaism means any form of figurative speech: comparison, allegory, fable, proverb, riddle, symbol, or jest. Similarly, the Greek word *parabolae* has the meaning not only of parable but also of comparison or proverb or riddle. Perhaps the description of C.H. Dodd captures best the meaning of parable in the New Testament:

> At its simplest the parable is a simile drawn from nature or common life, arresting the hearer by its vividness or strangeness and leaving the mind in sufficient doubt to tease it into active thought.

The emphasis is on the everyday element, vividly engaging the mind precisely because of the element of doubt in meaning. The sense of "teasing" the mind is important. Parables arrest attention and often surprise the listener since frequently the parable reverses the expected outcome.

■ Types of Figurative Speech ■

The simple comparison is familiar to all:

The kingdom of heaven is like leaven which a woman took and hid in three measures of meal until it all was leavened (Mt 13:33).

This is an everyday event in the making of bread and the comparison is evident: Just as leaven influences the dough, so the reign of God influences this world.

A parable strictly speaking is a freely composed story, with the force coming from a relationship to something else: do likewise. The story of the Samaritan (Lk 10:33–37) illustrates this parable, strictly speaking. The story takes its power from the conclusion to imitate the action of the Samaritan.

A third type of parable is an allegory which portrays truth by a series of images. *Gulliver's Travels* was meant to convey the truth of British political system of the time. The parable of the sower as recorded and interpreted, e.g. in Mark 12:1–11, conveys the truth of the falling away from the Christian community at the time of the composition of the gospel of Mark, as we have already seen. Each group refers to a particular group of people familiar to those in the Marcan community.

Finally, a parable may be any illustrative story, a free composition to prove a point but not with the injunction to do likewise. The parable of the workers in the vineyard (Mt 20:1–16) proves the point that no one should begrudge the good fortune of anyone else. If someone has worked less and been fortunate enough to receive a generous wage, then fellow believers should rejoice in the good fortune of another and not react grudgingly. Often enough this illustrative story brings a surprise ending. Surely that was true for the parable of the vineyard.

Many years ago I read a book which contained a parable that has stayed with me, even though I am not sure exactly in what book it was contained. It is a contemporary parable, and it illustrates the method of teaching by Jesus precisely because it teases the mind into active thought, uses commonplace elements and offers a surprise ending.

Once upon a time a wild goose lived with the flock and yearly traveled south for the winter. One year the goose noticed a barnyard and decided to stop. He saw the pond and the grasses and each day ate the feed offered by the farmer. He enjoyed the barnyard and decided to stay. Each year he grew more accustomed to the life and never bothered to endure that arduous journey south. After several years, one fall he heard the call of the wild geese flying south and all of a sudden he felt the yearning to join them and fly away from the confines of the barnyard. He flapped his wings again and again, but he had grown so fat that he could not get off the ground. So he settled down to the life of the barnyard, and the saddest part of the story is that he began to think of the barnyard as the world.

The reader probably expected a different ending. The surprise should have caused the reader to think of the meaning and learn something of the truth contained. Something similar happens with the teachings of Jesus in parables. We have heard them so often that we tend to get used to them and fail to see the rich meaning that he implanted. To look at them again with new eyes will help to unfold this richness.

■ Literary History of the Parables ■

Joachim Jeremias offers ten laws of transformation of parables which will also help in rereading these fundamental ways in which Jesus taught.

1. Translation of the parable into Greek: If Jesus spoke in Aramaic, then some changes will inevitably take place in the translation into Greek. No one who has suffered through translation will be unfamiliar to this event. Maria von Trapp experienced the problem when she attempted to translate the familiar New Testament quotation, "The spirit is willing but the flesh is weak," from German into her beginning English. She stated: "The ghost is anxious but the meat is soft." It was a possible translation into English from the German words, but failed to convey the meaning. We must admit that something is always lost in translation.

2. Representational changes: When Luke adds "putting the candle in a cellar" to the Markan parable, he is making a representational change, since there are no cellars in Palestine, but they do exist in other parts of the world.

3. Embellishments: Matthew has three servants in the parable of the talents, with five, two and one coins given respectively (Mt 25:15). Luke has ten servants with one hundred denarii (Lk 19:13).

4. Influence of Old Testament folklore: The parable of the vine-

yard in Mark 12:1–11 has elements taken from Isaiah 5:1–2. The parable of the mustard seed is found in Mark (Mk 4:31–32), Matthew (Mt 13:31–32), and Luke (Lk 13:18–19), and the Gospel of Thomas. Thomas has no reference to a tree and was probably original. Mark has the seed growing from a shrub to a tree with branches; in Matthew it became a tree; Luke omits the shrub and speaks of the tree. In each case the influence of the Old Testament, which used the tree as an image to convey the protection of God, has intruded into the parable (Ps 104:12; Dn 4:21).

5. Change in audience: The various conclusions to the parable of the laborers in the vineyard in Matthew 20:1–16 show the changes brought about as the parable is applied to different groups in different times.

6. Hortatory use: The parables of the unjust servant (Lk 16:1–9), the man before a judge (Mt 5:25–26; Lk 12:58–59) and several others exhort believers to respond to the moment, and the demands of faith for the time is brief.

7. Influence of the church's situation: The delay in the parousia has influenced the parable of the ten virgins, the thief in the night, the talents and the doorkeeper. Missionary requirements have influenced the parable of the great feast (Mt 22:1–14; Lk 14:16–24); the situation of the Marcan community has influenced the interpretation of the parable of the sower (Mk 4:3–20).

8. Allegorization: The parable of the wicked vinedressers (Mk 12:1–11; Mt 21:33–44; Lk 20:9–19) becomes allegorized after the death of Jesus, just as allegorical elements come into the interpretation of the parable of the sower.

9. Collection and conflation of parables: The collection of parables in Mark 4 and Matthew 13 affects their inter-relatedness—the combination of talents and the recollection of Archelaus who went to Rome for support against the rejection of his subjects and his return to punish them. This helps explain Luke 19:12–27.

10. Universal meaning: The parable of the sower in the early church eventually gave universal meaning as it was allegorized and interpreted.

The contribution of the historical critical approach to the Bible, exemplified by Jeremias, goes without question. Because of this approach in scholarship we have come to appreciate the various levels of meaning that are contained in a single passage, and we know the historical complications. A fundamentalist approach to scripture cannot survive in the historical study of a text.

With regard to parables, the ten rules of Jeremias give insights into individual parables and will make the student pause before coming to any definitive conclusion. At this point it might also be good to recall the contribution of A. Julicher. For this German scholar a parable has one meaning, one simple lesson that could be understood by all. The fundamental meaning of the parable of the sower, as we have seen, is that in the end there will be a harvest. That is the essential idea. The message of the talents is fidelity in all that God has given to a person. Whenever the parables get more complicated, we have evidence of a development beyond the teaching of Jesus.

Today we might criticize Julicher for what might appear to be oversimplification but his insight remains true: find the fundamental meaning and understand that first. When we follow the historical critical method we can come to the meaning as understood by the audience of Jesus. Surely an understanding of the parables must begin with this. Once we have understood the parable in its original meaning we can go further and understand it in its life situation in the preaching of the early church or even in the gospel and then make it applicable to the contemporary needs of the community. Fortunately, the study of the parables in the past twenty years has given us additional help in this hermeneutical approach to this fundamental way of teaching by Jesus.

The effort to understand the parables in their setting in the life of Jesus and the development in the early church made great progress in the scholarly approach to the parables. A severely historical approach, however, has its limitations. Dan Otto Via offers four criticisms: (1) the theological and non-biographical nature of the gospels makes it difficult to pinpoint the life situation of Jesus for the parables; (2) it tends to ignore the broad element of basic humanity in the parables; (3) this approach tends to leave the parables in the past with nothing to say to the present; finally, (4) this approach often ignores the aesthetic nature and function of the parables. The work of Via, and others, attempts to rectify these weaknesses in the historical approach.

■ Literary Interpretation ■

Ernst Fuchs was a student of Bultmann, and for him language is an event. Language has a performative function bringing into being a reality which was not present before. Great poetry performs and has its effect. When one hears the words of Gerard Manley Hopkins: "The world is charged with the grandeur of God. It will flame out like shining from shook foil," something has taken place; the words have had their effect and created an event.

The parables of Jesus verbalize his understanding of his situation in the world and his understanding of God. Listening to them created the possibility for the hearer to share that situation of Jesus. The parable can become a language event for the hearer, and the faith venture of Jesus can be the faith venture of the believer.

Amos Wilder was a poet-theologian, and for him the literary factor was essential in understanding the parables. Some parables may be exemplary stories, such as the good Samaritan, but others are revelatory. The good shepherd reveals, and as a poet Jesus reveals in his parables his own vision of reality. He used metaphors to shock the imagination, to convey immediately what was signified, and to unveil the mystery of the relationship to God. The emphasis on the revelational helps explain the power of the parable as a means of teaching.

Robert Funk continues this insight and speaks of the parable as metaphor which draws the hearer into itself. The metaphor is creative of meaning and represents the reality. The prophet Amos used a metaphor when he proclaimed:

And justice will roll down like water
and righteousness like a mighty torrent (Amos 5:24).

The language represents the reality and draws the listener within. When Jesus used parables, he used symbolic language, which as metaphor raises the potential for new meaning. This can be one meaning or many. Metaphor disallows one single meaning forever, and so the good Samaritan takes on new meaning as the listener at one moment in life becomes the good Samaritan, or at another time becomes the man who was in need, or even the robbers, or the priest or levite. Since the metaphor is unfinished reality, the hearers complete it when drawn into the story and must decide how they will comport themselves. As open-ended, a plurality of situations and audiences becomes possible. Each hearer hears in his or her own way. The future disclosed in the parable is everyone's future who listens to it.

Via not only criticizes the historical approach but also offers his own understanding of the parables as aesthetic object. He accepts the parables as language event and also sees the parables as an aesthetic object. The teacher carefully organized a self-contained coherent literary composition. He will not speak of the parable as referring to a reality beyond itself, but the literary word is autonomous, having meaning in itself. He uses the image of a window becoming a mirror and then a window again, first used by Murrary Krieger. The literary work first functions as a series of windows through which we see a world that we know and can recognize. Then the window becomes a mirror in which we see ourselves and recognize the familiar, giving us a personal understanding of existence. Finally, the mirror becomes a window again, giving us a new vision of the world in which we find ourselves.

The parable is a window onto life as Jesus understood life. We observe as he did. Suddenly we are not just an observer, for the parable has become a mirror in which we see ourselves. Finally the parable becomes a window again, and the familiar is now seen in a different way. The parable of the talents is a window in which we observe people taking a risk and a person who refuses. Then we face the mirror and the question of personal risk-taking. Finally, our own world has new possibility, as we no longer sit and observe but are willing to take a risk of faith. The good Samaritan is a window transformed into a mirror in which we see ourselves in the various characters. When it becomes a window again, our familiar world has been changed and we have a new vision of our understanding of life.

One of my favorite few verses in poetry is taken from *Four Quartets* by T.S. Eliot:

> *We shall not cease from exploration*
> *And the end of all our exploring*
> *Will be to arrive where we started*
> *And know the place for the first time*
> *Through the unknown remembered gate.*

Paul Ricoeur adds an important hermeneutical insight when he speaks of a post-critical or "second" naiveté. After we have learned all we can about a text, with the aid of critical tools, we have to return to the text and allow it to address ourselves. Although Via does not advocate this approach, it seems to me that it is a natural outcome of his method in dealing with the parables as aesthetic object. We return and see it again for the first time.

The last contemporary scholar who deals with parables is Dominic Crossan. He combines New Testament scholarship and poetic criticism. He begins by saying that one cannot simply distinguish parable from allegory. The allegory translates an abstract notion into picture language, and parables are picture language. Jesus could not express his ideas in any other way, since they reveal more than what can be reduced to language. We are involved with metaphor. Crossan offers two types of metaphors: the first is illustrative, in which information precedes participation. This is not metaphor properly speaking. The second type of metaphor is true metaphor, for participation precedes information and its function is to create the participation. This is the metaphor of the parables. We have a verbal level but also a non-verbal level. To understand Jesus we need the non-verbal, and this invites participation. Jesus had a fundamental experience of God which becomes paradigmatic for the meaning of Jesus and constitutive of him as an historical figure. The parables disclose this understanding. When the listener hears these parables he or she is united in the reality expressed. In a parable the listener experiences the advent of a new world with unforeseen possibilities. This advent causes a reversal of the past and brings about action, the expression of the new world and the new possibilities.

This new approach to the parables brings a new wealth to the scriptures. To see language as an event, which is revelational, raising the possibility for ever-new meaning causing participation and action, makes the parables alive. All of a sudden they reach out and demand participation and have their effect much as the word of God as proclaimed in Isaiah has its effect:

> So shall my word be that goes forth from my mouth;
> it shall not return to me empty,
> but it shall accomplish that which I purpose
> and prosper in the thing for which I sent it (Is 55:11).

Further Study

D. Crossan, *In Parables: The Challenge of the Historical Jesus.*
C. H. Dodd, *The Parables of the Kingdom.*
J. Jeremias, *The Parables of Jesus.*
N. Perrin, *Jesus and the Language of the Kingdom.*
D. Tracy, *The Analogical Imagination.*

7.

Eschatology

The future of human life, the destiny of creation, is God. We can think of individual futures and even conjecture about what lies in store for the planet earth, but for the Christian the ultimate future is God alone. Somehow when human history has been completed, when individual lives have fulfilled their destiny, God is the climax and culmination of the individual moments of this collective and individual history.

Eschatology, we learned from the study of the gospel of John, comes from the Greek word *eschaton* and means the study of the last things. Eschatology involves understanding God, not the God as creating but the final manifestation of the unifying and reconciling God. The last things are moments in that final reconciling in love. Traditionally theologians have spoken of eschatology as comprising: death, judgment, heaven or hell, the second coming and the final and general judgment which initiates the perfecting of the kingdom of God.

In the study of Matthew we have seen that this kingdom of God, or reign of God, is a communion that has been established through Christ, uniting God with humankind. We all know that this Christian God is a God of love, not an abstract and passive love but an active love that heals, renews and unites. God, as the final destiny of all, responds not just to the individual but to the individual as part of the family of creation. God loves the person individually but also as part of a common humanity. No one can possibly separate personal destiny from the future of the human race. The communion with God can never prescind from family, friends, associates and fellow Christians as well as men and women of good will whether or not they are part of a religious tradition.

In the study of the gospel of John eschatology was presented as

196

realized: the future had already taken place. The one who had come to the light had already passed from death to life (Jn 5:24); the believer does not come into judgment (Jn 5:24) and has already experienced resurrection and eternal life (Jn 11:25; 17:3). The author of this gospel emphasizes what has already taken place to the person of faith. He does not preclude some future eschatology, but, for reasons best known to him and his community, chose to concentrate on the present reality rather than look forward to a future reality. We can say that the church in its life, especially in its celebration of the eucharist, anticipates these future events in the present time. The church carries this divine reconciling and unifying Spirit and actually is accomplishing the future communion of all with God now, even if only in an inchoate stage.

While we should recognize the reality that has already taken place because of faith, the gospel of Matthew points toward a future which is demanded by people of faith. This future will give purpose and direction to our present lives. The human desire for ultimate fulfillment finds its release in the communion with God but never on a solely individualistic plane. We move toward the full reign of God throughout history and move as members of the human community. Certainly Matthew knew that in this movement toward the future the church community would encounter forces hostile to God and human destiny and working against Jesus and his church. Matthew presents his understanding of eschatology as a burning issue relating the final events, as recorded for us in chapters 24 and 25, to salvation history. (As with the sermon on the mount, I would suggest that the reader turn to these chapters and read them completely.) The author takes interest in the way that the eschatological events take their course, how they are present in the community of Matthew, and how the group of believers fit in the final sequence. Eschatology for Matthew is not completely realized, as in the gospel of John, but it already approaches.

By the time of the writing of this gospel the temple in Jerusalem has been destroyed. Matthew, however, does not join this destruction with the end of human history. Matthew sees no connection between the Jewish war with Rome and the beginning of the fulfillment. In his work, the historical references as seen in chapter 13 of Mark are missing. His future tense in his eschatological discourse shows his inclination to regard the events of the last time as historical. We cannot, however, conclude from these chapters how long the community, with its expectation of the end, has already existed, nor how long it will continue to exist as it points to a future. He knows that the second coming has been delayed. Matthew has announced in his gospel a long period to wait, and so no one should become anxious. The date of the parousia is uncertain. The followers of Jesus must not just watch, with a sense of an imminent return, but must remain watchful in life, in expectation for the goal of salvation which has come and which is yet to come. Eschatology is future but demands a watching in the present.

Matthew adds in his understanding of watchfulness the connection between expectation of judgment and the parousia (Mt 24:40–41, 51; 25:12, 21, 23, 30). This intimate connection of the two, judgment and second coming, strains the framework of the parables of watchfulness and points toward a future sifting in the final judgment scene (Mt 25:31–36). The actual judgment is the coming of the Son of man who will separate sheep from goats. The peculiar quality of Matthew's approach is the interpretation of the end in moral terms. Matthew's gospel announces the eschatological determination of the believer's task and the accountability of that task.

He also is concerned with universality. The final judgment takes place everywhere. According to Matthew 24 and 25 the ultimate event of human history will apply not to just a small band of believers in one place but to all within the jurisdiction of the Son of man, all peoples in all places.

The parables of the kingdom in chapter 13 present the working out of salvation history as the central theme. The parable of the tares among the wheat (Mt 13:24–30) and the net (Mt 13:47–50) brings salvation history to the fore. Even Matthew 13:41–43, when the angels gather out of the kingdom all evildoers, and the righteous shine like the sun, is not a warning. He offers his insights into the actual saving presence of God much like the parable of the mustard seed or the leaven (Mt 13:31–33). These are concerned with the history of salvation that is already taking place in human life now, even as the believers look forward to a future coming and judgment. These parables concerned with salvation history should be understood in relationship to the parables in chapter 24 and 25: the faithful and unfaithful servants (Mt 24:45–51), the ten virgins (Mt 25:1–13), and the talents (Mt 25:14–30). Salvation history takes place now, and demands a sense of watchfulness, for its completion will surely take place. Some of the goods of the kingdom have already been entrusted to the church, but this cannot instill a false sense of security. Watchfulness and diligent activity will guard and increase these goods until the Lord returns. Even if the time of his coming remains unknown, the church community must be aware of what is taking place now (hence the parables in chapter 13 on the kingdom). The church watches, guarding what it has received (hence the parables in chapters 24–25).

The parable of the faithful and unfaithful servants is directed toward the church leaders. Even if the parousia is delayed, the church leaders must not become lax in their responsibilities or their personal moral life. They are to be like the faithful servants who remain faithful even if the Lord delays (Mt 24:48).

The parable of the virgins stresses the demands on the church community. With the delay of the coming of the Lord the temptation exists for all to become lax and not to be prepared and not to be watchful. The whole community must accept the postponement but not allow this to change their fundamental commitment to the teachings of Jesus in action. They are to be prudent and vigilant even if they do not know when Jesus will come. Their sense of preparedness coexists with their Christian living, and so they will be able to go out to meet Jesus when in fact he does come.

The third parable, the parable of the talents, is also directed to the whole community. They not only will preserve what has been given but will work with it to increase the gifts with which they have been entrusted. Everyone does not receive the same talents or abilities, but each one works according to one's ability and each will be judged accordingly. This last parable depicts the judgment in greater detail than the others and conveys a sober warning.

The judgment, the exacting criteria, the separation and sifting, and the concluding dark side of condemnation culminate in the final great scene in chapter 25. Jesus, as Son of man, enthroned as king and judge, will come in glory attended by angels sitting on his throne. Before him are gathered all the nations. The separation will not divide just the church and unbelievers but will divide all humanity. The criteria is not church membership but deeds of love and mercy shown to the poor and outcast of humankind. He gives not anthropological or purely ethical reasons but christological criteria. That people are judged by the glorious Christ causes no surprise; that people are judged by their words and deeds is also no surprise. What startles in this final scene by Matthew is that this glorious judge identifies himself with the poor and the oppressed. The most lowly and often despised members of humanity become the presence of Jesus in this world. What is done for them, for better or worse, is done for the Lord. All morality for all peoples, and not just for believers, is interpreted in terms of what is done for the unfortunate, for in everyone God is present through Jesus. The just are those who offer mercy to those in need, for the christological reason that in the needy the believer, or the nonbeliever, will experience the presence of God. The presence of Jesus in suffering humanity renders forever invalid the distinction between duties toward God and toward humankind. Christian morality involves unlimited active love.

Often enough the gospel of Matthew has been depicted as too "ecclesiastical," too much concerned with hierarchy and organization and control. No doubt, as we have seen, this is part of the legacy of Matthew, but it can never be the only contribution. Matthew alone among the evangelists depicts the final judgment scene in terms of christology and relationship to those in need. Some may try to see in the least of these my brethren neglected Christians. It seems rather to refer to the poor and outcasts of humanity. The church of Matthew takes on a universal tone going far beyond the confines of Christianity. Jesus is the presence of God in human history offering a communion with God. This Jesus is present in the church and in the church leaders. On a more universal level, Jesus as the Lord of all is present in the outcasts and refuse of humanity demanding an acceptance and a love. On this criterion alone will humanity be judged: the love and care and compassion one for the other.

> And the king will answer them, "Truly I say to you, as you did it to one of the least of these my brethren, you did it to me" (Mt 25:40).

Further Study

J. Meier, *Matthew.*
E. Schweizer, *The Good News According to Matthew.*
J. C. Fenton, *Saint Matthew.*

8.

The Origin of Matthew

The gospel of Matthew probably has its origin in Antioch in Syria sometime between 80 and 90 C.E. The author wrote his gospel some fifteen or twenty years following the destruction of Jerusalem, alluded to in Matthew 22:7. With the destruction of Jerusalem in 70, and the death of James, the leader of the conservative church in Jerusalem, in the 60s, the church at Antioch lost its ties to its Jewish identity and past. The more liberal groups of Pauline and Hellenistic Jewish Christians and the Gentile Christians made progress against the conservative Jewish Christians which had looked to Jerusalem and James for support. The gospel, then, comes from a church which has its Jewish connection but sees the future of the Christian church directed toward the Gentiles.

Jewish Christians probably experienced persecution from Jews in Antioch. Some will cite the *birkat ha-minim,* the cursing of Christians in the eighteen benedictions of the synagogue, but such a formal separation was not necessary to explain the problems between the two groups. After the destruction of the temple, the Jews were involved in seeking a self-identity for the future just as the Jewish Christians were concerned with their identity. Since at Antioch Jews had experienced persecution from Gentiles during the time of the Jewish war, especially under the Jewish apostate Antiochus, no one would wonder if Jews had trouble dealing with Jewish Christians who associated with Gentile Christians. Tensions were bound to develop and surely found expression within the Matthean community. Probably some wanted to remain tied to the synagogue, but when the one remaining tie to Judaism, the local synagogue, was broken sometime in the mid 80s, the church of Matthew at Antioch became oriented to an exclusive Gentile future.

An additional problem facing this community was the possible persecution from civil authorities. With the break with the synagogue, Christianity lost its protection as a legal religion in the Roman empire. Both the missionary and the apocalyptic discourses in Matthew (chapters 10, 24, 25) speak of opposition from governors and kings as well as synagogues. Thus, the common experience of persecution would probably bring both Jewish and Gentile Christians together more closely. The more conservative members had a choice: either return to the synagogue or throw in their lot with the more liberal factions of Jewish Hellenists Christians and Gentile Christians. Those Jewish Christians who stayed were too Christian to return to the synagogue but still had misgivings about the influx of Gentiles. They also had concerns about being cut off from Jerusalem and the synagogue. How could they maintain those aspects of the Jewish heritage which in their view made Christianity the true fulfillment of God's promise to Israel? This community needed a sign of unity which would synthesize the various tendencies and groups within the community. The gospel of Matthew attempted to serve that purpose.

The author of Matthew offered a liberal conservative response to the tensions within the community. He used the gospel of Mark as a primary source. We have already noted that this gospel came from a period prior to 70 C.E. and probably from Rome. It was only natural that the Matthean community would turn to a gospel coming from the capital of the empire where the two significant figures of the Antiochean church, Peter and Paul, were martyred. Perhaps this gospel from Rome became the principle source used in the liturgy of the church of Antioch. Since this earliest of the gospels had a clear sympathy for Gentiles and was critical of the Mosaic law, the Hellenistic and the Gentile Christians would have found it quite acceptable. In time, however, the community of Matthew would have made its own additions and would have been interested in presenting some of its own theology to the theology of Mark.

We also know that the author of the gospel of Matthew had another source which scholars refer to as "Q." The nature of this document is somewhat hypothetical. Probably some early followers of Jesus in Palestine attempted to gather together the sayings of Jesus. Since "Q" never developed into a gospel, its eclectic nature would allow for a fluidity of content with various editions. The church of Antioch evidently accepted this collection since it could give support to the church from the actual sayings of Jesus. But if the gospel of Mark was open to interpretation and additions, the same thing was more true for a collection of sayings. The oral presentations allowed for many editorial changes.

We have learned of the existence of "Q" mainly through comparison with Mark and Luke. Matthew and Luke have some verses in common with Mark and some verses common just to each other. We can conclude that both Luke and Matthew knew Mark and "Q" while Mark did not know "Q." We can also detect in Matthew and Luke sections and material proper to each gospel. Thus, we can also speak of "Matthean material." This material embraces various traditions, each one reflecting the differing viewpoints within the church of Antioch.

The sayings which seem to reject a Gentile mission: "Do not go to the Gentiles and do not enter a samaritan city" (Mt 10:5–6), reflect the presence of extreme Judaizers who wanted nothing to do with Gentiles who did not first become Jews. The moral material in the sermon on the mount that does not run counter to the Mosaic law might have come from the conservative group of Jewish Christians anxious to preserve as much of Judaism and the law as possible. Such an emphasis on moral authority might counter the danger posed by the large number of Gentiles entering the church.

The traditions favoring the Gentile mission and opposing excessive devotion to the law would come from the more liberal Hellenists and Gentile Christians, e.g. the universal mission in the conclusion of the gospel in Matthew 28:16–20, or the coming of the magi in chapter 2 and the material in chapter 23 which criticizes both scribes and Pharisees.

The final form of the gospel reflects the practical needs of the church of Antioch. It would be a mistake, however, to think of these three sources, Mark, Q, and Matthean material, as three separate blocks of tradition combined for the first time by Matthew. The three would have interacted first in the liturgy, in catechetical instruction and in other church activities. Perhaps certain parts of Mark were altered by the oral tradition long before Matthew incorporated this material into his gospel. Also, some Matthean material might have been incorporated into the fluid collection called "Q." We might think of the origin of Matthew as coming from a school. The Old Testament citations in Matthew would have their origin in a scribal school which drew upon Jewish learning filtered through Jewish Christians. The prophets in the community would proclaim and apply this understanding of the Jesus tradition in homilies and catechesis. But in a larger sense the gospel of Matthew inherits the work of each bearer of the Jesus tradition at Antioch. The church faced a crisis of identity and unity. Varied elements struggled to relate to each other, experiencing pressure from the Judaism of the past and the Roman empire

of the present. Matthew interpreted and unified the competing traditions of Christian Antioch to make the Jesus tradition speak to a
new day.

Further Study

R. Brown, J. Meier, *Antioch and Rome.*
J. Kingsbury, *Matthew.*
J. Meier, *Matthew.*
————, *The Vision of Matthew.*

9.

The Meaning of Matthew

*F*ew people pick Matthew as their favorite gospel. In my experience with undergraduate, graduate and continuing education students, most people seem to pick the gospel of Luke or the gospel of John. Rarely does one pick Mark and, more rarely, Matthew. Since Mark seems to always have the pall of the cross hanging over the ministry of Jesus, I can well understand why many will not quickly turn to this first gospel. But for Roman Catholics, the gospel of Matthew was the most familiar gospel in the liturgy for many years. Until the reform of the Second Vatican Council the gospel of Matthew was read almost every Sunday of the year. It was ecclesial and catechetical and well suited to the needs of the Roman Catholic Church. People heard it frequently. They probably learned most of the teachings of Jesus through listening to this gospel and hearing preaching on the topics coming from the theology of this early community. Still, it is not the most favored gospel in the minds of most people.

I too shared this opinion and often thought of the gospel of Matthew as being too rigid and too controlled. I was more familiar with the other three gospels and seem to have avoided studying this gospel because of some built-in prejudice. The gospel is truly hierarchical with authority going from God to Jesus to the twelve and their successors. The gospel is organized with Peter as the leader, the eleven around him and all others falling in behind. The gospel also is catechetical. Answers are given to questions and most things seem black and white.

After reading what I have written about Matthew, however, I would presume that the reader knows that such a picture is misleading. The gospel of Matthew is hierarchical and authoritarian but it is not absolute. The presence of chapter 18 in this gospel modifies the overall approach. Matthew knew the need for organization and control but would not give any blank check to anyone, not even those who claimed the authority of Peter and the twelve.

Things are not so black and white. The various factions in this community are not condemned to silence but seem to have left their mark. What might appear as monolithic in fact is pluralistic. Even the authority given to Peter is modified by the authority given to the community in chapter 18. Matthew presents a hierarchical church, well organized but also tempered in its functions.

Peter is surely an authority figure in this gospel but not an absolute ruler. His position in the early church, with his openness to the Gentiles and his concern to preserve Christianity's Jewish origins, made him a centrist. The author of Matthew wanted evidently to be a centrist. He hoped to bring the new and the old from the same storeroom.

Being a centrist is troublesome. Usually such a person pleases few. Matthew makes a case for such a position. He does not exclude the extreme right or left unless they choose to exclude themselves. His gospel has evidence of great concern for Judaism and great concern for the Gentile mission. He knows that conflicts will inevitably arise but hopes that the Jesus tradition will be recognized as bringing a unity rather than a disunity. Peter historically bridged the gap between the party of James and the Jerusalem church and Paul and the Gentile church. Matthew then hoped that capitalizing on Peter's historical connection to Antioch would bring a sense of unity without destroying the new or the old.

Today when the church seems to be struggling with similar problems a centrist position might be the best that can be hoped for. Anyone who proposes either extreme will lose sight of the richness of the Jesus tradition and will fail to learn from the lessons of the past. Matthew stands forever as one who opted for a centrist position and offered his gospel not to put an end to differences but to see how these same differences can be part of the one tradition.

In a world that has become increasingly aware of the needs of the poor, the oppressed, the homeless, the people who live on the periphery of society, Matthew's gospel proclaims the presence of Jesus in all who are in need. That alone would make it relevant to a church that wishes to be identified with the outcasts and those in need. Since the Vatican Council spoke of a preference for the poor, the gospel of Matthew lays the proper foundation for this direction of the church.

Often enough the Christian church struggles to survive in a world of finance and order and neatness. It needs money and clout and buildings and investments; it needs liturgy, which needs music and appointments; it needs education, with teachers and textbooks and classrooms and lectures and workshops. It needs offices and committees and commissions and congregations. It needs shelter and food and clothing for its bureaucrats and leaders of prayer. It needs so much just to survive and even more to have an impact. But when it is all over, Matthew gives only one criterion to evaluate the presence of the faith commitment in an individual: Was Jesus recognized in those who were in need?

I do not propose that the church can do away with any of the above needs. I do not advocate the selling of great religious art works nor turning churches into shelters for the homeless; I do not advocate the simplification of life-styles of clergy or religious or the abandonment of papal trips which cost millions of dollars. I offer no program for the contemporary church but only for the contemporary believer: "As often as you did it for the least of my brethren, you did it for me" (Mt 25:40).

Lest one get discouraged in reading this gospel, when so much seems to depend on the recognition of Jesus in those who are in need, the author of Matthew reminds believers, in the sermon on the mount, just what they already are. If the sermon on the mount seemed too much it would have little impact on the lives of believers. Matthew solved the problem by reminding his listeners that already they have been peacemakers; already they have been the light of the world or the salt of the earth; in their lives they have experienced suffering for justice and have been pure of heart. If believers can look back and recognize what they have already become because of the presence of God in their lives, then they can always have hope for doing it again. You do not need to be perfect to be part of this gospel. You need only to recognize how much God has already done for you and with you. That gives the encouragement to continue the good work which Jesus has begun in each of his followers.

With this approach to Christianity the contemporary believer should feel good. Matthew does not want people to become discouraged. Rather, he wrote his gospel to lead people to an awareness of what is already within. We do not usually associate this gospel with realized eschatology, as we do the gospel of John. But if we pay attention to the sermon on the mount we recognize the good that has already taken place. In a world which needs to believe in the power of goodness, this gospel, especially this sermon, reminds Christians of what they already have become. If it has happened in the past it can and will happen in the future.

In the past the kingdom of God was too closely associated with the church and in particular with the Roman Catholic Church and the leaders of that church. Matthew says that the reign of God is a communion. God has entered into human history, and human history can never again be the same. Christians may be more aware of this nearness, but it can never be limited to Christianity. Nor can the Roman Catholic Church claim an exclusive identity with this kingdom. If the communion was established with Jesus, then all of humanity has been affected.

I do not think Matthew would have advocated a false irenicism in which all religions are the same, but he would have advocated the presence of God in human history through Jesus' establishing a communion. Once God has entered into human history, that history can never again be the same. There is no longer an order of nature and an order of grace. The order of grace alone exists. Christianity responds to the needs of the human race, to anyone who is open to receive its power. With such an understanding of the kingdom of God, the church, in particular the Roman Catholic Church, can be open to other Christian churches, to other religions and to all people of good will, for all have been blessed in some way by the presence of Jesus in history.

This gospel also calls for good teaching. Christianity needs good teachers who will maintain the Jesus tradition. Matthew knew this and taught. He also saw a need for other teachers to follow him, and they too must be in accord with the authentic teaching of Jesus. No one should be foolish enough to say that good teaching is not necessary but all we have to do is love Jesus. Such an approach is simplistic. The church cannot survive with an approach that concentrates on loving Jesus without at the same time devoting itself to the teaching of Jesus and the teaching of the apostles as described in Acts 2:42. People may not always agree on what is good teaching, but it seems clear from this gospel that good teaching is not without its differences. The conservative party of James and the Jerusalem church did not win according to this gospel; nor did the Hellenists and the Gentile Christians. Matthew tried always to bring the old as well as the new from his storeroom of knowledge. The same must be true today if we hope to have good teaching. The tradition is important, but the demands of the new age are equally important.

Matthew was open to the future. He never abandoned the past in his regard for what was coming. Christianity has changed over the centuries and will continue to change in the centuries to come. The Jesus tradition will remain the basis, but how this is translated into different societies, civilizations, economies and cultures will be never-ending. The church can never live in the past alone. If it does, it will die in the past and fail to fulfill its divine mandate to teach all nations. When the church accepts the stance of being open to the future, the church remains eternally vulnerable, precisely because the future is in the hands of God alone. Such a commitment to the open-ended acceptance of what will come fits well into the approach of Matthew. He accepted the presence of Jesus in the church and knew that the second coming might well be in the far distant future. With the assurance of the divine presence he also believed that the community could hold on to the past and embrace the new. Surely he also knew the dangers, but the presence of problems did not prevent this early community and its leader from trusting in the unknown. Just as people have to live their lives holding on to the past and accepting the future, so the church will follow suit. Matthew's gospel gives the example.

Finally, although the parables are present in all of the gospels, I have chosen to study them more thoroughly here in Matthew precisely because of the great significance they played in the actual teaching method of Jesus. For Matthew, Jesus was the great, new, teacher. Listening to the parables again and hearing them perhaps for the first time makes the teaching of Jesus alive and applicable to the present time. The various approaches presented, especially the literary approach, allow the parables to spill over into every aspect of the believer's life. They do not lie dead on the pages of a book, nor do they lose their impact after many hearings. As the listener changes, so the parables change and the teaching of Jesus continues. Any parable that one may pick unfolds its meaning when the reader becomes the object upon which the parable works its effects. The good shepherd from John allows the listener to be like a good shepherd or, at other times, like the sheep that needs protection and nurturing. The prodigal son may help the listener to understand when he or she becomes the father or the elder brother as well as the son. The richness of the parables continues to tease the mind into active thought.

What does this gospel mean? It means a need for an organized church but not without its parameters; it means good teaching but not closed teaching; it means a centrist position which emphasizes what has already taken place in faith with an openness to the future. Above all, this gospel means that in the end we will be judged on how we have lived faith and how we discovered the human face of God in Jesus, present in those who are in need. Matthew is not narrow. Matthew's gospel is the record of the Jesus tradition continuing to speak to the church today.

■ **PART V** ■

The Jesus Tradition and Mercy: Luke

1.

Historian and Theologian

*I*f San Francisco is everyone's favorite city and *La Boheme* is everyone's favorite opera, then if we have to pick a gospel which is everyone's favorite, the gospel is Luke. Centuries ago Dante referred to the author of the third gospel as "The Scribe of the Gentleness of Christ" (De monarchia 1.18). Ernest Renan, the nineteenth century French biblical critic, referred to this gospel as "The most beautiful book written . . . ." The above statements are exaggerations. They are, in the words of the Italian proverb, "Not true, but well founded." Most people do, in fact, like San Francisco and *La Boheme,* and most people like the gospel of Luke. The reader notices the qualities of mercy, love, joy, the kindness and compassion of Jesus. The gospel lifts people up and makes them feel good even if at the same time this gospel is demanding. Somehow the high level of expectation associated with Christian living in this gospel is overshadowed by the charm of the writing. Père M.J. Lagrange, the French Roman Catholic exegete who spanned the nineteenth and twentieth centuries, summed up his attitude toward Luke as follows:

> *In reading this gospel of mercy, but also of repentance, of stark renunciation, but with a view to charity, these miracles inspired by goodness, this forgiveness for sin which is not complacency but rather a divine gift for sanctification—in learning to appreciate how a virgin and tender mother gave birth to the Son of God and how He suffered to bring human beings to His Father, the noble Theophilus would have comprehended the reasons for the moral transformation at work before his eyes and undoubtedly already begun in his heart. And he would have recognized them as good and secure; the world has possessed a savior indeed (luc, xlvii).*

213

Luke combines the gentleness of the Christian savior with his call to radical discipleship in a most attractive way. Somehow the renunciation expected of the followers of Jesus is accepted without hesitation. The "hardness" of the cross becomes "soft" in the words of Luke without losing any of the demands. Luke's absolute renunciation required of the Christian, especially his statements of riches and poverty, leave no room to maneuver. Yet, they are accepted. For this same author has given us the wonderful songs: the Benedictus of Zechariah (Lk 1:68–79); the Nunc Dimittis of Simeon (Lk 2:29–32), the Magnificat of Mary (Lk 1:46–55). He alone has recorded for all Christians the story of the good Samaritan, the prodigal son and the gentle Jesus walking with two disciples on the road to Emmaus after the resurrection.

This author writes personally. He has an interest in people, especially those who feel outside or forgotten. The first people to come to recognize Jesus are shepherds. Throughout the gospel Jesus extends his hand to the outcasts. He called a hated tax collector, Levi, to be his disciple (Lk 3:24, 29), and responded to the sorrow of the widow of Nain by giving her back her son (Lk 7:11). Luke, the one who seems to expect so much from the rich, tells the story of Zaccheus, and once again the gentle Jesus responds to someone in need (Lk 19:2–10).

Some have seen in Luke an "ardent feminist." This gospel highlights the role of women in the ministry of Jesus. They follow him and care for him and are faithful to him to the end. Jesus used parables about women—the lost coin (Lk 15:8–10) and the women with the leaven (Lk 13:20–21). In the Acts of the Apostles women appear frequently and are called devout. They invited worshipers into their homes and seem to have held honored positions in the early community.

While everyone seems to have liked Luke, for centuries he was not considered a great New Testament theologian. Scholars would prefer the greatness of Paul or the author of John. In spite of writing approximately twenty-eight percent of the New Testament, Luke was not judged a great theologian. As late as 1952 C.H. Dodd could write:

> Among Christian thinkers of the first age known to us, there are three of genuinely creative power: Paul, the author of Hebrews and the Fourth Evangelist.

Part of the problem undoubtedly lies with the separation of the gospel of Luke from the Acts of the Apostles. Until very recently the three synoptic gospels were studied together in a homogenized fashion. The Acts of the Apostles was studied in conjunction with Paul. Only in recent days has Luke been given his due as a theologian who not only recorded the Jesus tradition in a gospel, but also carried this tradition into the development of the early church.

After these preliminary suggestions, many of which will become more developed as we unfold this gospel, some may think that the title of this chapter as a beginning of a study of the third gospel is unusual. Most readers know that the gospels are not strictly historical writings but works of theology, coming from a committed faith community. Why then speak of Luke as an historian? Would it not be better to begin with Luke as a theologian?

From the beginning of this century and up to the 1950s, Luke was considered precisely as an historian. He was the writer not only of the gospel but also of the Acts of the Apostles. The details mentioned in this, his second volume, seem to have considerable support from extra-biblical sources. An additional support for the thesis that Luke was an historian comes from the prologue itself. In the carefully formulated prologue Luke writes:

Inasmuch as many have undertaken to compile a narrative of the things which have been accomplished among us, just as they were delivered to us by those who from the beginning were eye-witnesses and ministers of the word, it seemed good to me also, having followed all things closely for some time past, to write an orderly account for you, most excellent Theophilus, that you may know the truth concerning the things of which you have been informed (Lk 1:1-4).

The account will be thorough, traced from the beginning, orderly and accurate. Any historian would be proud of such an assessment if made by another historian or reader. The question remains: Does the work of Luke live up to his protestation in the prologue?

At first reading people will be impressed with his use of a census under Quirinius (Lk 2:1-2; Acts 5:37), but actually we have no historical basis for such a census. Throughout his gospel the information on both history and geography is not accurate. In spite of his desire to be precise, Luke is far from accurate when compared to the methods of modern historical science. Some scholars (C.K. Barrett, N.A. Dahl) try to preserve Luke the historian and compare him to the ancient Hellenistic historians such as Plutarch, Josephus and Tacitus. But even these writers were careful to distinguish fact from fiction, and at times the contemporary reader may question whether Luke maintains the same distinction. Was there really a census, required by whomever, which prompted Joseph and Mary to go to Bethlehem, or is Bethlehem the creation of Luke? Fact or fiction?

History can never be completely objectively written since historians can give us only an interpretation of facts and past events. But even with such an admission, Luke does not fit the mold of historian, whether modern or ancient. He wrote from a perspective which interpreted events in light of a theological end; the events of which Luke writes are narrated as a fulfillment. Thus he subordinates his historical concern, whatever it was, to a theological purpose.

Like Matthew, he used Mark as a source for his gospel. When making the comparison it seems that he took very little liberty with Mark other than abbreviating his narrative and polishing his rough style. He seems to have no hesitation in making stylistic changes or modifications in endings or introductions. But when treating the words of Jesus, as recorded by Mark, he shows great reverence.

He also used "Q," as did Matthew as we have noted, and in use of both of these written traditions we can say that his history is as accurate as his sources. When we study the material proper to Luke ("L") we can conclude that he had independent sources of the Jesus tradition. Whether these were oral or written, or whether what we have in "L" is the result of Lucan editing, remains unknown. I suppose the most honest thing that can be said with regard to Luke and historical accuracy is that we just do not know. This will become more evident as we study the gospel and, in particular, the infancy narratives. People should overcome any hope of evaluating the historical accuracy of any biblical episode or tradition with some level of absolute certitude. Rather, readers of the Bible should look upon its meaning as more significant than any effort to sort out historical details.

Having qualified the note "historical" for the third gospel, we can concentrate on the theology involved and incorporate the history into the theology. Luke writes about salvation history and not the history as recorded by Toynbee, or Theodore White, or Barbara Tuchman.

No comment on Luke the historian can omit reference to the decisive work by Hans Conzelmann, *The Theology of Saint Luke* (a title in English quite different from *The Middle of Time,* the original German title). Conzelmann treats Luke as an innovator who responded to the delay in the parousia by a theology of salvation history.

The starting point for Conzelmann was Luke's emphasis on God's redemptive plan in three stages:

(a) the period of Israel and the Jews. "The law and the prophets were in force until John; since then the good news of the kingdom is preached . . ." (Lk 16:16).

(b) the period of the ministry of Jesus (The Middle of Time according to the original German title of the work), a peaceful period free from the influence of Satan (compare Luke 4:13 and Luke 22:3: the devil departs after the temptation and returns before the passion), composed of three sections: the time in Galilee (Lk 3:23–9:50), the journey to Jerusalem (Lk 9:51–19:27) and his entry into Jerusalem up to his death (Lk 19:28–23:56).

(c) the period of the church in the world (begun in the Acts of the Apostles and continuing). Now the Spirit becomes available to all.

Many individuals find fault with Conzelmann. He ignores, for example, the infancy narratives. He also sees symbolic interpretations in Luke's use of geography while in fact the journey to Jerusalem and the journey of Christianity to Rome were historical journeys and not just the results of a writer's imagination. Even the division into three sections is called into question by some. Might it rather be just two: the old and the new? Whatever one's position on Conzelmann, no one can study Luke without paying attention to his work. Even if we settle for an understanding of salvation history as divided into two periods, it still remains significant for Luke in his writing.

Conzelmann rightly related salvation to history and both to eschatology. I believe, unlike other critics, that it is also helpful to maintain the three divisions: Israel, Jesus and the church. Luke distinguished these phases to insist on a continuity among them. He also, however, accepts a discontinuity. The period of Israel is very different from the period of Jesus, and the time of the church differs significantly from the time of Jesus. If a shift has taken place, the shift concerns the daily existence of believers in the church as they await a sudden if distant parousia. The addition of the Acts of the Apostles to the gospel shows this change in emphasis. Now Christians must respond to the demands of a world far from perfect and even inimical to the Jesus tradition. The second coming remains part of the Jesus tradition in Luke but on the periphery. Luke has changed the crisis-oriented vigilance of the early Jesus tradition to a call to live in the world, taking up the cross of Jesus and following him. He has not eliminated the parousia from Christian teaching but has concentrated more on living the Christian life. Luke, like the other evangelists, is principally a theologian, adapting the Jesus tradition to yet another change of perspective. He includes some history in his works but writes more from the desire to preserve the Jesus tradition for future generations than to record accurate historical details.

Further Study

H. Conzelmann, *The Theology of St. Luke.*
J. Fitzmyer, *The Gospel According to Luke.*
S. Kealy, *The Gospel of Luke.*
I.H. Marshall, *Luke: Historian and Theologian.*

2.

Theology of Salvation

Over the years many people have attempted to write books and articles about Johannine or Pauline theology. I have already attempted in this work to write something about Marcan, Matthean and Johannine theology. To attempt writing Lucan theology creates more difficulty than for the other three evangelists. Some scholars think that the third gospel has no complete theological approach; others will treat Luke more as an historian than as a theologian. Mark can be remembered as the gospel which emphasizes faith and the suffering of the Son of man; Matthew, as the great catechetical gospel, with its liturgical and developing church, which easily pulls together the various parts of the gospel. Finally, the unusual approach in the fourth gospel to both church and christology distinguishes Johannine theology. Perhaps we could just say that in the third gospel we find an effort to relate the Jesus tradition to the Gentile world and present Jesus as the kind and compassionate messiah. This is true but does not present a complete overview of Lucan theology. I believe the greatest drawback in attempting Lucan theology is the failure to consider the Acts of the Apostles as an essential part of Lucan theology.

This work is principally concerned with the gospel of Luke. This chapter, however, must also consider the Acts of the Apostles if I am to be faithful to an overview of Lucan theology. I believe that the author presents Jesus as the bringer of salvation to the ends of the world. The journey begins in Galilee but will not be completed until the Jesus tradition takes root in Rome, the center of the known world.

Two concerns seem to have forged the Lucan approach: the acceptance of the delay of the second coming of the Lord and the need for the Christian community to get on with living. They learned to live in the midst of a real world as they continued to experience salvation. The community is becoming the church with the need for office and

219

established ministries; doctrine may not be left in the shadows but will need to be developed accurately, always maintaining a close connection to the Jesus tradition. The ethical code of Christians needs formulation. The particular theological approach of Luke responds to the church community toward the end of the first century. The Jesus tradition will take on a new format. The binding of these experienced needs, however, remains the saving presence of God through Jesus, offered to all who will respond.

Luke has a universal approach: the Jesus tradition that began in Galilee and moved to Jerusalem with the death and resurrection of the Lord. The preaching reached a plateau with the coming of the Spirit upon the apostles in the same city. Finally at the end of the Acts of the Apostles, this preaching of Jesus reached the city of Rome, the cultural, political and economic center of the world. There, Paul preaches the Jesus tradition,

And so we came to Rome (Acts 28:14).

And he lived there two whole years at his own expense, and welcomed all who came to him, preaching the kingdom of God and teaching about the Lord Jesus Christ quite openly and unhindered (Acts 28:30–31).

Luke has added geography to his theology in a way differing from the other gospels. Jerusalem is key. This city is the destiny of Jesus; it is also the starting point for salvation for humankind. The gospel begins in the city of Jerusalem with Zechariah offering incense in the Jerusalem temple (Lk 1:9) and ends with the eleven returning to Jerusalem to await the coming of the Spirit:

And they returned to Jerusalem with great joy, and were continually in the temple blessing God (Lk 24:53).

Even the first event recorded of the life of Jesus after his birth takes place in Jerusalem: the twelve year old must be in his Father's house in Jerusalem:

And he said to them, "How is it that you sought me? Did you not know that I must be in my Father's house?" (Lk 2:49).

The heart of the gospel is the journey to Jerusalem (Lk 9:51–19:27). Jesus arrives at his city of destiny and enters triumphantly (Lk

19:35–36). Alone among the synoptics, Jesus is proclaimed king as he enters the city:

Blessed be the king who comes in the name of the Lord!
Peace in heaven and glory in the highest (Lk 19:38).

After the resurrection Jesus appears only in the vicinity of the city. Luke writes as if once Jesus has entered the city, all previous references to Galilee are forgotten, and now the spotlight remains on Jerusalem.

The Acts of the Apostles opens with the apostles gathered in the city of Jerusalem: "And while staying with them he charged them not to depart from Jerusalem" (Acts 1:4). There they receive the Spirit and begin the preaching about Jesus that will be directed first to peoples of many nations. On Pentecost, Luke has Peter preaching to

Parthians and Medes, Elamites and residents of Mesopota-
mia, Judea and Cappadocia, Pontus and Asia, Phrygia and
Pamphylia, Egypt and the parts of Libya belonging to Cy-
rene, and visitors from Rome, both Jews and proselytes,
Cretans and Arabians (Acts 2:9–11),

and all hear the good news about Jesus and understand. The tower of Babel, when people are dispersed because their languages have been confused, has been reversed through the preaching of the Jesus tradition. Now all peoples of all languages can understand that Jesus has come to bring salvation to all. The universality of Christianity becomes crystallized in the city of Jerusalem.

The remainder of the Acts of the Apostles continues the spread of Christianity throughout Asia Minor. Luke narrates the missionary activity of Peter, John, Barnabas and, principally, the great apostle to the Gentiles, Paul. Many of the early controversies associated with early Christianity are narrated with various compromises proposed. Eventually Christianity looks to a future in which the majority of converts will be Gentiles. Christianity has broken out of its origins in Judaism to embrace the then known world. When Paul lays claim to his rights as a Roman citizen, the focus shifts from Jerusalem and Asia Minor to Rome.

"I am standing before Caesar's tribunal, where I ought to be
tried; to the Jews I have done no wrong, as you well know. If
then I am a wrongdoer, and have committed anything for

*which I deserve to die, I do not seek to escape death, but if
there is nothing in their charges against me, I appeal to Caesar." "You have appealed to Caesar, to Caesar you shall go"
(Acts 25:10–12).*

He arrives at Rome and begins his preaching of Jesus, "openly and
unhindered" (Acts 28:31). Luke has moved the preaching of the Jesus
tradition to the center of the world.

The opening section of this work narrated the origin of the primitive
preaching about Jesus as contained in the Acts of the Apostles. In that
section I noted that although Acts was written some fifty years after the
death of Jesus, it contains some earlier traditions which are found in the
various speeches. Luke used these traditions about the earliest preaching
to set the scene for the development of Christianity. He recorded for us
recollections of what the early preachers proclaimed about Jesus.

In many ways, the preaching about Jesus is common to all of the
evangelists as well as Paul. Each author, or preacher, however, has
distinctive characteristics and approaches. Fundamentally each
preacher proclaimed Jesus as crucified and risen, as God's act of salvation for all taking place in Jesus. To understand these two statements demands an appreciation that Jesus was the saving presence of
God in human history and proclaimed the nearness of God to all.
Then, after the resurrection, Jesus becomes the proclaimed. The salvation which Jesus offered now becomes salvation through Jesus.

■ The Preaching of Jesus ■

In the Lucan gospel, Jesus proclaims God's eschatological salvation. In an irrevocable and never-to-be-repeated manner, God has
entered into human history to offer his saving presence to humankind.
In a compelling and demanding manner, Jesus preaches and teaches.
In the scene at Nazareth Luke composed an account of Jesus which
becomes programmatic for the entire gospel. Jesus stands up in the
synagogue and applies to himself the words of Isaiah:

*The Spirit of the Lord is upon me, for he has anointed me to
preach the good news to the poor . . . to proclaim the acceptable year of the Lord (Lk 4:18–19).*

He continues with the bold statement:

*Today this scripture has been fulfilled in your hearing
(Lk 4:21).*

A new age has dawned; a year of God's favor has begun. Jesus will heal and release and call for belief and repentance. The result will be salvation. The emphasis on today calls for decision: one must accept or reject salvation, and experience release.

■ The Preaching of the Disciples ■

The Lucan emphasis on time and history does not mean, however, that this period of salvation is limited to the historical ministry of Jesus. Only in Luke does Jesus explicitly train his disciples to carry on his preaching when he states: "Whoever listens to you, listens to me" (Lk 10:16). The preachers of Jesus in the Acts of the Apostles were filled with the Spirit; they continued the saving preaching of Jesus who also was filled with the Spirit. The Spirit of God was given to Jesus so that he might proclaim salvation. At Pentecost this same Spirit is given to the apostles and they begin to preach Jesus, calling for belief, repentance and the acceptance of the Spirit of Jesus through baptism.

In the gospel itself Luke narrates the sending out of the twelve (Lk 9:1–6, 10) and the sending of the seventy-two (Lk 10:1–16). This double sending out increases the urgency of the mission and the importance of the activity of the disciples. It also will prefigure the preaching that will take place after Pentecost. The gospel concludes with a mission charge:

In his name repentance for the forgiveness of sins must be preached to all nations (Lk 24:47).

This charge is carried out throughout Luke's second volume, the Acts of the Apostles. Boldly and with urgency the disciples preach and proclaim that

salvation is found in no one else, for there is no other name under heaven given to human beings by which we are to be saved (Acts 4:12).

The preacher (Jesus) has become the proclaimed (risen Christ). In the past some scholars had problems with Jesus becoming the proclaimed in Christianity. They feared that somehow this elevated Jesus beyond his rightful state. Probably the period of public ministry of Jesus did not include on the part of his followers the exalted position they held after the resurrection. The resurrection itself explains the development. Jesus proclaimed salvation. With his resurrection Jesus became "Lord and Christ" (Acts 2:36), and now he was the means by which salvation could be offered to others. The acceptance of Jesus as messiah in power through his resurrection explains how the proclaimer became the proclaimed.

■ Content of the Preaching ■

Jesus proclaimed salvation; the disciples proclaim salvation. The fulfillment of the Isaian prophecy makes it possible for the preacher to become the proclaimed. In him salvation is made present in a way different from any other way in the past. The kingdom has come in Jesus. He is the herald of its presence. In the preaching of the disciples the saving presence of God, the kingdom, which has already taken place in Jesus now is offered to all who will respond in faith. Just as Jesus proclaimed salvation to the house of Zacchaeus (Lk 19:9) the disciples will proclaim salvation to all households in Acts. Sins are forgiven (Acts 2:38; 5:31; 10:43; 26:18). Forgiveness results from the saving presence of God in Jesus. People experience the Spirit of Jesus throughout the Acts of the Apostles. They repent, change their way of living and accept the way of the Lord.

Several times Luke summarizes what has taken place as a result of this preaching.

> And all who believed were together and had all things in common; and they sold their possessions and goods and distributed them to all, as any had need. And day by day attending the temple together and breaking bread in their homes, they partook of food with glad and generous hearts, praising God and having favor with all the people. And the Lord added to their numbers day by day those who were being saved (Acts 2:44-47).

They held all things in common; they prayed and praised God together; they found favor with all. In Acts 4:32-35 the same characteristics are mentioned. Salvation brought about a change in people. They turned over a page in the book of life and began to write differently. They accepted Jesus as Lord and messiah and allowed his Spirit to enter into their lives, changing their personalities as they attempted to live as Jesus lived. The salvation that Jesus proclaimed and experienced in himself was preached through his followers. They had received his Spirit and offered this Spirit to anyone who would respond in faith.

The Lucan theology is a theology of salvation. God has drawn near to people; God is interested in people; God wishes people to live in peace together so that no one is in need. Salvation is not something reserved for an afterlife for Luke. Salvation is *now*. People need to believe that God is present in human life, and Luke proclaims this. People also need to believe that no one group has a control over God and his saving presence. Luke preached precisely that. The Spirit of God knows no favorites. This salvation, as we shall see, is made present in the life of Jesus as he offers compassion and forgiveness to the outcasts as well as to the leaders of society. To the rich and especially to the poor, to those who depend upon God alone, Jesus proclaimed release. The same salvation is proclaimed in the Acts of the Apostles when Peter and John say to the lame man at the Beautiful Gate:

I have no silver and gold, but I give you what I have; in the name of Jesus Christ of Nazareth, walk (Acts 3:6).

Luke also narrates the activity of Paul. He proclaims the saving presence of God throughout his great missionary journeys. Gentiles of every nation accept belief in Jesus, experience his Spirit and change their way of living.

To understand Luke demands an appreciation of salvation offered and received. Luke knew that the parousia had been delayed; he knew that Christians had to begin to live a way of life based on the way Jesus lived. He wrote both of his works to respond to the needs of the delayed second coming and the demand for Christian living. His principal motif was the presence of salvation, first in the preaching of Jesus and then in the preaching of his followers. He also believed that this same salvation would continue to be present in the church through the same preaching from generation to generation. What had begun in Jesus would continue throughout human history through the presence of his Spirit.

Further Study

J. Fitzmyer, *The Gospel According to Luke.*
I.H. Marshall, *The Acts of the Apostles.*
————, *Luke: Historian and Theologian.*

3.

The Gospel of Mercy

Salvation, for Luke, has already taken place in Jesus. As an evangelist he has no great concern for abstract theological concepts. For him, salvation involves mercy and pardon for all. Often enough scholars and readers will characterize this gospel as the gospel of mercy, and rightly so. Matthew presents Jesus calling his followers "to be perfect as your heavenly Father is perfect" (Mt 5:48). The Lucan parallel states: "Be merciful as your Father is merciful" (Lk 6:36). Matthew's context is love, and for him love means being perfect like the Father. Luke says much the same, except he epitomizes love and perfection in mercy.

In the previous chapter I presented the central theme of the writings of Luke: Jesus offering salvation to all. A text which would sum up this theme and join it to the theme of this chapter is: "For the Son of man came to seek and to save the lost" (Lk 19:10). This verse concludes the story of the ministry of Jesus in Galilee and Judea. What follows is the entrance into Jerusalem which will lead to his death. This verse stands at the climax of the evangelistic ministry of Jesus; Jesus came to save the lost. His kindness, his compassion and his mercy become evident since he offers salvation to the lost.

Two principal signs of salvation offered by Jesus in this gospel are the performance of works of healing and preaching to the poor. No great emphasis is given to the miracles other than seeing them as a result of divine power (Lk 4:14, 36; 5:17; 6:19), which Luke ascribes to the Holy Spirit (Lk 4:14; Acts 10:38). These miracles, and especially the exorcisms, were also an attack upon Satan and the powers of evil. Jesus set people free. When the seventy-two return they tell Jesus that even the demons were subject to them. Jesus responds by remarking that he saw Satan falling like lightning from heaven:

226

And he said to them, "I saw Satan fall like lightning from heaven. Behold I have given you authority to tread upon serpents and scorpions, and over all power of the enemy; and nothing shall hurt you" (Lk 10:17–19).

Evil as depicted in the person and power of Satan is destroyed by the preaching and healing of Jesus. People who were under the yoke of sickness and sin are no longer bound. People have experienced the mercy and compassion of God through Jesus. They are free.

An outstanding blessing coming from Jesus is the forgiveness of sins. In Mark Jesus speaks of the need for forgiveness (Mk 3:28; 4:12; 11:25) but only once does Jesus actually offer forgiveness (Mk 2:1–10). Luke takes these references from Mark and adds the story of the sinful woman whom Jesus forgave (Lk 7:36–50). Zacchaeus also experiences mercy and forgiveness (Lk 19:1–10). In this second narrative two things are apparent: Jesus claimed that Zacchaeus was a son of Abraham, a Jew, and therefore entitled to salvation and mercy like any respectable member of society. Jesus addressed the Jews who considered sinful Jews as unworthy of divine mercy and forgiveness. Jesus treated them as members of God's people. The second point is that Jesus describes his concern for such people as Zacchaeus in terms of the activity of a shepherd, or more precisely as the shepherd of the flock of God (Ez 34:16). Luke uses the same image in 15:3–7 when Jesus justifies his eating with sinners to the Pharisees. He seeks out the lost and brings them back to God by offering mercy and forgiveness. The same blessing of forgiveness appears in the parable of the great banquet (Lk 14:15–24). The householder commands that the poor, maimed, blind and lame be brought in to his supper when the rich and respectable fail to respond to the invitation. The list here closely parallels Luke 7:22 and shows that the invitation of such people to the banquet is a sign of the fulfillment of God's promised salvation and mercy. We might even see in the meals held by Jesus with similar individuals an anticipation of the messianic banquet when all will experience the mercy and forgiveness of God. For Jesus, for Luke and for most people, table fellowship is important. When people eat together they find it difficult to withhold mercy.

Jesus also in Luke cares for women. The significance of this might easily escape the modern reader in most countries accustomed to the equality of women with men but in the ancient world it was otherwise. Often women were despised and considered inferior. Luke has two stories proper to his gospel in which Jesus brings forgiveness and

healing to women (Lk 7:36–50; 13:10–17). He also tells the story of
Mary and Martha (Lk 10:38–42) and the concern for the widow of
Nain in the loss of her son (Lk 7:11–17). Luke further relates the
healing of Mary Magdalene (Lk 8:2), and he especially emphasizes the
place of women who helped Jesus in his travels (Lk 8:1–3). He includes
women in the passion. They weep for him on the road to Calvary (Lk
23:27–31), observed his death from a distance (Lk 23:55), and finally
prepared spices and ointments for his burial (Lk 23:55).

For Luke, the compassion of Jesus did not stop at the boundaries
of Israel. Although it is well tested historically that for the most part
Jesus confined his mission to the Jews, Luke indicates a place for the
Samaritans, the particular enemies of the Jews, in his gospel. Jesus
healed a Samaritan leper (Lk 17:11–19), and the hero of the parable of
the good Samaritan is implicitly praised above the members of Jewish
society (Lk 10:30–37). Luke also narrates the story of the healing of the
centurion's servant and stresses the character of the centurion as a
godly non-Jew who showed great faith (Lk 7:1–9). The vision of Gentiles in the kingdom is also taken over by Luke from the tradition when
he includes the saying of Jesus about people coming from all over the
world to eat in the kingdom of God (Lk 13:28ff). Throughout the gospel
Luke presents Jesus as kind and compassionate, offering mercy and
forgiveness to all, Jew and Gentile alike. If one chapter, however, summarizes this gospel of mercy, that chapter must be chapter 15.

(As I have suggested previously, the reader should turn to chapter
15 and read it in its entirety. The length precludes the full quotation.)

For many scholars of Luke chapter 15 is the gospel within the
gospel. In the three parables Luke manages to express in language and
image the full meaning and importance of the meaning of salvation.
Mercy and forgiveness characterize God's relationship to people. This
is seen in the life and ministry of Jesus and will be found also in the
preaching and lives of his followers.

■ **Chapter 15** ■

God's love and mercy for the sinner, as we have seen, forms the
heart of the gospel of Luke. Salvation means just that. The response
on the part of the sinner is conversion and repentance. No one is
excluded from this offer, and each person is able to respond. For some
exegetes 15:1–19:27 is the gospel of the outcasts (some will not go as
far as 19:27 but will end at 18:14). In this section Luke presents Jesus'
concern for anyone who feels left out in any way. I do not think that

anyone would doubt this as part of the authentic ministry of Jesus, but it must also be admitted that Luke has added a particular emphasis that is not present in the other gospels. If salvation colors both the gospel of Luke and the Acts, then the theme of mercy colors the meaning of salvation.

The three parables—the lost sheep (vv 4–7), the lost coin (vv 8–10) and the lost or prodigal son (vv 11–32)—are distinctive of Luke. In all probability they were not uttered as a unit in the early Jesus tradition but came from different contexts. Luke has artistically constructed them into a single theme suiting his purpose. Love and mercy on the part of God and conversion and repentance on the part of the lost reach a climax in the note of joy in this chapter. Luke explicitly applied the joy to God himself in the concluding verse of the first two parables, and implicitly to God through the joy of the father in the final parable. Each parable seems to show a concern for those people whom others tend to despise or condemn.

Although the chapter is a unit, we can detect some divisions. Luke begins with an introduction (vv 1–3) followed by two parallel parables (vv 4–6, 8–9), each fitted with a concluding application (7, 10) and then a further developed parable (vv 11–32), with each one centering on joy over the finding of the lost.

The introduction sets the scene: people complain that Jesus eats with sinners. I have already mentioned that table fellowship is important for Luke. The concern for table fellowship may very well reflect the time of Luke himself when tensions remained among early Christians about who should be received and offered fellowship, as well as the ministry of Jesus. The parables will respond to this question: those who are lost are called home and welcomed.

We have a parallel in Matthew to the parable of the lost sheep (Mt 18:12–13), and it also has an application, although of a different nature (v 14—God does not wish any little one to perish). Probably the Matthean form of the parable is more original, and Luke has edited it to make the theme the same for all three parables. He has deliberately substituted the word "lost" for the word "wandered off" which we find in Matthew (both found this parable in "Q"). We have another form of the parable in the Gospel of Thomas. Here the emphasis is on the theme of the kingdom since Thomas begins by stating that the kingdom is like a shepherd. The concluding note refers to the love that the shepherd has for the sheep that have strayed.

The setting of the parable explains its meaning: the outcasts of first century Palestinian society come to Jesus and he receives them. The scribes and Pharisees grumble. Jesus, like the shepherd in the parable, will not only seek out the lost but will rejoice with them, and what more fitting way than to celebrate a meal with them? The application in verse 7 adds an additional note: the repentance of the sinner inaugurates heavenly joy. The parable concerns not only the graciousness of Jesus in calling sinners but also the joy of God over the repentance of a sinner.

■   The Lost Coin   ■

A woman has lost a silver coin. Diligently, with much energy, she searches and finds it. Then she calls in her neighbors to rejoice with her. This parable also has an application: repentance brings joy before the angels of God (v 10). The parable is proper to Luke; no parallel is found in the other gospels. The point of the parable seems to be the same as the shepherd with two additional notes. First the woman is depicted as diligently searching and seeking out the lost coin in a way different from the shepherd. The emphasis is on the divine effort to seek out the sinner. Second, Luke emphasizes the searching for one coin out of the ten. The reader would automatically wonder what was so significant about the tenth coin. Although not accepted by all exegetes (it is not explicitly in the text) Jeremias proposes that the ten coins are necessary for a woman's dowry. The loss of one coin would trigger her concern to retrieve the lost coin. Again this emphasizes the meaning of the application: Just as a woman would be anxious to have her dowry and would move mountains if necessary to find a missing coin to complete that dowry, so God will seek out the lost and, when found, the joy will not be limited to earth but will reach to heaven.

■   The Lost (Prodigal) Son   ■

Finally we come to the last parable in this chapter, which might also be titled "The Prodigal Father." Of all of the parables in the New Testament, perhaps this is the favorite of all. It involves freedom, responsibility, longing, return, grace, anguish, reconciliation and joy. Anyone who has ever witnessed the ballet titled "The Prodigal Son" has seen in movement, and listened in sound, to the meaning of the gospel of mercy in Luke. The ballet reaches its climax when the son crawls across the stage and ultimately is enveloped in the arms of a loving father. What a beautiful image to explain the relationship of God to his repentant son or daughter!

This parable, which many consider the greatest of the parables, has been the subject of painters and musicians and philosophers as well as of the great choreographer Balanchine. In Luke it expresses the great mercy of God. The presence of the elder son has long caused debate among exegetes. Some question his role and seek ways in which it can be considered as an appendage. It seems to me that the presence of the elder son is necessary for the full understanding of the parable. The love of the father is boundless and unconditional. He not only welcomes his lost son but will not allow the attitude of his elder and ever-faithful son to deter him from expressing his great joy. They feast, make merry and dine on the fatted calf. What was lost is found; what was dead is now alive.

The loving father in this parable stands as a symbol of God. The unconditional love and mercy of God toward the repentant sinner has already been hinted at in the previous two parables. Here the additional element, besides the poignant human story, is the rejection of any criticism of such a repentant sinner as seen in the additional element of the elder son. The cry of the young man: "Father, I have sinned against heaven and before you; I no longer deserve to be called your son," and the reaction of love and mercy on the part of the father reflects the meaning of salvation and the year of favor that Jesus proclaims in Luke's gospel. Some might prefer self-righteousness but such do not belong to the gospel of Luke.

Chapter 15 ends with the declaration of unconditional love, mercy, and forgiveness manifested to a sinner who turns to repentance. It matters little what a person has done or has failed to do. Jesus accepted the great sinners of his day, the tax collectors and public sinners, because all such persons can find acceptance by God. When we compare this parable to the earliest preaching in Acts we note that Luke also calls for repentance and belief as a response to the preaching about Jesus. The same merciful God responds to all those who will repent after hearing the preaching about Jesus, just as Jesus himself preached a merciful God. A continuity exists between the gospel and Acts. They are bound together by a theology of salvation and a theology of a merciful God ever anxious to respond to the needs of anyone who will turn and, like the prodigal son, confess: "I have sinned against heaven and against you." Then the repentant one will experience the loving embrace of a merciful and forgiving God.

Further Study

J. Fitzmyer, *The Gospel According to Luke.*

4.

The Infancy Narratives

Many Christians have clear ideas about the birth of Jesus. The stories have been imprinted into the memory through years of celebrating the season of Christmas. Most believers, however, do not distinguish the different origins of the stories associated with the birth of Christ and usually do not even notice that the birth and infancy of the Lord are described in Matthew and Luke and are not even mentioned in Mark and John. Moreover, the two gospels that do narrate the origin of Jesus differ significantly from each other.

Luke mentions a census under Quirinius which requires Joseph and Mary to go to Bethlehem where Jesus is born in a manger because there is no room for them in the inn. Matthew, as we have seen, gives no details of how Joseph and Mary came to be in Bethlehem. Nor does he give any details about the birth of Jesus.

In Luke, shepherds guided by an angel find Jesus in the manger and praise God. Matthew narrates the coming of the magi from the east, guided by a star. They come to worship and offer gifts, but not to Bethlehem but to Jerusalem. Herod hears of the magi and he sends them to Bethlehem to learn and report to him about the infant. Warned by an angel, the magi return to their own country instead of reporting to Herod. An angel then warns Joseph, and he flees to Egypt with his wife and child where they live until Herod's death when they return to Nazareth instead of Bethlehem. Luke has no mention of Egypt but instead describes how the child is brought to Jerusalem for the ritual of circumcision. Afterward the holy family return to live again in Nazareth. These and many other differences distinguish the two approaches to the birth of Jesus.

We have already studied the infancy narratives of Matthew. You will recall that in the past many Christians tended to regard these narratives as largely historical reports with the differences being re-

solved in various unsatisfactory ways. The approach taken here pur-
ports that these accounts are creative, literary accounts with the
differences arising for literary or theological grounds.

The central hypothesis for this study of the infancy narratives, as
well as for the general study of the New Testament christologies,
contends that the early church tended to work backward in its christology. The earliest Christian teaching about Jesus, again as have
seen, proclaims that Jesus was designated Son of God with his resurrection. As the Christian community reflected more on the meaning of
Jesus, this designation was projected back to his baptism which inaugurated his public ministry. Then a further projection took place, and
Jesus was designated Son of God at his birth and conception. Finally,
in the gospel of John, Jesus is the incarnation of the eternal Word of
God. With this as the background, we can study the infancy narratives
of Luke, attempting to see his particular theological perspective.

(At this time it would be helpful to read the first two chapters
of Luke.)

The first two chapters of Luke are the result of a two-stage literary development. In the first stage Luke created two parallel accounts:
one containing the annunciation narratives for John and Jesus (Lk
1:5–25; 1:26–45, 56); the other, the birth-circumcision-naming narratives for John and Jesus (Lk 1:57–66; 2:1–12, 15–27, 34–40). Later
Luke added to this balanced literary creation, the four canticles which
probably pre-dated Luke: the Magnificat, which Mary proclaims (Lk
1:46–55); the Benedictus, spoken by Zechariah (Lk 1:67–79); the
Gloria, sung by the angels (Lk 2:13–14); finally, the Nunc Dimittis
uttered by Simeon (Lk 2:28–33). Although we do not have any conclusive evidence, these hymns were probably composed by Jewish Christians and formed part of their prayer tradition before the composition
of Luke's gospel. At the same time that Luke added these canticles, he
also added the pre-Lucan account of the boy Jesus in the temple,
astounding the elders with his wisdom (Lk 2:41–52). This particular
account has its origins in some popular tradition of pre-ministry mar-
vels attested in John 2:1–11 and in particular in the apocryphal gospels which seem to delight in stories about the boy Jesus performing
wonderful miracles.

Luke patterns the annunciation of the birth of John in the same
manner as the annunciation of the birth of Jesus. How much history
involved is debatable. Perhaps the dating in the reign of Herod the
Great and the names of the parents of John are historical details. The
actual presentations of Elizabeth and Zechariah, however, are mod-
eled after two famous Old Testament accounts of births to barren

parents: Elkanah-Hannah in Samuel's birth (1 Sam 1–2) and Abra-
ham-Sarah in Isaac's birth (Gen 17–18). Luke utilized the theme of
barrenness, and the Old Testament annunciation pattern of the birth
of any great figure, as a bridge of continuity between the history of
Israel and the history of Jesus's life and ministry.

In the Jesus half of the annunciation account (Lk 1:26–56) Luke
reworked the pre-gospel annunciation of the birth of Jesus as the
Davidic messiah used by Matthew:

> He will be great, and will be called Son of the Most High; and
> the Lord God will give him the throne of David his father and
> he will reign over the house of Jacob forever (Mt 1:32–33).

And like Matthew, Luke will add the proclamation of the divine sonship of Jesus through the power of the Holy Spirit: The angels declares to Mary:

> The Holy Spirit will come upon you and the power of the
> Most High will overshadow you; therefore the child to be
> born will be called holy, the Son of God (Lk 1:35).

While some scholars have questioned the presence of the belief in
a virginal conception of Jesus in this account, a comparison between
these two annunciation events will highlight the superiority of Jesus
over John. If the birth of John was marvelous because of the barrenness of his parents, the birth of Jesus was more marvelous, since it was
through the power of the Holy Spirit and not through the ordinary
means of human conception.

Once he has completed the annunciations of John and Jesus,
Luke turns to the birth-circumcision and naming of these same individuals. The first section which describes the birth, circumcision and
naming of John originally closed with a summary statement of his
growth (Lk 1:80), which included two elements taken from the synoptic ministry of John: he was "strong in spirit" and he was "in the
desert."

The birth-circumcision-naming of Jesus is more complex. Luke
has added the temple scene (Lk 2:22–39) built around two Jewish
practices: the consecration of the first-born and purification after
birth. This section originally closed with a description of Jesus' youth
in Nazareth (2:39–40) as a transition to his later ministry (Lk 3:21).

In all probability the census described in Lk 2:1–5 is a Lucan device without historical basis. Luke probably knew a tradition that the birth of Jesus was associated with the end of a Herodian rule and he confused Herod the Great (died in 4 B.C.E.) with his son Archelaus (deposed in 6 C.E.). We do have a record of a census in 6 C.E. and Luke utilized this historical event as a means of bringing Mary and Joseph to Bethlehem. Actually the census took place some ten years after the birth of Jesus.

The appearance of angels to shepherds to announce the birth of Jesus is a typical annunciation form in which Luke utilized Isaiah 9:6 (describing a new born child who is to be heir of the throne of David) and Isaiah 52:7 (describing the messengers who bring the good news of salvation). In fulfillment of the Old Testament prophecy, the angels announce the Christian proclamation of Jesus as savior, messiah and Lord. The presence of shepherds foreshadows the outcasts who will recognize Jesus and believe in him. They come to see and rejoice and praise God.

The temple scene in Luke utilizes the model as found in Malachi 3:1: "The Lord whom you seek will suddenly come to his temple," and Daniel 9:24, which speaks of the anointing of a most holy one whom Luke sees as Jesus. The angelic announcement met the expectations of Israel, and now in the temple the Nunc Dimittis of Simeon reaches out to the Gentiles: "Lord . . . my eyes have seen your salvation . . . a light of revelation for the Gentiles."

Finally, his parents present Jesus at the age of twelve in the temple for Passover, and his wisdom astounds the elders. His parents do not understand him because they do not yet have the Easter faith in Jesus as God's Son. The insertion of this account here enables Luke to show the continuity from the infancy of Jesus as God's Son, through the boy Jesus in the temple, to the resurrected Lord.

This account, like that of Matthew, is not concerned with history. Whatever historical elements are present are incidental and inconsequential. In these chapters on the origin of Jesus Luke narrates a powerful literary composition, based principally on passages of the Old Testament with a set theological perspective. Luke has reflected, along with the broader Christian community, on the life of Jesus. The reflection takes place by using literary forms current and acceptable and part of the Old Testament tradition. In reading this narrative, like that of Matthew, the Christian community must progress in its understanding of the origin of Jesus. The thinking will move beyond the stage when every detail was accepted as historically accurate, beyond the position which questioned the whole statement on the origin of

Jesus as purely concocted material, to the position of asking: What does Luke wish to state theologically in his record of the origins of Jesus?

Certainly his wide use of the Old Testament to construct most of the actual material demonstrates a continuity between the Jewish messianic tradition and the origin of Jesus. Although the gospel is directed primarily to Gentiles, the historical Jewish roots of Jesus and Christianity are not forgotten. Moreover, the use of particular passages of the Old Testament will highlight the particular theology of Luke. He often alludes to the Old Testament but does not quote the passages in detail. The reader can compare specific sections of the gospel of Luke with Old Testament traditions to understand just how carefully Luke utilizes parts of the Jewish tradition.

Lk 1:26–33 compare with Zeph 3:14–17
Lk 1:32–33 compare with 2 Sam 7:16, 26
Lk 1:35 compare with Ex 40:34–35
Lk 1:39–44 compare with 2 Sam 6:2–11
Lk 1:46–55 compare with 1 Sam 2:1–10
Lk 2:1–14 compare with Mic 4:7–5:5
Lk 2:34 compare with Is 8:14

Luke proclaims that Jesus is Lord and messiah (Acts 2:32, 36). His origin is in the hands of God alone, for almighty God gives Jesus to the world as savior. Throughout his public ministry the poor and the outcast find acceptance in Jesus. At his birth the powerful are not present but only the poor shepherds who recognize him and praise God.

The chief character in this narrative is Mary. She has given herself to God, and God has responded to her faithfulness by calling her to become the mother of his Son. Mary as the model of faith in the ministry of Jesus lives as the model of faith in his origin. She trusts in God through the words of the angel, and once she has given birth of Jesus, she will offer his presence to the shepherds.

Luke depicts her kindness in his story of the journey to her cousin Elizabeth. Luke presents Mary as unmindful of her own needs but more concerned about the needs of Elizabeth. She makes the arduous journey. Luke also has her declaration of faith by having her speak the Magnificat.

Whatever historical memories the early church retained of Mary, they must have contained the image of a woman of great faith and great kindness. She does not figure in the public ministry of Jesus other than as one who has heard the word of God and kept it. Here in the infancy narratives she has responded to the word of God and has lived that faith in a kind and loving way. In the ministry of Jesus someone informs him that his mother and brothers are outside. Jesus responds: "My mother and brothers are those who hear the word of God and keep it" (Lk 8:21). Later, when a woman proclaims: "Blessed is the womb that bore you and the breasts that nursed you" (Lk 11:27b), Jesus responds: "Blessed rather are they who hear the word of God and keep it" (Lk 11:28). Mary bore Jesus in her womb because she was one who had heard the word of God and had kept it.

Luke even has a foreshadowing of the passion. Simeon declares that Jesus will be the cause of the fall and rise of many in Israel (Lk 2:34) and a sword will pierce through the soul of his mother (Lk 2:35). The author foreshadows the ministry of Jesus with acceptance and rejection in these opening chapters. The call to the outcasts is also present; the need for faith and hearing and keeping the word of God is present in the response of Mary. The overshadowing of the Holy Spirit, who figures prominently in the gospel, explains the origin of Jesus. Luke has taken his principal theological themes and gathered them together into an account of the origin of Jesus. Christians should read these chapters and ask themselves continually: What is the author saying about the meaning of Jesus? In doing this, the unfolding of the origin of Jesus will take place as the sign of God's salvation offered to all through faith.

Further Study

R. Brown, *An Adult at Christmas.*
————, *The Birth of the Messiah.*
J. Fitzmyer, *The Gospel According to Luke.*

5.

Jesus in the Gospel of Luke

Jesus "went about doing good" (Acts 10:38). He climaxed God's activity in Israel and brought salvation in himself to all:

> *And there is salvation in no one else, for there is no other name under the heavens given to human beings by which we must be saved (Acts 4:12).*

In a more complete fashion I could say that for Luke Jesus is the kingly Lord and prophetic man filled with the Spirit; Jesus preaches and lives as the kind and compassionate benefactor to all, especially to anyone in need. Luke sees him not as a figure of the past but as the risen Lord present now. Even in his ministry Luke gives to Jesus the title of Lord, not only in the sense of master or sir, but also in the full post-resurrection meaning of that title. He gives salvation to the Christian community now as he offered salvation to people in the time of his ministry. The unfolding of these ideas about the Lucan Jesus will help in appreciating why so many people turn to the gospel of Luke as their favorite gospel.

Jesus is a Jew, born in Bethlehem (Lk 2:6–7), of Davidic lineage (Lk 11:2; 2:4; 3:31), and raised in Nazareth (Lk 4:16). He was a man attested by God with mighty works (Acts 2:22). The Lucan Jesus is very human, filled with emotion. He responds to the widow of Nain (Lk 7:13), enjoys human friendships with Martha and Mary, celebrates meals with friends and even with sinners, with Levi (Lk 5:29) and Zacchaeus (Lk 19:2). He seems to enjoy life, and when faced with death he asks:

238

Father, if you are willing, remove this cup from me; neverthe-
less, not my will but your will be done (Lk 2:42).

The same dying Jesus will pray to God: "Father, into your hands I commend my spirit" (Lk 23:46). Jesus is the kind and compassionate savior, filled with human needs and emotions, who responds to people in a warm and forgiving manner. Jesus also lives and dies as the faithful one of God and always in a human manner.

Luke also presents the Jesus who transcends the human condition. We have already seen that his conception is through the power of the Spirit (Lk 1:34–35). His ministry is under control of the Spirit (Lk 3:22; 4:1, 14, 18; 10:21). He has a special relationship to God as his Father (Lk 2:49; 3:22; 9:35; 10:21–22; 23:46). Finally, through his resurrection he becomes Lord and messiah through the power of God (Acts 2:24, 32; 3:15; 4:10; 5:30; 10:40). All of these elements, taken together with the human dimension of Jesus, comprise Lucan christology. The very human Jesus somehow goes beyond the dimension of humanity and lives and acts in the divine realm without losing the human. Luke connects the human and the divine after the resurrection with his insistence on the importance of the ascension.

Unlike the other evangelists, Luke divides the time after the death of Jesus into set periods. God raised Jesus from the dead on the third day. The other evangelists end here. Then Luke adds forty days until the time when he ascends into heaven to sit at the right hand of God (Acts 2:33; 5:31). Then another ten days pass before the disciples experience the coming of the Spirit on Pentecost. Luke presents ministry, death, resurrection, ascension and exaltation, and, finally, the coming of the Spirit as the culmination of christology. Chronology figures prominently in his theology. He has had so much of an influence on Christianity that we use his time frame for liturgical celebrations. The Easter season continues with the celebration of the ascension forty days after Easter, and then Pentecost completes the cycle, ten days after the ascension. None of the other gospels have such a division. The gospel of Luke ends with a veiled reference to the ascending of Jesus (Lk 24:50), and the Acts of the Apostles opens with Jesus ascending (Acts 1:9–11).

Although never explicitly mentioned, Luke's christology also includes a return of Jesus as the final phase of his destiny. The angel who appears at the ascension tells the onlookers that Jesus will return in the same way that they saw him go (Acts 1:11). In the gospel Luke has also preserved the saying that Jesus will come in power and glory

(Lk 21:27). He sees, too, the exalted Christ as the one who pours out the Spirit (Acts 2:33) and who stands at the right hand of God (Acts 7:55–56), who is appointed as messiah to come (Acts 3:20–21) and will judge the world (Acts 17:31). Luke divides his understanding of Jesus into four phases: from conception to baptism; from baptism and ministry to the resurrection and ascension; from exaltation to the second coming; finally, the second coming itself.

Throughout this work on the Jesus tradition I have referred to many titles used by the various evangelists in referring to Jesus. Luke uses many of the same titles—sometimes with the same or similar meaning, other times with his distinctive nuance. Luke uses approximately fourteen titles. While I cannot hope to examine each one in detail, the more important titles need further study and should be related to the usage in the other gospels.

■ Lord ■

Luke used the title "Lord" most frequently for Jesus in both of his books. He used it for both God and Jesus. Pre-Christian Palestinian Jews did on occasion refer to YHWH as Lord, and it was generally used as a Greek substitute for the sacred name of God. Jewish Christians, probably the Hellenists, used the formula in reference to Jesus as a response to the earliest preaching. Such a usage would put Jesus on the same level as God but without identifying him with God. Luke will refer to God as "abba," for example, but never to Jesus as "abba." Jesus is Son. God the Father made Jesus Lord through his resurrection:

> Let all the house of Israel therefore know assuredly that God has made him both Lord and Christ, this Jesus whom you crucified (Acts 2:36).

In the public ministry of Jesus Luke has retrojected this title and has even used the title in the origin of Jesus. The angels announce to the shepherds that "Christ the Lord" is born in Bethlehem (Lk 2:11). In so doing, Luke has recorded the usage in the early Christian communities which saw Jesus on a par with God. This should not in itself, however, be regarded as an expression of divinity. The title as used by Luke connotes his otherness or his transcendent character, but not necessarily in a philosophical and metaphysical sense. The title, rather, expresses the influence that the resurrection has had on the followers of Jesus. For them, because Jesus has been raised, he has been elevated to the throne of God. Once Luke and the Christian community accepted this position of Jesus, Luke could read back into the ministry of Jesus an awareness of his proximity to God.

■ Christk/Messiah ■

Although not used as frequently as Lord, the title of Christ or messiah is the most important title for Luke in his two-volume work. Luke preaches salvation, and Jesus the anointed one of God brings this salvation. The gospel almost closes with the question posed by the risen Jesus: "Was not the Christ bound to suffer all this before entering into his glory?" (Lk 24:26). And it is Luke alone who tells us that the followers of Jesus were called "Christians" (Acts 11:26; 26:28).

The title is used approximately twenty-four times. Sometimes it is translated as "Christ" to suit the Gentile audience of Luke, and at other times it is translated as "messiah," conveying its basic meaning as one anointed by God. For modern believers the title has become almost the second name for Jesus, and even in Luke something similar has already taken place (Acts 2:38; 3:6; 4:10 etc).

In its Old Testament usage the title referred to certain historical persons chosen and anointed by God for the service of God's people. The kings of Israel were anointed. Also, at times the high priest was God's anointed. Even the Persian king Cyrus was the anointed of God to return his people to their land (Is 45:1).

At the time of Jesus, messiah indicated either someone sent by God in the kingly Davidic and political tradition, or someone in the priestly tradition. The political overtones for the title would have been known to Jesus and his followers. This would account for the Lucan and Matthean correction to the admission of a messianic role for Jesus as attested before the high priest in the gospel of Mark:

> *Again the high priest asked him: "Are you the Christ, the Son of the Blessed?" And Jesus said: "I am; and you will see the Son of man sitting at the right hand of power, and coming with the clouds of heaven" (Mk 14:62).*

Both Matthew and Luke present the same scene with a refusal on the part of Jesus to respond: "If I tell you, you will not believe, and if I ask you, you will not answer" (Lk 22:67).

After his death and resurrection, Christ or messiah became a principal title for Jesus in the Lucan writings. Jesus was crucified as "king of the Jews" (Mk 1:16; 5:26) but for his followers he became the messiah. Within a few years after his death, Christians began to use "Jesus Christ," "Christ Jesus" or "Jesus the Messiah" as an honorific designation that suited Jesus alone. Jesus is God's anointed agent announcing a new form of salvation to humankind.

■   Savior   ■

A third title important for Luke is "savior." The title actually occurs only once in the gospel (Lk 2:11) and occasionally in Acts, but it is significant since Luke presents Jesus as one who brings salvation to the world as its great benefactor. The title itself was used frequently in the Greco-Roman world, applied to gods, philosophers, physicians, kings and emperors. In the Old Testament it is used for individuals whom God has raised up for the deliverance of his people as well as for God himself (1 Sam 10:19; Is 45:15, 21). The Christian use of the title may be influenced by both traditions. In the gospel the meaning of savior denotes deliverance from such evils as sickness, infirmity or sin. In Acts it denotes the complete process: the effect of Jesus on human history and humankind. It is not just deliverance but the actual experience of God's presence in love, seeking out what was lost and bringing the lost home.

■   Son of God   ■

The title "Son of God" for contemporary Christians usually connotes that Jesus was divine. Such need not always be the case when the title is used in the New Testament. Actually, Luke also uses "Son of the Most High" and, in other places, just "my Son." Whatever conclusion one might draw from the use of these various titles, Luke does imply a special relationship to God. Like the other synoptics, he recognized the special character of the baptism of Jesus in which a voice speaks:

> When Jesus also had been baptized and was praying the heavens were opened and the Holy Spirit descended upon him in bodily form, as a dove, and a voice came from heaven, "You are my beloved Son (here some ancient sources add:

"today I have begotten you"); with you I am well pleased"
(Lk 3:21–22).

The title itself was used frequently in Greek circles and in other cultures in the ancient near east and can mean divine favor or divine adoption or even divine power. In Israel, kings were called God's sons, as were the angels and other individuals who were righteous in the sight of God. Nowhere can we find either in the Old Testament or in Palestinian Judaism the title "Son of God" with a messianic nuance.

When Luke used the title he seems to have predicated to Jesus a unique relationship to God. Gabriel declares to Mary that her son will be "the Son of God" (Lk 1:35), and when we couple this with the same declaration that the Holy Spirit will overshadow her (Lk 1:35), the uniqueness cannot be missed. No one can say much more than this. Whatever the title meant to Luke and his readers, it surely did not mean anything on a philosophical or metaphysical plane. Jesus was Son of God because of his special relationship to God, and he manifested this sonship by his willingness to live according to the will of God, even to the point of the acceptance of death.

■ Son of Man ■

Elsewhere in this work, I have discussed the title "Son of man." Perhaps more than any other title used of Jesus in the New Testament, this one causes the most confusion. Volumes have been written on it. What does it mean in the Old Testament? Did Jesus use it of himself in his ministry? If so, what did he mean? What does it mean in each gospel? All four gospels use the title with various nuances. It can mean human being in a generic sense, or in an indefinite sense, such as someone. It can mean "everyman" and it can also suggest a heavenly figure. We have already seen these meanings. Most times it is found on the lips of Jesus himself. An exception is Acts 7:56 when Stephen sees Jesus as a Son of man standing at God's right hand. As I have previously stated, it seems to me that originally the title was used in a generic sense, such as everyman. This use can actually be found in Mark 2:28, originally implying that everyone can be lord of the sabbath because the sabbath was made for everyone. In the early church the title was overlaid with the meaning as found in Daniel 7:13, and possibly similar to the usage in 1 Enoch 46–69. Like Mark, Luke used the title sometimes in association with the passion of Jesus (Lk 9:22,

44; 18:31; 22:22; 24:7), and he also used it in the sense of future coming (Lk 9:26; 11:30; 12:8, 40; 17:22, 24, 26, 30). A tentative conclusion will see the title in Luke similar to the other synoptics. It refers to Jesus as everyman, as human, but also as one who transcends everyman. In some ways it is similar to the title Son of God and might even transcend that title. Luke does not have the highly developed understanding of John, but he recognizes the manner in which Jesus transcends humanity, and he used the title to convey both the human and the closeness to the divine.

■ Conclusion ■

For Luke, Jesus is the kind and compassionate savior. He does not offend. He is kind to all in need and responds to specific people with kindness. This savior is filled with the Spirit and frequently will turn to his Father in prayer: at his baptism (Lk 3:21), in the desert (Lk 4:42; 5:16), before he chooses the twelve (Lk 6:12), at the transfiguration (Lk 9:28) and finally from the cross (Lk 23:46). All of the titles used by Luke support this fundamental meaning of Jesus. He came to bring salvation to humankind, and he accomplished this precisely because of his unique relationship to God and his possession of the Spirit. Luke makes Jesus most attractive to all, calling all to accept the saving presence of God, especially those in need. Since most people feel left out, at least sometimes in life, a kind and compassionate friend who reaches out to invite everyone inside makes the hurt disappear. The Jesus of Luke is everyone's friend.

Further Study

F. Danker, *Luke.*
J. Fitzmyer, *The Gospel According to Luke.*
S. Kealy, *The Gospel of Luke.*

6.

Discipleship: Lucan Ethics

Luke may be everyone's favorite gospel but it is also the most demanding. Jesus is kind and compassionate but also calls for a profound personal renunciation. Perhaps the tone of the gospel is such that believers tend to overlook just what Luke says about discipleship. On a careful reading, the follower of Jesus might even become worried with such stringent demands.

In one sense every Christian can say that no one saves oneself. Salvation is offered by God or, even more simply, if one has to do something then the simple answer is what Paul responded to the jailer at Philippi: "Believe in the Lord Jesus and you will be saved, you and your household" (Acts 16:31). Such answers, however, are not sufficient. God initiates and people respond by living according to the teaching of Jesus.

■ Divine Calling ■

Although some may claim that Luke does not emphasize the divine calling and the human response in specific terms, the idea is present in both works. God takes the initiative in the church:

> But at night an angel of the Lord opened the prison doors
> and brought them out and said: "Go and stand in the temple
> and speak to the people all the words of this life" (Acts 5:20).

The sending of the missionaries both in the gospel and in Acts is also done under divine guidance. Divine providence caused the Ethiopian to be reading Isaiah 53 in his chariot (Acts 8:32), and surely Paul was under divine providence when he experienced the vision of the risen

Christ (Acts 9:1–6). Salvation depends upon God who has sent his word Jesus. God also prepares the hearts of people to receive the gospel of Jesus. The gospel is the gospel of God's grace (Acts 20:24), and through grace people come to faith (Acts 18:27). The grace of God also directs Jesus in his presence to the church (Acts 14:3). In truth, God alone offers salvation through Jesus his Son.

Divine initiative figures prominently in Luke's theology. Some think that in his gospel he comes close to promoting a doctrine of salvation by works. Alms secure inward cleansing (Lk 11:41); the pious gain salvation (Lk 7:4ff). It almost seems that devout Jews who keep the law qualify for salvation and Jewish Christians accomplish salvation through their piety. Such a conclusion, however, is unwarranted. Luke knows that salvation is through faith alone even if he will not present this teaching as apodictic as does Paul (Rom 3:20, 28). The presence of piety and good works in a believer is not the accomplishment of salvation but the indication of an attitude of trusting and serving God:

> And Peter opened his mouth and said: "Truly I perceive that God shows no partiality, but in every nation anyone who fears him and does what is right is acceptable to him" (Acts 10:34).

Piety prepares for the gospel but it is God who offers salvation through the preaching of the gospel.

■ Repent, Believe, Be Baptized ■

The response to the primitive preaching about Jesus is repentance, belief and baptism.

> "Brethren, what shall we do?" And Peter said to them, "Repent and be baptized, every one of you, in the name of Jesus Christ for the forgiveness of your sins; and you shall receive the gift of the Holy Spirit" (Acts 2:37–38).

This is the human side of receiving salvation. People first hear the word preached about Jesus, for apart from hearing the word, no one experiences salvation. They may accept the word or reject it. The acceptance is belief, both in the message and in the messenger (Jesus). The believer accepts Jesus as messiah and Lord and savior. Once a person has believed, that person becomes a disciple. Such people have accepted their savior and stand in a personal relationship to him, as their Lord.

Repentance is the second element in the human response. People have to turn over a new page in the book of life and live life differently. The content is moral as well as religious. People must turn away from evil and sin and wickedness:

> God, having raised up his servant, sent him to you first, to bless you in turning every one of you from your wickedness (Acts 3:26).

Then they will express this conversion in outward acts which indicate the reality of an inward change of heart:

> They should repent and turn to God and perform deeds worthy of repentance (Acts 20:26).

Disciples give up sin (Acts 19:18ff) and begin a new way of living (Lk 19:1–10). Some may still question if Luke has returned to a sense of accomplishing one's own salvation, since he seems to moralize the nature of repentance. Again, this opinion misinterprets Luke. Repentance is an attitude that follows belief and involves a moment of turning away from sin and evil and attempting to live a new life. Repentance does not accomplish salvation; rather, repentance is the fruit of the acceptance of salvation.

These internal and personal attitudes of the disciple are inseparable from the Lucan idea of baptism. Here the outward act of the church expresses the inner reality. People are baptized into the Spirit of Jesus when they live according to his teaching. The early church community expressed this internal conversion and commitment to the gospel through the ritual of baptism. In Acts, in almost every record of conversion, baptism is mentioned (Acts 2:47; 4:4; 6:7; 9:42; 11:21–24; 13:48; 14:1; 17:34). For Luke, baptism was indispensable. Such must have been the practice of the early church.

The immediate effects of baptism are forgiveness of sins and the reception of the Spirit (Acts 2:38). People can forget about their past sins. They are forgotten. The concept was present in the gospel of Luke, and since he expresses it again in Acts, it would appear that Luke has preserved a term characteristic of the early preaching. The immediate effect of salvation and the acceptance of Jesus is the forgiveness of sins. People need not look forward to repeating the mistakes of the past, nor should they maintain a sense of guilt over the past. What God has forgiven is forgotten.

The other blessing associated with baptism is the reception of the Holy Spirit. The disciples experienced the Spirit on Pentecost (Acts 2:1–4). God continues to pour out his Spirit on Jews and Gentiles. Luke associates the Spirit with water baptism but he also will record some anomalies. The people who shared in Pentecost were not baptized with water. They experienced the Spirit as tongues of fire (Acts 2:3). In Acts 8:14–17 the converts from Samaria who were baptized with water did not receive the Spirit until Peter and John subsequently laid hands upon them. No one can discover precisely what lies behind these varied reports. For Luke, the Spirit is associated with baptism but not always in the same pattern. What Luke first demands is the internal conversion. The water baptism and the laying on of hands signifies that these outward acts relate the experience of the individual believer to the Christian community.

Once the individual has experienced the Spirit, the believer is equipped for mission. The Spirit gives the believer a special gift which makes the disciple capable of certain additional expressions of faith in preaching the gospel to others. Since all partake of the Spirit, all partake in the mission of the church. The Acts of the Apostles is filled with stories of people who have received the Spirit and then partake in missionary activities. Stephen, Peter, John, and especially Paul take the message of Jesus to others, driven by the power of the Spirit. Such should be the activity of all believers. Once a person has experienced the healing power of God through Jesus, that person should be anxious to offer what has been received to others.

■ **Praise and Prayer** ■

The Christian has begun a new life, having experienced forgiveness and baptism and been filled with the Spirit. Joy is the immediate effect. Christians are happy because of what God has done for them in Jesus (Acts 5:41; 11:23; 15:3; 12:14). Rejoicing accompanies the hearing of the message of salvation (Lk 2:10; 8:13), and to receive Jesus as one's guest is an occasion for joy (Lk 19:6). Such earthly joy is an echo of the heavenly joy over the return of the lost (Lk 15).

Luke associates this joy with praise of God. People who are happy will thank and praise God for what has happened to them. Angels and shepherds praise God at the birth of Jesus (Lk 2:13, 20). Jesus performed mighty works as signs of God's nearness, and people praised

God (Lk 5:26; 7:16; 13:13; 17:15 etc). Even his death caused the centurion to glorify God (Lk 23:47). Finally, after Jesus had ascended, the disciples returned to Jerusalem with great joy and they were continually in the temple praising God (Lk 24:52ff).

Praise of God leads naturally to prayer. The first followers prayed until they received the Spirit (Acts 1:14), and prayer accompanied the sending out of missionaries (Acts 13:3). Prayer was the normal activity of the church when its members gathered. Peter and John go to pray in the temple (Acts 3:1). Paul and Silas sing and pray in prison (Acts 16:25). Through prayer the members of the church committed themselves to God (Acts 14:23; 20:36; 21:5), and God responded to prayer by signs and mighty works (Acts 4:31; 9:40; 28:8).

One final note should be made with regard to prayer. A characteristic of the common life was "the breaking of the bread" (Acts 2:42). In this summary statement the breaking of bread is associated with devotion to the apostles' teaching, fellowship and prayers. Such juxtaposition of these elements probably constituted the early Christian worship. The followers of Jesus celebrated the Lord's supper. The same idea seems to be present in the gospel when the two disciples recognize Jesus in the breaking of the bread:

> When he was at table with them, he took the bread and blessed and broke it, and gave it to them. And their eyes were opened and they recognized him; and he vanished out of their sight (Lk 24:30–31).

The followers of Jesus, having expressed their commitment in faith and experienced the Spirit, find joy in their hearts as they pray and praise God and celebrate the presence of Jesus among them in the breaking of the bread.

■ Wealth and Possessions ■

Luke includes in his gospel considerable teaching on wealth and the role of the poor. Jesus preached the good news to the poor and warned the rich about the danger of possessions. Christians should learn to use wealth in the proper way. Luke gives an injunction to give alms (Lk 11:41; 12:33), which is assumed by Jesus to be a normal religious activity that his followers should practice (see also Mt 6:2–4; Mk 14:4–7). This act of self-denial Jesus intensified when he commanded his disciples to give up everything to follow him. Mark records for us the story of the rich young man called to sell all he had and give to the poor (Mk 10:21). Luke makes this injunction more stringent. His disciples left their homes to follow Jesus (Lk 18:28). Disciples must make decisive breaks with the past (Lk 9:57–62) and must renounce all (Lk 14:25–33). Following Jesus demands a sharp decision and Luke allows no compromise.

The picture in Acts, however, is not quite the same. They had all things in common but did not distribute their possessions and their wealth to the poor (Acts 2:45). They kept it for each other. In Acts such activity was voluntary. They lived a common life, meeting together and eating in each other's homes even to the extent of sharing their property so that they had resources to help the poor. They probably lived as a family with goods at the disposal of others without an adoption of a system in which no one owned anything. We need not think that Luke describes an ideal situation or an imaginary community. In all probability such was the practice of some early Christian communities. These ideals of the proper use of wealth and the need for generosity and care for the poor were taught throughout the early church and are relevant for the church at all times.

■ Tribulation and Suffering ■

The joy and praise of God may hint at a theology of glory associated with Jesus and his gospel, but Luke also has his theology of the cross. The Christian carries in the body the death of Jesus so that the life of Jesus may also be manifested in the body. Christians may experience something of the blessings of salvation, but the fullness of this blessing is possible only at the end of the pilgrimage.

Luke announces the theme of suffering early in the gospel. A sword will pierce through the soul of Mary his mother (Lk 2:35). The solemn note of the experience of Mary as she witnessed the suffering and death of her son is sounded in the midst of the joy of his birth. The followers of Jesus will experience persecution and deprivation and through tribulation they will enter the kingdom of God (Acts 14:23). Luke also narrates the sufferings of Paul who knew that imprisonment and affliction awaited him in every city (Acts 20:23; 9:16). Stephen perished through stoning (Acts 7:58); James dies by the sword. Peter is imprisoned and Christians have to flee for their lives. Paul preached and was persecuted continually, and finally he is arrested and sent captive to Rome.

Nor is the early church free from internal sufferings. Ananias and

Sapphira sin (Acts 5); tensions exist among the Hebrews and Hellenists (Acts 6); even missionaries quarrel and go their own way (Acts 15:39). Trouble multiplies. But the word of God is not limited. In spite of the pain and suffering, salvation triumphs in the lives of believers. "The word of God grew and multiplied" (Acts 12:24). The story is not failure but triumph, but not without the presence of suffering. The hope in final victory sustains the believer who often groans in the present state. Luke always sees hope in the midst of persecution. The church lives confidently in the power of God who will bring the community through its sufferings. The church will pray not necessarily to be delivered from pain but rather that, despite the threats of opposition, the church will speak the word of God boldly:

And now, Lord, look upon their threats, and grant to your servants to speak your word with all boldness (Acts 4:29).

When a martyr looks death in the face, as did Stephen, the martyr will see beyond death to the welcome of the Lord into the presence of God (Acts 7:55ff). This is the theology of the cross for Luke: pain with a hope for glory.

The work of salvation continues in the church, in the community of believers. Salvation embraces men and women of every nation who have responded in faith. They will not always find peace, for ultimately peace is God's gift. But joy and praising God will always characterize the follower of Jesus, since they characterized the life of Jesus himself. Jesus began his journey to Jerusalem knowing that his death would culminate his journey. Along the way he taught his disciples the meaning of discipleship. They accepted the challenge he offered them, and, once filled with the Spirit, they preached the good news of the saving presence of God to all who would listen to them. Luke wanted to show everyone what must be done to experience this salvation. The gospel and the book of Acts record the offering and acceptance of this salvation. People heard the gospel in the teaching of Jesus and the teaching about Jesus. They heard and continue to hear the good news of salvation, for they know they must: "Believe in the Lord Jesus and you will be saved."

Further Study

F. Danker, *Luke.*
J. Fitzmyer, *The Gospel According to Luke.*
S. Kealy, *The Gospel of Luke.*

7.

The Origin of Luke

*C*hristians read the gospel of Luke today because it forms part of the New Testament, expressing the rule of faith of early Christianity. But just how this gospel managed to be included in the canon of New Testament books remains a mystery. We know now that many others wrote gospels, some of them earlier than that of Luke, and they were not accepted into the canon of New Testament writings. We know also that Luke was not one of the twelve and makes no greater claim than to state that he wished to write an orderly and accurate account. He alone among the four evangelists has a prologue, just as he alone wrote a second volume on the development of the church.

Contemporary historians and even just ordinary Christians have many questions resulting from Luke's unusual prologue. Who is this author? Who is Theophilus? From where is he writing? Did he have a larger audience in mind when he wrote? What sources did he use? How did he use his sources? What was his church community like? All such questions arise in the mind of the contemporary believer, but unfortunately we will never be able to answer all of them, and many of them will find only a possible or probable response.

Perhaps two reasons formed the foundation for the acceptance of the writings of Luke being included in the canon of the New Testament. Tradition associates him with Paul, especially the "we" sections of the Acts. Secondly, his own ministry within the early church would have influenced the acceptance of his writings. Paul and his gospel quickly received acceptance in the early church, especially the Gentile church. Thus, anyone associated with Paul would have found a ready audience.

Irenaeus (c. 180 C.E.) insists that to find perfect knowledge of the gospel of Jesus one must go back to the writings of the apostles. Then he identifies Luke as "the follower of Paul who put down in a book the gospel preached by that one (Paul)." Earlier Justin Martyr (c. 160 C.E.) had commented that the memoirs of Jesus were composed by "apostles and by those who followed them." Luke was identified with Paul, and Mark, as we have seen, was identified with Peter. The witness of Tertullian in the early third century was similar. By the fourth century the remark by Paul, "my gospel," was widely believed to refer to the writings of Luke. It is more interesting, however, that Luke does not refer to Paul in his gospel as any source for his writings. Rather, in his prologue he introduces his gospel as the narrative of the word of God delivered to him by eye-witnesses and ministers of the word. The precise relationship between Luke and Paul will remain forever in shadows. Evidently the early church associated the two. The earliest testimony comes from the Muratorian Fragment (c. 170 C.E.):

> The third book of the gospel: according to Luke. This Luke was a physician. After the Ascension of Christ, when Paul had taken him along with him as one devoted to letters, he wrote it under his own name from hearsay. For he himself had not seen the Lord in person, but, insofar as he was able to follow (it all), he thus began his account with the birth of John.

The epistle to the Colossians (4:10–14) describes Luke with Paul in his Roman prison as the "beloved physician." From 2 Timothy 4:11 we also learn that he was a companion of Paul. Origen in the third century identified him with Lucius in Romans 16:21, and in the fourth century Ephraim Syrus identified him with the Lucius of Cyrene in Acts 13:1.

The tradition of Lucan authorship clearly exists in the beginning of the third century and it was never disputed. The second century tradition of authorship also carries considerable weight, especially because it identifies the author with a relatively unknown person in early Christianity.

From the New Testament we can deduce that Luke, a sometime companion of Paul, perhaps a physician, a disciple who had not witnessed the ministry of Jesus, wrote a gospel for Gentile converts. He also composed the Acts of the Apostles and wrote in a good Greek style. It seems to me that this tradition should be accepted. If the gospel and Acts were not written by Luke, then the early church had no reason to associate them with a relatively unknown early church figure.

Was Luke a Gentile Christian or a Jewish Christian? Like many of the other questions associated with this gospel, we may never know. Some say he was a Gentile Christian because of the superiority of the Greek used in the works, the avoidance of semitic words, the omission of gospel traditions about Jesus' controversies with the pharisaic understanding of the law, and the changing of Palestinian local color and details into Hellenistic counterparts (e.g. the parable of the light in the cellar: there are no cellars in Palestine—Lk 11:33).

Others will claim he was Jewish Christian because of his interest in the Old Testament, his alleged Palestinian language, and the Epiphanian tradition that he was one of the seventy-two disciples sent out by Jesus.

Most recently J. Fitzmyer regards Luke as a Gentile Christian—not, however, as Greek but as a non-Jewish semite, a native of Antioch where he was educated in Hellenistic culture. He bases his theory on the form of Luke's name, the New Testament passages in which he is mentioned, and the ancient tradition about his Antiochean origin.

Again, I would conclude that the ethnic background of Luke will never be satisfactorily solved. Whether he was a Gentile Christian or a Jewish Christian or a non-Jewish semite, we know that he was well acquainted with Greek and with Hellenistic culture. We also know that he was not an eye-witness to the ministry of Jesus. Perhaps we know more about him than the authors of the other gospels, but even here much remains unknown.

Was he the companion of Paul? Some might presume that by this point I have accepted without reservation this theory. Such is not the case. First we have no evidence that Luke ever read any of Paul's letters. We also know that the journeys of Paul, as depicted in his letters, differ in many instances from what was presented by Luke in Acts. Some have solved these discrepancies by believing that Luke was associated with Paul but only for a brief period. Once again, I leave the readers with a quandary. I personally see no reason not to accept Luke as the sometime collaborator of Paul but realize that no matter what position I would hold, I have not solved all of the problems in an authoritative or unqualified manner.

Was he really a physician? Some will find special details given to medicine in his works which will support this theory. Others will find no evidence for such a position. Whether he was a physician or not makes no difference to the understanding of the gospel. He is called a physician in Colossians 4:14, and for anyone who identifies this same Luke with the author of the third gospel, it is enough.

And so, who was Luke? Whether the author of the third gospel was really called Luke, really a companion of Paul, really a physician, really a Gentile Christian, really well educated in Greek, makes little difference. What matters is the text of the third gospel and what this gospel means to Christians of every age, regardless of who wrote it.

■ Date and Place of Composition ■

We know that the gospel of Luke was written after Mark and before the Acts of the Apostles. Most will also see the gospel written after the destruction of the temple in 70 C.E. But how much later? We also know that Luke did not use the Pauline letters, and so his gospel should be dated before the formation or the circulation of the Pauline corpus of writings. The best solution, favored by most today, is to date the gospel between 85 and 90 C.E.

As for the place of composition, the individual reader might as well choose for oneself. Ancient tradition locates the origin of the gospel in Achaia (Greece) or Boeotia or Rome. Modern guesses include Caesarea, or the Decapolis, or Asia Minor. We have another unanswered question.

■ Theophilus ■

For some, Theophilus is a representative figure with no historical foundation. The name means "beloved of God." Thus, Luke writes for anyone who is "beloved of God" or interested in God and especially open to Christian faith. Others see Theoplilus as a pseudonym for the emperor Domitian's cousin, T. Flavius Clemens, who was interested in Christianity. Still others see Theophilus as a prominent person of high rank who perhaps helped Luke with the cost of publishing his book. Maybe he was a catechumen and Luke wanted him to grow in his understanding of his faith. Maybe he was someone who was misinformed about Christianity and Luke wrote for him to offer him the correct information. By now the reader knows that we have another unanswered question. Since I believe that the gospel was written not just for an individual but for a community, it seems best to me to regard Theophilus as a representative figure. Whether or not such a figure had indeed some historical foundation matters little.

■ Luke's Intended Audience ■

Luke wrote his gospel for a predominantly Gentile Christian audience. Such a conclusion arises easily from his concern for salvation for all. He attempted to relate the Jesus tradition to a Greco-Roman literary tradition as evidenced in the prologue. He even dedicated his works to someone with a Greek name. He wrote his gospel eliminating material which was predominantly concerned with Jewish preoccupations. He wants to show a continuity between Judaism and Christianity, but he also sees that the future belongs to the Gentile church.

The community probably was urban, in a Greek speaking part of the Roman world. Note that the sophisticated Luke remarks that the Gerasene demoniac did not live in a house (Lk 8:27). Repeatedly Jesus is a guest in people's homes. He mentions the word "city" thirty-eight times. These and other Lucan asides support the theory of an urban site for the gospel and the Lucan community.

It also seems that the people for whom he wrote were at some distance in time from the ministry of Jesus. They had some knowledge of the life and ministry of Jesus but Luke was not satisfied with this knowledge. He wished to give them an accurate and orderly account of the Jesus tradition. Then they could remain in continuity with Jesus through the writings of Luke, the testimony of ministers of the word, and the eye-witnesses themselves.

The community had many problems. The second coming of the Lord was delayed and may be pushed into a distant future. By now, the church had been separated from the synagogue. Some sections even read like warnings to a persecuted community (Lk 12:1–12). His frequent remarks about wealth indicate the presence of many poor. The temptations that wealth often brings must have been evident in the community. The role of women was also of great importance. We can also add the problem of culture, of reconciliation between gospel and the Hellenistic milieu as well as the relationship between the acceptance of Christian faith and citizenship in the world.

Like other Christian communities at the end of the first century, the Lucan community stood on a threshold of change. Unlike Matthew, he was not too concerned with the past. He wanted to push out into the future but in such a way that the tradition remained firmly rooted in Jesus. He knew that Christian faith would develop and expand as it experienced a greater world and welcomed thousands of Gentiles into its midst. He never feared for the future as long as people could feel secure about the past. Once he has Paul reach Rome, he concludes his second volume. From then on, what will happen will depend upon the preaching of others, like Paul, equally filled with the Spirit of Jesus and equally committed to a new world.

Luke did not solve all of the problems facing his church. The role of women in the community was not resolved by Luke; the problem of Christians with wealth continues in every century. The expansion of Christian faith to other cultures and civilizations continues into the twentieth century as it has done for the intervening nineteen. Luke offered a witness to the Jesus tradition which continues to have relevance to the church today. This brings us to the final chapter.

Further Study

F. Danker, *Luke.*
J. Fitzmyer, *The Gospel According to Luke.*

8.

The Meaning of Luke

The word of God exists more in the hearts of people and in the preaching of the Christian church than in the actual record in the Bible. This word lives and moves and has its effect, bursting out of the time and space limitations bringing about changes in the lives of all who will listen. This one word has been refracted in many ways in history, and in each gospel this word finds its own expression and power.

One of the reasons so many people like the gospel of Luke is due to the gentle power of God's word as recorded by this first century Christian. He writes with an appeal that transcends the twenty intervening centuries. We can read and become part of that first century church community, enjoying the call to repentance and belief, feeling part of a movement that overwhelmed the world. The gospel has its own characteristics which give it this distinctive meaning.

■ Mercy, Compassion and Kindness ■

The study of Luke, or even a casual reading, leads the reader to love this kind and compassionate Jesus. He reaches out and offers salvation and comfort. Jesus seems to enter into the sorrow that people experience, and because of his presence the sorrow is able to be borne with greater ease even if not without its pain. Jesus equally enters into the joy of people, and with his nearness the people doubly enjoy their happiness. Somehow Jesus never seems distant from human life in this gospel. What people experience, Jesus has experienced. He knows their needs and problems and joys and celebrations, and Jesus makes himself personally present.

The kindness of Jesus leaps out of every page of this gospel. He always seems to bring out the best in people and emphasizes their good qualities while often overlooking those qualities which are not so good. Jesus is always the perfect gentleman who does not offend but rather makes people look good. He treats them nicely because he believes in their value and worth. We recall his attitude toward women and his treatment of Zacchaeus; even his manner of dealing with Judas shows the same kindness. The stories that Luke preserves for future generations always seem to bring out these qualities which are universally appealing precisely because they make people feel good.

■ Forgiveness ■

Perhaps the overwhelming quality of this gospel is forgiveness. Jesus never seems to hold any grudges. Rather he continually extends the forgiveness of God to all people. No one is beyond the need for forgiveness and mercy, since all fall short of the mark. Jesus seems to be so attuned to the human condition that he knows human weakness and appreciates just how much people need to experience the words and gestures of being reconciled and forgiven. The parable of the prodigal son stands as the great narrative monument to forgiveness and joy which accompanies reconciliation. Everyone can identify with the prodigal son at some time in life, and Luke insists that not only will the prodigal be welcomed home, but when the prodigal returns, the occasion demands celebration. Even the attitude of the older son can never dampen the joy. With characteristic kindness God and Jesus and Luke question the elder son, encouraging him not to hold any ill feelings in his heart but to join in the celebration by offering his own forgiveness. What was lost has been found. If people remember chapter 15, the gospel within the gospel, and recall the power of forgiveness, they will have remembered forever the meaning of the gospel of Luke.

■ Outcasts ■

I remember going to a new school, not knowing anyone, and wondering how I would be accepted. I recall leaving the warmth and comfort and security of home and with great anxiety putting out tentative steps into a different world. So many of the other kids seemed to know each other. Old friends greeted each other with enthusiasm. It was like standing on an outer circle and watching all those within the circle having a good time. I knew what it meant to be an outcast. But then (I still recall it vividly) someone reached out to me, told me his name, and all of a sudden I was no longer on the outside but I was in the circle.

So many times in life people experience being outsiders, whether in a school, a job, a neighborhood, or a social gathering. No matter how long we live or how many experiences we have in life, until the day we die we will experience moments of being on the outside. Sometimes we never get invited in, and the pain never goes away from that moment of rejection. When we no longer feel like an outsider, we somehow forget that we ever felt differently. Someone, or some group of people, erased the pain of being an outcast and welcomed us in.

Luke knew the meaning of being an outcast. He himself might very well have been an outsider in early Christianity. Certainly he was not an eye-witness to the Jesus tradition, and he evidently knew some who were. He never followed Jesus in his public ministry and never had the joy of his company. His gospel is filled with people who were outsiders whom Jesus made feel welcomed. From the shepherds in the beginning of the gospel to the two disciples on the road to Emmaus, Luke wrote of the experience of rejection and disappointment. Each time the hand of Jesus, or the words of Jesus, touched people, and the pain of being an outcast was forgotten and people felt as if they belonged. Jesus was their friend even if the world offered little friendship. Lepers, those sick in mind and body, tax collectors, and publicans all received the offer of friendship from Jesus. They were not left on the outside of the circle looking in, but Jesus himself drew them in and made them feel at home. The Lucan church did the same. They found favor with people and continually added to their own numbers. The lost were found; the people who lived on the periphery of society were brought into the circle. The outcasts were welcomed home.

■ Universalism ■

The third gospel, more than any other, is the gospel of universalism. Everyone is invited: Jew and Gentile, slave and free, man and woman, rich and poor. He began his gospel by telling us that the genealogy of Jesus extends back to Adam. He ends his second volume with Paul preaching the Lord Jesus in Rome, the center of the then known world. No group or territory will hold a favored position on salvation. God extends his saving presence to all peoples of all times, and if one group has a special election, the choosing expects responsibility and not privilege.

In a society which had its strata, Jesus did away with distinctions. Salvation is not something different for men than for women, or more powerful for Jew than for Greek. Salvation is God's presence in life bringing about a sense of happiness and peace and contentment, and such a blessing extends to all peoples. Luke could deal with Greek culture and Jewish religious traditions. He could move from Jerusalem to Asia Minor to Rome. All along the way the good news of Jesus affected people. The people differed from one city to another, but they became united in the one belief in a gracious God who had manifested himself in Jesus of Nazareth. Luke would never be content with exclusivity or an elitism. Jesus broke down the barriers that separated people and classified them into groups. God knows no distinctions in love and treats people alike, offering the same experience of salvation, whether Jew or Gentile. Universalism denies the hubris of nationalism and emphasizes the common humanity of peoples. Universalism destroys the distinction of races and celebrates the unity that can be found in diversity. Universalism refuses to acknowledge classes, for all are brothers and sisters under the one God, who makes his sun shine on all and rain fall on all.

In a world that sees too much that separates into nations and races and classes, the gospel of Luke cries out with a universal appeal. God knows no distinctions among people, and the saving presence of God, human happiness and fulfillment, takes root and flourishes in the hearts of all people: black or white or yellow or red, rich or poor, male or female, old or young. The world would be a better place if the universal teaching of Luke became the banner under which nations walked.

■ Women ■

After two thousand years of Christianity women still struggle to be accepted as equals with men in the Christian church. The American bishops have begun a long road for this equality in their recent pastoral on women in the church. Luke, I am sure, would have applauded such a decision and would also have asked: "Why so tentative a step after so many years?"

Like John, the author of this gospel seems to have a special place for women in Christianity. They remained faithful to Jesus and evidently held important positions of leadership in the early community. Luke can never answer the question of ordination of women, but neither can he answer the question of ordination of men. There is no New Testament evidence that only the twelve apostles were present at the last supper. Luke seems to imply that many disciples were there. There is also no New Testament evidence that Jesus ordained anyone at the last supper. Luke presents women as part of the ministry of Jesus, and then in the Acts of the Apostles they continue to perform important functions in the early community. In a society that places women in defined positions and roles, Jesus refused to be so limited in his dealing with women. Greek society afforded women a greater role than in Jewish society, but even here the limitations confined women to set roles. Following the tradition of Jesus, Luke expanded the position of women, allowing them, and probably encouraging them, to assume their proper roles in the early church. Once he had established the precedent, the church could follow his lead and make additional adjustments as society woke up to the importance and need for a rightful role of women. Things changed for Luke; development took place in the early decades of Christianity. If such things happened in the past, then continual development will take place in the present and in the future.

■ Tradition ■

Everyone needs roots. We need to know where we have come from so that we have a direction for the future. Luke wanted the Christian community to have its roots. He carefully tied his experience of God through Jesus back to the experience of the earliest followers of Jesus. One generation passes on to the next and so forth. If, somewhere along the line, things get confused, then future generations will suffer. Luke wanted to avoid such confusion. The Christian of his community would know the security of being part of a continued faith tradition back to the actual experience of Jesus.

The church needs a sense of tradition today as well. People have to feel secure that what they are experiencing is part of the continuation of the same Jesus tradition. Sometimes, however, people confuse tradition with no change. What is passed on is actually affected in the passing and not left unchanged. Luke knew this. The demands made upon his community were different from the demands made upon a predominantly Jewish-Christian community. Greco-Roman culture was not the same as Jewish-Palestinian culture. The tradition must remain but will adapt itself to new situations.

I often use the image of a Bible being passed on from generation to generation in the original wrapping, having never been opened, never been read, handled or even abused with the oil of hands and the roughness of turning. I compare this to a Bible well read and even worn by the loving touch of devoted readers. Tradition is like the latter and not the former.

Today tradition continues its adaptation, giving people the same security that what is part of the Christian experience now was part of the same Jesus tradition, even if changes have taken place. Luke made his changes. He could read Mark and decide that only some of Mark's understanding of the Jesus tradition would make sense to Luke's predominantly Gentile audience. He could change the words of Jesus, add stories and add explanations, convinced that the tradition remained intact. To change without losing roots is the continual challenge to Christianity. Luke gives a good example of how to do it.

■ Cost of Discipleship ■

Finally, Christians must pay the cost of following Jesus. It does not come cheaply. Luke knew the demands made upon the disciples. Riches can cause problems. Forgiveness makes demands. Mercy takes its price daily; kindness often goes unrewarded. Accepting rejection and persecution and misunderstanding was the lot of Jesus and has been the destiny of Christians ever since. No one can get through life cheaply, and surely no one can follow a crucified Lord without paying the price. Luke knew what was involved and never shunned the payment. People will continue to follow Jesus and will not be overwhelmed by the demands of discipleship. They know that what a person gives up pales in the light of the power and goodness of the gospel.

Christianity can tend to become leisure time activity. People have to do something with their free time, and so why not add a generous amount of Christianity? Luke would reject such an approach to the Jesus tradition. Christianity demands sacrifice and brings its own amount of pain as people try to learn to serve each other. I do not intend to nail people on a mystical cross of suffering. I do not believe that Luke wanted to emphasize the sorrow of following Jesus. He was realistic enough to know that the pain will come and no one need go looking for it. He was not afraid to give up anything, for in fact he believed that no one ever loses in following Jesus. The pain that one experiences never destroys the joy of being part of the community. Discipleship may cost, but such an investment pays greater dividends than any other human endeavor.

What does the gospel of Luke mean? It means that Christianity is for all; mercy and pardon belong to the church, since these qualities formed the heart of the Jesus tradition. Outsiders should always feel welcome. Even if the cost of discipleship is great, the rewards are magnificent. Everyone's favorite gospel does it again. No matter how many times people read this witness to the Jesus tradition, the power of its gentleness pervades the spirit and people feel good. The testimony of Luke lives on in his gospel. What a marvelous man he must have been to have created such a gospel.

Bibliography

■ **Mark and the Primitive Teaching** ■

Achtemeier, Paul J. *Mark.* Proclamation Commentaries. Philadelphia: Fortress, 1975.

Barclay, William. *The Gospel of Mark.* Philadelphia: Westminister 1956.

Best, Ernest. *The Temptation and the Passion: The Markan Soteriology.* Cambridge: University Press, 1965.

Blanch, Stuart. *The Christian Militant: Lent with St. Mark's Gospel.* London: SPCK, 1978.

Brown, Raymond E. *The Churches the Apostles Left Behind.* Ramsey: Paulist Press, 1984.

Burkill, T. *New Light on the Earliest Gospel.* Ithica: Cornell University Press, 1972.

Dodd, C. H. *The Apostolic Preaching and its Development.* London: Hodder, 1936.

Farmer, W. *The Synoptic Problem: A Critical Analysis.* New York, 1964.

Hahn, F. *The Titles of Jesus in Christology: Their History in Early Christianity.* London, 1969.

Jeremias, J. *The Parables of Jesus.* New York: Scribner, 1963.

Jones, Alexander. *The Gospel According to St. Mark.* New York: Sheed and Ward, 1963.

Kee, Howard C. *Community of the New Age: Studies in Mark's Gospel.* Philadelphia: Westminister, 1976.

Kelber, W. *The Kingdom in Mark.* Philadelphia: Fortress, 1974.

———. *The Passion in Mark.* Philadelphia: Fortress, 1975.

Martin, Ralph. *Mark: Evangelist and Theologian.* Grand Rapids: Zondervan, 1973.

Marxsen, Willi. *Mark the Evangelist.* Nashville: Abingdon, 1969.

Nineham, D. E. *Saint Mark.* Philadelphia: Westminister, 1963.

Perrin, N. *Jesus and the Language of the Kingdom.* Philadelphia: Fortress, 1975.

————. *A Modern Pilgrim in the New Testament Christology.* Philadelphia: Fortress, 1974.

————. *The Resurrection According to Matthew, Mark and Luke.* Philadelphia: Fortress, 1976.

Quesnell, Quentin. *The Mind of Mark.* Rome: Biblical Institute Press, 1969.

Rohde, J. *Rediscovering the Teaching of the Evangelists.* Philadelphia: Westminister, 1971.

Schweizer, Edward. *The Good News According to Mark.* Richmond: John Knox, 1970.

Smith, Morton. *Jesus the Magician.* New York: Harper and Row, 1978.

Todt, H. E. *The Son of Man in the Synoptic Tradition.* Philadelphia: Westminster, 1965.

Trocme, E. *The Formation of the Gospel According to Mark.* Philadelphia: Westminster, 1975.

Weeden, Theodore J. *Mark, Traditions in Conflict.* Philadelphia: Fortress, 1971.

Wrede, W. *The Messianic Secret.* Cambridge, 1971.

■ John ■

Barrett, C. K. *The Gospel of John and Judaism.* Philadelphia: Fortress, 1975.

Brown, Raymond E. *The Community of the Beloved Disciple.* New York: Paulist, 1979.

Collins, Raymond. "The Representative Figures in the Fourth Gospel." *Downside Review,* 94 (1976), 26–46, 118–132.

Cullman, Oscar. *The Johannine Circle: A Study in the Origin of the Gospel of John.* London, 1976.

Culpepper, R. Alan. *Anatomy of the Fourth Gospel.* Philadelphia: Fortress, 1983.

Forestell, J.T. *The Word of the Cross: Salvation as Revelation in the Fourth Gospel.* Rome: Pontifical Biblical Institute, 1974.

Harner, Philip, B. *The "I Am" of the Fourth Gospel.* Philadelphia: Fortress, 1970.

Kysar, Robert. *The Fourth Evangelist and His Gospel.* Minneapolis: Augsburg, 1975.

———. *John: The Maverick Gospel.* Atlanta: John Knox, 1976.

Kasemann, E. *The Testament of Jesus According to John 17.* Philadelphia: Fortress, 1968.

Lindars, Barnabas. *The Gospel of John.* Grand Rapids: Eerdmans, 1972.

Martyn, J. Louis. *History and Theology in the Fourth Gospel.* Nashville: Abingdon, 1979.

MacRae, George. *Faith in the World: The Fourth Gospel.* Chicago: Heralds Biblical Booklets, 1973.

Maloney, Francis. *The Johannine Son of Man.* Rome: LAS, 1976.

O'Grady, John F. *The Gospel of John.* New York: Pueblo, 1982.

———. *Individual and Community in John.* Rome: Marino, 1978.

Perkins, Pheme. *The Gospel According to St. John.* Chicago: Franciscan Herald Press, 1978.

Schnackenburg, Rudolf. *The Gospel According to St. John.* Vol. III New York: Crossroad, 1982.

Taylor, Michael, ed. *A Companion to John.* Staten Island: Alba House, 1977.

■ **Matthew** ■

Bornkamm, G., G. Barth, and H. J. Held. *Tradition and Interpretation in Matthew.* 2nd rev. ed. London: SCM, 1982.

Brown, Raymond E. *An Adult Christ at Christmas. Essays on the Three Biblical Christmas Stories.* Collegeville: The Liturgical Press, 1975.

Brown, Raymond E. and John P. Meier. *Antioch and Rome.* New York: Paulist Press, 1983.

Brown, Raymond E. *The Birth of the Messiah. A Commentary on the Infancy Narratives in Matthew and Luke.* Garden City: Doubleday & Company, Inc., 1977.

Crossan, D. *In Parables: The Challenge of the Historical Jesus.* New York: Harper and Row, 1973.

Dodd, C. H. *The Parables of the Kingdom.* New York: Scribners, 1965.

Fenton, J. C. *Saint Matthew.* Philadelphia: Westminster, 1978.

Harner, Philip B. *Understanding the Lord's Prayer.* Philadelphia: Fortress Press, 1975.

Jeremias, Joachim. *The Parables of Jesus.* New York: Scribners, 1963.

———. *The Sermon on the Mount.* Philadelphia: Fortress Press, 1963.

Kingsbury, Jack Dean. *Matthew.* Philadelphia: Fortress Press, 1977.
_____. *Matthew: Structure, Christology, Kingdom.* Philadelphia: Fortress Press, 1975.
Lambrecht, Jan. *Once More Astonished. The Parables of Jesus.* New York: Crossroad, 1981.
_____. *The Sermon on the Mount.* Wilmington: Michael Glazier, 1985.
Meier, John P. *Matthew.* Wilmington: Michael Glazier, Inc., 1980.
_____. *The Vision of Matthew: Christ, Church and Morality in the First Gospel.* New York: Paulist Press, 1979.
Nolan, Brian M. *The Royal Son of God. The Christology of Matthew 1–2 in the Setting of the Gospels.* Göttingen: Vandenhoeck & Ruprecht, 1979.
Perrin, Norman. *Jesus and the Language of the Kingdom. Symbol and Metaphor in the New Testament Interpretation.* Philadelphia: Fortress, 1976.
_____. *The Resurrection According to Matthew, Mark, and Luke.* Philadelphia: Fortress, 1977.
Schweizer, Eduard. *The Good News According to Matthew.* Atlanta: John Knox, 1975.
Senior, Donald, C. P. *The Passion of Jesus in the Gospel of Matthew.* Wilmington: Michael Glazier, 1985.
Tracy, David. *The Analogical Imagination.* New York: Crossroad, 1981.

■ Luke ■

Barrett, C. K. *Luke the Historian in Recent Study.* Philadelphia: Fortress Press, 1961.
Brown, Raymond E. *An Adult Christ at Christmas. Essays on the Three Biblical Christmas Stories.* Collegeville: The Liturgical Press, 1978.
_____. *The Birth of the Messiah. A Commentary on the Infancy Narratives in Matthew and Luke.* Garden City: Doubleday & Company, Inc., 1977.
Caird, G. B. *Saint Luke.* Baltimore: Penguin Books, 1963.
Conzelmann, Hans. *The Theology of Saint Luke.* New York: Harper & Row, 1960.
Danker, Frederick W. *Luke.* Philadelphia, Fortress Press, 1976.
Ellis, E. Earle. *Eschatology in Luke.* Philadelphia: Fortress Press, 1972.

————. *The New Century Bible Commentary: The Gospel of Luke.* Grand Rapids: Eerdmans, 1966.

Fitzmyer, Joseph A. *The Gospel According to Luke. Introduction, Translation, and Notes.* 2 vols. Garden City: Doubleday, 1981, 1985.

Karris, R. J. *Luke: Artist and Theologian. Luke's Passion Account as Literature.* Mahwah: Paulist, 1985.

Kealy, John P. *The Gospel of Luke.* Denville: Dimension, 1979.

LaVerdiere, Eugene. *Luke.* Wilmington: Michael Glazier, 1980.

Marshall, I. Howard. *The Acts of the Apostles.* Grand Rapids: Eerdmans, 1981.

————. *Luke: Historian and Theologian.* Grand Rapids: Eerdmans, 1971.

O'Toole, R. F. *The Unity of Luke's Theology. An Analysis of Luke–Acts.* Wilmington: Michael Glazier, 1984.

Perrin, Norman. *The Resurrection According to Matthew, Mark, and Luke.* Philadelphia: Fortress, 1977.

Schweizer, E. *The Good News According to Luke.* Atlanta: John Knox, 1984.

Talbert, C. H., ed. *Luke-Acts. New Perspectives from the Society of Biblical Literature Seminar.* New York: Crossroad, 1984.

Index

For Carol Susan Roth *z"l*
1947–2010

How's this?

The God Upgrade:
Finding Your 21st-Century Spirituality in Judaism's 5,000-Year-Old Tradition

2011 Quality Paperback Edition, First Printing
© 2011 by Jamie S. Korngold
Foreword © 2011 by Harold M. Schulweis

For information regarding permission to reprint material from this book, please mail or fax your request in writing to Jewish Lights Publishing, Permissions Department, at the address / fax number listed below, or e-mail your request to permissions@jewishlights.com.

Library of Congress Cataloging-in-Publication Data
Korngold, Jamie S.
  The God upgrade : finding your 21st-century spirituality in Judaism's 5,000-year-old tradition / Jamie S. Korngold. — 2011 quality paperback ed.
    p. cm.
Includes bibliographical references.
ISBN 978-1-58023-443-6 (quality pbk.)
1. God (Judaism) 2. Spiritual life—Judaism. I. Title.
BM610.K67 2011
296.3'11—dc22

2011000079

10 9 8 7 6 5 4 3 2 1
Manufactured in the United States of America

Cover Design and Art: Tim Holtz
Interior Design: Kristi Menter

For People of All Faiths, All Backgrounds
Published by Jewish Lights Publishing
A Division of LongHill Partners, Inc.
Sunset Farm Offices, Route 4, P.O. Box 237
Woodstock, VT 05091
Tel: (802) 457-4000   Fax: (802) 457-4004
www.jewishlights.com

To Gilda

Love —

THE
GOD
UPGRADE

Finding Your
21st-Century Spirituality
in Judaism's
5,000-Year-Old Tradition

Jamie

Rabbi Jamie S. Korngold

Foreword by Rabbi Harold M. Schulweis

For People of All Faiths, All Backgrounds

JEWISH LIGHTS Publishing

Woodstock, Vermont

www.jewishlights.com

I believe in Spinoza's God who reveals Himself in the orderly harmony of what exists, not in a God who concerns Himself with fates and actions of human beings.

ALBERT EINSTEIN

CONTENTS

FOREWORD

Can you pray to God without God? Can you praise or petition God without believing in God? Can you question God's fairness without knowing what may properly be expected of God? Can you study the prophet's claim to revelation without an idea of God's intention, or intervention or abstention?

Can there be spirituality, ritual observance, without thought or moral reasoning? It can be done. It's being done. Prayer recitation, the chanting of the tropes of the sacred texts, fluency with words and cantillation replaces religious inquiry. The ritual gesture turns surrogate for theological meaning.

For some, prayer is poetry—but poetry not believed. Rhyme without reason, ritual without rationale, responsive readings without the response of heart or mind. When theological discussion is ignored in class or at home or in the seminary, the vacuity yields feelings of boredom and irrelevance. While some suggest that finer poetry, more popular instrumentation, or larger choruses will reinvigorate the synagogue, the truth of the matter is that aesthetics cannot replace belief. Too often, the melody in the liturgy distracts from the lyrics of the theology.

The religious educator must anticipate the harder questions young and old have even when they are not openly articulated. In Judaism, the dignity of the question is often more important than the regal dogmatic answer.

Questions are to be revered. I mean not the questions about the translation of a Hebrew term in the text or the proper sound of a trope in the cantillations. I mean the kind of theological questions we asked as young people and still ask as adults, for example, questions that challenge the fairness of God's judgment in visiting the sins of the fathers upon the sons, or questions about the meaning of "chosenness" and whether chosenness insinuates rejection of other traditions.

To such theological questions, when I dared asked my grandfather, he would extend his hand, pinch my cheek indulgently, and deflect the question with the Yiddish expression *"Shpeter"*—"later." Later, when I would be older, he assured me, I would be answered. Only "later" never came. The procrastination created a hole. And like nature, religion abhors a vacuum.

This is one of the welcome contributions Rabbi Jamie Korngold makes in her book *The God Upgrade*. It anticipates the questions of the readers, young and old, and encourages them to freely open the prematurely buried inquiries of their minds and hearts. Rabbi Korngold exposes the reader to the diversity of Jewish responses within the Jewish tradition and frees the seeker from the erroneous monolithic myth that Jewish tradition is static, immutable, only to be obeyed and never to be changed. In her discussion, the questions are raised to a higher plateau.

Pedagogical legend tells of a teacher in a confirmation class who asked how many of the students believed in God. No hands were raised except that of one young person. Asked how she had come to believe in God, she answered casually, "I don't know. I think it just runs in my family."

In our days, God-talk is unheard around the table, in the classroom, or even in the seminary. That theological silence must be broken. Old questions must be renewed, and new answers must be tried. Credit the author of this energizing book who knows that we have nothing to fear but rigidity and emptiness itself.

Rabbi Harold M. Schulweis
Valley Beth Shalom, Encino, California

Introduction

RUNNING GOD SYSTEM 1.0
IN A 2.0 WORLD

We shall require a substantially new manner
of thinking if mankind is to survive.

ALBERT EINSTEIN

My husband, Jeff, who owns a high-tech Web development firm, has a manual Hermes 3000 typewriter on his desk. It was his mother's typewriter from her college days in the 1960s. Remember the ones that made a "bing" sound at the end of a line alerting you to manually move the carriage return?

One day our five-year-old daughter Sadie noticed the typewriter and asked what it was. Jeff explained it was for typing. Sadie walked over and easily typed in "Sadie," then her sister's name, "Ori," and then asked, "Now what?" She was dumbfounded when he explained that was all it did. No touch screen, no mouse, not even a monitor. The point of the contraption eluded her and she returned to a build-your-own roller coaster game on Jeff's iPad.

As I watched her, it occurred to me that God, as explained in the Bible, fits into our modern world about as well as a manual typewriter from the 1960s does. That's not to say great things were not created based upon the ideas presented in the Bible, just as the PC ultimately evolved from the typewriter. But the interface between our world and the biblical concept of God works about as well as trying to upload videos to YouTube on your typewriter. (Good luck with that.)

The typewriter was a great improvement on what came before it (What did come before it? Movable type? Scribes?) just as the biblical God was a great improvement upon the God ideas that preceded it. For one, the new God banned child sacrifice, a practice often required by pre-biblical God. Presenting this change in practice is the primary point of the *Akeida*, the biblical story in which Abraham takes his son Isaac up Mount Mariah to sacrifice him, but is stopped when an angel of God tells him to kill a ram instead. Through the narrative, God lets it be known that He no longer demands or desires child sacrifice (Genesis 22:1–19). (I refer to God as a He here because the authors of this story certainly viewed their God as a male even if I do not. When I am discussing my own God concept you will notice I do not use gender. If you are bothered by my use of "He," please be aware that I use it ironically and pointedly, further displaying why this concept does not fit with our modern world.)

But let's face it: despite the improvement from sacrificing children to sacrificing animals to please God and stay on God's good side, the whole biblical idea of God rewarding and punishing us based on our obedience is no longer believable to many of us. We look around our world and see that bad things happen to good people all the time. Certainly the equation cannot be so simple as God takes care of those who please God.

Fortunately, there have been numerous upgrades to our God concept over the centuries. But all too often the people with whom I interact don't know about them and think Judaism still subscribes to the God in the sky who writes down our deeds and rewards and punishes us accordingly. Who can blame them? That is what our prayer book says on Yom Kippur, the only day many Jews step foot in a synagogue. Why would they know about the other theologies? By the time the rabbi gets around to the sermon when he or she might explain modern God concepts, all too many of the congregants are bored, busy counting ceiling tiles, or too tuned out to listen.

My goal in this book is to introduce you, in a very approachable way, to some of the God upgrades that have been introduced over the years. We will start with the early Jewish God concepts we read about in the Bible and move on to big innovators like Maimonides (1138–1204), who brought rational thought to Judaism, and Spinoza (1632–1677), who took it a step further, advocating that we throw out anything that doesn't make rational sense. Next we will explore some of the most influential modern theologians, such as Martin Buber (1878–1965), who taught that we access God through relationships, and Harold Schulweis (1925–), who teaches that God is in our actions.

My aim is not to be the ultimate source on each of these theologians (there are plenty of books by and on each of them) but rather to give you a taste of their belief systems in order to better inform you of their thoughts, and to remind you that you are part of a long line of people who have interpreted and reinterpreted our tradition to make it their own. I don't advocate throwing out meaningful history and tradition. Rather, let us build on the thousands of years of wisdom we have inherited. Let us reclaim and interpret our Judaism so that our tradition can help us make sense of our world and our lives. In this way, Judaism is far more like an iPad than a typewriter; Judaism is interactive, urging us to move beyond the limitation of typing static words on a page, to engage deeply with our narrative in myriad ways.

I will share my own theological struggles and my own God concept, one that is deeply intertwined with my relationship with nature. I'll model for you how my study of other theologians combined with the development of my personal practice has enabled me to create a God "version 2.0" that works for me. I have never given up on the belief in God, but I did need to move away from the classical definition of God presented in the Torah and the old prayer books and develop my own answer to the question "What is God?"

The act of reclaiming our religion and updating it is a very Jewish concept. I hope that this conversation will give you the vocabulary to talk about God and explore ideas that work for you. My agenda is not to convince you that my God concept is right for you, although it may be. My agenda is to help you start thinking about what God is to you. Despite what my detractors may tell you, I am not trying to start a theological revolution or dismantle Judaism as we know it. I am simply trying to remind you that it has long been the Jewish tradition to upgrade our God concepts as we learn more about the world around us.

Through learning, discussion, and debate, we can shed some of the baggage the term *God* has collected over the centuries (and it is not carry-on baggage!) and come to understand God in a way that is relevant in our modern lives.

Dr. Neil Gillman, professor emeritus of philosophy at the Conservative movement's Jewish Theological Seminary, insists that each rabbinical student should be required to develop and articulate his or her own concept of God, a study culminating in the writing of a personal theology statement. Consider this book your invitation to take part in this valuable assignment, without the anxiety of being graded by the esteemed Dr. Gillman!

Not surprisingly, once we have reclaimed the word *God* and redefined God in a manner that makes sense in our world, Judaism itself is altered; how we live as Jews and how we practice as Jews require redefinition. Once God changes, Judaism changes. In the last section of the book we will explore some of the pressing questions related to Judaism 2.0 and explore how Judaism is still relevant to our lives today.

My first book, *God in the Wilderness*, described the spiritual lessons we can learn outdoors and the unique nature-based work I do to make Judaism relevant, accessible, and meaningful. This book in some ways serves as a continuation of that book in that it addresses the question, "Why bother?" Why bother bringing Judaism up to date so that it can fit into our lives? Why bother recreating this archaic culture that has its origin in animal sacrifice and fear of a wrathful God?

This takes us back to Sadie's typewriter experience. Clearly, Sadie was quickly bored by the limited capability of a typewriter. You can't make the letters blue or pink and it doesn't read the words back to you, let alone read them to you in different languages. (And, frankly, at five years old, Sadie can't spell that many words.) But if based on her disappointing experience she tossed out the entire technology thing altogether, she would miss out on so much that makes her life fascinating, fulfilling, rewarding, and fun. So, too, we need not toss out all of Judaism simply because the God concept we hear about in the Torah doesn't resonate with our worldview. We just have to get the upgrades.

It pains me when I see Jews jettison their Judaism because they have not experienced anything beyond cookie-cutter bar or bat mitzvahs ("Today you are a man; tomorrow you go back to seventh grade"),

Federation fundraising campaigns ("I wouldn't be calling if the situation were not so dire and the need so great") or the *30-Minute Seder* (amusing and accurate but not particularly thought provoking). Judaism offers us so much more.

I should explain that my goal as a rabbi is not to keep people Jewish for the sake of maintaining Judaism. It's not to get more members for synagogues or more people to come on my Adventure Rabbi retreats or even to get Jews to marry Jews. Those outcomes may be results of the way I present Judaism, but they are not my goal. My goal as a rabbi is to keep people Jewish because I believe Judaism can make our lives better: more meaningful, fulfilling, and peaceful.

Judaism has so much to teach us about how we treat ourselves, each other, and our planet. What Judaism is about is teaching us how to build community and how to be good companions, how to cultivate our courage and our compassion, how to be content and kind. Of course, you can learn these values elsewhere. But as a people, Jews have thousands of years of experience turning this kind of stuff over and over. We've made hundreds of upgrades and have had millions of users working to debug the system. Rather than look to other sources for guidance, let us turn to our own people's past to discover what it has to say about our present and our future.

Our people used to talk about a covenant with an almighty deity. I don't think we have that kind of covenant anymore, but we do have a covenant with each other: to learn with each other, to look out for each other, and to care for each other. Judaism helps us understand what being part of that covenantal group means.

So join me on this mind adventure as we explore the changes we Jews have made to our God concept over the many centuries until we arrive at a Judaism for today—a religion that is inspirational, encouraging, and thought provoking.

Part I

THE ISSUES WITH GOD 1.0

CHAPTER 1

Looking for Lightning

If triangles had a God, God would have three sides.
YIDDISH PROVERB

The biggest stumbling block when it comes to religion is God. There, I've said it. Any lightning strikes? No? Okay. So far, so good.

What keeps people away from religion? Expensive fees? Rambling sermons? Boring religious schools? Pushy fundraisers? Inconvenient holidays? Religious zealots? None of those help, but I believe the biggest problem is God.

If you believe that God can heal the sick, mend a broken heart, or bring peace to Earth, please do us both a favor and go read a different book. This is not the book for you.

This is a book for people who equate religious services with counting how many pages are left in the service or counting windowpanes or noticing how many people are wearing the same outfit. This book is for those who are as likely to willingly join a prayer circle as to go bowling on the moon.

Often, when I am sitting in a Sabbath service at another rabbi's congregation, diligently reading the responsive prayer in sync with the other congregants, I feel like I must have missed a very crucial explanatory meeting. It feels like the congregation has reached an agreement on how to understand the God in the prayer book and I am the only one who doesn't know it. Did they all agree to say words they don't believe?

The other day we came to these words in the prayer book: "You are our God and our Shepherd; we are Your people and Your flock: If only today we would listen to Your voice."

Everyone reverently read along with the rabbi and I wanted to stop and ask someone to explain it to me.

I could imagine myself raising my hand and saying, "Excuse me, man in the third row with the blue sweater and khaki pants, do you really believe God looks out for us like a shepherd protects his flock?"

Or, "Sorry for the interruption, but woman in the fabulous red dress and black heels with the two adorable kids, do you really believe that God has a voice we can hear? Have you ever heard it?"

The rabbi would probably turn to me and say, "Jamie, it's not literally a voice like we have a voice. God doesn't have vocal cords, obviously! But as humans, our descriptions are limited to the words of our language. It's a metaphor."

I would look around at the congregation and ask, "Does everyone know that when we talk about God in the prayer book that it's a metaphor? When we praise God's 'wondrous creative power [that] filled Heaven and Earth…. Awesome and Holy God be praised!' and when we ask God to 'cause peace to reign among us,' that this is all a metaphor? Did you all agree to that when I was in the bathroom? What is the metaphor anyway?"

That might be a good cue for the rabbi to have us turn to page 97 for the silent prayer. We Jews don't like to talk about God.

"It's a metaphor" is one of the common answers I hear when I ask questions about the God concept that I read about in our prayers and other holy books. It's one of the answers that sounds really spot-on when someone, especially someone you admire or think is smart, says it. But when you think about it afterward it doesn't really tell you much, does it? Later, maybe you try to explain what was just explained to you to a thirteen-year-old, who isn't afraid to challenge you, and you suddenly realize you're not quite sure what the metaphor is.

But I don't raise my hand and the service continues along uninterrupted. We read from the prayer book, "I, the Eternal One, have called you to righteousness, and taken you by the hand, and kept you; I have made you a covenant people, a light to the nations."

No one else seems the least bit perplexed by these words, which we read week after week. I look left; I look right. Why does this make sense to everyone else but me?

Sometimes I wonder if we are all too intimidated to ask questions about God because we fear that we might be the only one in the room who doesn't "believe." The entire congregation might turn around and glaringly point to the door and tell us to leave.

If my situation sounds at all familiar to you, either about yourself or someone you know, then this is a book for you. This is a book for people who feel puzzled when a friend says, "I'll pray for you," and cringe when a politician says, "I'll pray about that," or wonder when a sports team prays for God to lead it to victory. This is a book for people who don't believe that God cares if I have a ham sandwich for lunch. (I actually had a peanut-butter sandwich for lunch in case it matters to you.)

This is also a book for people who, despite all their doubts and questions, feel an inexplicable connection to Judaism. There are many of us who don't buy into the idea that God split the Red Sea or spoke to Moses on Mt. Sinai, but still love a good Passover Seder with its discussions, debates, and matzah ball soup. How is that possible?

I can introduce you to thousands of Jewish people who don't believe God dictated the Torah to Moses and who don't believe the Torah is an accurate historical record, but are still moved to tears when we read from the Torah on the summit of a Colorado mountain. What is that about?

I propose that if we resolve the God piece so it doesn't trip us up, Judaism will become meaningful and relevant. In my work as the Adventure Rabbi, I have made it a priority to explore a different concept of God, a God that is congruent with our modern sensibilities. Where do we begin to "meet" this God?

Do you know those sudden moments of connection, where you feel linked to something bigger than yourself? Perhaps standing on top of a mountain? Sailing on a quiet lake? Talking with a dear friend? Watching the birth of your son or daughter? Touching the Torah for the first time? These are the moments in which we meet God.

If you have participated in the Adventure Rabbi Program, you have experienced the way we use the outdoors to experience God. For those of you who have not joined us yet, imagine the sense of awe that is generated by standing in a desert canyon, surrounded by towering red rock walls, and joining your voice with your community as we sing out the *Shema* (a central Jewish prayer that talks about the oneness of God). The feeling of connection in such a moment is beyond the realm of words. That, too, is God.

If we choose, these are the kind of moments that can lead us to a different, more palatable understanding of God. If we can let go of the concept of an anthropomorphic God, a God who loves us and takes care of us, a God who intervenes and interferes with us, we can discover that our lives are infused with God encounters. It is just a different kind of God. This is a God we can't describe very well, but we can experience in moments such as those I've just mentioned. This is a God of connection, a God that motivates us to action, but not a God who acts.

But of course it is not so easy. For centuries our teachers have tried to tell us that God is not a man in the sky, and yet the myth that this is what Jews believe persists. Why? Perhaps because we want it to. Perhaps because part of us is not ready to give it up. Maybe, despite our adamant insistence that we do not believe in God, we don't really want to be presented with an alternative understanding. Could it be that what we unconsciously want is to be convinced that an omnipotent God actually does exist? That way, He can swoop down here and fix the mess we have made of the world.

Cultivating an alternative understanding of God, one that builds on the wisdom of the generations who came before us yet is consistent with our modern world, takes work and the willingness to ask questions, seek answers, and wrestle with concepts. We must be willing to lay down the theology of a personal God of agency who is very easy to describe yet difficult to experience, and trade in that theology for a less tangible God concept that we can more easily experience but can describe only inadequately. It's hardly a fair trade, and I recognize that many of us are not ready to do this.

I began to write this book as a story about my personal struggle with faith, my envy of those who believe in a God that can intervene in their lives, and my resolve to find meaning in Judaism without sacrificing my rational intellect. But over the many months of research and writing, after long animated conversations with the members of the

Adventure Rabbi community, on hikes and chairlift rides, in lecture halls and classrooms, through e-mails and Facebook, the book expanded beyond my personal struggle and has come to reflect the struggle many of us face with Judaism.

Many of us feel alienated from Judaism and religion precisely because we have had it with being preached at about a God concept that makes no sense to us. We want Judaism to be part of our lives, but we are not willing to check our rational minds at the door.

I submit that if we are willing to look carefully at our Judaism and understand what works and what does not, if we are willing to upgrade our God concept to one that is aligned with our modern sensibilities, then we will be able to reclaim and modernize Judaism at every level.

Once upon a time our ancestors believed the world was flat and that demons caused strokes. But our understanding of the world around us has evolved and so, too, should our concept of God and our religion. We need not be tethered to a God concept that does not reflect the world as we know it.

It is my hope and expectation that these pages will spark conversations and controversy, so that you and I, and the people around us, will be prompted to discuss and debate, question and converse, and explore how to make Judaism relevant and meaningful for ourselves and for generations to come.

CHAPTER 2

They Taught You That in Sunday School?

It is a miracle that curiosity survives formal education.
ALBERT EINSTEIN

Although this is not a parenting book or a book geared for teachers, I would like to share with you a little about what I have learned about God when confronted by my daughters' and students' questions about God. Interactions with children have an incredible capacity to force us to own up to what we truly believe.

There is an odd hypocrisy in the world of Jewish professionals. Behind closed doors, many (although certainly not all) of the Jewish professionals I know do not believe that there is a God in the sky who keeps an eye on us, rewarding good and punishing bad. In a recent Harris poll, only 9 percent of American Jews claimed to believe in a God who makes things happen in the world.[1] Yet, in many classrooms this is what we continue to teach our children.

I frequently visit communities and lecture on my innovative approach to Judaism. In preparing to write this book, I invited audiences to share their questions about God. Adults consistently ask questions such as "Does God hear our prayers?" and "How could God let the

Holocaust happen?" and "Does healing prayer work?" and "Whose prayers does God decide to answer?"

I am accustomed to adults struggling with the idea that God can come down here and intervene with our lives, so their questions rarely surprise me. But children's questions continue to shock me. You see, I errantly expected that with so much adult ambivalence about this God in the sky who watches us and records our deeds like a Jewish Santa Claus, we would teach something different to our children. Apparently, I was mistaken.

One particular talk stands out. The audience was mostly adults but some inquisitive children had accompanied their parents. I was stunned by the words of two bar mitzvah students, one from California and the other from Colorado.

The first boy said, "My Sunday school teacher taught us that God is everywhere and sees everything. That means God is watching me while I am showering and that kind of gives me the creeps."

The second student shared, "My Sunday school teacher told us that God is always watching us and knows everything we do. She said God is like those cameras on top of traffic lights, catching you at every moment. But what I want to know is why doesn't God ever send us speeding tickets?"

Both of these students attend well-run, highly regarded religious schools. How is it possible that we continue to teach students a theology like that? Yet so it is. A religious school textbook still advertised in 2010 as "the consummate Confirmation course for the religious school" teaches: "God is all-powerful. He can do anything He chooses and nothing can prevent Him from so doing…. God knows all."[2]

Eventually, these kids will realize that the anthropomorphic theology they have been handed doesn't make rational sense and is contradicted by what they experience in the world. Will they have the tools to create a new theology for themselves? Or will they simply toss the God idea in the trash and Judaism right along with it?

Why *are* we teaching this God concept to our children? Part of the reason is that we adults don't know what we believe. If we Jewish professionals and parents are not clear in our own God concepts, how can we expect to teach our students and children about God?

Add to our lack of clarity the exhaustion and frustration that are all too often part of teaching and parenthood and you have a teaching moment disaster in the making.

When my daughter Sadie was about three years old, the lightbulb above the washer and dryer blew out. It was late at night and already well past her bedtime, which meant it was past my bedtime because I go to bed very early. But there was a little problem in our nighttime routine. I had washed Sadie's favorite blue flannel sheets with the little sheep and clouds on them, and she insisted that she could not possibly fall asleep on the blue-and-white checkered sheets that were now on her bed. After I tried to compensate for her loss by reading two extra Maisy stories by Lucy Cousins, getting her a glass of cold water, putting more ice in the glass of water, and putting more stuffed animals in her bed, I relented and we trooped to the laundry room to get the little sheep and cloud sheets out of the dryer so she would go to sleep.

I pulled the cord dangling from the light fixture and felt that satisfying click, but the light did not come on. Standing in the dark room, Sadie asked me, "Mama, who broke the light?"

"Nobody broke it," I answered. "It just broke."

As a three-year-old will, she asked again, "Mama, who broke the light?"

"Nobody," I answered. "It just broke."

Again she asked, "Mama, who broke the light?" And as I pulled the sheets out of the dryer, she continued to ask the same question, with the same exact wording, and the same exact tone, because that is what three-year-olds do when the answer they are given makes no sense to them.

I tried to explain electricity as best I could to her, but the truth is that I am not really sure how electricity works. Something about pulses through a wire and a vacuum in the bulb and then the light goes on. Predictably, with each attempt to answer the now very grating refrain, "Mama, who broke the light?" I became less and less clear and more and more frustrated.

At the exact moment my handsome husband Jeff walked into the room, finally, in exasperation I said, "God broke the lightbulb because He was mad at it."

"Who is God, Mama?" she asked

"Can we talk about it in the morning?" I said.

Completely shocked, my husband asked me, "What are you teaching our child?!?!" Then he rescued me with, "Honey, why don't you go ahead and go to sleep and I'll put Sadie to bed."

Now this was a bad parenting moment in a lot of ways. Mainly this statement is so contrary to my theology that it is comical that such words would come out of my mouth. It is exactly what I do not want our daughter to learn. The last thing I want Sadie to think is that God comes down here and breaks people's lightbulbs, or their hearts, or their bodies, or their lives. I certainly don't want her to think God is this powerful force that gets angry at people and makes bad things happen to them.

For weeks afterward, Sadie asked me, "Mama, who is God?" I tried to answer the best I could in language a three-year-old could understand. I tried, "You know that special feeling of connection between you and Bubbe? That feeling is God." Or, "You know how happy you feel when your favorite nanny, Tara, comes over? That special feeling is God." Or, "You know how much you love when we sing our Shabbos songs and we're all together as a family? That feeling is God."

But the explanations all fell short and so the question continued: "Mama, who is God?"

I've learned a few things in this process. First, I now completely and utterly understand how people came up with an all-powerful God who makes things happen on Earth. How else do you explain things that happen when you don't understand them? How do you explain thunder and rain if you don't have the Weather Channel to tell you about high-pressure and low-pressure systems? How do you explain drought or premature death or any other unexpected occurrence? It's convincing and believably simple to say, "Our crops failed because God was displeased with us. We must try to please God."

It certainly was easier to say to Sadie, "God broke the lightbulb because He was mad" than to explain the truth, which made no sense to her. And now the next time Sadie doesn't want to go to bed I can simply say, "Remember what God did to the lightbulb? You don't want to make God angry, now do you?" (But of course, I am not going to do that.)

The second thing I learned is that we can't explain anything well if we don't understand it fully ourselves. Electricity has been explained to me countless times. But I still don't get it. If explaining electricity is an intellectual challenge, then no wonder it is hard to explain God. Explaining to a three-year-old means you have to understand something fully enough to be able to translate it into her terms.

God concepts are something I think about more than most people, and yet when the question came, I had no simple response. I realized that it was time for me to struggle with it for a bit, to turn it over and over, until I could really explain what I thought to a three-year-old or, equally challenging, to a twelve-year-old bar mitzvah student.

Enter Zachary. Shortly after the lightbulb incident, I fielded a call from an exasperated Jewish educator at a neighboring synagogue. "We've tried everything with this bar mitzvah student," she said. "His Hebrew is great but he refuses to say the prayers. He doesn't want to read from the Torah. He says he doesn't believe in God and our rabbi can't seem to make it make sense to him. Would you please take him into your bar mitzvah program?"

A week later, I sat in my office with Zachary and his demoralized mother, Denise. "I've been planning his bar mitzvah since his bris," Denise said. "Now he says if I want him to have a bar mitzvah at that synagogue, I'll have to tie him to a chair and drag him in. We did everything we were supposed to, so what went wrong? Should I force him, or let it go? I don't know what to do."

Zachary had no ambiguity, no doubt, about where he stood. "I won't say, 'Baruch atah, Adonai, Eloheinu melech ha'olam, Blessed are You, my Lord, King of the Universe.' God isn't the king of the universe. God didn't create the heavens and the earth. The Big Bang did that," he said.

He continued adamantly, "There is no God listening to our prayers or commanding us to do things like light the candles. God doesn't bring forth bread from the earth. These blessings are absurd, and I am not going to read from the Torah, which tells all those far-fetched stories that sound like ancient mythology."

Finally, "I'm not going to be a hypocrite and stand on the bimah and say all that nonsense just to make my parents proud."

Despite years of Jewish education, Jewish Community Center preschool, weekly religious school at an excellent religious school, and a father on the board of directors of their synagogue, his rabbis, teachers, and parents had failed to present Zachary with a God concept that made any sense to this inquisitive, rational twelve-year-old mind.

"Now this is a kid I'd like to work with," I thought to myself. So I borrowed a favorite old rabbinic phrase and said to Zachary, "What if I told you that the God you don't believe in, I don't believe in Him either?"

To prepare myself for my conversations with Zachary, and for the many inquisitive students (both adult and b'nei mitzvah) who followed him, I returned to studying the writings of the theologians I had learned about in seminary. Before I started outright rejecting what I thought was standard Jewish theology, I owed it to our people to delve a bit deeper into what others have suggested about God. After all, I'm not the first to ask these types of questions. I follow a rich tradition of scholars who have wrestled with God concepts.

I discovered that although none of the theologians fully satisfied my existential itch, pieces that each of them offered worked for me and have contributed to my ability to build a belief foundation and ritual structure on which I can stand comfortably and with integrity in my Judaism. Thus began a year of study with Zachary, unpacking the purpose of prayer, the power of community, and the heart of Judaism as I know it. We reexamined the juvenile concept of God he had been taught in Sunday school and explored an evolving concept of God that was congruent with his (and my) rational worldview. When Zachary finally stood in front of his community, the words he spoke were sincere, relevant, and meaningful.

CHAPTER 3

God Envy

I find your lack of faith disturbing.
DARTH VADER

I realize this next thought will probably cause some people to unfriend me on Facebook, but I may as well be blunt. I don't think God is listening to our prayers, nor do I think God commanded us to leave the Swiss cheese off our burgers, and I don't think God asked us to pray three times a day, to wear yarmulkes on our heads, or to cover our mirrors when people we love die.

I will confess that I am envious of people who do believe in that type of personal God, a God who cares about us and reacts to our actions and behaviors. I have a serious case of God envy. How I wish that I believed in that God!

But I believe the planets and stars were created by the Big Bang, not by some omnipotent, omniscient force called God in six admirably efficient days. I don't think that if we pray to God, we will be healed any more than I think I can pray to God for good book sales. (Although I might try. It never hurts!)

Herein lies the contradiction. Did I mention that I am an ordained rabbi? That I am a religious person who never fails to begin the Sabbath by lighting the candles, and always says good-bye to it with the prescribed pungent scents, sweet wine, and braided candle of Havdalah (the ceremony ending the Sabbath)?

Every nook and cranny of my life is infused with Jewish teachings, law, ethics, customs, history, ritual, and, yes, prayer. Yet I completely understand Zachary's aversion to Torah stories, prayer, and "rabbi-speak." How do I make that work?

Frequently, at conferences, services, and classes, while we are praying, studying text, or listening to a *D'var Torah* (speech on a section of the Torah), I find myself whispering under my breath, "Do they really believe that?" My handsome husband likes to respond, "Yes, Rabbi!" with the emphasis on "rabbi." The irony and perhaps the contradiction between my belief and my career confront me in the oddest of places. My office floor was one of the more unusual places to elicit introspection.

Remember when your sixth-grade teacher told you (and told you for the last time!) not to tip back in your chair? Well, it turns out that was pretty good advice, because last winter, I fell back in my office chair, elegantly catching myself with my right hand and tearing two ligaments and the triangular fibrocartilage complex in my wrist. For the record, I was not tilting back in my chair. I was rolling backward when it tipped over. My backward trajectory was caused by a caster catching on the uneven carpet, propelling me backward onto my office floor. I lay there for a moment, staring at the ceiling and taking an inventory of my body parts and knowing that all was not well.

A month later I finally admitted that my wrist was not going to heal itself. My doctor referred me to an acclaimed hand and wrist surgeon. Soon I was sitting across the examination table from him, surrounded by diagrams, charts, my MRI results, and a plethora of sketches of my hand and wrist bones from a multitude of angles, through which he wished to convey the magnitude of my injury.

We scheduled my surgery for ten days later, just after I was to lead the Adventure Rabbi spiritual skiing retreat, a weekend of skiing and learning. I had to laugh when my surgeon gave me these instructions, "You can ski, but don't fall. On second thought, you're getting surgery anyway. I'll fix whatever damage you inflict."

Later that day a friend e-mailed suggesting that before I agreed to surgery, I should see the kabbalistic healer who had changed his life. "Thanks," I e-mailed back, knowing I would never even look into it.

Then it hit me. Why wouldn't I see his mystical healer? Why? Because I—a rabbi, a religious person who would never dream of working on Yom Kippur—was not a believer. At least not a believer in a God that will heal my hand. I am a believer in finding a good surgeon.

I like religion staying firmly ensconced in its own domain. I do not feel that religion or God has much of a place in the healing of my torn cartilage and severed ligaments. Sure, I won't say "no" if you want to say the prescribed prayers for my rapid healing and complete recovery, but really I would prefer if you would drop off a big macaroni-and-cheese casserole at the house, so my kids have something to eat while I am recovering and can't cook. When I told my husband the story about not wanting to see the Jewish mystical healer, he declared my fall from faith complete.

My surgery went well and my wrist healed almost completely. Recovery is always a slow process marked by milestones, and mine was no different. I exulted when I could finally twist open a jar by myself, lift a tea mug, and type with both hands. One moment that stands out was the first Shabbat after the bandages came off my wrist. We always bless our children, Sadie and Ori, on Shabbat, and that week I savored the feeling of placing my hands on their heads to bless them, without a bulky dressing beneath my palm.

Oh, the tenderness of blessing my children before the Shabbos meal! I love to feel Sadie's soft hair beneath my hands and the warmth of Ori's little face close to mine. Whatever disquiet the week brings—perhaps a looming deadline, a disagreement with a friend, or words Sadie picked up from playground playmates—when I place my hands on their heads, all the week's worries are pushed out of my world, if only for a moment.

I held my daughters close. As always happens during this moment, I was flooded with good thoughts—hopeful thoughts of who they are and who they may become, of all their world could and might be.

I prayed as I do every week, with all my heart, for God to protect them, to be with them, and to grant them lives filled with peace.

I chanted the ancient formula, "*Yevarechecha Adonai v'yeshmarecha.*"

My husband recited the English, "May God bless you and keep you."

Our voices alternated, "*Ya'er Adonai panav elecha veyichunechah.*"

"May God's countenance shine upon you and be with you."

"*Yisa Adonai panav elecha veyasem lecha shalom.*"

"May God be with you wherever you journey and may God bless you with the greatest of all blessings, the blessing of peace."

As I do every week, I meant it. I sent every word of this plea, petition, and supplication sincerely from my mouth to God's ears. But of course, I don't think God has ears and I don't believe God is listening to me. So what is this moment about? One of the most powerful moments of my week is infused with a deeply rooted, heartfelt prayer to the Almighty, a prayer I don't believe will be heard. What am I doing?

In part, my prayer is wishful thinking—wishful praying. Oh, how I do wish I believed that God could heal my wrist, bring peace to the Middle East, and keep my daughters safe when they cross the street. I envy people who have that relationship with God.

My friend Janet does. She understands God. "You see," she explains, "God is like a parent who gives us what we need. Even if we can't quite see the whole picture, God can." Janet has serenity in her life because she knows that even what appears to be a catastrophe is really God's way of guiding her where she needs to go. In her view, nothing is ever truly bad because when God's ultimate plan is revealed, we will discover that what we thought was bad actually enabled the good to happen. When I listen to her, I am reminded of those who believe the Holocaust was a necessary part of God's plan to create the State of Israel.

I'm willing to see the silver lining in the cloudy day and to make lemonade when life gives me lemons. But I don't think bad things have to happen in order for us to see the silver lining or drink the lemonade. I think bad things just happen because they happen. Period.

How I wish I could buy into the common words of comfort, "Things always work out for the best." But I can't. Sometimes bad things happen and it's just bad. Our job is to deal with it, not to use God to excuse or explain the situation.

When I officiated at the funeral for an eleven-month-old baby, I felt sick to my stomach when the boy's aunt eulogized that God needed him more than we did. I had to stop myself from jumping into a side conversation to disagree with a guest I overheard saying that God was sparing the baby future pain by taking him now. There was nothing good about that tragic situation.

These are all the kinds of explanations that give my friend Janet so much comfort. She deals with such tragedies with composure because she is confident that it is all part of God's great plan. I envy the certitude and serenity that accompany her unwavering faith.

Janet lovingly calls me the "heretic rabbi" and likes to tease me that the seminary faculty must have been distracted the day they ordained me as a rabbi. When I am not busy teasing her in return, I envy her faith. How comforting to go through life knowing that everything happens for a reason.

My friend Andrew also has a personal relationship with God. "God tests us," he explains to me. "God lets us struggle just to make sure we keep the faith. But if we do right by God, God will do right by us." Andrew points out passages from the Torah and the prayer book that explain in detail our responsibilities toward God. He reminds me, "When we fulfill our obligations to God, we are rewarded with abundant crops, good health, and long life."

I don't dare tell Andrew that I think that sounds like a juvenile way to be a god. He would be mortified. But to me, his god sounds like my fickle junior high school classmate who was my best friend one week because I helped her do her hair, but then hated me the next week because Richard asked me out instead of her.

Or maybe I pray like this just in case they are right and I am wrong. Sometimes I think God really *is* listening. I like to think God is amused by my lack of faith. I imagine that God shakes His head and laughs when He hears me ranting about His lack of ears. He says, "Okay, Jamie-the-Doubting-Rabbi. You go ahead and doubt, but just keep bringing people back to Judaism like you're doing." (On the other hand, if God is not laughing, I might really be in trouble when I get to the other side.)

I'll admit I've been known to take some things as a sign of God's approval. Last year on Yom Kippur, I risked trying something new with my community. On the holiest night of the year, at the holiest moment, the chanting of *Kol Nidre*, I dared to experiment with tradition. Controversy was in the making. Usually the rabbi calls the congregation's president to come forward to hold the Torah in front of the congregation while the cantor chants *Kol Nidre*. Instead, I handed out flashlights and led my group of more than two hundred people outside into the dark, cold Colorado night, where we made a circle beneath the star-filled sky. I then unrolled two Torahs (something that is never done on Yom Kippur evening) and asked everyone to hold the scrolls (also something that is not done on Yom Kippur). "It's your Torah," I said. "Come claim it. Hold your Torah."

Menstruating women, non-Jews, and all sorts of people forbidden to touch the Torah held it that holiest of nights. There were no lightning strikes.

The sound of the rushing stream accompanied the piercing chant of *Kol Nidre*. As if two hundred people standing shoulder to shoulder, holding their Torah, many for the first time, beneath the stars, beside a roaring river wasn't spiritually elevating enough, just as we reached the climax of *Kol Nidre*, a fox bolted through the center of our circle!

I was only 85 percent joking when I remarked that the fox was God's sign of approval of our innovative service.

Here is the real reason I bless my children each Friday night. Even though I don't think God has anything to do with the well-being of my children (much to my chagrin), the ritual of blessing them remains powerful. Placing my hands on their heads, hearing my voice mingle with my husband's voice, saying those ancient words spoken by Jewish parents for generation upon generation, and repeating that ritual week after week after week without pause—that alone is remarkably potent.

For my children, here is a moment when they are assured of my full attention and reminded of my deep devotion. The ancient words flow into their souls, strengthening the bonds between us and with their Jewish tradition.

The words carry trace memories of all the people who have said them before me and all the past weeks that I have said them myself. With each added recitation, I am reminded and emboldened. I am reminded of my commitment to care for my children. I am emboldened to continue to be a good mother, despite the frustrations and self-doubt that are a normal part of parenting. These are the connections—to my children and to all the parents who have said these words before me—that I invoke with these sacred words.

In weighty Jewish theological terms, you might say that blessing my children is part of reminding myself and recommitting myself to the Jewish covenant. Some theologians, such as Eugene Borowitz (one of the great theologians of our time), insist that you can't have a Jewish theology without a covenant. What is a covenant? The original Jewish covenant was made between God and the Jewish People. The deal was that we promised to keep His commandments, and He (because He was a He to the people who bought into this theology) promised to keep us safe, fed, and watered.

I don't know about you, but when I think of the word *covenant*, I think of the dreaded homeowner's association covenant at my old condo, which mandated my grass could not be more than three inches high and that I could only paint my house one of three authorized shades of beige. Oh, mourn the deterioration of the covenant from a sacred relationship between a deity and His people to a neighborhood pact that supposedly creates community but seems to generate contention and matching beige houses. (Hmmm, maybe that *does* sound like the God 1.0 concept that keeps many of us away from synagogue, causes contention, and gives us beige Sabbath services.)

But the concept of covenant and its essence as a sacred agreement may in fact be part of what makes blessing my children something more powerful than just putting my hands on their heads and reading a poem. I do not have a covenant with an all-powerful deity. But I do have a covenant with my religion and God as I understand God (more on that later). My covenant also has a give and take. I agree to live responsibly and ethically in relationship with my family, the Jewish People, and the planet. Judaism, with its time-tested rituals and teachings, agrees to help me navigate life in a way that is purposeful and meaningful.

This is but one example—and we will explore more—of how Judaism can remain meaningful to you even if you do not believe God makes prayers come true. To be clear, I am not going to suggest we jettison the concept of God completely, because among other problems, that would make this a very short book. But by upgrading our God concept to one that is aligned with our modern sensibilities, we reclaim and modernize Judaism at every level.

We can come to understand God in a way that makes sense to us and does not conflict with our rational understanding of the world. Once we learn how to decouple the concept of an all-powerful, all-knowing God from religion, we will suddenly discover that Judaism is an amazing, potent, dignified, delightful, and meaningful religion.

Part II

UPGRADES THROUGH THE CENTURIES

CHAPTER 4

God 1.0

When the World Was Flat, God Had It Easy

I do not feel obliged to believe that the same God who has endowed us with sense, reason, and intellect has intended us to forgo their use.

GALILEO

Maybe our relationship with God could have remained simple if Ferdinand Magellan had simply sailed off the end of the Earth as he was supposed to.

When the world was flat, God had it easy. God would wake up just before sunrise, put a pot of coffee on to brew, and then get the sun started rising through the sky. Next, He would take down the moon and stars and tuck them away until He needed them again the next night.

God would then pour a nice big mug of coffee. (Organic, shade-grown, of course. God has always advocated protecting the Earth.) God would sit down in His favorite celestial easy chair and read the newspaper. He needed to keep up with all the goings-on down on Earth, but back when the world was flat there were not so many people, so it didn't take very long.

God had given the people an instruction book, so they knew what was expected of them. He liked to call it the Good Book because it taught them how to be good. If the people obeyed the rules, God gave them rain in its season, so their crops would grow. But when they did not obey the rules there was pestilence, drought, blight, barrenness, and a whole host of wrathful retributions. (See Deuteronomy 11:11–17.)

But when Magellan proved the Earth was spherical by sailing around it, all sorts of things fell apart between us and God.

Soon after that discovery, Galileo came along to tell us that the Earth was not the center of the universe. Now, God was no longer in charge of getting the sun up into the sky because the Earth's eastward rotation took on responsibility for the sunrise and sunset.

On the heels of that cosmic disruption, Darwin declared we were descended from apes, not created on day six. Then, before you could say, "Monkey see, monkey do," Freud deduced that human behavior was simply an unconscious manifestation of the subconscious mind.

Before a person had time to ask, "Mother, may I?" all sorts of things that used to be the domain of God were outsourced to science.

Soon drought and the withering crops it caused were due to climatic fluctuation, not sin. Strokes were due to blood clots, not demons. Other illnesses were caused by microbes and genetic mutation, rather than by not fasting on Yom Kippur. Comets were not harbingers of God's wrath but rather dust and ice careening through the solar system. Ice storms were created by a layer of warm air being trapped between two layers of cold air, rather than by forgetting to pray after meals. The common cold was inflicted by touching infected shopping cart handles, but maybe that was always the case.

Once science moved in, there was little left for God to do, so He packed up and moved south to Florida. There He bought a condo in Century Village and now He spends His days playing golf and catching early-bird dinner specials. Sometimes He takes half His portion home to have for lunch the next day. It's a lot of work to cook for One.

Science and technology have in many ways dethroned God as the Creator and Ruler of the universe. In our society, awe has been replaced by rationalism. We look to science and technology, rather than God, to repair our lives and mend our hearts. Prozac has replaced prayer. Medicine has replaced *Misheberach* (the Jewish prayer for healing). Social networking has replaced synagogue communities. Search engines have replaced Talmudic inquiries.

Disappointingly, technology and science have turned out to be false gods. Our technological advances have solved many dilemmas, but, much to our mortification, they have also caused others, such as climate change, pollution, and deforestation, to name just a few.

How about those great tools, which some of us (i.e., me) rely on so heavily: Facebook, Tweeting, texting? These innovations were designed to connect us, creating easily accessible virtual communities that could diminish our need for physical community (one of the main reasons people seek out religion). But do they connect us or separate us as we wear out our thumbs texting to avoid talking face to face?

It turns out that as wonderful as science and technology are, they cannot solve all our woes. Neither can they provide us with a road map for life. They cannot teach us values or priorities, give us direction, or help us make good choices. They cannot bring meaning to our existence. This, then, is still the task of religion.

Interestingly, for many decades Jews celebrated assimilating into mainstream culture and becoming secularized. Families with names like Skolnick, Schwartzstein, and Sarnotsky readily changed their names to Smith, Stewart, and Sloan, moved out of the Jewish parts of town, and perhaps even joined the country club. But after a few decades masquerading as goyim (non-Jews), we collectively realized that the secular world did not answer the essential question of life, the questions of identity—who we are, what is expected of us, and how we should be in the world.

Today, many intelligent, successful, worldly adults are still trying to find the answers to life's persistent questions and are willing to give Judaism, the rejected religion of their childhood, another look. And for good reason—our collective history, wisdom, and culture have a lot to say about such questions. Those who are fortunate enough to have access to thoughtful, creative communities will find their curiosity nurtured and they will join an exciting Jewish "thought renaissance" that is emerging in pockets around the country. But those who do not may not fare as well. Regrettably, if they start their forays into Judaism by looking at the Torah without a skilled interpreter, they might not be so excited about the God concept they find there.

CHAPTER 5

God 1.1

Therapist with Superpowers

It is the theory that decides what we can observe.
ALBERT EINSTEIN

The theology of the Bible appears very straightforward. If you obey God's commandments, all will be well with you; if you disobey God's commandments, you had best buckle up because you are in for a turbulent ride.

In the Bible it appears that the ancient Israelites, eking out a living on their rocky terraced gardens, believed quality of life was dictated by this simple equation: Good Deeds – Bad Deeds = Quality of Life.

I love the simplicity of this worldview. How comforting it must have been to know that you would get *only* what you had coming to you. At least when times were tough, you could take solace in knowing that your own deeds were the cause of your pain and suffering.

Unfortunately, the equation doesn't seem to work anymore. We need only click on CNN.com to see the tragedy that befalls good and righteous people. Our hearts break as we see homes swept away in floods and watch buildings crumble as an earthquake trembles.

We live in a culture that often teaches us the exact opposite: that dishonesty and deception bring rewards and riches, despite what we may tell our children. We see athletes lying about steroid use and still being lauded as heroes. We see CEOs deceiving customers and shareholders and being paid millions of dollars in bonuses.

My favorite high school teacher, Judy Cook (may her memory be a blessing), tried to counter this trend. One of her few classrooms rules was, "Take responsibility for your actions and be prepared to deal with the consequences." As far as I can see, our CEOs, bankers, and politicians have demonstrated that our culture rewards those who avoid responsibility for their actions. They take risks, and if they succeed they reap the rewards; if they fail, we bear the cost of their mistakes. I certainly don't see much evidence that God holds us accountable for our behavior.

When we read the Bible, this formula—Good Deeds – Bad Deeds = Quality of Life—is clearly articulated time and time again. How did the ancients develop this viewpoint, which is so very different from our own?

One of the fascinating facets of the Bible is how much God's role seems to change from chapter to chapter and even verse to verse. We might assume that Judaism has fixed ideas about important things (such as God, for example), but in actuality our beliefs have changed through the years. Ours is a very fluid religion.

In the book of Genesis, God is like a therapist, but better. Not only can He give good advice but He also has superpowers to make things come to fruition. When the patriarch Abraham is seventy-five, God counsels him to stop living in his dad's home and under his influence, saying, "Go! Go forth!" (Genesis 12:1), as if to say, "Abe, don't you think it's time that you grow up and strike out on your own? Your father has died. You can't live in his house forever. Go see the world. Do something with your life! Become the patriarch of a new religion, or maybe even three religions."

Later, God counsels Abraham not to worry about his son Ishmael's future. However, God doesn't merely dole out emotional support and guidance like a therapist would. There is none of the normal therapist banter, "It's just a stage," and "All teenagers go through this," and "Just respect who he is and show him love."

Instead, God reaches down the divine big hand and fixes the problem (a therapist no-no) by promising to make Ishmael's descendants into a great nation, and the cool thing is that God can do that. Talk about assuaging a parent's anxiety! I'd love a therapist like that. To top it off, God never says, "Well, our time is about up. You made great progress today. See you next week. That will be $200."

By the time we get to the book of Exodus, God's role changes dramatically. Why? Because we change. In the Egypt- and Sinai-based narratives of the book of Exodus, the Israelites grow from a family into a nation. The family began with Joseph and his brothers, Abraham's great-grandsons. We read in the Passover Haggadah (a special prayer book used at the Passover Seder) that the brothers migrated to Egypt to survive the famine caused by a drought. During their time in Egypt, "the Israelites were fertile and prolific; they multiplied and increased very greatly, so the land was filled with them" (Exodus 1:7). When they left four hundred years later, they were poised to become a nation.

Think about that for a moment. This is a big change. For example, recall what it takes to get your family packed and into the car for vacation, and then imagine what it takes to get 600,000 people packed for a forty-year GPS-free trek across the wilderness.

Nations need rules by which to live and rituals to bring them together. Now that they were becoming a nation, their relationship with God had to change. God transforms into the Giver of the Law and becomes the focus of ritual. God becomes what we need God to be.

God's role vis-à-vis humanity continues to change throughout the Bible as our needs changed. Likewise, our understanding of God continues to change through time as we learn more about the world and ourselves.

What strikes me as odd is the absence of God between these two eras, between the intimate God the therapist, and the God who directs the nation. What is God doing between the death of Joseph (end of therapist era) when the book of Genesis ends, and the arrival of Moses at the beginning of the book of Exodus (beginning of lawgiver era)?

According to Exodus 12:40, the Israelites were in Egypt for 430 years: "Now the sojourning of the children of Israel, who dwelt in Egypt, was 430 years." My friend Michael irreverently jokes that during this time God was scouring the desert in search of a telephone booth in which to change identities.

What was God doing all this time? One of the first things you will no doubt notice is that God didn't seem to help with the farming. (Okay, maybe it's not the first thing you notice, but now that I point it out, it is odd, isn't it?) The God of the later Bible stories is so intricately involved in farming, especially the rain needed for agriculture, that it seems like a dereliction of duties.

Now I could understand this if God had other things on His godly to-do list, like freeing the slaves, but for most of the Israelites' years down in Egypt, God didn't seem to be doing that either. So what was He doing? It occurred to me, maybe the Israelites didn't need help with the gardening! The Bible tells us that "the Israelites were groaning under the bondage and cried out" for God to free them (Exodus 2:23). But during all those weary, difficult years in Egypt, they never seemed to pray for rain for their gardens.

Life in Egypt was tough in many ways. (Okay, saying life in Egypt was tough is sort of like saying the Nile in its flood stage is damp.) But at least in Egypt you could count on the Nile to water your little vegetable plot behind your hut. They were slaves, but they were slaves with cucumbers and melons (Numbers 11:4). Let's be fair about the situation.

The Egyptians prayed to their God Hapi to bring the correct level of flooding to the Nile each year so that it would bring fertility to the land. If the flood was too low, it left meager amounts of silt, resulting in poor crops and famine; if the flood was too high, the powerful force of the water could sweep away their homes. While the Egyptians used prayer to try to get the flood just to the sweet spot, Joseph, a nice Jewish boy with a trendsetting coat of many colors, used another technique. He advised the Pharaoh to deal with the variable flood levels and subsequent variable harvests by going into the warehousing business. Rather than praying to God, he counseled filling storehouses with grain during the seven years of plenty so they would have ample grain to distribute during the seven years of famine. Now, doesn't that sound like a solid Jewish theology? It does to me. Don't wait for God to fix it; do it yourself! I call this the Home Depot theology. (An interesting note: Home Depot was founded by another nice Jewish boy, Bernard "Bernie" Marcus, who, like Joseph, came from an immigrant family.)

There is a great joke that reminds me that Joseph's technique is still culturally accurate today. A Buddhist monk, a Christian priest, and a Jewish rabbi are meeting together in an interfaith chapel when the lights go out. The monk takes the opportunity to teach the others about the importance of meditation as a pathway to finding our inner light.

The priest follows with words about the power of Jesus to illuminate our path. The rabbi goes and gets a flashlight.

Even in biblical times, our ancestors seemed to be developing a vague awareness that God wasn't going to fix all their problems. They began to realize what we know today—that prayer is not enough—that it was incumbent upon them to take control of their lives. But this concept was still in its infancy. In the bulk of the biblical stories, as we will explore in the next chapter, God remains the potent force for change, upon which the Israelites relied.

CHAPTER 6

God 1.2

On the Farm with God

In the middle of difficulty lies opportunity.
ALBERT EINSTEIN

When the Israelites first came into the Promised Land, it was just a vast desert with unreliable rain patterns. There was no towering Temple, no orchards overflowing with oranges. It must have been tough being a farmer in ancient Israel. The water sources were more random and unpredictable than they were in Egypt. Can you imagine farming the dry desert expanse without sprinklers or greenhouses? Of course I suppose there were the rivers flowing with milk and honey, but I've never known milk or honey to be very helpful for watering crops.

Natural springs were hard to come by, so the Israelites became dependent on the sparse rainfall. Talk about high-risk, stressful farming! If the autumn rains came too late, it was difficult to plow the sunbaked land and sow the seeds. If the spring rains came too late, the cereal crops could not mature, and if the spring rains fell during the harvest, the moisture would destroy the barley. No wonder Jewish mothers, to this very day, urge their sons to go into medicine!

Fortunately, the Israelites figured out how to control those unpredictable rains. I'm not talking about drip irrigation, although it was two Israelis—Simcha Blass and his son Yeshayahu Blass—who invented drip irrigation in 1959. Nor did the ancient Israelites figure out how to seed clouds to make it rain. Life was much simpler back then and much less technological.

In those days, or at least how it looks from the Bible, if you stayed on God's good side, God made it rain. Conversely, if you made God angry, God closed up the clouds. If God was happy, you had plenty. Slide out of God's favor and you had a famine on your hands. I do love simplicity, don't you?

Isn't it interesting that this is the God concept that evolved in this extreme environment? It was in the rocky, terraced hillsides of ancient Israel that the idea that our behavior affects how God intervenes in our everyday lives began to take hold. Of course, in the past God stepped in now and then, sometimes in big ways (creating the world and parting the sea) and sometimes in little ways (lighting bushes on fire and turning people into salt pillars). But it is at this transition in our history, when we became farmers in the desert and dependent on seemingly random rainfall for our survival, that we as a nation connected our everyday behavior to God's everyday response—in this case, to God delivering rain. It makes sense if you look at the world through the ancients' eyes.

Today, if you and I wanted to figure out what caused a drought in Israel, we would Google "cause drought Israel," and we might be directed to an article about climate change or a shift in the jet stream.

How do we react to bad weather? I recently took my annual ski trip with thirty rabbis, and this year instead of floating through knee-deep powder, we were scraping over stumps and gouging our skis on rocks! Did it cross my mind that the terrible snow conditions might be due to a lack of sincere prayers by my esteemed colleagues and myself? No, I blamed it on a high-pressure system hovering in our area.

But the ancient Israelites, for whom even the *Farmer's Almanac* would have been a technological advancement, had to turn to other sources for explanation of their world's problems. "Why did the spring rains not fall?" "Why did she have a baby and not me?" "Why isn't there good snow for my ski trip?" (Okay, maybe they didn't ask that one.) "Why me?" So they turned to their version of Google, the recepta-cle of all knowledge: the Bible. When they entered "cause drought Israel," the answer came back:

> If you shall listen diligently to my commandments which I com-mand you this day, to love the Lord your God, and to serve Him with all your heart and with all your soul, then I will give the rain of your land in its season, the early [autumn] rain and the late [spring] rain, that you may gather in your grain, and your new wine, and your oil. I will give grass in your fields for your cattle, and you shall eat and be full. Take heed to yourselves, lest your heart be deceived, and you turn aside, and serve other gods, and worship them; and the anger of the Lord will be kindled against you, and He will shut up the sky, so that there shall be no rain, and the land shall not yield its fruit; and you shall perish quickly from off the good land which the Lord gives you.
>
> DEUTERONOMY 11:13–17

The belief that fulfilling God's commandments resulted in reward while ignoring them invoked punishment was a core tenet of the early versions of Judaism. The concept was so strongly integrated into early Judaism that it has retained its place in Judaism throughout history. Even today, traditional Jews recite these lines as part of the *Shema* prayer twice a day. If you have a mezuzah (a case containing a small parchment scroll) on your door, guess what verses are inside? These same verses are also on the scrolls inside tefillin (small boxes worn by some people on the head and left arm during prayer).

But even in those days the Jews must have been sharp enough to observe that the equation Good Deeds – Bad Deeds = Quality of Life didn't always work. What did they think when they obeyed all of God's commandments and still the rain did not come? At this juncture, we can see the introduction of another concept, demonstrating our contin-uing tradition of adjusting and amending our belief system so that it corresponds to reality. Here comes the afterlife!

CHAPTER 7

God 1.3

Discovery of the Afterlife

If people are good only because they fear punishment,
and hope for reward, then we are a sorry lot indeed.

ALBERT EINSTEIN

Rabbi, what does Judaism teach us happens when we die? Buddhists get reincarnated, Christians go to Heaven or Hell, but what about us? What are we supposed to believe?"

Ask ten Jews what happens when we die and you may get ten different answers.

Mr. Freidman, an Orthodox man I met in hospice, was certain he was going to Heaven to study Torah with Moses.

My grandmother, Mrs. Fay Wolfe (may her memory be a blessing), believed our bodies decompose, but we live on through our children.

Mrs. Shillerman, a generous woman from the Midwest, teaches that we live on through the good acts we perform.

Mr. Rabinovitz asked to be buried with dirt from Israel because he subscribed to the belief that bodily resurrection will come first to those buried in Israel, and then next to those buried elsewhere but with dirt from Israel.

Actually, Judaism has at different times held each of these beliefs. If you read the Bible carefully, the afterlife is not a hot topic. Leviticus, which is so full of rules for how to care for a corpse, is surprisingly reticent on what happens after we die. Even Moses's death is accompanied by little information about the afterlife. God tells him only, "You shall die on the mountain that you are about to ascend, and shall be gathered to your kin" (Deuteronomy 32:50).

It is only later that afterlife concepts are slowly added and adjusted through the centuries. The concept of resurrection, for example, is only mentioned twice and in two rather late books, Daniel and Isaiah.

The concept of "Heaven" as a place where you go and dwell in the presence of God was invented by the Jewish leaders around the year 200 BCE. They used the power of the Jews' reverence for God and the promise of Heaven, where one spends an eternity with God, as a tool to persuade Jews not to assimilate into the Greek culture. They enticed them by promising, "If you remain Jewish, you will go to Heaven and be with God forever."

Heaven is one of the first big adjustments we see in the equation Good Deeds – Bad Deeds = Quality of Life. This modification comes out of our people's effort to reconcile their understanding of God with the reality of their lives on the ground.

If you believe that God rewards good people with good, and punishes bad people with bad, but your life experience does not reflect this, what are you supposed to think? If a person is good his whole life and yet tragedy befalls him at each corner, clearly Good Deeds – Bad Deeds ≠ Quality of Life. What are we supposed to make of that?

We can either change the equation or change the premise of the equation that God makes things come out right. Today, you and I are willing to toss the equation out altogether and say that bad things happened because of bad luck, bad timing, or bad choices. We generally don't blame God for the flat tires and stubbed toes of life. (Although we sometimes do still fault God and ask "Why me?" when it comes to big tragedies.)

But for the most part, rather than bring in God, we alter the foundation of the equation. We alter our understanding of God's role in our lives. We contend that life just doesn't work like that. We, with our modern sensibilities, are willing to entertain the idea that perhaps God isn't a force that can intervene in our lives, or an entity that rewards and punishes us based on our actions. But, if you are not willing to alter the presupposition that God rewards and punishes—and our ancestors were not—then historically the common way to deal with the inadequacy of the equation was to add the afterlife:

Good Deeds – Bad Deeds = Quality of Life + Afterlife.

Heaven is a great way to balance the equation and still keep your belief in an interventionist God intact. For millennia, suffering people have comforted themselves by saying, "In the afterlife, I will be rewarded for my misery here." People in poverty or living in oppression often cling to this belief. Twenty-one percent of Americans (but few Jews) still hold this belief today.[3] How encouraging and comforting it must be to believe, "God may be causing me to suffer here, but it is only so that He can reward me fivefold in the world to come, where I will be in His presence for eternity." Pastor Del Whittington of the Open Door Church in Rifle, Colorado, explained this idea succinctly to his parishioners, "Wait until heaven, and accounts will be settled."

The afterlife is a fabulous mechanism for keeping people content in poverty. Remember the phrase "The meek will inherit the Earth"? Keep quiet about your anguish here and you will be rewarded in the hereafter. Many have found comfort in the belief that their suffering would ultimately lead to reward, which is a powerful device for those vested in keeping others suffering.

The Jewish concept of Heaven was unique among afterlife concepts because this Heaven was open not only to the great heroes (as was the Norse concept of Valhalla) and royalty (as was the Egyptian concept) but also to the common people. It was the first afterlife concept for which entrance was based on a person's fidelity to God.[4]

It seems to me that many of the most pervasive and perhaps pernicious God images we have—including God on a throne with a long white beard and a staff—originate from this concept of God in Heaven, our eternal resting place. Despite centuries of theologians trying to explain to us that the Jewish God is not a person or like a person, and despite our vehement rejections of the idea of God in the sky, the picture of God in Heaven is tenacious. It stays in our stories, prayers, jokes, and children's textbooks. Perhaps this is because as much as we love to reject it, we still unconsciously or consciously take comfort in this irrational, unprovable, but emotionally appealing idea.

Even as we reluctantly retain this image of God in the sky, our discomfort with God is apparent in our changing expectation of Heaven. Today, our common vision of Heaven no longer focuses around God. Lisa Miller, religion editor of *Newsweek*, points out an interesting shift in the vision of Heaven in contemporary culture. Heaven has become a place where you will be reunited with your loved ones and where you can do whatever you love to do, but God is largely absent. You can eat hot fudge sundaes with mounds of whipped cream and sprinkles on top and you will not gain an ounce of weight. You can run for hours and you will never get tired and your knees will never ache. You can read long novels in a steaming bath and the pages will never get wet, the water will never turn cold, nor will the phone ring and interrupt you. Stephen Colbert during the *Colbert Report* describes God's role in Heaven like this: "It's like Mom and Dad are upstairs and we're playing in the basement."[5]

Most of us don't talk much about Heaven these days and would probably be startled if a friend said, "Will you sponsor me in the Avon Walk for Breast Cancer? God will reward you for your donation in Heaven." A fascinating trend that the student of Jewish history will no doubt notice is that when life is pretty good for the Jews, as is currently the case in the United States, we hear very little discussion about what happens after we die. But when persecution is rampant and anti-Semitism makes life difficult for the Jews, our texts show that discussions about the afterlife abound. Not surprisingly, different concepts developed based on the information absorbed from the community and circumstances in which Jews lived. For example, during the Spanish Inquisition (1478–1834), Jews living under Christian rule in Spanish lands incorporated Christian ideas, which contradicted more long-standing Jewish ideas held by Jews living freely in other countries.[6]

At that time, who would get into Heaven was the subject of heated debates in Amsterdam. Once again, this was a conversation about their relationship with God and what God expected from them. Amsterdam was one of the few places where Jews could live safely, and many Jews left the Inquisition lands in which they had been forced to live as "secret Jews" and fled to Amsterdam. But usually they left behind friends and relatives who still lived secretly as Jews, and this influenced their thinking about the requirements for afterlife in Heaven.

The debate was divided like this: those who had family and friends living in lands as hidden Jews argued that God didn't require us to live a Jewish life to go to Heaven. They held that all that was required was to proclaim your Judaism internally; you could live outwardly as a Christian and still be admitted to Heaven. This is similar to the Christian belief that faith in Jesus is the most important among the prerequisites for entering Heaven. These Jews needed this belief. Imagine how horrible it would be to think that your friends and family, who were able to survive the Inquisition by masquerading as Christians, would be eternally barred from Heaven and God's presence.

On the other side of the argument were Jews who were accustomed to living freely as Jews. They argued that what you professed internally was not sufficient, a more traditional belief. You are required to live life as a Jew in an open relationship with God, obeying the mitzvot, the commandments God requires of us. These Jews had worked hard to establish and maintain a viable Jewish life in Amsterdam. They felt that the requirement to live an openly Jewish life for entrance to Heaven would be an incentive for the hidden Jews to leave their wealth and possessions behind in the Inquisition lands and flee to Amsterdam to live a truly Jewish life.

Who is right? I know I am not so interested in conducting the necessary "field research" to find out by leaving this world. But what we can say is that each side "discovered" a truth about what God requires of us that served their needs and reflected their worldview. Both sides were adamant, and the division ripped the community in two.

The Jews in Amsterdam, like the early Israelites, used God as a way to explain what they did not understand and to create what they needed for their mental well-being. It is in this environment of textual commentary and debate that the great philosopher and rationalist Spinoza (see chapter 10) was born and raised.

We can see how the afterlife can be used to explain God's intervention or lack thereof in our lives and as a tool to entice people to be faithful to God. But what is equally important to recognize is that our ancestors were willing to disagree with each other, to create totally new religious concepts, and to wonder and argue about God.

We are not part of a static tradition, but rather a continually changing one. This is why the Jewish Reform movement is not called the

Reform*ed* movement. It is not in the past tense because we are not done reforming! The change continues, and you and I are called upon to be part of the process. As we look at our ancestors' struggles and questions, we need not agree with how they balanced the equation by adding the afterlife. But we can learn from their process and feel empowered to develop the vocabulary to tackle our own theological questions.

CHAPTER 8

God 1.4

Arguing with God

Sagittarius *(November 22–December 21): After decades of soul-searching and inward reflection, you'll finally realize this week that the question of God was always intended to be rhetorical.*

THE ONION

If there were a biblical Academy Award for "Best Arguer *with* God," I would nominate our matriarch Sarah. Sarah blatantly laughs at God, scoffing at the idea that God could enable her to have a child long after she has entered menopause. She does ultimately conceive and gives birth to a son. Abraham names him Isaac, which means "he laughs."

What is of more interest to me are those who argue *about* God. The award for "Best Arguer *about* God" goes to Job, a man from the land of Uz. He courageously argues about God with his friends Eliphaz the Temanite, Bildad the Shuhite, and Zophar the Naamathite.

The book of Job established the precedent for debates about God. Job begins a tradition that continues and expands into the many questions we ask today. "Why did God do this to me?" "Does God intervene in our lives?" "Does God hear our prayers?" And so on.

Job of Uz expresses his doubts that he is being treated fairly by God and challenges the idea that he is getting what he deserves. Remember,

Job has been taught that there is a direct, causal connection between his actions and the events God creates in his life. Unlike his fabulously named friends, Job is not afraid to admit that the reality of his life does not match what he has been taught about God. He has obeyed all the commandments, and yet his life is filled with tragedy.

To review the story, Job was the wealthiest man in the East. He was "blameless and upright; he feared God and shunned evil" (Job 1:1). God had rewarded his loyalty by blessing him with abundance. Job had 7 children, 7,000 sheep, 3,000 camels, 500 oxen, 500 she-asses, and a very large household (Job 1:2–3).

One day, the text tells us, God was bragging to Satan (the Adversary) about how faithful his servant Job was to Him. The Jewish concept of Satan differs from the Christian concept. Also called "the Adversary" or "the Accuser," the Jewish Satan does not create evil. Rather, he points out people's evil inclinations and actions to God. In chapter 9 we will see how Tashlich (a New Year's custom of casting bread into water, symbolically casting away sins) originated as a ritual to bribe Satan so he would not report back to God about humans' sins.

Satan scoffs at God's praise of Job, saying, "You give him everything a man could want. No wonder he is faithful." Then Satan challenges God: "Would Job remain faithful if he lost all his worldly goods?" Confident that Job would continue to praise God's name even if evil befell him, God gives Satan the go-ahead to mess with Job's life, and horrific events unfold.

Sabeans attack and steal Job's oxen and kill the herdsmen. Fire falls from the sky and burns his sheep and the shepherds. Chaldeans raid and steal all Job's camels and kill the herders. In case taking his worldly wealth is not terrible enough, a house collapses, killing all seven of Job's children. Finally, a terrible itchy inflammation infects Job's body from the soles of his feet to the crown of his head.

You can imagine Job's anguish. He cries out to God, saying, "Why me? I didn't deserve this!"

His friends, who have come to console him, say to him, "You must have deserved it! God is always fair."

They say, "Think now, what innocent man ever perished? Where have the upright been destroyed?" (Job 4:7).

Job retorts, "Are you kidding? Bad things happen to good people all the time! I did nothing wrong! God is acting unjustly. Why are you defending God's actions as justified? Are you really going to stand here and ignore the truth?" Or converted into Bible-speak, "Will you speak unjustly on God's behalf? Will you speak deceitfully for Him?... Will it go well when He examines you? Will you fool Him as one fools men?" (Job 13:7–9).

Job is adamant. He says, "I did not deserve this. I fulfilled my part of the covenant. I obeyed the mitzvot."

The idea that our lives are not necessarily a reflection of our behavior represents a huge paradigm switch for the Bible, and here is the cool part of the conversation. At the end of the book, when God finally comes out and settles the score, He isn't angry with Job for questioning; God is angry with the friends. The Bible tells us, "After the Lord had spoken these words to Job, the Lord said to Eliphaz the Temanite, 'I am incensed at you and your two friends, for you have not spoken the truth about Me, as has my servant Job'" (Job 42:7).

The book of Job teaches us that it is appropriate, acceptable, and even valuable to question how God's intervention affects our lives. Job's friends are unwilling to reconcile reality with the God concept they have been taught. Only Job is willing to suggest that the equation Good Deeds – Bad Deeds = Quality of Life is not adding up. Job takes a first difficult step in questioning the equation. Although he only takes the process of redefining the equation so far, others come after him throughout history to pick it up from him. Thus begins the long line of questioning and questioners, a mantle we still proudly should take on today.

In the next chapters we will jump ahead in time to meet two theologians who built on Job's questions about God and pushed the envelope of thinking about what God is: Maimonides and Spinoza. They set the stage for integrating rational thinking with religion. We take a look at both of them to understand and develop a modern sense of God.

CHAPTER 9

God 1.5

Maimonides on What God Is Not

I forgive everyone who speaks ill of me through stupidity.
MAIMONIDES

You should thank Maimonides if you have ever said something like, "One thing I love about being Jewish is that Judaism teaches us that if we don't understand the reason for something, we are supposed to ask, and ask, and keep on asking until we understand." You and I may take Judaism's emphasis on inquiry and rational thought for granted, but it was Maimonides who infused Judaism with these concepts. Maimonides' work had such a pervasive effect on Judaism that we often don't realize what we learned from him.

Maimonides (born 1138 in Spain, died 1204 in Egypt) is one of the most revered Jewish thinkers of all time. He was a devout and erudite Jew, as well as a scholarly philosopher and an esteemed physician. He was highly regarded in non-Jewish circles as well as a leader within the Jewish world.

Philosophers, who like to stress his rational side, call him Maimonides (meaning son of Maimon). But many rabbis, who like to stress his Torah piety side, refer to him as Rambam, an acronym created from the initials of his Hebrew name, Rabbi Moses ben Maimon.

Maimonides is one of a handful of rabbis who created the bedrock of Judaism as we know it. He gave us works called the *Ladder of Tzedakah*, *Thirteen Principles of Faith*, and the Mishneh Torah, which is a summary of Talmudic law that governs Jewish daily life. Each of these alone could have been an achievement worthy of a life's work. This must have come as a big relief to his father, a judge, who was worried that his son was a lazy slacker who never was going to amount to anything!

Because Maimonides was a rabbi and a philosopher, a pious Jew and a broad thinker, he taught us that we learn about God not only through the written words in the Torah but also by studying anatomy, astronomy, and the world at large. I like to refer to this as studying Torah in the largest sense. In a religion that is so often focused on text, Maimonides' understanding—that we learn about Judaism not just from engaging with text but also by exploring the world at large through a Jewish lens—is refreshing even today!

One of the reasons that the Bible has had such remarkable tenacity through the centuries is that, from the very beginning, it has required interpretation and commentary. Maimonides' commentary took this tradition to a new level. There are many places where his commentaries reveal that Maimonides walked a tenuous tightrope between his remarkable commitments to both Jewish tradition and intellectual reason. For example, Maimonides taught that the Torah was the word of God, but that we should not need to throw out reason to understand it. Thus, when he encountered an irrational teaching in the Torah, he felt compelled to reinterpret it so that it made rational sense.

His inquisitiveness and deductive thinking brought reason to a superstition-laden tradition. For example, on Rosh Hashanah, the Jewish New Year, the Jews of his time blew the shofar (a trumpetlike instrument made of a ram's horn), as we still do today. But their intention was to scare off evil spirits with the loud blasts of the ram's horn. Maimonides reinterpreted the required shofar blasts as a call for worshipers to awaken to the importance of the day.

Another example of his influence on our rituals, also from the Jewish New Year, has to do with the intention behind the ceremony of Tashlich. Thanks to Maimonides, we teach that as we toss bread crumbs into a lake we symbolically cast our sins into the water. In contrast, in

Maimonides' day, Jews understood the ceremony as an opportunity to bribe Satan not to tell God about their sins.

Despite my admiration for Maimonides' respect for reason, I find his theology perplexing, although I like his starting place. Maimonides taught that it is impossible to say what God is. He explained that our language and intellect are too limited to allow us to understand or convey the fullness of God. He wrote, "God's essence as it really is, the human mind does not understand and is incapable of grasping or investigating" (Mishneh Torah, *Hilchot Yesodei HaTorah* 1:9).

He is probably right about that, but avoiding talking about what God is does make it a tad difficult to teach, write, or discuss the subject! Although I agree that we cannot hope to come up with a definitive answer to the question of what God is, neither can we allow the conversation to cease. Maimonides must have come to the same conclusion because he eventually deigned to elaborate, saying that although we cannot say what God is, we can say what God is not.

This methodology—of defining something by process of elimination—is similar to what occurs in scientific study. Scientists can never prove something is absolute, but they can disprove things. Falsifiable hypotheses are critical to scientific study.

Maimonides summarized:

- God is not composite.
- God is not physical.
- God is not corporeal (i.e., God has no body).
- God has no beginning and no end.

So far, his theology makes sense to me and fits nicely with what I know intuitively. But then we get to the crux of his theology and I get a little lost.

"God is pure intellect." Now what on earth does that mean? My mathematician friends explain to me that pure intellect is similar to understanding the world mathematically. All the forces and interactions of the world can be represented through mathematical equations, such as $E = mc^2$. It must be amazing to be the kind of person who can reduce the world to mathematical equations. But sadly, I am not one of those people. I opted out of calculus after my freshman year at Cornell University and I will admit I never made it to the level where you see the beauty of mathematics. I thought those chalkboards that were stacked about seven chalkboards high up to the fifty-foot ceiling so that the professors could do these huge long equations were totally cool, but as for the squiggles that they put on the boards? What can I say? I liked forestry classes.

I don't doubt that there is a profound connection between equations and understanding God, but frankly, despite my admiration of the fictional characters Don and Charlie Eppes on the television show *Numb3rs*, it's just not how I see the world.[7]

When I think of pure intellect, I go directly to Data on *Star Trek* before he had his emotion chip installed. Data was 100 percent rational thought. As such, he would be great to have on board if your turbo thrusters failed, but he's not exactly who you want to ask for dating advice. This can't be what Maimonides meant, can it?

Part of my inability to imagine pure intellect stems from a paradigm shift in the 800 years since Maimonides' time. He believed, as did Spinoza, who followed 400 years later, that eventually reason would lead us to a single truth that would explain life, the universe, and everything. These brilliant thinkers were ultimate reductionists, believing there was nothing that eventually would not be solved by rational thought and equations.

In the twenty-first century, we have in fact reached a vastly new level of knowledge. But not only has rational thought not produced all the answers Maimonides assumed it would, but also ironically, today's physicists tell us that even rational thought is based on faith!

According to Dr. Noah Finkelstein, professor of physics at the University of Colorado, "We have to believe in reason and order to believe in science. But those are just that—beliefs. Reason and order are both *unprovable* first principles from which we begin our scholarly and scientific investigations. At a bare minimum a scientist must have a fundamental belief—a faith—that the world is rational (subject to order), and that this rational world is knowable (susceptible to our investigations of it). Without those fundamental postulates, science cannot continue."[8]

It has long been fashionable to draw a clean delineation between science and religion. Science, we say, is based on provable rational thought and religion is based on faith. Science addresses "how" questions, as in how the world works. Religion answers questions of "why." But in reality, there is more overlap than this.

Finkelstein and Maimonides share the understanding of science and religion as intermingled. For both of them, intellect is a pathway to understanding God.

Another way Finkelstein explains the cohabitation of science and religion is that they naturally lead to questions for one another: Where did the Big Bang come from? How does the world work? These questions lead to more questions, which is a very Jewish way of thinking!

In the end, science and religion are both mechanisms for humans to make sense of the world and their place in the world; science and religion are in dialogue, and in this sense are woven together, rather than defined at strict boundaries, not limited by notions such as religion begins where science ends.

Academy Award–winning actor Morgan Freeman, who interviewed hundreds of cutting-edge scientists involved in cosmology as the narrator of the Science Channel's show *Through the Wormhole with Morgan Freeman*, finds the dialogue between science and religion to be a common view among physicists and cosmologists. Freeman's series uses astrobiology, string theory, quantum mechanics, and astrophysics to help us understand the universe and our place in it.[9] Having immersed himself in this world of scientific exploration and worked with hundreds of scientists, Freeman explains that scientists reach different conclusions about the origins of the universe. But there is one element in which they are consistent; when the scientists reach the part of cosmology that they don't understand and that is beyond their knowledge and understanding, they credit the hand of God.[10]

Maimonides would have appreciated this relationship between intellect and faith. Even as he reveled in reason, he was adamant that reason had its limits. Maimonides taught that God gave us intuition, emotions, tradition, and personal experience and therefore each of these should be used in concert with reason to help us understand the world. His personal experience and devotion to Jewish tradition left Maimonides no doubt that a personal God created the world and then revealed to us His Torah. Maimonides' emotions and intuition enabled him to understand that God still interacts with the world, albeit infrequently. Ultimately, he believed that humans have mere glimpses in the dark into the reality of the Divine. This may be why physicists see beauty in their work.

His steadfast belief in God and God's revelation, alongside his love for God's Torah in the largest sense, enabled Maimonides to live a life infused with meaning and learning. Maimonides passed on to us a deep respect for inquisitiveness and debate, as well as a yearning for God and love of tradition.

Studying Maimonides' commitment to finding God through his scientific pursuits alongside Jewish text empowered me to create a Jewish practice based on wilderness experience. Although I do take Jewish text with me, I also move beyond the text. It is there, in that place beyond the words, in that state of awe and connection that nature so readily creates, that I have discovered God and a Jewish practice that is meaningful in the twenty-first century. I speak about this experience at length in *God in the Wilderness*, where I discuss how the spirituality many of us easily experience outdoors can be used as a springboard to a new understanding of God.

Maimonides' discernment that we cannot describe what God is should serve as a warning to people like me and dissuade us from attempting to put words together to describe God. Yet at the same time, it is essential that we engage in a discussion of God, *even if there is no answer*, rather than write the conversation off as beyond our intellectual and spiritual capacity.

Just because we can't find the words to explain something does not mean we cannot understand. Judye Groner, who edits my Jewish children's books, told me I couldn't write a young children's book called *Shehecheyanu*, the name of a common Jewish prayer of thanks, because kids can't say *Shehecheyanu*. (I did a quick survey in our preschool and she is correct.) So instead I wrote a book called *Kids Can't Say the* Shehecheyanu *but They Can Feel It*. The book is filled with photos of children in "*Shehecheyanu* moments," such as hearing the first shofar blast, eating the first peach of the season, and lighting the first Chanukah candles. The story explains that although children can't say the *Shehecheyanu*, they can hear it, taste it, see it, and so on.

I think what Maimonides was trying to tell us about God is similar to this. Although we can't write down a description of God, we can experience God through our studies of the wonders of the world. As we look to create our own God concepts, let us remember that Maimonides relied on a mixture of reason and intuition, rational thought and experience, philosophy and tradition to help him formulate his theology. So, too, we should not limit ourselves to one school of thought, but rather integrate a variety of types of intelligence to create a believable and sustainable theology.

CHAPTER 10

God 1.6

Spinoza's Spin on God

We feel and know that we are eternal.
BARUCH SPINOZA

The first time I remember hearing the name Spinoza, I was sitting beneath a tree, planning a Rosh Chodesh ceremony, the Jewish celebration of the new moon. The particular tree against which my back rested that autumn afternoon grew in a hidden courtyard, sequestered in the rear recesses of the high-walled compound of Hebrew Union College on King David Street in Jerusalem.

I was a first-year rabbinical student, still finding my way around our campus, which was built with glistening white Jerusalem Stone. Howard, a third-year student, had already noticed that I seemed more comfortable among forests of pine trees than stacks of library books. So one afternoon when my friends and I were looking for a place to study, he casually tossed me the key to the hidden courtyard. "Check it out," he said. "You'll love it. It's the nature preserve of the campus." When we unlocked and opened the gate I was awestruck to discover a secret garden of grass, flowers, and trees hidden within. Why was this inner sanctum of greenery locked away?

After my friends and I had made ourselves comfortable in this little green oasis amidst the stone, Howard stuck his head in and, looking at me, called out, "What do you think, Spinoza?"

"Why is he calling me a 'spinoza'? What's a 'spinoza'?" I asked my classmates. I thought it was some kind of Sephardic pastry, a cheese-stuffed phyllo dough thing like spanakopita that you might serve on Sabbath. One of my friends answered, "You don't know who Spinoza is? He was a famous Jewish thinker who taught we could find God in nature. He was excommunicated for his heretical beliefs."

Since my early days in the seminary, people have frequently told me that my thinking was like Spinoza's. Usually this was meant encouragingly, as in, "You like nature? You should study the great philosopher Spinoza because he found God in nature, too." But sometimes it was more derogatory, such as, "You're a pagan just like that heretical Spinoza!"

As I learned more about Spinoza, I secretly liked the idea of being aligned with this thinker from the seventeenth century whose ideas so diverged from the traditional establishment and whose passion for nature was so deeply intertwined with his religious understanding that he was ultimately excommunicated.

It's true that I was an outlier when I was in rabbinical school. For example, during our first year of school while living in Jerusalem, I attended morning services every day before classes started. So since Sabbath (our only day without classes) was supposed to be different from the rest of the week, I left campus and went mountain biking. I spent a year of Sabbaths riding my bike through the Jerusalem forest, over trails and roads in what is now the West Bank and even riding from Jerusalem to the Dead Sea on hidden desert trails. You could not safely ride these routes today. Without a doubt, my rugged desert mountain bike rides were some of the most spiritual experiences of my year in Israel.

But with the exception of one classmate who actually bought a bike and rode with me on our vacations, the rest of the class thought I was nuts. You see, when I was a rabbinical student my passion for combining Judaism and nature made me an enigma. You have to understand that although today the connection between nature and Judaism is more common, back then, it was unheard of. Hazon, the force today behind the new Jewish food movement, didn't exist. Teva, now the leader in Jewish environmental education, was a tiny organization. And I, who would later become the Adventure Rabbi and found the nationally renowned Adventure Rabbi Program, was busy struggling through biblical Hebrew and trying never to tilt my head to the side lest all the Aramaic I had crammed in there would fall out of my ear. My peers and many of my professors (with a few very important exceptions who kept me going during my school years!) didn't have the least interest in my burgeoning connection between Judaism and the environment. Even the chancellor, Alfred Gottschalk *z"l*, affectionately called me "the Pagan." Understandably, Spinoza seemed to me to be an oasis of theological sanity.

When I was in seminary, my knowledge of Spinoza could be summarized with this:

Baruch Spinoza (1632–1677) was born in Amsterdam. At the time, Amsterdam had a thriving Jewish community because it was a central gathering place for Jews who had escaped the Inquisition in Spain and Portugal and sought to return to living a Jewish life. Spinoza's father, for example, had been living in Portugal as a secret Jew before his family fled to Amsterdam when his father was a youngster.

Spinoza was a brilliant philosopher. He found God in nature. But he was excommunicated because the traditional leadership found his thinking to be a threat to the cohesiveness of the community and the integrity of the Bible. Living in the shadows of the Spanish Inquisition, the Jewish leaders felt it was vital that the Jews stick together with uniformity of ideas and attitudes.

After Spinoza was excommunicated, rather than seek out another community, he lived a quiet life as a lens maker and died young, at forty-four. He died of a lung disease, which was likely the result of inhaling the glass dust, an occupational hazard of the grinding required for making glass lenses. His great works were published anonymously and celebrated posthumously. In recent years there has been an effort to un-excommunicate him, but the current Amsterdam community does not feel it has the authority to overturn the decree of past leaders.

It turns out that although none of that information is actually wrong, it's not completely accurate either. For example, he wasn't *just* a lens grinder. He made some of the best lenses of his day. His telescope lenses were sought after by Christiaan Huygens, who used the lenses to explore the rings of Saturn and to discover Saturn's moon, Titan.

Being kicked out of the Jewish community didn't mean he lived a completely isolated life, as I had imagined. No, he had peers with whom he exchanged ideas and a circle of students who sat at his feet. He kept up multiple radical correspondences and wrote a plethora of treatises, some published after his death, which continue to influence us today. For example, Spinoza lived a secular life, meaning that once he was excommunicated he did not identify with any other religious community. This might not seem like a big deal, but in his day it was unheard of not to be affiliated with a religious community. Your religious network determined what career you could have, whom you could socialize with, where you shopped, and more. Spinoza's audacious act of independence from a religious community, and his writing that emanated from this experience, set the stage for the establishment of the separation of church and state as we know it today.

But the most important aspect of his life and thought that I had misunderstood was that when he was talking about God and nature as being one and the same, he was not talking about God and nature in the way that I talk about God in nature. If Spinoza were alive today, would he come on an Adventure Rabbi Sabbath hike? I'm not so sure he would.

Here is an example of the kind of moment I write about to convey the experience of God in nature:

It was the week after Passover and spring had truly arrived in Boulder. The first big rain of the season had fallen. My daughter Sadie grabbed my hand and pulled me outside into the garden to smell the sweet fragrance of fresh rainfall and feel the cool drops on our faces as we watched the storm move over the mountains. Moments later, we laced on our boots and headed up to the trail behind our house.

Here, spring abounded. Delicate slivers of green pushed their way through the heavy brown grasses, remnants of last year's growth. Vibrant yellow clusters of Oregon-grape blossoms burst out from cozy conclaves nestled in the hillside, safe from the chill of spring winds. I spotted tiny white bells, so small I had to lean down to see them, their small unfurled flowers too tiny to identify.

It is in that place, amidst the burgeoning forest, that I feel the presence of God. It is the feeling of connection with That Which Is Greater Than Myself. Immersed in nature, I feel exuberantly connected to the Oneness of Life, to the cycles of seasons, to eternity, and to God.

It is through such moments and such encounters that I discovered the language of awe and gratitude that enables me to talk about the idea of God. In nature I freely use words like *spirituality, awe, reverence,* and *sacred space,* words that seem corny and contrived to me when I hear them in other settings. Nature is my portal to God and religion. It provides me with tools, such as a spiritual vocabulary, that I can then use to interact in more normative Jewish settings.

One of the major Jewish prayers is called the *Shema.* The words are taken from the Bible: "*Shema Yisrael: Adonai Eloheinu, Adonai Echad.* Hear, O Israel: the Lord is our God, the Lord is One" (Deuteronomy 6:4). When I sing the *Shema* outside, standing among the tall ponderosa pines, I *feel* the oneness described in the prayer. Then, when I return to the synagogue, the *experience* of the prayer follows me, infusing the prayer with meaning even as I stand in a chapel, walled off from my beloved pines.

Is this what Spinoza meant when he found God in nature? Is this what he meant when he said God and nature are one? As much as I would like to claim an alignment with Spinoza, I don't think it is. Spinoza was a rationalist through and through. When he talked about knowing God, he was talking about an intellectual communion with God via an understanding of how the world works. He believed that our intellect would eventually enable us to understand everything there is to know. Can you imagine how enraptured he would have been with the discovery of genes, DNA, and quantum physics?

Physics professor Dr. Noah Finkelstein teaches about the intersections between science and religion. He recalls an experience he had that enabled him to bridge an emotional response he felt in nature that was similar to those I experience, with an intellectual understanding similar to Spinoza's. Prior to attending graduate school, Finkelstein and his friends frequently met to sit and watch the sun set over the Pacific Ocean. It was a joyful time of camaraderie, conversation, and wine, combined with the thrill of watching the setting sun slowly dip into the Pacific Ocean. A few years later, as a graduate student in laser physics, he returned to San Diego, bringing with him a scientific understanding of what causes the effect we call "sunset."

He says, "In graduate school, I had gained new understanding of the sun and light, and I proceeded to explain to my friends the oscillations of electric dipoles and the nature of Rayleigh scattering as a cause for the diffuse patterns and brilliant hues (blue scattering far more than red due to its shorter wavelength)."

"Suddenly I stopped," recalls Finkelstein, "fearful that by layering all this physics and mathematics atop, that I had just ruined the gorgeous sunset that my friends were trying to experience. I had pushed God out of the moment. But then as our subsequent conversation unfolded, and we had time to reflect, I realized my new knowledge was not displacing but enhancing the experience. I realized that the emotional/spiritual and intellectual/spiritual are both meaningful ways that we can engage with the sunset and intensify the godliness of the moment. The sunset didn't change. I did. I now had more ways to engage with the same phenomenon."

At first Finkelstein thought his science depleted the God moment of the experience. But then he realized it actually added to it because both the emotional/spiritual and the intellectual/spiritual pathways can bring us to the same God. Finkelstein says that "both science and religion are human constructs; each provides us with a lens with which we may view and engage with the world."[11]

So, too, some people misunderstand Spinoza's commitment to rational thought and misrepresent Spinoza as an atheist. But clearly he was not an atheist. Rather, his love for God was so infusive that he is often referred to as a "God-intoxicated man." He simply held a different belief in God than the traditional concept of a personal God who interacts in our lives and is influenced by our prayer.

You see (and get ready for the radical part), Spinoza didn't conceive of God as an entity that was separate from the world and therefore something that could act on the world. Rather, he believed God was the source of all, and since all things come from God, everything is God. In his great book *Ethics*, he writes, "Besides God no substance can be granted or conceived" (1:14).

It's too bad that Spinoza was excommunicated and that his theological line of thinking was discarded for so many centuries. For me, discovering Spinoza's God concept was like rummaging around in my grandmother's attic and discovering a dusty brass lamp with beautiful ornate curves, delicately etched flowers, and a pink fringed lampshade, something that no one had wanted for decades, but is completely fabulous, trendy, unique, and useful!

Spinoza's conception of God describes the world as I see it. There is no God that works from the outside, no God who can come in here and change this or fix up that. There is not a God demanding we do A and not B, doling out punishments based on our actions. God is not an external force with an intelligence and a consciousness acting on the world. Rather, God *is* the world. God is in everything.

Spinoza was the original pantheist, before the word *pantheist* was invented. Pantheism is the belief that God and the material world are one and the same and that God is present in everything. Spinoza didn't simply find God in nature; he thought God was nature and nature was God, all one and the same. (Panentheism, in contrast, posits that God is greater than the universe and the universe is one aspect of God.)

Spinoza believed that the understanding that all things are God led one to live a life of righteousness filled with love for God. But (and here is where he gets even more radical) he had no expectation that God would or could love us back. Because God is not separate from the world, God cannot intervene or interact with us in a personal and conscious way any more than a flower can choose to grow to please us or a snowstorm can decide to close city streets to stymie our plans. This is the most refreshing and realistic theology I have ever encountered in Judaism!

To Spinoza, the idea of praying to God for a certain event to unfold or believing that God will create an outcome based on our behavior was absurd. It would be similar to me thinking the crab apple tree in my backyard will have an abundant year of blossoms because I was especially kind this year. Or that last year's lack of fruit was due to my bad behavior, rather than the late snowstorm that killed off the magenta blossoms before they could mature. The crab apple tree does not make a conscious decision not to burst forth in an exuberant celebration of purplish pink. It did not stop and consider, "Hmm, Jamie has been xenophobic this year. I think I won't produce fruit."

With these kinds of beliefs, it is not surprising that Spinoza came to loggerheads with the Jewish community.

Spinoza consistently argued that if something did not make rational sense, we were duty-bound to reject it as false. This even applied to the Bible. Spinoza did not believe the Bible to be a divinely written or divinely dictated document. Rather, he believed, as do I, that the Bible was written by men as a record of their striving toward God, and therefore contained all the biases, agendas, and intellectual limitations of its human authors.

He thought the Bible's main purpose was to teach us kindness. Spinoza summarized the basic teaching of the Bible as "to love God above all things, and love one's neighbor as one's self." We can see how this line of thinking may have influenced Martin Buber's theology (see chapter 13) that we experience God through our relationships. If God is in everything, then we can experience God through our connection to other people, animals, and nature in general. As we grow cognizant of the godliness of all beings, then the only plausible outcome is for us to live our lives with kindness and respect.

When Spinoza came to passages that did not make rational sense, he felt quite comfortable turning the page and moving on. This is one of the critical differences between Maimonides and Spinoza. The former believed in the divine authorship of the Bible, so he was compelled to do intellectual gymnastics to make it correspond to his rational understanding of the world.

Another difference between the two thinkers is that Maimonides thought the prophets of the Bible were on a higher plane of communion with God than ordinary people were. Spinoza thought the prophets were delusional. While Maimonides thought that intuition and experience could guide us alongside intellect, Spinoza thought they were emotional nonsense.

I imagine Spinoza would have scoffed at what we call "spirituality." Much to my chagrin, if he saw me leading my Adventure Rabbi hikes with a backpacking Torah and a guitar carefully strapped to my pack, I imagine he would have turned and strode off purposely in the other direction.

When Spinoza talks about learning about God through nature, he's not talking about climbing a mountain and having a transcendent moment with sky and wind. I am forced to admit that I am not Spinozian in the way I meet God. Pure intellect has not been my path, as it was Spinoza's. He wrote, "Thus in life it is before all things useful to perfect the understanding, or reason, as far as we can, and in this alone man's highest happiness, or blessedness, consists."[12]

But despite our different mechanisms for meeting God, Spinoza's path being the rational/intellectual and mine being the emotional/experiential, we arrive at the same place. Ultimately, we share a concept of a God who can be recognized in the interconnectivity of the world, rather than a God of agency or action.

Spinoza has been an important teacher for me in many ways. I admire his rational thinking and his willingness to throw out parts of the Bible that contradicted his intellect. I am relieved to learn that this great thinker, once reviled and now celebrated, was confident that God does not intervene or interact in the world. Knowing that I share this belief with a man of such astounding intellect reassures me in my own concept of God.

And so, even if he would not have gone hiking with me, my colleague Howard, who in my early days at the seminary called me "a Spinozian," might be right after all.

Let's jump now to the twentieth and twenty-first centuries and see what sprouted from the seeds planted by Job's questioning, Maimonides' rational thought, and Spinoza's willingness to leave behind elements that conflicted with his understanding of the world around him. What do contemporary theologians teach us about God in our world?

Part III

TWENTIETH-CENTURY UPGRADES

CHAPTER 11

God 1.7

Rabbi Harold Kushner on
When Bad Things Happen to Good People

If a kid asks where rain comes from, I think a cute thing to tell him is "God is crying." And if he asks why God is crying, another cute thing to tell him is "Probably because of something you did."
JACK HANDEY, SATURDAY NIGHT LIVE

Whenever a massive tragedy strikes, especially "acts of God" such as hurricanes, tsunamis, and earthquakes, we clergy are inundated with calls from reporters asking us to explain why bad things happen to good people.

The standard voice mail message goes something like this: "Hi, Rabbi Korngold. This is so-and-so from such-and-such newspaper. I'd like to interview you about the recent catastrophe. Could you please explain the suffering in the world to me? Oh, and my deadline is at 5 p.m., so if you can call in the next half hour that would be great."

Why do bad things happen to good people? The answer to this question is probably the most obvious differentiator among the various theologies and their practitioners.

I'm always a little reluctant to answer these calls, because I'm nervous about the response I'll get from the reporter when I tell her what I truly believe: God has nothing to do with it.

I remember one interview, when first I explained that I believe bad things happen to good people because of things like unfortunate timing, inadequate building codes, warped cultural priorities, lead in children's toys, and so on. Then I discussed the intricacies of my faith, and how, like Spinoza, I believe in a non-conscious, non-interventionist God. The reporter, apparently having not heard a word of what I said, asked, "But you do believe in God, Rabbi, right? I mean, you pray to Him to help you, right?"

No wonder I don't like to talk about it!

A Reconstructionist rabbinic colleague of mine points out that those of us who live in theological uncertainty seem to have ceded the arena of God and belief to two groups. The first group consists of people who are adamant that this God stuff is all bunk, a big deception, and we should get over it and move on. The second group is made up of those who are confident in their belief. People with steadfast belief love to talk about their faith. They will talk to you about God's comforting presence and healing powers. They don't pretend to have all the answers, but they are comfortable not having all the answers because for them God has all the answers and they are happy to cede that domain to God.

Meanwhile, many of us are somewhere in the middle. We are not so confident about God, so we stay mute and let the other folks return the phone calls. We often don't even have the vocabulary to comfortably talk about God.

Usually, when we hear from clergy in the news, we hear the views of those who are not hesitant in their beliefs and are happy to answer the media's phone calls.

Some people preach that bad things happen to people because they are not good people. I am always shocked by how many people subscribe to the biblical theology that the bad things that happen in life are God's punishments for our actions. I'm not sure why these things happen, but the fundamentalists seem to know: the people deserved it.

So for example, when a horrific earthquake hit Haiti, killing upward of 300,000 people and shattering the lives of millions more of the poorest of the poor, Pat Robertson, the television evangelist, had a simple explanation: it was the Haitians' own fault. They practiced voodoo and made a pact with the devil.

In case you are wondering what he is talking about, nearly all Haitians are Christian, but about half of them also practice voodoo, which is an adaptation of their African ancestors' native religion. According to the strict scriptural interpretation preached by Robertson, this practice violates the first commandment of the covenant, "You shall have no other Gods before me."[13]

Dr. Robertson has a lot of followers. But I'm not one of them, and I can't agree. Does it make sense that sin would determine who lives and who dies? Are the people who survived so much more pious than those who died? I don't buy it.

It is hard to stomach this type of explanation, especially when we are living in a world where so many "religious" people have done despicable things and when we all know so many nonreligious people who are living lives filled with good, kind, charitable acts. Yet for many, this thinking makes sense to them. All too often I get hate mail from Orthodox Jews who are angry at the updates I make to Jewish practice. One vengeful critic took consolation in the fact that I will ultimately face divine retribution for my sins, writing, "The only consolation of knowing that people like you exist is the promise of divine punishment for spreading lies and falsehoods to Jews who don't know any better."

Oh, the mighty arrogance of religious zealots! At least it is consistent across religions. After the Haitian earthquake, my local television news channel interviewed a missionary from Colorado Springs who had been trapped for several days in a crushed building. When he was eventually rescued, the reporter asked him why he thought he lived when so many others had died. He said, "I prayed and prayed, and God answered my prayers."

How I wish the journalist had asked him, "What about your missionary friend who was ten feet away from you, but was killed? Do you think his prayers weren't sincere enough?"

Rabbi Harold Kushner, author of *When Bad Things Happen to Good People*, responded to Robertson's remarks by saying, "I think that it's supreme hubris to think you can read God's mind."[14]

Kushner's theology, which is among the most commonly embraced Jewish theologies, involves the idea that God does not make bad things happen, but God helps us respond to and cope with the disaster. God is present with us through the love and support of our friends, family, and community. God gives us inspiration and hope, and thereby fills us with strength to cope with life.

I was watching a discussion on television with a panel of clergy explaining God's presence after horrific tragedies, and the first participant's comments echoed Rabbi Kushner's concept of God.

"God couldn't stop the tsunami," one rabbi explained. "But what He can do is bring us the strength and hope to deal with it."

All the panelists nodded in agreement.

But I thought to myself, what is up with a God who can't intervene to stop a tsunami, but can intervene to give us strength and hope? If God is going to come on down here and help, God should roll up the divine sleeves and stop a tornado from a hitting a town or heal an infant or two.

Another rabbi expanded on the first comment, saying, "God set the world in motion and can't interfere with the natural order. Think of God more as a counselor who can help us deal with the emotions of the situation. God is there with you, beside you. When you cry, God cries. When you suffer, God suffers. When you know you are not alone because God is right there with you, you can cope with any situation." I know a lot of people find satisfaction in this answer and comfort in the concept, but I do not. The idea of God as a personality who is powerful enough to create the universe but who today can do no more than sit by our sides and weep with us when we suffer seems paradoxical.

This answer reminds me of a biblical text I struggle with. Remember the part we read at Passover where Moses, at God's request, goes to Pharaoh and begs him to free the enslaved Israelites? God punishes the Egyptians with horrible plagues, and repeatedly Pharaoh is ready to relent and let the Israelites go. At one point Pharaoh gives this impassioned speech: "I stand guilty this time. The Lord is in the right, and I and my people are in the wrong. Plead with the Lord that there may be an end of God's thunder and of hail. I will let you go; you need stay no longer" (Exodus 10:28).

But then he changes his mind. Why? Because God hardens Pharaoh's heart so that he will not relent and let the Israelites go free. Moses pleads and pleads, but we know that Pharaoh is going to say no because God hardened his heart: "The Lord had stiffened the heart of Pharaoh's so that he would not let the Israelites go from his land" (Exodus 11:10).

I find it troubling to think that God can mess with our emotions. It hardly seems reasonable, let alone fair. How can we possibly hope to build a society based on the biblical injunction "Justice, justice shall you pursue" (Deuteronomy 16:20) if God is controlling our actions through emotions?

If God can affect our emotions, then why are we so cruel to each other? Why doesn't God change our emotions for the good? God could make all parents feel love, patience, and respect for their children, and God would eradicate child abuse. God could make Christians, Jews, and Muslims feel tolerant of each other so we could live peacefully side by side. Peace on Earth, just like that! Surely if God could, God would. Because God doesn't, it confirms my belief that God cannot tinker with our emotions.

CHAPTER 12

God 1.75

Rabbi Harold Schulweis Says
God Is in the Grammar

God is a verb.

BUCKMINSTER FULLER

Another rabbi on the panel offered a different explanation to the question of where God is in a tragedy: "God is present in the response of the community. Look at the outpouring of generosity! We find God in the verbs, in the loving, the giving, and the consoling. We need to stop looking at God as a person or as the subject or noun of the sentence."

Rabbi Harold Schulweis, one of our generation's great teachers and a personal favorite of mine, calls this "Predicate Theology." He says God is in the gerunds, which is such a theologian thing to say. Only a theologian can take a good concept and then complicate it by naming it after some grammatical term that I have to look up every time I reread his books. (A predicate is the part of a sentence that is not the subject. A gerund is a noun formed from a verb, such as *loving*.) It is an interesting concept, albeit a bit ethereal for me to wrap my head around, probably because of the grammar thing. I wonder if Stephen Colbert could explain it to me. After all, I finally understand how to use the Oxford comma after he explained it during *The Colbert Report*.

The concept suggests we should stop searching for a God who is like a person. Schulweis proposes God is neither the noun, nor the subject, but rather God is the action of the sentence and is knowable through those actions. He writes, "I propose a shift of focus from noun to verb, from subject to predicate, from God as person to Godliness, in Hebrew Elohuth. Not the qualities of divinity but the divinity of the qualities is essential to belief."[15]

I like the concept that when we are interacting with each other in godly ways, that is God. We can see a little Spinoza here, in that God is not an external being but rather an aspect of our interaction with each other. If we stretch way back to chapter 3 when I talked about covenant, we can recognize that in this theology, the covenant would not be a hierarchal one between us and a divine creator, but rather a communal covenant, to interact with each other and the planet in godly ways.

This serves a perfect bridge to the next clergyperson, who spoke about the relationships forged by the crisis.

CHAPTER 13

God 1.8

Rabbi Martin Buber's I-Thou

When two people relate to each other authentically and humanly, God is the electricity that surges between them.

MARTIN BUBER

When I saw people who didn't even know each other," explained the next clergyperson, "clawing through the rubble to save people they didn't even know, I was reminded of Buber's teaching that we meet God in relationships." He continued, "This was one of those situations where people interacted with each other on such a human level, not thinking what they could do for themselves but just valuing each human life."

Martin Buber (1878–1965), one of the great modern Jewish thinkers, taught that we encounter God through our relationships with others. He described two kinds of relationships: I-It and I-Thou.

I-It is when you deal with someone on the level of what he can do for you. A basic example would be my interaction with a customer service representative whom I called because I was having trouble with an online order. I called the 1-800 number, then followed a complicated phone tree asking me to push 3, then 1, then 4, then "insert your order number," then 2, then 5, then "insert your order number" again, then 0, and then a real person answered and asked me for a third time for the order number, because it was not relayed through to her. I didn't want to answer, "How are you today?" or hear how her day was going. I wanted to know why the green swim goggles were on sale for $9.99 but when I clicked them into the shopping cart it said they were $19.99.

Another example of I-It is my relationship with the checkout clerks and baggers at our local supermarket. I've seen the same checkers and baggers at least once a week for ten years. I call them all by name, without having to glance at their name tags anymore, and they recognize me and my children and will even ask where my kids are if they are not with me. They have seen me more regularly than some of my best friends. They have seen me pregnant, then with a newborn. They have witnessed my children learning to walk, run, and squeal with delight when presented with the store's red helium balloons.

On my end, I always ask how they are doing and try to make some kind of light conversation. I treat them with respect and we are mutually friendly, but the truth is my interaction with them is based on buying groceries. As much as I appreciate them, we're not going to go out for lunch and talk about what is going on in our lives. Most of them have no idea I am an author and a rabbi. There is nothing wrong with these relationships; in fact, in many ways they are what make our world work. But they are based on a utilitarian interaction, or as Buber would say, I-It.

The other kind of relationship Buber called I-Thou. This is when we interact based on the essence of who a person is, not what she can do for us. Buber explained that we could have these encounters not only with people but also with anything in nature. He gives examples of his I-Thou relationships with a tree, a horse, and a piece of mica. We have all experienced these special relationships.

Here is the cool piece. Buber explained that every time we experience an I-Thou moment, we are encountering God. God is something we feel, something we experience in our relationships, not an external being to whom we pray. God is not a God of action but a God of interaction. This is not a hierarchical God, but rather a God revealed by companionship.

What does I-Thou feel like? Think of someone you love dearly and you will be able to remember tender moments of I-Thou. Perhaps it was when you shared an important idea and your friend listened quietly, without trying to solve or interject his experience. Or perhaps it was with a running or hiking partner with whom you spend hours on the trail, sometimes sharing your deepest thoughts and other times saying nothing at all but simply listening to the sound of your shoes striking the dirt. There is the tender moment of holding an infant, for whom you feel such a deep love that you never realized you could love that much. Those are I-Thou moments.

I speak of I-Thou moments because I-Thou relationships move in and out of I-Thou and I-It. Even our most loving, intimate relationships may seem to have more I-It moments than I-Thou moments. "Honey, can you please take out the trash?" "Sweetie, what time do you need to be picked up at school?" "Can someone please walk the dog!" If we were in I-Thou all the time, we would not get anything done. We would sit on a rock and gaze lovingly into each other's eyes. Buber taught that I-Thou is preferable to I-It. I think one is not better than the other; they are different and we need to have both in a meaningful, functioning life.

Striving to be in I-Thou all the time is sort of like trying to always "live in the moment." Although it is important to be fully present and live in the moment as much as possible, if I always lived in the moment I would never empty the dishwasher, pay my bills, or listen to voice mail messages. I would eat milk chocolate bars with hazelnuts continually.

Buber's God concept is one of the most popular theologies of young rabbis today. Rabbis love to explain that we meet God in our encounters with others. We preach (and preach and preach) about the importance of creating time to have meaningful interactions so that we can find God through our relationships both with people and the Earth. This outlook fits well with Jewish communal priorities because it promotes community, social justice, and taking care of the Earth. At the same time, it kind of gets us off the hook with dealing with the whole God thing directly. We get rid of the hierarchal God, the God of action, the God of agency, and move to a more internal relationship that jibes better with our modern sensibilities.

I will admit that despite the number of these types of sermons I have given, Buber has never quite satisfied my theological itch. He comes close, but it's not quite what I experience. Perhaps the terms "I-Thou" and "I-It" simply lose too much in the translation from German to English to be effective. For me the distinction is not whether a relationship is based on utilitarian purposes but whether an interaction is respectful or rude, playful or painful, caring or disconnected.

I believe that we can experience God in completely utilitarian I-It relationships, when the interactions are respectful and kind. My relationship with the checkers at the supermarket is a great example. They are completely utilitarian, I-It. I select whose line to go on not based on "the essence of the checker's being" but on who is quick and efficient and will carefully place my peaches onto the conveyer belt after scanning them rather than dropping and bruising them. But I believe I do experience God in those moments, because they are genuine meetings of two people who share the same moment in time.

I believe experiencing God has nothing to do with using someone or not, because I *am* using those clerks. Meeting God in an interaction has to do with being present and engaged. Think back to Moses and the burning bush. In chapter 1 of *God in the Wilderness*, I wrote at length about the biblical passage that says God waited until Moses noticed the bush, and then God called out to him. I theorized that in today's world Moses would have missed the bush because he would have been distracted by a text message. So, too, in our interactions, we can experience God through connections, but only if we are aware.

I return to Spinoza's idea that God is all things and his conclusion that we must then approach our interactions with kindness and justice. (And not check our cell phones while our children show us their latest dance moves!)

When I disconnect from that which is greater than myself, when I have forgotten or disregarded Spinoza's idea that we all came from God and therefore are all part of God, then I do not feel compelled to be kind or attentive. Some days I am far too cranky and exhausted to experience any sort of ubiquitous connection. In fact, some days I feel so in demand, depleted, and used up that I don't want to feel a connection with anybody. On those days I ask someone else to answer my e-mails. Perhaps this theology should be called I-Thou, Cranky-It, emphasizing the change in myself.

On those days I am glad Buber taught that I-Thou could also be experienced with nature. These are the days that I head up to the ponderosa forest behind my house, to be nurtured by the pines and the purple lupine flowers. Here in the wild, no one asks anything of me. Rather, it is my soul that is nourished by the sounds of wind blowing over the grasses and the water tumbling down the rocks as it carves its way over the rocky riverbed. I am reminded that I should be more like the water, knowing which rocks to flow around, which rocks to flow over, and which to slowly carve my way through. I feel calmed, connected, and confident. These are some of my most powerful God moments and I cherish them.

What resonates most for me about Buber's theology is that he, too, moves away from a hierarchical, anthropomorphized God. He suggests that God is an experience we have through our relationships, rather than a force we pray to, hoping for a response.

CHAPTER 14

God 1.9

Rabbi Abraham Joshua Heschel and Praying with Our Feet

People who rely most on God rely least on themselves.
LEMUEL K. WASHBURN

I want to return to the panel because the last clergyperson on the panel moved away from the Buber theme and spoke about how the tragedy had spawned an outpouring of prayers for healing. "Because of this crisis," she explained, "people all over the world are praying for healing. Perhaps placing the tragedy in a spot with such limited medical care is God's way of reminding us to pray, and of the power of prayer to heal."

There does seem to be a lot of praying going on after tragedies. I wish someone had raised these questions: Do we come together so God can hold us, or so we can hold each other? Do we pray so God can intervene and fix our world, or to remind ourselves that we can fix our world? Do we pray to God for answers, or so that we can learn to ask the questions? I will discuss these themes in detail in chapter 20.

The idea that a tragedy was designed by God to remind us to pray was more than I could take. I thought of Rabbi Abraham Joshua Heschel (1907–1972), one of the most influential theologians and philosophers of the twentieth century, who taught that prayer could consist of actions, rather than words.

Heschel explained that there are three ways to reach God: through the natural world, through the study of sacred texts, and by performing mitzvot. He reassured his students to not be troubled if faith seemed difficult. Rather, he encouraged them to take action, which would then lead to faith. Heschel was a strong advocate of the civil rights movement and a powerful voice of opposition to the Vietnam War. When he marched alongside Martin Luther King Jr. in a protest march for voting rights for blacks, he said, "In Selma, I prayed with my feet."

Inspired by Heschel, I shut off the panel discussion program and went to write a check to an aid organization. Other people can send their prayers calling on God to intercede with healing and help. As for me, I'm praying with my checkbook; I'm sending money.

Part IV

GOD 2.0

God in the Twenty-First Century

CHAPTER 15

God and the Big Bang

Science conducts us, step by step, though the whole range of creation, until we arrive, at length, at God.
MARGUERITE DE VALOIS,
SIXTEENTH-CENTURY QUEEN OF FRANCE

Physicists tell us that when the universe began, there was a singularity. One. In religious terms, we call this God.

But whatever you call this oneness, so it was. One.

Then something happened! Bang! A bang of such tremendously big proportions, it became known as the Big Bang.

The cause of the Big Bang is unknown and remains a hotly debated and researched topic. Scientists can map out the sequence of the Big Bang to billionths of a second, but there is still a moment when they do not know what happened.

We understand there was a Big Bang, but why? What made it happen? Where science ends, is that where God begins?

Maimonides and other theologians say God is the force that set the universe in motion, the Eternal that existed before anything else. They said this even before the idea of the Big Bang theory was created. They would call the singularity that preceded the Big Bang and set it in motion the Primary Mover or the Unmoved Mover. In the book

America's Four Gods: What We Say about God—and What That Says About Us, Paul Froese and Christopher Bader, sociologists at Baylor University, explain that 24 percent of Americans believe in this type of God, termed a Distant God, who set the world in motion but since that time has remained hands-off.

The Unmoved Mover is aligned with classical physics, which says that a body at rest will remain at rest unless acted upon by an outside source. Quantum physics counters the Unmoved Mover theory. Stephen Hawking, in *The Grand Design*, explains that there are particles that can move freely forever and without beginning or end, and so there is no need for a Primary Mover to set the whole process in motion.

Frankly, for my theology, any of the scenarios is fine. Whichever concept works for you—scientific or theological, classical physics or quantum physics—we began with a singularity.

One. The universe began as one. At some point, that singularity, that oneness, divided into many. Light and darkness! Heavens and planets! Water and air! Mountains and valleys! Fish and frogs! Plants and trees! Creepy crawly things and cattle! You! Me! This book!

Everything began as that one singularity—in Hebrew we say *echad* (one)—and then divided into many.

As I mentioned earlier, one of the major Jewish prayers is called the *Shema*. This prayer is often called "the watchword of our faith." The *Shema* is so important that it is the first prayer we are supposed to teach our children. The sequence of words is supposed to be the last words we say before we greet death, and so we say them each night before we fall asleep, in case we don't awaken in the morning. Besides the prayer over the bread, *Motzi*, *Shema* is probably the most widely known Jewish prayer. (To hear these two prayers, visit www.GodUpgrade.com/motzi and www.GodUpgrade.com/shema.)

Although I love these words and sing the *Shema* with my children each night before I tuck them into bed, the prayer had always puzzled me, until one day a physicist described the Big Bang theory to me and then suddenly, it clicked: our One is that one! Everything is one! Everything began as one and so remains connected in some primal way. The very idea of monotheism, of one God, now made absolute sense to me on an entirely richer level.

I'm not saying anything about a God who talks to people, or a God who makes things happen in our lives. I'm not talking about pure intellect or intellect at all. I'm not talking about a blueprint for the world. I am talking about the God of ultimate connection among all beings, which has been there since the beginning of time. This God does not necessarily have a consciousness or interact in our lives, yet it connects us all. That is what I understand by "Hear, O Israel: the Lord is our God, the Lord is one."

What are the consequences of such a ubiquitous connection? When we realize that we are connected to everything, that we are part of everything, what does that mean?

When we experience moments of transcendence—watching a child being born, singing with our community in a synagogue, climbing a mountain peak, reading Psalms, or listening to a Mozart concerto—we are accessing our line to this elemental connection. When we "hook up" to this line, we are motivated to be kind, gracious, and compassionate, and to look out for each other, the planet, and future generations. We are inspired to protect each other from those who act destructively.

Interestingly, Spinoza summarized the entire corpus of Jewish teachings as a call to be kind to others. I would argue that when we are violent, selfish, or greedy, we have lost our sense of connection to the oneness of the universe. When we realign ourselves with the omnipresent connection, not only do we become more kind and our lives become more meaningful, but we also experience eternity, because we are part of something that has always existed.

When our texts say that we are made in God's image, I don't understand that to mean God has two eyes and a mouth like I do. I understand that to mean that because everything began as a unified whole, we sustain an internal and abiding similarity, which should enable us to experience empathy.

My theology is very basic. The world began as one and therefore we are all of one. When we can transcend the separateness of our lives, and go deeply into our eternal connection, we experience God.

I know this sounds simplistic. My theology does not offer us a man in the sky, commanding us to do this and refrain from doing that. Neither does my theology offer us divine intervention to heal the sick and support the poor. My theology cannot purport to explain the purpose of life or what happens when we die.

But neither does my theology require engaging in intellectual gymnastics and putting our rational minds into storage. Here is a God concept that coincides with our intuitive experience yet does not collide with or insult our intelligence. My theology offers a new way to look at our covenant, our holy books, and our culture, as I will do in the final section of this book.

This is a God we can experience right here, right now, on this Earth. I have designed the Adventure Rabbi Program retreats, classes, and services to facilitate our participants' God experiences. As I am fond of saying, I may not be able to succinctly articulate what God is, but I can help you experience God. In the next chapter, I will share with you how I came to experience God.

CHAPTER 16

Finding God on a Mesa

One cannot help but be in awe when he contemplates the mysteries of eternity, of life, of the marvelous structure of reality.

ALBERT EINSTEIN

There is a popular story that Sir Isaac Newton discovered gravity while sitting under an apple tree. I discovered God while powder skiing in Utah.

After many frustrating years of trying to help congregants find God in the synagogue, I had a powder skiing epiphany. I was telemark skiing down the steeps of Great Scott, a chute along the Upper Cirque of Snowbird Ski Resort in Utah. The snow was light as air and literally up to my waist. It was Saturday morning, but I was on vacation and it was a powder day, so I didn't think twice about skipping Sabbath services.

I launched off the cornice and landed softly in the chute. After a night of incessant snowfall, the powder was so deep it sprayed my face with every turn. My skis sliced effortlessly through the soft snow. I floated left, right, left, right, left. As I turned right, I saw Felicia, who flashed a smile and jumped in behind me with her long, sinuous

S-curved ski tracks. As I turned left, I saw Ron gracefully floating down on his snowboard.

The sky was blue and the sun was warm. It was one of those magical moments when I felt intensely connected to the mountain, to my friends, and to the universe. At the base of the cirque, where the terrain momentarily flattens out, the three of us exchanged knowing smiles, laughing aloud that anything could be quite this awesome. Then we struck out in search of more untracked powder.

If we think about holiness according to the Jewish definition—something that is sacred because it is differentiated from the mundane—then this was clearly holy time. Skiing that day with my friends, I experienced a sacred moment of connection among us and with the mountain. Here we were, three Jews on Sabbath, on the mountain, and I felt closer to God then I ever did with three hundred Jews reading responsively on Sabbath in my walled-in sanctuary. Through those connections, I experienced God.

"*Shema Yisrael: Adonai Eloheinu, Adonai Echad*," I quietly sang into my purple fleece neck warmer, feeling that, "Yes, God is one, and we are all part of the one."

Suddenly it hit me. My epiphany. Why do I work so hard trying to create transcendent God moments through prayer books and psalms when it is remarkably easy to have a God moment here in the snow? Why do I preach about God in the sanctuary on Saturday mornings when most of my congregants are out skiing, far away from the reach of my words, however clever I think my sermons are? Why am I trying to cram God into a synagogue when my own God moments are so frequently outdoors? Why not take the "Jewish thing" outdoors, to God? Why not show people like Felicia and Ron how this remarkable experience we are having is actually Jewish? Why not take the spirituality we so readily experience out here, and bring to it a Jewish twist?

I wrote in depth about the creation of the Adventure Rabbi Program in my first book, *God in the Wilderness*, so let me focus here specifically on how nature has shaped my understanding of God.

I have taken thousands of Jewish people outdoors for Sabbath services on hikes, High Holiday retreats in the mountains, and even outdoor weddings and bar and bat mitzvahs. (Unlike Moses, however, I do not take 600,000 at once, because Boulder Open Space would never grant a permit for such a high-impact event.)

I have discovered that with careful guidance, even adamant atheists are able to experience God outdoors. Through my work as the Adventure Rabbi, I have discovered it's not that these people don't believe in God; it's that they don't believe in the man they have been taught is God.

I'm not talking about a man in the sky named God. I am not talking about a God with a consciousness, an awareness, or an intellect. No, those are attributes our ancestors layered onto God so they could relate to God and explain the mysteries of their lives. The God I experience in the wilderness can neither talk to me nor grant me the wishes of my heart. But this God can help me connect to the deepest level of my existence and help me create a meaningful paradigm in which to live my life.

My personal theology is deeply seated in the experience of wilderness. The outdoors is what has taught me what God feels like. Expressing my Judaism outdoors enabled me to learn to use words like "God," "spirituality," and "holiness" in ways that feel authentic rather than contrived, as they did in synagogue. Wilderness reacquainted me with "awe," a concept vital for religion but hard to find in our modern technological world, and certainly difficult for many of us to find in a prayer book. (For a more detailed discussion of awe, read chapter 3, "Rediscover Awe," in my book *God in the Wilderness: Rediscovering the Spirituality of the Great Outdoors with the Adventure Rabbi*.)

Rabbi Abraham Joshua Heschel taught that we meet God in places and moments of awe. He described awe as the state we enter when we run out of words with which to express ourselves.[16] We frequently have moments like this in nature, times when all we can muster is a simple "Wow!" or perhaps even an unconscious prayer of gratitude, "Oh my God!" Hopefully, we can all recall such a moment, perhaps while watching a vibrant sunset, seeing a powerful wave crest into the ocean, or spotting a pair of hawks soaring on the thermals. Heschel proposed, and I concur, that these moments when we are moved beyond words are holy times in which we can encounter God. Heschel advocated finding awe in three ways: (1) in nature, (2) in the Bible, and (3) through the performance of mitzvot.[17]

There are many different spiritual portals, but I prefer the first one Heschel suggested: nature. How does this work? Wilderness brings us beyond ourselves and connects us with something greater than ourselves. Wilderness creates God moments, moments in which we transcend the surface meaning of our lives and connect to something deeper, the elemental levels of our existence. Maimonides might be right that these awesome God experiences are beyond the purview of words, but were I to try I would suggest the terms *pristine, primal,* and *divine.*

One of my colleagues keeps a journal in which she writes to God and asks God questions and God answers by guiding her writing. She knows it is God because she says the voice is clearly not her own. As much as I appreciate my colleague, I can't relate or believe in a call-and-response God. The meeting with God I am going to describe here is not dramatic. There is no clear voice. The best I can do for you is to describe the situations that evoke my experiences of God.

I spent my freshman year of college in an outdoor program that involved camping out every night. In our lingo, "sleeping inside" referred to sleeping in a tent while "sleeping outside" meant sleeping under the stars. For my sophomore year, I matriculated at Cornell University in Ithaca, New York. After one sleepless night in the noisy dorm room, I craved the calm of sleeping outside. After two sleepless nights, I went into our backyard and strung a simple tarp between two tall white pine trees. Much to the bewilderment of my resident advisor and classmates, I declared the tarp to be my new bedroom.

Transitioning from a full year of field studies to indoor classes and labs was difficult for me. As a freshman, I studied geology in the field with an instructor who interpreted the landscape for us. For example, we were taught about glaciers by climbing mountains and envisioning ice fields moving across the landscape, bulldozing huge boulders out of their path. Now as a sophomore at Cornell, I sat in a classroom, studying slides, maps, and charts, and highlighting passages in heavy textbooks.

The social scene was equally daunting. I had come from a tight-knit community of twenty-five people, united by our extreme environmental passion. Now I had to seek out new friends on a huge and diverse college campus. I didn't know the social rules by which college students played. My new life was lonely and overwhelming.

Late at night, when I felt crushed by the demands of textbook ornithology and plant physiology, and confused by the social mores of bars and fraternity parties, I would lie down on the soft ground beneath the white pines, inhaling the pungent sweet scent of the needles and feeling the Earth cradle me. Slowly, as I lay there, my apprehension melted away and was replaced with calm confidence that I could face the challenges of this new lifestyle I had chosen. I had the reassuring sense that I was not alone in this. I did *not* get the sense of assurance that everything works out for the best, nor that there was a divine plan behind my struggle. But I did feel connected to something larger than myself. I was acutely aware of the energy of the Earth supporting me, nourishing me, and holding me.

If someone had told me then that what I felt was God, I probably would have written him off as a New Age hippie. (I was happy being a vegetarian and environmental extremist, but I was adamant that I was not a New Age hippie.) Now in hindsight, at twice the age I was then, with five years of rabbinical seminary education, two published books, and four more in the publishing queue, and ten years as an ordained rabbi behind me, I realize that description is correct. What I experienced lying beneath the tall white pines was God. I felt the universal connection of all beings, including myself, and that experience of connection is what I understand God to be.

What is it about the outdoors that is so powerful? Why does it enable us to find God? I have asked thousands of people this question, and all of their answers can be distilled into one word: connection.

We live in a society that conspires to separate us. Not only are we separated by technology and distance, but we are also divided and subdivided. Many of us live close to neighbors we hardly know and collect hundreds of friends on Facebook but have few friends that we actually make time to have coffee with. Our culture divides us into wealthy and poor, conservative and liberal, married and single, white and nonwhite, gay and straight, with children and without children.

Transcendent experiences, such as watching the sun set over the ocean, seeing a meteor shower, or walking beside a lake, overcome these artificial differences and remind us of our connection to each other and to all aspects of the universe. Nature brings us together and helps us feel part of something larger than ourselves and connected to God. With this steadfast connection, we are able to face the stifling demands of life and the ultimate chaos of death. The continuity of cycles and seasons, so evident around us, reminds and reassures us of eternity.

One of the most readable (and most pessimistic) books of the Bible is Ecclesiastes. The author of Ecclesiastes, Kohelet, writes, "Only the Earth abides forever" (Ecclesiastes 1:4). He intends this as a despondent comparison between the longevity of the Earth and the short life of humans. But once we understand ourselves to be part of the system that includes the Earth and the universe, then we, too, abide forever and this becomes an optimistic observation. We have a place in a system that surrounds us and envelops us; we are never truly alone. When we experience this sense of connecting to something greater than ourselves, which permeates place and time, we are experiencing God.

My idea of God is so different from what appears in many traditional prayers that you might wonder why I bother with the traditional liturgy. I do, in fact, find it meaningful, even if I internally reinterpret the meaning to match my understanding of God. For me, the first step toward making traditional prayer meaningful was to move the service into the wilderness. When I pray with traditional liturgy outdoors, I am using the springboard of spirituality that I already feel outside to animate my Jewish prayers. Out there, prayers that I may have said thousands of times before suddenly become infused with meaning. Because outside, even if I can't properly express what God is, I can feel God's presence. This feeling, this intuition, is what enables me to experience prayer with sincerity.

I was once leading a group of Jewish sixteen-year-olds on a month-long backpacking trip. We had services every morning and evening. The students took turns as service leaders, but despite their efforts to be creative, most of the time the services were rushed and we said the prayers by rote. In the morning, we hurried through the assigned sequence of prayers so that we could finish them quickly and start hiking. In the evening, we again hurried through the prayers, this time because we were too exhausted to devote much energy to the enterprise. Services were boring and repetitive, and we much preferred to go down to the river, soak our feet in the icy water, and share funny stories about our day.

But one evening, our service was profoundly different. We found God.

After ten days of backpacking through Dark Canyon, we finally ascended out of it, carefully making our way up the steep embankment, past the loose rock, and up to the mesa top. From this vantage point we were able to look back at the meandering river we had followed for days. We could see the spot where we had bravely helped each other leap across the stream, the white current raging beneath us. We could see where we had hiked away from the river and run out of drinking water, and where we had found it again. We could make out where we had slept on slabs of rocks by the river because the trail to the campsite was too dangerous to navigate as the day's light faded to darkness.

Standing on the mesa, looking back at our journey, we all experienced a sublime sense of accomplishment and unity. Every member of our group had contributed to the success of this adventure.

As the sun began to set over the canyon, the beauty of this divine place moved even these sixteen-year-olds beyond words. The red and orange of the rocks seemed to glow with the setting sun. The river far below seemed to shimmer, despite the distance. The sounds of the wind played on some cottonwood leaves, gently rustling, as night fell. As our evening service began, I suggested, "Let's pray tonight as if God is the connectivity of all of us and this place, the glow of the rocks, the shimmer of the water, and the sound of the cottonwood leaves. Let's give thanks to the God of this canyon, the God of this river, and the God within each of us that enabled us to see this awesome spot, to stand here right now, together."

So we prayed. We said our usual prayers, the same prayers that we said each morning and each night: the *Shema*, *V'ahavta*, *Amidah*, and so on. But they felt drastically different. After we were done, we sat in silence for a long time until Ben, one of the students, whispered, "I've never actually done that before. I mean, say a prayer and mean it."

"Is that what it's like for people who really pray? Do they feel that connected to God every time they say these words?" asked Lisa.

"Wow. I had no idea Jewish prayer could be that expressive," said Adam. "I felt like I was Navajo Indian giving praise to the Earth. I've always envied them, the Native Americans. I didn't realize we could pray like they did."

It went on into the night: the discovery of God in the canyon. What a profound introduction to the power of prayer, and to prayer's ability to help us express the latent feelings of our hearts.

I have since had similar experiences with many groups and I know now that these intense God experiences linger on for weeks, months, and years. Every time those kids say the *Shema, V'ahavta,* or *Amidah,* whether it is under a tree or inside a sanctuary, the prayer carries with it traces of their desert experience. Every time they repeat the words, the echo of what they felt standing on top of that mesa reverberates through the canyon, through time, and meets them wherever they are.

Finding God in nature can be easier than finding God in a text or in a temple. But once we know what God experiences feel like, we can connect with God wherever we are. I can have deeply spiritual moments inside a sanctuary, even if stained-glass windows block out the view of trees and forests beyond, and I can have a God moment in a supermarket, with the checker who scans the parsley and radishes I have purchased. My Jewish outdoor experiences have helped me identify what I am looking for so that today I can notice those holy moments everywhere.

CHAPTER 17

According to What Authority?

Chutzpah even towards Heaven is effective.
BABYLONIAN TALMUD, *SANHEDRIN* 105A

After I shared one of the chapters of this book on a recent hike in Boulder, Colorado, a member of my community, Sarah, asked me, "How can you contradict everything I've been taught about God? Do you have the right to do that?" "Yes," I told her, "I do." And so do you. This is why.

There is an old Jewish saying that "standing beneath the wedding chuppah (Jewish wedding canopy) is not the best place to have an epiphany." Fortunately for me, that piece of wisdom refers to the bride and groom, not to the rabbi performing the ceremony.

What happened was this: the wedding was in some ways like every other. I stood beneath the chuppah in my formal black robe, my elegant tallis (prayer shawl) draped over my shoulders. The bride, Alison, looked radiant and proud in her white beaded gown. Beside her stood Jason, tall and confident. Behind them was a mountain meadow teeming with wildflowers, an unrestrained celebration of magenta paintbrush, scarlet foxfire, and pink shooting star, as if the whole world were celebrating this union.

The wedding proceeded as usual. I chanted this and said that, we drank two glasses of wine, beautiful words were spoken, tears of joy were shed, and so on. When we came to the vows, I said to the groom, as I always do, "Please take this ring and, placing it upon the finger of your bride, say to her the words that establish your covenant of marriage."

Jason placed a delicate gold wedding band on Alison's finger and then, clasping her hands in his, recited the ancient formula: *Harai at mekudeshet li b'taba-at zo h'dat Moshe v'Yisrael.* Be consecrated to me with this ring as my wife according to the law of Moses and Israel."

That was the moment when both of our worlds changed. Jason's because he was now married to Alison, and mine because I had an epiphany.

The last words of the Jewish wedding vow, "according to the law of Moses and Israel," startled me. For the first time, standing beside Alison and Jason, staring at the backdrop of the ancient Maroon Bell Mountains, I wondered, "What do we mean by 'according to the law of Moses and Israel'?"

Before Jason and Alison's wedding, I assumed "according to the law of Moses and Israel" meant marrying within the Jewish faith. Somewhere during my rabbinic education I had learned to take the line out when performing interfaith weddings, because a wedding between a Jew and a non-Jew is not allowed according to the law of Moses and Israel. I was taught, and I insisted, that interfaith couples change the vow to "*Ani l'dodi v'dodi li.* I am my beloved's and my beloved is mine."

When Jason said, "according to the law of Moses," for some reason I flashed to thinking about Moses's wedding to his bride Zipporah. Did Zipporah hold flowers? What kind of flowers can you get in the Sinai Desert? Yellow spiky acacia flowers? Did she and Moses stand beneath a chuppah? Who officiated? Did she wear white?

Then I realized, with a quiet but dramatic gasp, that Moses's wedding was different because Moses didn't marry a Jewish woman. Whoa! Wait a second. How could "according to the law of Moses" mean marrying a Jew? That doesn't make any sense at all! Why would Moses's law contradict Moses's behavior?

Later, between passed appetizers of smoked duck and pistachio dumplings and some fabulous mushroom caps with sun-dried tomatoes and herbs, I realized that what is even more fascinating is that the vow does not say, "according to the law of God." Why not? For centuries, Jews have understood that the traditions of our community are created not by divine authority but by the authority of the community. That is actually what we mean by "the law of Moses and Israel"—the accepted practice of our Jewish community. Guess who has the authority to determine that?

Well, not surprisingly, we mix it up a bit. We take a bit of learning from traditional texts and sprinkle in some from modern society. We give a great deal of say to the rabbinic authorities we as a community appoint. And, we admirably give a large amount of credence to the views held by concerned laypeople who are actively involved in the community. Jews do not have a pope commanding us from above; rather, we hash it out among ourselves.

One of the great examples of the power of the laypeople as it applies to Jewish tradition is in the Talmud. In this passage, two rabbis are debating which blessing should be said before drinking a glass of water. The rabbis argue and argue, and finally one says to the other, "Go and see what the people are doing" (*Berakhot* 45a).

The rabbinic scholars don't only sit around discussing the fine points of the law. (Although, admittedly, they do in other places! That is a favorite Talmudic pastime.) Rather, they go and check out the reality on the ground. What are the people doing? The Talmudic Rabbis realized that sometimes the law is based on what people are doing rather than the other way around. They understand that for a law to be embraced by the people, it has to be accepted by them. This is what we mean by "Israel."

Now there are times when some of "the people" don't want change, and they need the wisdom of governance to push them in the right direction. Think about the changes brought by the civil rights movement in this country, or women's suffrage, or even gay marriage. It takes people and governance to make effective change happen, although not always smoothly, and not always with one immediately following the other. This is why the wedding prayer does not say "according to the law of Israel," but rather "according to the law of Moses *and* Israel."

When I read "Moses and Israel" today, I understand it as this: the word *Moses* represents the historical and contemporary authorities, such as Torah, Talmud, Responsa, and our rabbis. Israel represents the people, the Jews of yesterday and today. Together we determine "the law of Moses and Israel."

When Sarah asked me, "How can you contradict everything I've been taught about God? Do you have the right to do that?" I answered yes, I believe I do, "according to the law of Moses and Israel." I follow a long Jewish tradition of questioning, as we discussed in chapter 8, and I have taken the Talmud's advice to "go and see what the people are doing" (*Berakhot* 45a). When I talk to "the people" and see what they "are doing," it rapidly becomes clear that the God they believe in is not the God we hear about at services or in the Torah. The majority of the Jews with whom I work are much more aligned with the ideas put forth in these chapters, and it is my privilege and responsibility to give these ideas a voice.

I know not everyone is going to agree with me. I know a lot of people will take exception with what I have said, and I understand that the already disturbingly large volume of hate mail I receive will increase. Tellingly, before I even signed the contract to write this book, the publisher and I had an intense conversation about whether writing such a blunt questioning of contemporary portrayals of God would be detrimental to my career as a rabbi. Ultimately, he encouraged me to write the book, saying, "I don't necessarily agree with you, but I think more people may agree with you than disagree with you."

My hope is that my writing, my work, and my teachings will help you find a God concept that echoes your experience but does not insult your intelligence and that therefore, you will be able to access the rich tradition of thought, culture, and community of our Jewish heritage. Let me be clear: I do not seek the destruction of Judaism; rather, I seek to make Judaism relevant, meaningful, and accessible.

My colleague Rabbi Jessica Zimmerman explains it another way: "Part of the difficulty of writing a book about theology is that no one can ever prove if you are right or wrong. Remember, the task is not to give an answer. The task is to provide us with the vocabulary to ask the questions. Give us the tools that enable us to talk about God, then set us loose to debate, experience, and wonder, and we will each be empowered to come up with our own understanding of God. Teach us—model for us—that it is acceptable Jewishly to break out of the confines of the God concepts that don't work for us and create something that does."

Part V

JUDAISM 2.0

*A New Understanding of God Enables
a New Understanding of Judaism*

CHAPTER 18

Why Do I Feel Attached to Judaism Even Though I Never Go to Synagogue?

I considered atheism, but there weren't enough holidays.

ANONYMOUS

Each year at Rosh Hashanah, the Adventure Rabbi Program holds a retreat combining Judaism and outdoor activities. We hike through golden aspen trees, sing *Avinu Malkeinu* on the banks of an alpine lake, and tell stories around a campfire late at night. People fly in from all over the United States to join us as we build a remarkable community in a surprisingly short amount of time.

Ironically, the only facility in Colorado that is large enough to hold our group is a Young Man's Christian Association (YMCA) camp. It is a beautiful camp, run by a delightful and accommodating staff. We cover the wooden crosses, ignore the ubiquitous references to Christianity, remember that we are their grateful guests, and make it work.

As a YMCA camp, it hosts many Christian programs at the same time as ours. The camp can hold up to 5,000 people at a time, and because we haven't reached that number of Jews attending our High Holidays retreat, we share the camp with many Christians. We have our own dining room for our 200 people, but we have to walk through the main dining hall to get to our meal.

On the way to lunch one afternoon, Rabbi Jordie Gerson, one of the other rabbis on our faculty, pointed out to me that every time she walked through the main dining hall, she overheard someone discussing his relationship with Jesus.

I wondered, "Why don't Jews sit around at lunch and talk about God?" So, abiding by the Talmudic advice to "go and see what the people are doing," I made my way into our dining hall to see what we Jews talk about.

Can you guess what I heard? I caught tidbits of a conversation between a man and a woman, both describing how their mothers had e-mailed them an article about my book and said they should go on the Adventure Rabbi Rosh Hashanah Retreat. Another woman was animatedly trying to set up a new friend with her single brother in Chicago. Several couples were planning a Sabbath potluck to keep their families together after the retreat. Two women were talking about two "hot" guys on the other side of the room and figuring out how to sit next to them during the closing circle.

Our group was talking about relationships. I suppose if we think about God in terms of Martin Buber's theology—that God is the feeling we experience in relationships—the conversations in the Jewish side of the dining hall were about God, too. Many of us access Judaism through our relationships with people, with nature, and with ritual.

Rabbi Harold Kushner, in his book *To Life!*, explains that one of the most important differences between Judaism and Christianity is that Jews were a family and a people before we developed a religion.

In contrast, he explains, "Christianity begins with an idea—the incarnation of God in Jesus, the crucifixion and resurrection of Jesus as a way of redeeming people from sin. If a person believes that idea, he is Christian. If he doesn't have that belief, however literally or metaphorically he may understand it, one might question whether he is in fact a Christian."[18] His point is that you have to have belief in Jesus Christ to be a Christian, but you don't have to have a belief to be a Jew. Instead, all you need is a sense of connection to your community.

Of course, as we know, Christians do create communities, and they do an excellent job of it! But faith is a primary commonality uniting the participants. That is why it is so common to hear Christians sitting around the YMCA dining room sharing their thoughts about their relationships with Jesus. Their conversations about Jesus deepen their connection to each other.

If a Jewish person sat down at a table in the Jewish dining room and started to talk about her relationship with God, I think she soon would find herself at a very empty table. Jews sit down and play Jewish geography. "Oh! You're from Kansas City? Do you know Danny Simon?" We connect with each other through family, food, history, and tradition. It's rare for a Jewish person to openly talk about a personal relationship with God.

Another fascinating difference between Judaism and Christianity is that Judaism began as a family, instead of an idea or a belief. We are all the great, great, great, great … grandchildren of Sarah and Abraham. Before there were prayers, scriptures, rituals, and laws, we were a family. This is a different unifying force than the unifying force of an idea.

When we meet Jewish people, we feel an instant connection that doesn't always make sense. Why? We are *mishpacha* (family)! This is not only our myth; in fact, recent genetic testing has revealed that most Jewish people share a common ancestry as descendents from only six women. We *are* family. Sometimes it feels a bit uncanny how instantly comfortable we often are with Jewish people. Is it how we talk? What we talk about? What we don't talk about? What causes we tend to support? I don't know. I know that when I meet Jewish people, even if their accent or skin color is different from mine, there is a sense of already knowing and accepting each other.

When I was living in Israel, I landed in a heated argument with an Israeli about my progressive religious stance. He had no tolerance for women being rabbis and basically felt that I and "those other Reform Jews like me" were corroding Judaism "like rust on metal." We were standing on a Jerusalem side street and all of a sudden a car came careening around the corner and almost hit me.

The Israeli grabbed me and pushed me out of the way. Then, without missing a beat, he resumed berating me. I remember thinking, "Wow! That is so uniquely Israeli. He saves me so that he can yell at me some more." If we were in Manhattan, he would have pushed me in front of the car.

Because we Jews are first and foremost a family, we can tolerate differences of belief and practice. I have rabbinic colleagues with whom I completely disagree when it comes to theology, *halacha* (Jewish law), and a whole host of other things. But I still treasure their friendship. They are family! In a family, you can have very little in common with others, but you are still family.

This also explains why the process for becoming Jewish is so different from becoming a Christian. Christian parents must baptize their child for him or her to be Christian. Traditionally, to be Jewish, you need only be born to a Jewish mother. The Reform movement controversially made this stricter by declaring a person is Jewish who is born to a Jewish parent and *raised as a Jew*. Yet even many Reform rabbis cleave to the less strict traditional law (despite its problematic gender issues) because within it a person is considered automatically Jewish solely by being born into the family. No special ceremony or education is necessary.

Have you ever wondered how Jews can feel resolutely Jewish and not participate in synagogue life at all? Because Jews are a family first and a religion second. What do people mean when they say, "I am culturally Jewish"? That they go to Jewish museums? No. Or how about, "I'm a bagel and lox Jew." They mean, "This is my tribe and these are my people."

My friend Paul Andersen, an insightful journalist based in the Roaring Fork Valley of Colorado, laments, "Why can't we all be part of one group? Why so much division?" Maybe the need to be part of a subset is in the human DNA. It feels instinctual to want to be a "M.O.T." (Member of the Tribe).

Often this familial connection makes conversion to Judaism for marriage problematic. You can't take bagel and lox classes on how to be culturally Jewish, although the field trips sure would be tasty. "Now this is Zabar's," the instructor would say. "Zabar's is Jewish, but not necessarily kosher, as you can see by the meat and cheese selection behind the counter. Have you ever tasted such good rugelach?"

They might need to teach you how to order from a New Yorker who tells *you* what you want: "Nah, you don't want that. You want a nice pastrami on rye. Look at how nicely marbled and fatty it is today! Have that with a little mustard."

You can't teach someone the comfort a child feels baking challah with her *bubbe* (grandmother) or a little boy's glee upon finding the *afikomen* (piece of matzah hidden for children to find) that his *zayde* (grandfather) hid under the sofa cushions. You can teach the recipe for challah baking and the rules for conducting a Seder, but how could you possibly transmit the cumulative years of memories or the feelings that the smell of fresh-baked challah and the taste of matzah kugel evoke?

Instead, potential converts take religious classes and fulfill religious requirements such as attending synagogue, keeping the dietary laws, and then for fun they learn to conjugate Hebrew verbs. Often converts end up being more ritually observant than their born-Jewish spouses. We've all heard stories about a born-Jewish person saying to his Jew-by-Choice spouse, "Well I wanted you to be Jewish, but not THAT Jewish."

At the Yom Kippur service I lead, we hang signs all over the rooms with common reasons people come to services. We begin the evening by inviting people to break into groups based on the reasons they came to *Kol Nidre*. The posters read:

I come because my (husband/wife/boss/partner/parent) asked/told me to.

I come to connect with the Jewish community.

I come to connect with Jewish culture and history.

I come because this is what Jewish people do.

I come to connect nature with Judaism.

I come to pray to God, to repent my sins against God, and to ask forgiveness from God.

I come to repent for my sins against other people and to make *teshuvah* (atonement).

I come to connect with my family who is not here (i.e., my family is in New York, but going to services makes me feel connected to them).

I come to connect with my family who is here.

I come for a spiritual Jewish experience.

The smallest group is always the God group. Overall, for most of us, the underlying reason we come to Yom Kippur services is to be with our Jewish community, our extended family.

Yom Kippur is said to be the holiest day of the year. The evening service, with its bone-chilling chanting of *Kol Nidre*, has the power to draw in Jews who don't set foot in a sanctuary for the other 364 days of the year. What is it that brings them there? The connection to family.

The image that I find most appealing for Yom Kippur is not of God sitting in Heaven with ledger in hand, nor of scales weighing good versus bad deeds, nor even of gates closing. The image that works for me is this:

On Yom Kippur, Abraham and Sarah look down at us from Heaven to see how the family is doing. It is they, our great, great, great ... grandparents, not God, who recount our deeds.

Sarah looks down and says, "Oy, such *naches* (joy)! Do you see what our Jeanette did this year? God promised our offspring would be as numerous as the stars, but who knew Jeanette would be a rocket scientist making machines that fly amongst the stars?"

Abraham joins in, "Do you see our sweet Bobby? He is in college and is studying the family history, they call it Jewish studies! He is teaching the *kinderlach* (children)!"

Sarah points out, "Do you see our Molly, Jennah, Emma, Jacob, Dan, Scott, and David—can you believe they are in the Adventure B'nei Mitzvah class already? They will each be learning about a chapter of the family scrapbook. They call it the Torah!"

"I'm so glad we left them such a good family album so they can know what we did and what we saw. I know I pestered you about collecting those postcards every place we stopped, but now I am so glad we have them all together in one book!" adds Abraham.

"Look at the new babies!" says Sarah.

"They call that little one Sarah! They named her after you!" says Abraham.

"What a *mechaieh* (delight)!" says Sarah.

Abraham and Sarah look down at each of us, lovingly *kvelling* (proudly boasting) over the good, tenderly pushing us to correct our ways when we go astray, and quietly consoling when things go awry.

Perhaps, when we get that urge this time of the year to come to synagogue, it is because while we slept, Sarah and Abraham quietly whispered in our ears, "It's time to come home! Come be with the family! I know you are busy, but only for one night. It would mean so much to us. Your cousins want to meet you."

Although Abraham and Sarah's tent has grown too small to hold us all, we still gather together, shake hands, and embrace. We are family. We may not all believe the same things, we may not all practice in the same manner, but we are family, to be welcomed and to be embraced. Welcome home!

CHAPTER 19

Who Wrote the Torah?

If there were no God, it would have been necessary to invent him.

VOLTAIRE

Traditional Jews believe that the Torah (the first five books of the Bible) was revealed to Moses on Mount Sinai. Literalists believe that God dictated the Torah word for word to Moses. God said, "Moses, jot this down. It's dictation time." Moses whipped a stone chisel out of his back pocket and carved it in stone, word for word, so that you and I can read God's words today.

An interesting aside: the reason Hebrew reads from right to left is that it was easier to chisel words into stone if you chiseled right to left. Imagine you are chiseling words into stone. Your dominant hand (usually right) would hold the hammer and your less strong hand would hold the chisel. Because of the angle, it works best if you move from right to left. Once we started writing with ink, writing from left to right worked better, so righties (the statistical majority) wouldn't smudge the ink as the right hand moved across the page. Moses was probably a righty, if he had to chisel that whole big book.

Other people believe that God only dictated the Ten Commandments on Sinai and that the rest of the text was gradually revealed later. In this case, Moses may have been a lefty.

Others hold that God gave Moses the entire Torah and the Talmud (a legal code for daily life, considered the most important Jewish text), the latter of which was then passed down verbally from generation to generation and thus called the Oral Law.

The Reform movement, in which I was ordained, teaches that rather than being the literal word of God, the Torah is a record of our people's experience of God. We believe that the Torah is an exquisite book, from which we can drink deeply. But although the text remains central to our practice, we recognize that it was written by multiple authors, fallible people whose vision was inspired and limited by the time in which they lived.

Scholars have been able to look at the text and, by tracking different names for God, divergent writing styles, and distinct themes, identify individual authors who wrote segments of the Torah at different times. We teach that the Torah's teachings are influenced by the agendas and biases of its authors. Consequently, there are segments we are duty bound to reinterpret or even disagree with.

The Torah's concept of commandments (mitzvot) and of God as the "commander" have served as effective shortcuts for commanding actions that lead to a meaningful life. But the Reform movement would say that the true command comes from inside ourselves and from those within our community whom we have appointed as experts and authorities.

As you can see, even within normative Judaism, we have radically different thoughts about the divine revelation. As they say: two Jews, three opinions. If that's not confusing enough, sometimes it's one Jew, two opinions.

For example, Maimonides, whom we learned about in chapter 9, preached publicly that the Torah was revealed by God to Moses on Sinai. But some students of his works believe that this was only his belief as written for the public. In private, they argue Maimonides doubted the possibility of revelation at Sinai because it didn't make rational sense. What is this dichotomy about?

The Jews of Maimonides' time lived in Islamic-ruled lands. The Muslims were very critical of the Jews and accused them of tampering with the original texts. Jews and Muslims have different interpretations of the same story. For example, in the Muslim tradition, Abraham's eldest son Ishmael is the hero, but in the Jewish story he is the villain, while his younger brother, Isaac, is the hero.

Conceding that the Bible was an interpretation might have had terrible consequences for the Jews. Therefore, some scholars believe that Maimonides asked himself the age-old question: "Is it good for the Jews?" Deciding the answer was "No," he taught that the Bible was the word of God in order to keep Muslim critics at bay.

Believing that the Torah is the literal word of God has some perks. It certainly reduces the number of decisions you have to make. It gives you security and answers many of your questions. It gives you a clear path, and lets you know how to live your life and where you are going. If God said you should do something a certain way, you should do it that way. It's pleasantly unambiguous and appeals to people who crave guiding authority in their lives.

I don't believe that our sacred texts are the literal words of God, because I don't think that God has words. But I do believe there are sacred words. What do I mean?

Different people experience God differently. Each of us translates our experience into language we can understand. When I say language, I am speaking broadly, including words, art, music, and so on. When a great musician accesses his connection with divinity, he might express it as a concerto. Ludwig van Beethoven is quoted as saying, "Music is a higher revelation than all wisdom and philosophy."

But when a kindergarten teacher taps into her connection with the divine, she might write on the blackboard in language a five-year-old can understand: "When someone is not nice to you, it's hard to be her friend." For some of the five-year-olds in Mrs. Jenak's kindergarten class, *these* are sacred words.

Tapping into divinity is like digging a well into groundwater. If you and I both dug wells in our backyard, the water might taste and look different. It would have absorbed the unique minerals of the rock that surrounded it beneath the ground. It may or may not have been contaminated by pollutants or other chemicals. The water is still water, but it will look and taste differently, depending on the environment. So, too, a Jew, a Muslim, a musician, and an artist each tap into divinity and come out with different teachings.

Just as some sources of water are less altered—such as melted ice from an ancient glacier—and others are more adulterated by additives—such as water in a flavored water drink, so, too, some God sources are more pure and others are more diluted.

Thousands of years ago the Rabbis tapped into their connection with divinity and wrote the Torah, the Talmud, and our other great texts. The words themselves are not God's words, but the writings are powerful because they reflect our ancestors' effort to understand and explain God.

Sometimes the way a person experiences God tells us more about the person than it does about God. What do we learn about our ancestors from reading the Torah? What did they know that can help us live more meaningful lives? How did they view God and religion as a force to bring peace and contentment into their world?

Strikingly, the biblical experience of God is laden with legal metaphors. The lens with which our ancestors experienced God was covenant and command. It's as if they were all lawyers out there in the desert, writing the biblical narratives. (It must have been a Jewish mother's dream come true. I can almost hear the moms *kvelling*, "Oy, such *naches*! Oh! Such joy! A whole tribe of lawyers! Now, if only we had a few doctors!") But, jokes aside, what our ancestors created was a legal system to guide our lives. We take that for granted, noting that the Torah contains 613 mitzvot (commandments), rules requiring us to do this and not that.

Doesn't it seem odd that the biblical emphasis is more on rules than on faith? The Rabbis explain that we can't command faith but that the mitzvot (commandments) are actions that lead us to faith. Rabbi Abraham Joshua Heschel (chapter 14) prayed with his feet by participating in a civil rights march in Selma, emphasizing the importance of actions as a pathway to God. To paraphrase his teachings, "Act now, and you may eventually come to faith." Much of our traditional emphasis on social justice, civil rights, and environmental action stems from the priority we place on action.

There is also a more pragmatic reason. The Torah was written by a community that was expanding from a family into a nation. Remember: Joseph's family went to Egypt as a family group composed of twelve brothers and their father, Jacob. When the freed slaves came out 400 years later, there were 600,000 of them. The family had transformed into a nation.

Now that they were a nation rather than just a family, what did they need at this juncture? They needed laws to structure their community. They needed a code to bring stability and meaning to their lives. They needed 613 mitzvot, rules telling them to do this and not do that.

Historically, the next really big book, the Babylonian Talmud, expands on these rules. The Talmud is also not a book about belief. Interestingly, one of the common debates among Talmudic Rabbis was about which should take precedence, studying the *halacha* (the rules that govern our actions) or praying to God. Study generally won out.

The Talmud and the Torah, arguably our most sacred books, teach us to be kind, compassionate, and thoughtful people despite living in a dog-eat-dog world. The Torah text inspires and challenges us to fill our lives with meaning. It offers us the prospect of holiness, time that is elevated and set apart from the frenetic discourse of life. It teaches us how to create sacred times, such as Sabbath and holidays, much needed insulation from the fray of modernity.

Meanwhile, the Talmud builds on the Toraitic discourse. The Rabbis in the Talmud debate among themselves and with other rabbis throughout history, and establish the laws through which Judaism guides our everyday lives. It explores and further explains concepts set forth in the Torah. Examples are discussions on what constitutes forbidden work on the Sabbath and acceptable reasons for granting a divorce, as well as more intangible considerations, such as judging someone by his inner qualities, not his outer appearance (*Pirke Avot* 4:27).

The Rabbis of the Talmud were living in the Diaspora and trying to establish modalities of ritual and practice that could keep Judaism relevant outside the boundaries of a sovereign Jewish nation. When we read through the laws they created, many of them are as relevant today as they were in their time. In some ways, our ancestors' struggle is not so distant from our own. Judaism remains relevant today not because of our relationship with a divine being, but because our religion provides us with an interpretation of life that brings meaning to our everyday actions. Through the Torah, Talmud, and other texts, Judaism creates order, establishes priorities, and builds values in an otherwise chaotic world.

Because I am involved in so much outdoor, nature-based work, I interact with many people who argue that we would be better off learning how to behave from the natural world. They explain that we would learn how to be part of an interactive web, how to participate in community, how our actions affect others, and so on. One of the Jewish lessons I love to point out is that Judaism actually implores us to rise above the call of nature. In nature, "survival of the fittest" rules. The strong thrive and survive, while the weak are marginalized and perish. In contrast, Judaism teaches us to overthrow this natural order.

Centuries before Thomas Hobbes (1588–1679) famously described life without law as "solitary, poor, nasty, brutish, and short," Judaism had already introduced the need to impose moral order onto humans' natural instincts. As Jews, we seek justice for the vulnerable and protect the orphan, the widow, and the stranger. The Torah commands us thirty-six times to protect the stranger, who symbolizes all the vulnerable members of the community. As Jews, we strive to create a world that serves not only our own best interest but that is also built on justice, where even the defenseless are cared for.

So who wrote the Torah? Our ancestors wrote the Torah—and we continue to "write" it today. At b'nei mitzvah ceremonies, I tell students that the Torah contains two kinds of letters. The black letters are those scribed onto the parchment. These are the stories of our ancestors, the shared narrative of our people.

But if you look at a Torah scroll closely, you will see that there also appear to be other letters. White letters are created by the spaces between the black letters. If you haven't seen this for yourself, ask a rabbi to show you. It's similar to the black-and-white drawings in which you see a woman or a vase, depending on your focus. For an example, visit www.GodUpgrade.com/white. I tell my students that these white letters are the stories we write with our own lives, as we continue the tradition of interpreting Torah and building it into our very existence.

If we accept or believe that people wrote the Torah and that the commandments (mitzvot) are not coming from the commander (God), but instead from years of writing by various Jewish people, then the next question we might ask is, does God hear our prayers?

CHAPTER 20

Does God Hear Our Prayers?

I cannot conceive of a God who rewards and punishes his creatures, or has a will of the kind that we experience in ourselves.

ALBERT EINSTEIN

It was one of those typically gorgeous Colorado days with our famous big blue skies above and fresh snow below. After a morning of exhilarating skiing, thirty-five or so of us gathered at Copper Mountain's outdoor chapel site for a slopeside Sabbath service. As is my custom, I gave a brief three-minute talk about some of the writing I have been working on. That day, I talked about my God concept and then asked for questions. A man, visiting from New York, quickly raised his hand and asked, "Does God hear our prayers?" I answered, "I don't believe so."

He continued, "So what are we doing here?" I answered, "We are here so I can hear your prayers and so you can hear mine."

"I do not pray to God when I pray," I explained. "I *experience* God through my prayers. Through my voice and yours joining together, and through the timeless echoes of those who came before me, I imagine my prayers joining those of my ancestors as I speak the same words they did, layer upon layer."

How does this work? Sometimes prayer is like a meditation. I repeat a Hebrew phrase over and over and suddenly find myself descending below the tumult of my life to a place of quietude, reassurance, and calm. Prayer is the tool I use to loosen the binds of my life and to submerge myself in a sea of calm and connection.

Other times I experience God through the communal encounter prayer provides. As I described to the skier from New York, hearing my voice join with others is a very powerful God experience for me. The shared language of prayer, even (or perhaps especially) saying words in a language we do not understand, enables us to connect with each other in a unique way. Saying the same exact words that I know my grandmother said when she lit the Shabbat candles with the same exact candlesticks I now use, or that 1,807 miles away in New York my parents are saying, is another type of God experience.

Other times—for example, when I say a quick prayer before eating or upon spotting an exceptionally beautiful flower, or when arriving safely at the end of a long trip—a prayer is a speed bump in my day, a reminder to slow down and be aware of what is happening in the moment. A man in my Pilates class has a tattoo on his arm that says "breathe." I imagine he occasionally catches a glance of the tattoo and remembers to take a deep breath and relax. Prayers work like that, except they don't usually hurt as much as getting a tattoo.

Still other times, prayers give me words to express my emotions when I can't find the words myself. A similar experience that might be more familiar is when you hear a songwriter's lyrics express an idea that describes exactly what you feel, but you just couldn't say it quite as well. The truly great liturgists are like great poets and composers. Their poetry, melodies, even the cadences of their prayers, enable us to express our deepest emotions—our longing, despair, gratitude, anger, hope, and joy.

Of course, I can write my own prayers, and I do. Judaism has a long tradition of spontaneous and personal prayer. I also write my own poetry and my own songs. But, as much as my children love me, they insist that their favorite children's singer, Jeff Kagen, has much better lyrics than I do. I am no Mozart and I am no Robert Frost. I am not even as good a lyricist as Jeff Kagen. That is why I use prayers written by talented and time-tested liturgists. The timeless prayers of great liturgists who wrote beloved prayers like *Kol Nidre*, *Avinu Malkeinu*, and *Oseh Shalom* coax emotions from within us, as they take us deep within ourselves and beyond ourselves.

In Hebrew the word "to pray" is the reflexive verb *lehitpallel*. It literally means "to judge oneself, to evaluate oneself." Reflexive verbs are actions you do to yourself, such as "I feed myself," "I bathe myself," "I berate myself." "I pray myself" seems like a funny construct, until we realize that praying is not about asking God for something. Prayer is an inner and a communal dialogue. Prayer is about reminding ourselves of our priorities and about connecting ourselves with our community.

Of course there are plenty of prayers that have been written specifically to ask God to do something, including the first prayer uttered in the Bible. Moses asks God to heal his sister Miriam, who was stricken with leprosy, saying, "O God, please heal her" (Numbers 12:13).

The types of petitionary prayers that I find the most challenging are healing prayers. Prayers for healing are among the most complicated prayers for many of us, and so I want to devote some time to those prayers in particular. There have been studies that indicate healing prayer works. According to these studies, people who are prayed for, even if they don't know it, get better faster and have a more complete recovery. Unfortunately for those who practice healing prayer, there have been many more studies recently undermining the theory that prayer works and explaining why all the original studies were wrong. But not surprisingly, there are people who choose to ignore whichever set of studies they disagree with.

Let me tell you about an interaction I had earlier this year with my friend Maureen, a deacon. It was early in the morning and already she looked distracted and distraught. She shared with me that one of her parishioners, a nineteen-year-old, had just died of leukemia. Maureen's grief was palpable and so was her spiritual tumult.

She told me, almost pleadingly, "We prayed and prayed. We prayed for God's healing power. We prayed for the light of God to be with him. We laid hands on him. We prayed for hours and hours, for days and weeks, with sincerity. We prayed with all of our hearts. And he died. What am I supposed to do with that?"

She paused to wipe her tears away, then continued, "One of my colleagues says God did answer the prayer, and the answer was 'No.' What kind of answer is that? What am I supposed to do now when someone comes to me and asks me to pray for healing for her? One of the ministers I work with said God's answer was to take him to Heaven, where he is needed more than he is needed here. Try telling that to his little sister. 'Sorry, honey, but God needed him more than you did.'"

She was looking for explanations, but I think she knew she would not find them with me. Instead we sat together. We struggled together. We commiserated together. The rabbi and the deacon. Some say that experience of togetherness is God, a Buber I-Thou moment. Maybe it is. Or maybe it is just two people being kind to each other, sharing our hurt, our frustration, and our spiritual turmoil.

She asked me about my thoughts on prayers for healing. I explained that the traditional Jewish prayer for healing makes little sense to me theologically, although when I am leading a service, I almost always read it. I ask for God's blessing on the sick, saying, "May the one who blessed the ones before us bring complete healing of body and soul to our loved ones."

I admit I am often tempted to leave this prayer out of a service, and sometimes I do skip it. More often than not, I say it because it brings comfort, hope, and strength to so many people. And, I do like to provide the opportunity for people to share the hurt in their lives so we can comfort each other, as communities do.

For people who are ill or injured, sometimes I'll make a video of myself singing the prayer and e-mail it to them or sing a blessing on a voice mail message that can be played repeatedly. People do play it again and again and again. They are so grateful when I do this because they feel remembered. Do they feel touched by God? I don't know.

Reverend Beverly Fest is the chaplain at our local hospital. She says patients often ask, "Why would God do this to me (give me this illness)?" and "How does God choose who to heal and who not to?" She tells them that she doesn't think God works that way. She adds, "And if God did, why would you want to be in a relationship with that kind of God?"

If you look at synagogue services today, my skepticism about healing prayers seems not to be shared. The healing prayer is among the most popular of all the prayers. Even people who don't care to come to services will call in names of sick friends and ask that they be put on the list. In some synagogues, the list gets so long (because by human nature many people forget to call back to let the rabbi know that the name can be taken off) that it threatens to take over the entire time allotted for the service!

The name we use for healing prayers, *Misheberach*, is indicative of the central place the prayer has taken in our services. Jews have a whole category of prayers called *misheberach* (literally, "the one who blesses"). For example, we say a *misheberach* for a birthday, for an anniversary, or for a person who reads from the Torah. Yet, *Misheberach* (with a capital M) has come to mean a prayer for healing, just as Kleenex has come to mean a tissue.

I will admit that when my father was having open heart surgery, I called his cantor, Benjie Ellen Schiller, to ask her to make a *Misheberach*. Certain events appear to override my doubt about the efficacy of prayer, and one of them is open heart surgery on my father. Another is when I am backcountry skiing too close to an avalanche-prone area. Besides, Cantor Schiller's voice is so beautiful and her prayers so sincere that God surely must take her calls.

My father had a heart attack the day my husband and I came back from our honeymoon. He could have had it when we asked our family and friends to hike a mile uphill in three feet of snow to our Colorado wedding. He could have had it while my charming husband and I were on our honeymoon hiking overseas. But my dad is a truly thoughtful man, and so he kindly waited until our plane had safely landed on U.S. soil. We had barely unpacked our bags when we got the call. We rushed back to the airport and boarded a plane to New York City.

We arrived in time to see my father before the surgery. He was in intensive care. You know the drill—lots of tubes everywhere, machines that beep, nurses rushing in and out, and thin curtains separating each patient in a feeble gesture of privacy.

I stood next to my father and held his hand as he prepared to go into surgery. He asked me to say the *Shema* with him before he went under. The *Shema* is the prayer we are supposed to utter with our dying breath, the last words we say and hear before we die. My father wanted to be prepared just in case. His request shook me to my core, but I prayed the *Shema* with him. "*Shema Yisrael: Adonai Eloheinu, Adonai Echad*. Hear, O Israel, the Lord is our God, the Lord is One," we said.

I could see in his eyes that the ritual gave him some strength to face what was ahead. Not that he was ready to die. He was not. But hearing the words, *"Shema Yisrael: Adonai Eloheinu, Adonai Echad,"* which so many people have said before him, gave him strength. He was not alone in his fear or pain. He was not the first, and he will not be the last. He was connected to something larger, a community that resounded through time and steadied him in this moment.

Saying ritualized words of oneness and connection like these gave both of us comfort and hope. We were reminded of the oneness of all. And the ritual itself created order. Saying a prescribed prayer helped us to combat the suffocating fear of the ultimate threat of chaos—death.

The act of asking his cantor to pray the traditional prayers for him put my father's community on red alert. Asking her to say a *Misheberach* was kind of like testing the emergency broadcast system. "Are you there for us?" Okay, they are there for us. I tested the system and now I know that even if the worst came, my family and I would not be facing it alone. My parents' congregation would support us every step of the way, comforting us, bringing us meals, sharing stories with us, and so on. I drew strength from the knowledge that a community stood beside us, as is traditional for a Jewish community to do, and would catch us if we needed them to.

After the surgery, my father told me, "Jamie, I made a deal with God. I told Him, 'God, if You let me live, I promise I will go to shul (synagogue) every Shabbos.'"

"But Dad," I said, "you already go to shul every Shabbos."

"Ah!" he said. "Yes, I do. But I never *promised* to go."

My Dad does in fact go to shul every Shabbos, as promised. As for me, I didn't pray to anyone to do anything. I didn't make any deals or ask for intervention, because I don't think it works that way. I did hope that the surgeon had a good night's sleep. And that no one ate the last scoop of the Ben and Jerry's Cherry Garcia ice cream that the anesthesiologist was planning to eat the night before, thus putting her in a bad mood.

Although I did not pray for God to do this or that, I did find comfort in hearing and saying those ancient words, passed on from generation to generation. I found strength in abiding by an ancient ritual that gave me handholds in a precarious moment.

It is in this, the ritual, based on a solid tradition, passed lovingly from generation to generation, that Judaism is made relevant and meaningful to me. We are inheritors of wisdom, collaborated on for centuries by people sometimes wiser than and sometimes not as wise as you and me. It is our task to study what we have been taught, to sift through it carefully, and then to add our own learning to this collective effort.

CHAPTER 21

My Life Is Already Overbooked. Why Should I Make Time for Judaism?

The important thing is not to stop questioning.
ALBERT EINSTEIN

I was sitting at my computer, writing, when all of a sudden I realized, with a sinking feeling in my gut, that I had missed my daughter Sadie's kindergarten end-of-the-year Fun and Fitness Day. She had mentioned it at dinner the night before and I meant to look it up to see what she was talking about, but then I answered a phone call, which led to writing a follow-up e-mail, and then I forgot all about it.

When I finally remembered to check, I found in an announcement in a previously unread newsletter, "Fun and Fitness Day! Come share what your children have learned in kindergarten this year! 8:30 to 9:30 a.m." Unfortunately, it was now 10:30 a.m.

While all the other kids spent the morning with their parents, jumping across logs and crawling through tunnels, showing off their dexterity and speed for their parents in running races and tower climbing, my daughter and her friend held hands and did it together because neither of their parents showed up. Ouch.

There are moments of parenthood in which I feel like I am acting like the busy father in Harry Chapin's song "Cat's in the Cradle." Time after time he promises that soon he will make time to be with his son. "We'll have a good time then, son, you know we'll have a good time then," the father repeats again and again. Most of the time I remember that I am a great mother who does spend lots of quality time with my children, but I only volunteered in Sadie's classroom for three days during the whole school year. In my defense, she only goes to kindergarten for three hours a day, which means my precious quiet time for writing is very limited. That is irrelevant to Sadie, when Lia's mom comes to school every Thursday for book bag day.

It is hard to write a book, a paragraph, or even a sentence if all you hear in your mind is: "When are you coming home? I don't know when, but we'll have a good time then, you know we'll have a good time then."[19]

Do you know what I have never forgotten this year? Not once? Making Havdalah, the ceremony that concludes Sabbath. For me to forget to say good-bye to Sabbath with a braided candle, spices, and wine would be like Larry, our mailman, forgetting to bring us the mail.

I sit here trying to understand the difference.

Life is chaotic. We are overwhelmed by information and activity choices. What do we read thoroughly and what do we skim quickly? What do we file away for future reference and what do we discard even before reading? How often should I go to my children's myriad activities and when should I let the babysitter take them?

Let's not forget about the hundreds of people at work who need my attention, the plethora of voice mails and e-mails. Who do I call first and who can wait a few days? Who do I need to call myself, and who can I have another staff person call back?

I am what they call a "well-boundaried person." I carefully reserve time for my family, time for my work, and time for my daily exercise. Yet I still find the onslaught of needs—both my children's and my congregants'—demoralizing and paralyzing. How do we figure out what to do first and second and third? How do I decide what time to take for work and what time for family?

Judaism gives me a framework; it includes a weekly and yearly schedule. Judaism uses ritual to provide structure to our otherwise unpunctuated lives. Judaism moves my life from chaos to contentment. Each week, time is built into my schedule and integrated into my life's rhythm. That established schedule is why I never skip Havdalah, because I don't have to decide every week if I should do it or not. No one needs to send me a flyer or an e-mail. Every single week when Sabbath arrives, I turn off my computer and create time with my community, my family, and myself. I have unburdened moments to reflect on the week that has passed, as well as an intentional ritual to leave the week behind. When Havdalah arrives, I am ready to look optimistically ahead to the week to come.

Judaism has centuries of practice creating order out of chaotic lives. We think we are the first generation to experience sensory overload. What would the authors of the Torah have to say about declaring e-mail bankruptcy as a solution for feeling overwhelmed? But our ancestors also experienced the world as overwhelming. Let's look at what they wrote about.

The creation story from the Bible may tell us more about the creators of the story than about the creation of the Earth. The first lines read:

> When God began to create Heaven and Earth—the Earth being unformed and void, and darkness was over the surface of the deep, and a wind from God was sweeping over the water—God said, "Let there be light"; and there was light.
>
> GENESIS 1:1–3

When our ancestors imagined the beginning of the world, before God began to create, what did they picture? A deep, dark, shapeless, chaotic, undefined something. Nothing is ordered or bordered.

Then God began His cosmic work. God created order out of chaos. God took the big primordial soup and put the planets into solar systems and the stars into constellations. God separated light from darkness, water from land, land from sky, day from night. God created boundaries, six days for work and one for rest.

Sometimes when I am reading the creation story from Genesis, I look at consecutively larger circles in my life, first around at my desk, then out to my yard, and then beyond to the world news, and I feel like very little has changed, except, of course, the scale. I'm upset about my books not being put away on the shelf, the weeds overtaking my garden, and armies seemingly irrationally invading other countries, while the creation story is talking about the universe being in disarray. These situations all invoke the unsettled feeling that accompanies disorder.

The creation story expresses our ancestors' discomfort with living in an overwhelming, disordered world. They asked the same questions we do. What am I supposed to be doing here? What is my place in the universe? How do I live a meaningful life? What do I do first? How do I pick and choose my priorities in order to create a meaningful path through life?

One of the ways in which religion makes our lives meaningful is by creating boundaries and separation. Judaism takes our unpunctuated lives and inserts the punctuation. We have Sabbath for commas, Rosh Hashanah for periods, bar and bat mitzvah for exclamation points, and so on. Judaism gives structure to our days, weeks, months, and years.

Now if another rabbi were writing this book, this next section might be about how to make your life meaningful by separating your Swiss cheese from your hamburger, setting Saturday aside from the rest of the week by going to synagogue, and making a distinction between Jewish people and non-Jewish people by not marrying the non-Jewish ones. But I'm not going to do that. In order for Judaism to work, in order for Judaism to effectively bring meaning to our lives, we also have to let our lifestyle influence the way we practice Judaism.

Remember my self-righteous example of never missing Havdalah? It wasn't always like that. When our second daughter, Ori, was about eighteen months old, I experienced a miracle. I slept through the night. I went to sleep and then I woke up. It was morning. There was nothing in between. No crying, no screaming, no 2 a.m. or 4 a.m. or 6 a.m. diaper changing, no 1 a.m. or 3 a.m. or 5 a.m. bottle. I was nothing short of euphoric.

The next morning was Sabbath and I was sitting in the living room with the clarity of mind that a full night's sleep delivers, when I noticed that our Havdalah candle was the same height it had been a few months earlier. The braided candle should steadily burn down week by week and need to be replaced every few months, but ours was keeping a steady height. Either there was something magical going on in our home, or we had missed a week or two of Havdalah. Suddenly it occurred to me that I could not even remember the last time we had celebrated Havdalah.

Friday night blessings are easy to remember because you set the table and prepare a special meal, and the whole exercise leads up to that beautiful moment of song and prayer. Or even if you don't make a special meal, the point is that you still have to say the blessings before you can eat. It's like stopping at the tollbooth before you drive over the bridge. After a while you do this reflexively. It is kind of like using an automatic toll pass instead of digging for loose change under your car seat.

But Havdalah stands alone. It is attached only to the appearance of three stars in the Saturday night sky. In a house with little kids, Havdalah is especially difficult. Havdalah has this pesky habit of coming late at night. Even when Havdalah is reasonably early, it still competes with a packed evening lineup: bath, teeth brushing, face washing, pajama time, rounding up favorite stuffed animal time, reading time, and bedtime.

I guess forgetting Havdalah was a gradual thing. As the days grew longer and Havdalah grew later, I said to myself, "We can do Havdalah after the kids are asleep." Then I would fall asleep putting them to sleep, and that was that.

There I sat on the couch and realized that Ori, who knew the sequence of the Sabbath prayers perfectly, thought Havdalah was something we do on very special occasions, not every Saturday.

We keep our Havdalah set on a table in the living room next to the Sabbath candles that my grandmother brought over on the boat from Europe. Looking at them together, I suddenly had the solution. We light the Sabbath candles when we sit down for dinner. The official candle-lighting time is completely irrelevant to me. I don't even know when it is. In my house, Sabbath begins at 5 p.m., winter, summer, spring, or fall. So why wait for three stars for Havdalah? Why not do Havdalah before dinner, the same way we do Sabbath blessings?

That very night, overriding protests of "Why do we have to do Havdalah? I'm hungry!" that is what we did and have done every Saturday since. We have adapted the Jewish practice to fit our lifestyle. Now, each week, my family gathers before dinner for Havdalah. There are no longer complaints; it is just what we do. Bathed in the soft light of the braided candle, we sing the blessings and optimistically look forward to a week of peace. Ori and Sadie each proudly pass around a spice box. Havdalah has become such a part of Ori's life that she even named her stuffed lion "li-li" after the Debbie Friedman melody we sing. (Visit www.GodUpgrade.com/havdalah to learn this prayer.)

I should have been at Fun and Fitness Day. Of course I should have. But in a world of overwhelming choices, I am thankful that there are certain moments built into my week when without fail I know I am there for my children.

Shortly after I wrote this, my friend and I were commiserating about our struggles as working mothers and how hard it is trying to divide our attention and energy between children and work. I was going on and on about how great Havdalah is as a weekly time to be together. We sing songs, we light the long braided candle, we sip the sweet grape juice, and we smell the pungent spices. I explained that it only takes a few minutes, is much simpler than welcoming Sabbath or making the whole day special (which we also do as a family but I knew she did not), and that she, too, could bring it into her family life. She looked at me like I was nuts. "I wouldn't know what to do with a Havdalah candle if I had one, which I don't," she said.

"Oh, but it's so easy," I said. "I can teach you."

"Jamie, for someone who gets it, you really don't get it," she said. "Havdalah makes no contextual sense for my family. We don't do anything for Sabbath and we are not going to, so what are we ending? Besides, at your house, Havdalah is lovely because you can sing. Without song, it's not quite as lovely."

She continued, "If you want Judaism to be meaningful to me every day, give me something else. Give me something that fits into the interstitial spaces of my very ordinary life and fills it with meaning. Don't ask me to buy something, or go somewhere, or learn something complicated."

She was right and I knew it, and I was a little annoyed because I was raring to go with my "Havdalah in Every Home!" campaign. But nonetheless, I started looking for something for her.

I found my answer while I was studying the Torah portion of that week. The Torah contains a classification of laws called *chukat*, laws that have no rational reason but that we are supposed to obey anyway.

The kashrut (kosher) laws are examples of *chukat*. Now, there are a lot of reasons we can make up for why it's good to keep kosher, but they are not the biblical reason. In the Bible, God uses the perennial parental favorite, "Why? Because I said so, that's why!"

The brilliance of creating laws around food is that we eat every day, several times a day! Suddenly, a very mundane act like eating a peanut butter and jelly sandwich becomes a Jewish activity.

If we are looking for simple Jewish moments to interject into our days, to make Judaism more relevant and our lives more meaningful, we need look no further than the prayer before we eat, the same prayer we say over the challah. There are distinct prayers mandated for different foods, but if you are just getting started I suggest saying the mainstream prayer, the *Motzi*: *Baruch atah, Adonai, Eloheinu melech ha-olam, ha-motzi lechem min ha-aretz.* Blessed are You, Creator of the Universe, who brings forth bread from the Earth." (To hear the *Motzi* visit www.GodUpgrade.com/motzi.)

Saying a prayer before we eat gives us a momentary pause before we dig in. We notice who we are with and what we are about to eat. We are thankful. We connect with each other and with something larger than ourselves. Although it only takes ten seconds, don't underestimate the cumulative power of this prayer. Pausing to say this prayer is a spiritual portal that can open you to the power of Jewish ritual. Most spiritual traditions teach that a spiritual practice begins with awareness—with noticing, pausing, and appreciating. The *Motzi* offers a simple and accessible way to incorporate awareness into your day.

If you are fortunate enough to eat with others who know this prayer, it is a lovely way to accentuate your shared heritage. We stop and we notice with whom we are seated and what food we are about to enjoy. We pause to express our gratitude with a prayer our people have said for generations.

If you are alone, or with people you are not comfortable saying a prayer in front of, say it quietly to yourself. Even said silently, the prayer prompts you to notice and then express your gratitude for the food. The formulaic recitation reminds you of your connection to your heritage, to the planet, and to God.

Remember Zachary, who refused to say *"Baruch atah, Adonai"*? This is one prayer he might not have objected to. A powerful element about this blessing is that it makes sense even without a belief in a hierarchical God in the sky.

Let's look at the last phrase of the *Motzi*, "who brings forth bread from the Earth." Have you ever passed a bread field or a bread orchard? Is there a God in the sky who miraculously brings forth fields of bread from the Earth?

No. Rather, this prayer is about admiring and appreciating the connectivity of the different parts of the system that create bread. What does it take to make bread? Soil, sun, rain, seeds, the intellect to grow wheat and then to mill it. Fossil fuels to power the trains and trucks for shipping, the business interactions among farmer, miller, grocer, and so on.

If you believe, as I do, that God is not an external power intervening in our lives, but rather the connectivity of all beings, then there is no better prayer than this to remind yourself of your connection to something larger than yourself every day, several times a day.

So there it is, a little bit of Judaism I promise will make your life more peaceful and more meaningful. You don't have to buy anything. You don't have to go anywhere, and you don't have to learn anything very complicated.

Judaism is filled with gems like the *Motzi* and Havdalah, beautiful rituals developed and refined over the centuries. When we make them part of our lives, when we say the words and perform the gestures that have been shared by so many people through the years and across the miles, we link ourselves to our ancestral chain as well as to Jews the world over. These rituals have been designed to enable us to transform mundane moments of our lives into holy time. Holy moments await you in every nook and cranny of your life!

CHAPTER 22

What Happens When We Die?

Now he has departed from this strange world a little ahead of me. That means nothing. People like us, who believe in physics, know that the distinction between past, present, and future is only a stubbornly persistent illusion.

ALBERT EINSTEIN

When I was six years old, I discovered death. My grandfather Sam Wolfe died of a heart attack after a day of spring skiing. Our phone rang sometime in the middle of the night while I was sleeping. My parents lifted my sister and me out of our warm beds and put us into the car, still in our pajamas, to drive the two hours to our grandparents' house in upstate New York. I can still see myself walking into my grandmother's kitchen, where she was seated at the kitchen table, head bent into her hands, sobbing.

Only a short time later, my father's uncle, Al Samisch, died in his sleep. His sister found him the next morning in his New York City apartment, in his ornately carved, turn-of-the-century bed, the heavy, velvet curtains closed, his cane hanging smartly from its hook.

A few days after that, his sister, my grandmother Sadelle Korngold, died while sitting in her neighbor's armchair drinking her favorite brand of Martinson's coffee, brewed on the stovetop in a two-cup percolator. I can still picture the red high-backed armchair where they said she died.

I refused to go to the third funeral. Even though I had discovered that graveyards made a great place to run around and play with my cousins, turning cartwheels in the grass and hiding behind headstones, I had had enough of bodies being lowered into the cold ground.

My mother arranged for me to go home after school with my teacher, Ms. Joan Altman, so I could miss the funeral and have a pause from my family's understandable focus on death. Unfortunately, at Ms. Altman's house I discovered a book about the Holocaust sitting on the side table. I had learned about the Holocaust in religious school, so I knew what it was, but the horror of the murder of six million individuals finally sunk in as I looked through the book. It was nothing but pages and pages filled by six million dots representing the six million Jewish men, women, and children who were killed by the Nazis. Six million more dead people.

Too much death, too little understanding. Too many lifeless bodies.

I became terrified of dying. A few months later, my mother was driving me home from violin lessons when the unresolved fear erupted. I don't know what set me off, but I do remember screaming, "I don't want to die! I don't want to die!"

My mother parked our yellow Pinto station wagon in front of the neighborhood pond. She wrapped me in her arms while I cried and wailed, "I don't want to die! I don't want to die!"

I can pinpoint exactly what frightened me. I didn't want to stop existing. I didn't want to not exist forever. An eternity of nonexistence seemed dreadfully long.

Somehow, my mother must have comforted me, or maybe I just grew tired out as a child will. I recall her saying, "It won't happen for a long time."

Her words must have worked on some level, because the issue abated for many years, until I arrived at rabbinical school. Here, once again, my fear of death consumed me. I read texts about afterlife. I wrote essays about it. I sought out funerals to hear what rabbis would say in their eulogies. But I was still scared.

Finally, I went for help. Frequently, new rabbis and rabbinic students have a more experienced clergyperson who serves as their pastoral supervisor. They function very much as therapists and help the newer rabbis process the pastoral turmoil of rabbinic life. However, there is one notable difference between a therapist and a pastoral supervisor. A therapist is supposed to help you figure out the right answer for yourself without giving you direct advice or instruction, but a clergyperson can tell you what to do, especially if something is morally wrong.

When my fear of death threatened to overwhelm me, I went to see my supervisor, Rabbi Julie Schwartz. She tried different methods to help me work through my panic, none of which worked. We kept going deeper and deeper into my fear and I always came back to, "I don't want to not exist forever."

Eventually, she sent me to her supervisor, Henry Marksberry. I sat with him for many months, working on different aspects of my fear. He gave me breathing exercises to do, prayers to recite, papers to read, and texts to study. He was a wealth of wisdom, but nothing worked. Finally, one day he told me simply, "When you start thinking about death, don't go there."

What I wanted from him was to hear, "Don't worry about dying. We all go to Heaven. You'll be with all the people who died before you. I know this with certainty. So stop worrying. It will all be okay." But he didn't.

I'm still terrified of dying, but as it turns out, his advice, "Don't go there," has actually been very helpful. About twice a year I still have an attack that I can't stop, but now I just call my husband on his cell phone and he says, "Don't go there." I am soothed, and that seems to work.

No matter how many texts I study, theologians I read, or eulogies I hear, I am not going to be able to convince myself about the afterlife. I am green with envy of people who do believe in it, but it does not appear that I am going to. So, my other option, "Don't go there," seems to work for me. The truth is, there are some things we just don't have the answers to.

What do I think happens when die? If we are all part of the One, then we stay part of the One. We have always been, and we will always be, part of the One, which is God.

Will we keep our individual consciousness? I don't know. I hope so. But maybe not. Is this concept strong enough to take the edge off the fear? Not really. But it is congruent with my theology, my intuition, and my intellect, and that, my friend, is all I know. Sorry to go no further, but I'm not supposed to go there.

CHAPTER 23

Judaism 2.0

The Upgrade

The idea that God is an oversized white male with a flowing beard who sits in the sky and tallies the fall of every sparrow is ludicrous. But if by "God" one means the set of physical laws that govern the universe, then clearly there is such a God. This God is emotionally unsatisfying ... it does not make much sense to pray to the law of gravity.

CARL SAGAN

Centuries ago, our patriarch, Abraham, left his homeland and his father's house to go forth and create a new religion. He needed to make a clean break from his family life and the culture in which he was raised in order to found something fresh.

Many of us have unknowingly followed Abraham's model, as we left our communities and our parents' homes to strike out and create new lives for ourselves. We live very different lives from our parents—we have different careers, concerns, priorities, and goals.

Like Abraham, we, too, tried to create a new religion. Our religion was based on technology and celebrated our secular morals. Science, we believed, would ultimately save us from ourselves, cleaning our polluted waters and skies, or maybe even whisking us off to a new planet. Doctors would banish malaria and cancer, and economists would figure out a way to finally have chicken in every pot.

But much to our horror, we have discovered that our new religion has failed to make our lives better, more peaceful, or more meaningful. Our weapons of mass destruction have made the world more dangerous, not safer. Technology has filled our oceans with oil and our air with toxins. The moral code of our society has created a culture built on dog-eat-dog competition, marketing deception, and self-aggrandizement. Even as we rejected religion, we were forced to notice what happens in societies that outlaw religion: Communist regimes in the twentieth century murdered far more people than were killed in the name of religion. There have been 100 million killings on four continents in states that reviled religion when controlled or influenced by Communism.[20]

Disillusioned, we turn back for one last look at Judaism. We crave guidance to help us order the chaos of the world around us. We yearn for wisdom from people who have navigated this path before us. We pine for comfort, familiarity, community, and family.

Even those among us who have relegated Judaism to a relic of the past have moments when in our *kishkes* (our guts) we wonder what answers Judaism might offer and what wisdom Judaism might provide. After all, isn't it telling that the old melodies from our childhood still evoke a reaction? We still light candles on Chanukah and remember the melody of the blessing and look forward to the taste of crispy latkes. For some inexplicable reason, we still ask our bosses for the day off on Yom Kippur and go to synagogue in search of meaningful connection.

Judaism has a tenacious ability to lie dormant for many years in the recesses of our memory and then suddenly move to the forefront of our consciousness. What creates the change? Perhaps we pick up a book like this, or attend a Passover Seder. Maybe we come across an article about how much Judaism has influenced our country's legal code, or hear a klezmer band (traditional eastern European music) at a concert. Whatever the spark, suddenly a portal opens and we catch a glimpse of a Judaism that is meaningful, relevant, and accessible. Here is a Judaism that does not insult our intelligence, but rather calms our spirits, excites our minds, and connects us to something larger than ourselves.

A new journey begins as we take on the challenge of exploring Judaism as adults. We try a ritual, perhaps saying the *Motzi*, and notice that the meal feels different. We wonder, "Is *this* what it is like to connect to God?" It's less dramatic than we envisioned.

We take a walk in the woods and imagine that the spiritual feelings we have there are actually a connection to God. Our internal dialogue begins: "There is no booming voice, not even the still small voice. There is no voice at all. But there is this feeling. What is this feeling? Is this God?"

We meet a friend for lunch and ask what she believes about God, and suddenly the lunch becomes a long afternoon conversation that lingers into the evening. For the first time in our lives we feel empowered to join the God conversation, to ask the question, "What is God?" Or perhaps, "When is God?" or "Where is God?"

In these pages, I have given you the tools you will need on your adventure into Judaism 2.0. I have shown you how great minds who lived long before you and I were even born began the tradition of wrestling with God and questioning Jewish practice. I have shared with you my own struggle with the God so often represented as the "Jewish God." I have spotlighted what some of the leading theologians of our day teach us about God, as they understand God. I have shown you where and how I experience God and how that enables Judaism to enrich my life.

This upgraded concept of God allows us to alter our approach to Judaism so that this ancient religion can be meaningful to us today, as we face the challenges of the twenty-first century: loneliness, information overload, and superficiality, to name a few.

The name *Israel* literally means "God wrestler."[21] Now it is your turn to wrestle with Judaism, to create your own God concept. It is your time to turn it over and over,[22] to question, to ponder, and to wonder. Let me know how it goes for you, because I love to hear new ideas for how people bring Judaism into their own life. Please, come join the conversation at www.GodUpgrade.com.

God sends Abraham from his father's home to innovate, create, and discover. God says to him, "*Lech lecha*. You! You go forth!" (Genesis 12:1). Now I say to you, "*Lech lecha*. You! You go forth!" Upgrade to an understanding of God that resounds with your experience, your intuition, and your intellect. Fashion a Jewish lifestyle that works for you. You need not abandon your modern life, sensibilities, and intellect to draw from the ancient wisdom, traditions, ritual, and spirituality of our Jewish heritage. These can and should be intertwined, enhancing one another.

One of my favorite lines in the daily morning services comes from the *Amidah* prayer: *"Kadosh, Kadosh, Kadosh Adonai tz'vaot, m'lo chol ha-aretz k'vodo.* Holy, Holy, Holy is God! The whole Earth is filled with Your glory!"

As Spinoza taught us, the whole Earth truly is filled with God's glory, and holiness abounds. God is the spray of a waterfall and the pattern of geese flying overhead. God is the buzz of bees pollinating the apple trees and the giggles of children running under a sprinkler. God is the profound conversation of two people sharing their essential truths and an impromptu group of people singing together.

As you walk along your way on this God-filled Earth, as you lie down, and as you rise up, may your connection to *this* God and to *this* Judaism inspire you, bring you comfort, and fill your life with peace.

ACKNOWLEDGMENTS

There are moments when I write when the words flow easily and artistically. But other times, I feel like a character in this Hasidic tale: A young, uneducated shepherd comes to the synagogue to pray. Not knowing the prayers of the established liturgy, he sits in the back row and sings the alphabet over and over. The men of the synagogue confront him: "Why do you disturb our prayers with your gibberish?"

The boy explains, "I do not know the prayers. But I wish to thank God for my sheep and the stream, for the warmth of the sun and the silver moon that keeps me company as I sleep. I am singing the alphabet, and surely God can put the letters in the correct order to make the prayers."

My sister, K.T. Korngold, is a far better writer than I am. In my world, it is she who took my jumble of words and set them in the correct order for you, the reader. She elevated my writing, and I am grateful for her help and her friendship.

This book is dedicated to Carol Susan Roth *z"l*, who passed away in January 2010. She was my mentor and literary agent and she drastically changed my life with one phone call, asking me to write a book. Carol, who also represented the Dalai Lama, was a woman of great vision, deep loyalty, and spiritual passion. She believed in the power of my voice to make Judaism meaningful and relevant for people who do not resonate with conventional Jewish practice. She believed in my ability to create community in a world all too often bereft of meaningful connections. I missed Carol with every page I wrote, and I miss her still.

I am grateful to Stuart M. Matlins, publisher of Jewish Lights, for his interest in my rabbinate and for asking me to write this book. Thank you for your support and guidance throughout the process. Thank you to Emily Wichland and Lauren Hill for shepherding the book through the publication process with such grace and attention to detail. Thanks to Tim Holtz for the perfect cover design and Jenn Rataj for her creative and far-reaching publicity work. Jewish Lights is an important part of the landscape of religion, and I am proud to be part of the Jewish Lights team.

Darya Porat was the editor of my first book and agreed to work on this manuscript as well. I am grateful for her continued support, editorial guidance, and confidence in my work.

I'd like to thank Annie O'Driscoll for taking care of my children as I wrote. Not only were Sadie and Ori happy and well taken care of, but also whenever I was in an intense writing frenzy, she always came into my study with a reassuring smile and a fresh glass of cool water for me to drink. Thank you for caring for them and me.

It would have been impossible to write a book like this without sincere friends who were willing to help with the project. My friends Rabbi Jessica Zimmerman and Dr. Noah Finkelstein were open with their feedback, suggestions, and quotable contributions. Rhoda Lewin read the early drafts of this book and responded with both patience and encouragement. I am grateful to my friends and rabbinic colleagues at the Oneg Conference who shared their thoughts about God on the chairlift rides and helped guide my reading selections.

Thank you to Stephen Colbert for the grammar lessons.

The Adventure Rabbi community heard each chapter of this book as I wrote it. Thank you all for your support and feedback and for enabling me to have the best rabbinic job in the world.

My parents, Bob and Carole Korngold, have been a continual wellspring of encouragement and inspiration. I hope this work brings them much to *kvell* about.

No words can properly express my love for and gratitude to my husband, Jeff Finkelstein. Without his emotional support, editorial assistance, marketing expertise, and unwavering commitment to me and this manuscript, I would never have undertaken such a project. How fortunate I am to experience such love and partnership!

APPENDIX

36 Large and Small Ways to Make Judaism Relevant
and Meaningful in Your Life, Especially If You Don't Believe
There Is a God Up in the Sky Who Can
Come Down Here and Fix Things!

1. Shul hop. Jewish practice is varied in ways both subtle and dramatic. Your town or city may offer the following types of Jewish religious services (this list is alphabetical): Conservative, Humanistic, Independent Minyan, Modern Orthodox, Reconstructionist, Reform, Renewal, Orthodox, Ultra Orthodox. Try something new. It might not be the right fit for you, but it might still be an interesting way to learn about and link you to *Am Yisrael*, the Jewish People. After the service, ask one of the regulars what it is he loves about his community.

2. If you find a community that feels like it could be a Jewish home for you, but the God talk just doesn't work for you, ask to meet with the rabbi. You might find that he or she can "translate" his or her God interpretation in a way that works for you.

3. Take a class from one of the Jewish teachers in your town. Perhaps there is a class on one of the theologians discussed in this book. Jewish Community Centers (JCCs) and universities often offer adult learning programs. Generally, you do not have to be a member to attend a synagogue's classes. (This can be a great way to get to know people, too.)

4. To supplement your in-person involvement, or if there are no suitable classes where you live, great institutions like the 92nd Street Y in New York City (www.92y.org) offer lectures and other opportunities to connect to the larger Jewish world via the Internet.

5. If you are in your twenties or thirties, see whether there is a Next Dor Rabbi (which means Next Generation Rabbi) in your town. Next Dor Rabbis create innovative programs to engage people in their twenties and thirties in the future of the Jewish community (www.nextdoronline.org).

6. Create a meaningful Sabbath for yourself. You might consider:

   - Inviting a friend to attend a synagogue service with you.
   - Having lunch with someone whom you rarely make time to visit.
   - Setting a goal, such as not complaining, not saying anything negative about anyone, or not e-mailing all day.
   - Having friends over for Sabbath dinner.
   - Spending contemplative time alone.

7. Tour the other Jewish institutions in your town and see whether any of them feel like a community you could be a part of. Google any of the following words, for example, plus your town, to see what is offered:

   - Jewish Community Center (JCC)
   - Moishe House (www.moishehouse.org)
   - Jewish Federation
   - Anti-Defamation League
   - Jewish book and film clubs
   - Jewish groups especially for women (Hadassah and Women of Reform Judaism, for example)
   - Jewish groups especially for men
   - Jewish social action groups (American Jewish World Service, for example)
   - Jewish environmental action groups (Hazon and the Coalition on the Environment and Jewish Life, for example)
   - Jewish single groups
   - Jewish outdoor groups

8. Find a group in your community—or start one—that takes over community support responsibilities from Christians on Christmas Eve, Christmas Day, and Easter in a homeless shelter, shelter for battered women, hospital clerical area, and so on.

9. Support a Jewish charity that takes care of needs in the Jewish community in your area, nationally, or internationally; support a charity in Israel; or support an organization such as American Jewish World Service that actualizes Jewish values in the world outside the Jewish community.

10. Participate in a mitzvah day at a congregation in your area.

11. Subscribe to a Jewish newspaper or magazine (hard copy or online), such as the *Forward, Moment, Zeek, Jerusalem Post, Tablet, Jerusalem Report, New York Jewish Week,* or *LA Jewish Journal,* or a local Jewish newspaper or publication.

12. Visit Israel. There are myriad tours geared around different interests.

13. Read news articles about Israel. Try to be informed about both sides of whatever is being argued. For example, today some people view the occupation of the West Bank as a violation of basic human rights. Others believe it is necessary for Israel's security. Still others view the Israeli presence as a biblical mandate.

14. Some Jewish activities require you to have certain items on hand. Consider purchasing the following (or knowing where to get them) so you can use them when you want them:

    - Candlesticks
    - White Sabbath candles (sold in most supermarkets near the matzah)
    - Matches
    - Wine or grape juice
    - Kiddush cup (a wineglass also works)
    - Challah cover (a cloth napkin also works)
    - Chanukiah (nine-branched candle holder used on Chanukah)
    - Chanukah candles
    - Kosher salt
    - Matzah meal
    - Havdalah candle (or use two regular candles and hold them so the wicks touch when burning)
    - Spice kit (you can just use a tea bag or a flower)

- Yahrtzeit candle (to light on the yearly anniversary of the death of a loved one)

15. Integrate a Jewish calendar into your regular calendar. There are free downloads for most calendars. Or, if you use a paper calendar, buy one with Jewish dates. I like the Jewish calendar supplements created by www.jewishcalendartools.com. They include information about the holiday and commentary on the Torah portion. This powerful tool was created by my seminary classmate Rabbi Dan Moskovitz.

16. Plan ahead for Jewish holidays so you can take time off when appropriate or make plans to celebrate some other way.

17. Create Jewish-only or Jewish-majority space for a dinner, a trip, or a movie so that people feel comfortable expressing themselves as Jews.

18. Invite Israeli college students studying in your community over for dinner or a holiday.

19. Learn how to say the *Motzi* and say it before you eat. To learn, visit www.GodUpgrade.com/motzi.

20. Bake traditional Jewish dishes with an elder. (This might be your grandmother, mother, or aunt, or someone you meet in the community.) Write down their recipes. (Ignore when they say, "Oh, honey, it's not exact. Just add a little of this and a touch of that." Tell them your rabbi said you need the exact measurements!)

21. Check out Jewish architecture and art in public spaces, such as Marc Chagall's windows at Lincoln Center in New York City. Often old synagogues have been converted to new uses but you can still see the beautiful architecture.

22. Listen to Jewish comedians or watch them on YouTube. Judaism has a long history of humor. After all, humor is one of the finest ways of dealing with tragedy. Jews were instrumental in the start of the cartoon and comic industry in the United States and have a disproportional presence in the comedic world.

23. Read autobiographies about Jewish people. From Ruth Bader Ginsberg to Albert Einstein, Jews have had a profound impact on our world. Twenty-two percent of the individual recipients

of Nobel Prizes between 1901 and 2009 have been Jewish, although Jews make up only approximately 0.2 percent of the world's population.[23]

24. When traveling, find and visit the Jewish community, museums, cemetery, or other sites and tour the Jewish part of town. Attend a synagogue for worship service.

25. Light candles on Friday evening. If it feels lonely, call a friend and do it together over the phone or on Skype.

26. Host a Passover Seder with a friend. If you like to cook, let your friend lead the service. If you like to lead, let him cook.

27. Seek out Jewish-themed stories, books, and films. You can learn a great deal about Jewish history, culture, and practice through our literature and films. It is also a wonderful way to connect with the language and vocabulary of the Jewish People.

28. If you have children in your life, sign them up for PJ Library (www.pjlibrary.org), an award-winning initiative of the Harold Grinspoon Foundation that mails free, quality Jewish-content books and music to children age six months to eight years. It a great way to build Jewish identity.

29. Instead of making New Year's resolutions at the beginning of the secular year (January 1), make them for the start of the Jewish New Year, Rosh Hashanah.

30. Hang Jewish art in your home.

31. Display Judaica, such as a menorah, dreidel, and shofar, around your house.

32. Hang a mezuzah on your doorway. (For instructions and the *klaf*, the prayer that goes inside, visit www.GodUpgrade.com/mezuzah.)

33. When buying gifts for Jewish people, buy Jewish books, Jewish art, menorahs, challah covers, and the like.

34. When writing a check for a charity or as a gift, give denominations of $18 ($18, $36, $54, $3,600, and so on). The Hebrew language predates the Arabic numeral system. So, since the ancient Hebrews didn't have 1, 2, 3, each letter was assigned a number value. The letter aleph = 1, bet = 2, and so on. Therefore, it is

possible to take a word and replace each letter with its numeral equivalent. The Hebrew word for life, *chai,* if converted to numbers, equals 18. Therefore, to celebrate life, Jews use the number 18 and denominations of it. By giving in denominations of $18, you link your gift to Jewish teachings, such as caring for others and celebrating with each other.

35. Learn to make matzah balls. (They are actually very easy to make, and who doesn't love a good matzah ball? My favorite recipe is at www.GodUpgrade.com/matzahball.) Perhaps you would enjoy collecting favorite Jewish recipes from family or friends and make a gift book to share.

36. Figure out who sells challah in your town and which is the best one! Make challah French toast with the leftovers. (Buy an extra loaf so there are leftovers!)

NOTES

1. Humphrey Taylor, "Most Americans Believe in God but There Is No Consensus on His/Her Gender, Form or Degree of Control Over Events," Harris Poll #60, October 16, 2003, www.harrisinteractive.com/vault/Harris-Interactive-Poll-Research-Most-Americans-Believe-in-God-but-There-Is-No-Cons-2003-10.pdf.
2. Louis Jacobs, *The Book of Jewish Belief* (West Orange, N.J.: Behrman House, 1984), pp. 16–17.
3. Cathy Grossman, "Americans' Views of God Shape Attitudes on Key Issues," *USA Today*, October 7, 2010.
4. Lisa Miller, interview by Stephen Colbert, *Colbert Report*, Comedy Central, June 3, 2010.
5. Ibid.
6. "The Inquisition," Jewish Virtual Library, www.jewishvirtuallibrary.org/jsource/History/Inquisition.html.
7. Full disclosure and claim to fame: Rob Morrow (who plays Don Eppes) and I both attended Edgemont High School.
8. Noah Finkelstein, lecture, "When Science Meets Religion: Intelligent Perspectives on Our World" (lecture, Adventure Rabbi 2009 Rosh Hashanah Retreat, September 20, 2009).
9. PRNewswire, "Science Channel and Morgan Freeman Invite Viewers to Journey through the Wormhole," May 11, 2010.
10. Morgan Freeman, interview by Jon Stewart, *The Daily Show*, Comedy Central, June 2, 2010.
11. Finkelstein, "When Science Meets Religion."
12. Spinoza, *Ethics*, part IV, appendix, para. 4, trans. in Rebecca Newberger Goldstein, *Betraying Spinoza: The Renegade Jew Who Gave Us Modernity* (New York: Schocken, 2006), p. 236.
13. Lisa Miller, "Why God Hates Haiti," *Newsweek*, January 25, 2010.
14. Ibid.
15. Harold M. Schulweis, *For Those Who Can't Believe: Overcoming the Obstacles to Faith* (New York: HarperCollins, 1994), p. 133.

16. Abraham Joshua Heschel, *Man Is Not Alone* (New York: Noonday Press, 1951), p. 98.

17. Abraham Joshua Heschel, *God in Search of Man* (New York: Noonday Press, 1955), p. 31.

18. Harold Kushner, *To Life! A Celebration of Jewish Being and Thinking* (New York: Warner Books, 1994), p. 10.

19. Harry Chapin, "Cat's in the Cradle," lyrics, www.harrychapin.com/music/cats.shtml.

20. Stéphane Courtois et al., *The Black Book of Communism: Crimes, Terror, Repression* (Cambridge, Mass.: Harvard University Press, 1999), p. 4.

21. In Genesis 32:29 Jacob wrestles with God, earning him the new name Israel, meaning "God wrestler."

22. *Perek* 5, *Mishnah* 26: "Ben Bag Bag says: Turn it [Torah] over and over, for everything is in it. See with it, grow old and gray with it, and do not budge from it, as there is no better measuring rod than it."

23. "Jewish Nobel Prize Winners," Jinfo.org, www.jinfo.org/Nobel_Prizes.html.

BIBLIOGRAPHY

WORKS CONSULTED

Angel, Marc D. *Maimonides, Spinoza and Us: Toward an Intellectually Vibrant Judaism.* Woodstock, Vt.: Jewish Lights, 2009.

Bader, Christopher, and Paul Froese. *America's Four Gods: What We Say about God— and What That Says about Us.* New York: Oxford University Press, 2010.

Borowitz, Eugene B. *Liberal Judaism.* New York: URJ Press, 1984.

———. *Renewing the Covenant: A Theology for the Postmodern Jew.* Philadelphia: Jewish Publication Society, 1991.

Buber, Martin. *I and Thou.* New York: Simon & Schuster, 1970.

Comins, Mike. *Making Prayer Real: Leading Jewish Spiritual Voices on Why Prayer Is Difficult and What to Do about It.* Woodstock, Vt.: Jewish Lights, 2010.

Courtois, Stéphane, Nicolas Werth, Jean-Louis Panné, Andrzej Paczkowski, Karel Bartošek, and Jean-Louis Margolin. *The Black Book of Communism: Crimes, Terror, Repression.* Cambridge, Mass.: Harvard University Press, 1999.

Dawkins, Richard. *The God Delusion.* Boston: Houghton Mifflin, 2006.

Feiler, Bruce. *Where God Was Born: A Journey by Land to the Roots of Religion.* New York: HarperCollins, 2005.

Gillman, Neil. *Doing Jewish Theology: God, Torah & Israel in Modern Judaism.* Woodstock, Vt.: Jewish Lights, 2008.

Goldstein, Rebecca Newberger. *Betraying Spinoza: The Renegade Jew Who Gave Us Modernity.* New York: Random House, 2006.

———. *36 Arguments for the Existence of God: A Work of Fiction.* New York: Pantheon Books, 2010.

Hawking, Stephen, and Leonard Mlodinow. *The Grand Design.* New York: Bantam Books, 2010.

Heschel, Abraham Joshua. *God in Search of Man: A Philosophy of Judaism.* New York: Farrar, Straus and Giroux, 1976.

———. *Man Is Not Alone: A Philosophy of Religion.* New York: Farrar, Straus and Giroux, 1976.

———. *The Sabbath.* New York: HarperCollins, 1951.

———. *Who Is Man?* Stanford, Calif.: Stanford University Press, 1965.

Hoffman, Lawrence A., ed. *Who by Fire, Who by Water*—Un'taneh Tokef. Woodstock, Vt.: Jewish Lights, 2010.

Jacobs, Louis. *The Book of Jewish Belief.* West Orange, N.J.: Behrman House, 1984.

———. *A Jewish Theology.* West Orange, N.J.: Behrman House, 1973.

Korngold, Jamie S. *God in the Wilderness: Rediscovering the Spirituality of the Great Outdoors with the Adventure Rabbi*. New York: Doubleday, 2008.

Kravitz, Leonard, and Kerry M. Olitzky, eds., trans. Pirke Avot: *A Modern Commentary on Jewish Ethics*. New York: UAHC Press, 1993.

Kurtz, Paul. *Science and Religion: Are They Compatible?* Amherst, N.Y.: Prometheus Books, 2003.

Kushner, Harold S. *To Life! A Celebration of Jewish Being and Thinking*. New York: Warner Books, 1994.

——. *When Bad Things Happen to Good People*. New York: HarperCollins, 1983.

——. *When Children Ask About God: A Guide for Parents Who Don't Always Have All the Answers*. New York: Schocken Books, 1976.

——. *Who Needs God*. New York: Simon & Schuster, 1989.

Maimonides. *Mishneh Torah: Hilchot Yesodei HaTorah*. Translated by Eliyahu Touger. Jerusalem: Moznaim, 1989.

Martin, James. *How Can I Find God? The Famous and Not-So-Famous Consider the Quintessential Question*. Rev. ed. Liguori, Mo.: Liguori Publications, 2004.

——. *The Jesuit Guide to (Almost) Everything: A Spirituality for Real Life*. New York: HarperCollins, 2010.

McFee, Marcia, and Karen Foster. *Spiritual Adventures in the Snow: Skiing & Snowboarding as Renewal for Your Soul*. Woodstock, Vt.: SkyLight Paths, 2009.

Miles, Jack. *God: A Biography*. New York: Knopf, 1995.

Miller, Lisa. *Heaven: Our Enduring Fascination with the Afterlife*. New York: Harper, 2010.

Nadler, Steven. *Spinoza: A Life*. New York: Cambridge University Press, 1999.

Nelson, David W. *Judaism, Physics and God: Searching for Sacred Metaphors in a Post-Einstein World*. Woodstock, Vt.: Jewish Lights, 2005.

Olson, Richard G. *Science & Religion, 1450–1900: From Copernicus to Darwin*. Baltimore: Johns Hopkins University Press, 2004.

Polish, Daniel F. *Talking about God: Exploring the Meaning of Religious Life with Kierkegaard, Buber, Tillich and Heschel*. Woodstock, Vt.: SkyLight Paths, 2007.

Schachter-Shalomi, Zalman. *Jewish with Feeling: A Guide to Meaningful Jewish Practice*. With Joel Segel. New York: Riverhead Books, 2005.

Schroeder, Gerald L. *God According to God: A Physicist Proves We've Been Wrong about God All Along*. New York: HarperCollins, 2009.

Schulweis, Harold M. *For Those Who Can't Believe: Overcoming the Obstacles to Faith*. New York: HarperCollins, 1994.

Sonsino, Rifat, and Daniel B. Syme. *Finding God: Selected Responses*. New York: UAHC Press, 2002.

——. *Finding God: Ten Jewish Responses*. New York: UAHC Press, 1986.

Stern, Chaim. *Gates of Prayer for Shabbat and Weekdays*. New York: Central Conference of American Rabbis, 1994.

——. *Gates of Repentance: The New Union Prayerbook for the Days of Awe*. New York: Central Conference of American Rabbis, 1978.

Wade, Nicholas. *The Faith Instinct: How Religion Evolved and Why It Endures*. New York: Penguin Press, 2009.

Warren, Rick. *The Purpose Driven Life: What on Earth Am I Here For?* Grand Rapids, Mich.: Zondervan, 2002.

Wolpe, David J. *Why Be Jewish?* New York: Henry Holt, 1995.

———. *Why Faith Matters.* New York: HarperCollins, 2008.

SUGGESTIONS FOR FURTHER READING

Borowitz, Eugene B., and Frances W. Schwartz. *A Touch of the Sacred: A Theologian's Informal Guide to Jewish Belief.* Woodstock, Vt.: Jewish Lights, 2007.

Cosgrove, Elliot. *Jewish Theology in Our Time: A New Generation Explores the Foundations and Future of Jewish Belief.* Woodstock, Vt.: Jewish Lights, 2010.

Dosick, Wayne D. *The Business Bible: 10 New Commandments for Bringing Spirituality & Ethical Values into the Workplace.* Woodstock, Vt.: Jewish Lights, 2000.

Gillman, Neil. *The Death of Death: Resurrection and Immortality in Jewish Thought.* Woodstock, Vt.: Jewish Lights, 1997.

———. *Traces of God: Seeing God in Torah, History and Everyday Life.* Woodstock, Vt.: Jewish Lights, 2006.

———. *The Way Into Encountering God in Judaism.* Woodstock, Vt.: Jewish Lights, 2000.

Herberg, Will. *Judaism and Modern Man: An Interpretation of Jewish Religion.* New York: Atheneum, 1951.

Hoffman, Lawrence A. *The Art of Public Prayer: Not for Clergy Only.* 2nd ed. Woodstock, Vt.: SkyLight Paths, 1999.

———. *The Way into Jewish Prayer.* Woodstock, Vt.: Jewish Lights, 2000.

Lyon, David. *God of Me: Imagining God throughout Your Lifetime.* Woodstock, Vt.: Jewish Lights, 2011.

Ross, Dennis. *God in Our Relationships: Spirituality between People from the Teachings of Martin Buber.* Woodstock, Vt.: Jewish Lights, 2003.

Schachter-Shalomi, Zalman. *First Steps to a New Jewish Spirit: Reb Zalman's Guide to Recapturing the Intimacy & Ecstasy in Your Relationship with God.* Woodstock, Vt.: Jewish Lights, 2003.

———. *A Heart Afire: Stories and Teachings of the Early Hasidic Masters.* Philadelphia: Jewish Publication Society, 2009.

Schulweis, Harold M. *Conscience: The Duty to Obey and the Duty to Disobey.* Woodstock, Vt.: Jewish Lights, 2008.

Shapiro, Rami, trans., ann. *Ethics of the Sages: Pirke Avot—Annotated & Explained.* Woodstock, Vt.: SkyLight Paths, 2006.

Sonsino, Rifat. *Six Jewish Spiritual Paths: A Rationalist Looks at Spirituality.* Woodstock, Vt.: Jewish Lights, 2000.

Steinberg, Milton. *As a Driven Leaf.* Reprint, West Orange, N.J.: Behrman House, 1996.

Strassfeld, Michael. *A Book of Life: Embracing Judaism as a Spiritual Practice.* Woodstock, Vt.: Jewish Lights, 2002.

Teutsch, David A., ed. *Kol Haneshamah: Shabbat Vehagim.* Wyncote, Pa.: Reconstructionist Press, 1994.

———. *Mahzor LeYamim Nora'im: Prayerbook for the Days of Awe.* Wyncote, Pa.: Reconstructionist Press, 1994.

Congregation Resources

Empowered Judaism: What Independent Minyanim Can Teach Us about Building Vibrant Jewish Communities
By Rabbi Elie Kaunfer; Foreword by Prof. Jonathan D. Sarna
Examines the independent minyan movement and the lessons these grassroots communities can provide. 6 x 9, 224 pp, Quality PB, 978-1-58023-412-2 **$18.99**

Spiritual Boredom: Rediscovering the Wonder of Judaism *By Dr. Erica Brown*
Breaks through the surface of spiritual boredom to find the reservoir of meaning within. 6 x 9, 208 pp, HC, 978-1-58023-405-4 **$21.99**

Building a Successful Volunteer Culture
Finding Meaning in Service in the Jewish Community
By Rabbi Charles Simon; Foreword by Shelley Lindauer; Preface by Dr. Ron Wolfson
Shows you how to develop and maintain the volunteers who are essential to the vitality of your organization and community. 6 x 9, 192 pp, Quality PB, 978-1-58023-408-5 **$16.99**

The Case for Jewish Peoplehood: Can We Be One?
By Dr. Erica Brown and Dr. Misha Galperin; Foreword by Rabbi Joseph Telushkin
6 x 9, 224 pp, HC, 978-1-58023-401-6 **$21.99**

Inspired Jewish Leadership: Practical Approaches to Building Strong Communities
By Dr. Erica Brown 6 x 9, 256 pp, HC, 978-1-58023-361-3 **$24.99**

Jewish Pastoral Care, 2nd Edition: A Practical Handbook from Traditional & Contemporary Sources *Edited by Rabbi Dayle A. Friedman, MSW, MAJCS, BCC*
6 x 9, 528 pp, Quality PB, 978-1-58023-427-6 **$30.00**

Rethinking Synagogues: A New Vocabulary for Congregational Life
By Rabbi Lawrence A. Hoffman, PhD 6 x 9, 240 pp, Quality PB, 978-1-58023-248-7 **$19.99**

The Spirituality of Welcoming: How to Transform Your Congregation into a Sacred Community *By Dr. Ron Wolfson* 6 x 9, 224 pp, Quality PB, 978-1-58023-244-9 **$19.99**

Children's Books

Around the World in One Shabbat
Jewish People Celebrate the Sabbath Together
By Durga Yael Bernhard
Takes your child on a colorful adventure to share the many ways Jewish people celebrate Shabbat around the world.
11 x 8½, 32 pp, HC, 978-1-58023-433-7 **$18.99** *For ages 3–6*

What You Will See Inside a Synagogue
By Rabbi Lawrence A. Hoffman, PhD, and Dr. Ron Wolfson; Full-color photos by Bill Aron
A colorful, fun-to-read introduction that explains the ways and whys of Jewish worship and religious life.
8½ x 10½, 32 pp, Full-color photos, Quality PB, 978-1-59473-256-0 **$8.99** *For ages 6 & up*
(A book from SkyLight Paths, Jewish Lights' sister imprint)

Because Nothing Looks Like God
By Lawrence Kushner and Karen Kushner Introduces children to the possibilities of spiritual life. 11 x 8½, 32 pp, Full-color illus., HC, 978-1-58023-092-6 **$17.99** *For ages 4 & up*

The Book of Miracles: A Young Person's Guide to Jewish Spiritual Awareness
Written and illus. by Lawrence Kushner
6 x 9, 96 pp, 2-color illus., HC, 978-1-879045-78-1 **$16.95** *For ages 9–13*

In God's Hands *By Lawrence Kushner and Gary Schmidt* 9 x 12, 32 pp, Full-color illus., HC, 978-1-58023-224-1 **$16.99** *For ages 5 & up*

In Our Image: God's First Creatures *By Nancy Sohn Swartz*
9 x 12, 32 pp, Full-color illus., HC, 978-1-879045-99-6 **$16.95** *For ages 4 & up*

The Kids' Fun Book of Jewish Time
By Emily Sper 9 x 7½, 24 pp, Full-color illus., HC, 978-1-58023-311-8 **$16.99** *For ages 3–6*

What Makes Someone a Jew? *By Lauren Seidman*
Reflects the changing face of American Judaism.
10 x 8½, 32 pp, Full-color photos, Quality PB, 978-1-58023-321-7 **$8.99** *For ages 3–6*

Holidays/Holy Days

Who by Fire, Who by Water—Un'taneh Tokef
Edited by Rabbi Lawrence A. Hoffman, PhD
Examines the prayer's theology, authorship and poetry through a set of lively essays, all written in accessible language.
6 x 9, 272 pp, HC, 978-1-58023-424-5 **$24.99**

All These Vows—Kol Nidre
Edited by Rabbi Lawrence A. Hoffman, PhD
The most memorable prayer of the Jewish New Year—what it means, why we sing it, and the secret of its magical appeal.
6 x 9, 300 pp (est), HC, 978-1-58023-430-6 **$24.99**

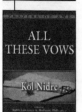

Rosh Hashanah Readings: Inspiration, Information and Contemplation
Yom Kippur Readings: Inspiration, Information and Contemplation
Edited by Rabbi Dov Peretz Elkins; Section Introductions from Arthur Green's These Are the Words
Rosh Hashanah: 6 x 9, 400 pp, Quality PB, 978-1-58023-437-5 **$19.99**; HC, 978-1-58023-239-5 **$24.99**
Yom Kippur: 6 x 9, 368 pp, Quality PB, 978-1-58023-438-2 **$19.99**; HC, 978-1-58023-271-5 **$24.99**

Jewish Holidays: A Brief Introduction for Christians
By Rabbi Kerry M. Olitzky and Rabbi Daniel Judson
5½ x 8½, 176 pp, Quality PB, 978-1-58023-302-6 **$16.99**

Reclaiming Judaism as a Spiritual Practice: Holy Days and Shabbat
By Rabbi Goldie Milgram 7 x 9, 272 pp, Quality PB, 978-1-58023-205-0 **$19.99**

Shabbat, 2nd Edition: The Family Guide to Preparing for and Celebrating the Sabbath
By Dr. Ron Wolfson 7 x 9, 320 pp, Illus., Quality PB, 978-1-58023-164-0 **$19.99**

Hanukkah, 2nd Edition: The Family Guide to Spiritual Celebration
By Dr. Ron Wolfson 7 x 9, 240 pp, Illus., Quality PB, 978-1-58023-122-0 **$18.95**

The Jewish Family Fun Book, 2nd Edition
Holiday Projects, Everyday Activities, and Travel Ideas with Jewish Themes
By Danielle Dardashti and Roni Sarig; Illus. by Avi Katz
6 x 9, 304 pp, 70+ b/w illus. & diagrams, Quality PB, 978-1-58023-333-0 **$18.99**

Passover

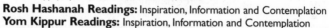

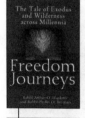

My People's Passover Haggadah
Traditional Texts, Modern Commentaries
Edited by Rabbi Lawrence A. Hoffman, PhD, and David Arnow, PhD
A diverse and exciting collection of commentaries on the traditional Passover Haggadah—in two volumes!
Vol. 1: 7 x 10, 304 pp, HC, 978-1-58023-354-5 **$24.99**
Vol. 2: 7 x 10, 320 pp, HC, 978-1-58023-346-0 **$24.99**

Freedom Journeys: The Tale of Exodus and Wilderness across Millennia
By Rabbi Arthur O. Waskow and Rabbi Phyllis O. Berman
Explores how the story of Exodus echoes in our own time, calling us to relearn and rethink the Passover story through social-justice, ecological, feminist and interfaith perspectives. 6 x 9, 288 pp, HC, 978-1-58023-445-0 **$24.99**

Leading the Passover Journey: The Seder's Meaning Revealed, the Haggadah's Story Retold By Rabbi Nathan Laufer
Uncovers the hidden meaning of the Seder's rituals and customs.
6 x 9, 224 pp, Quality PB, 978-1-58023-399-6 **$18.99**; HC, 978-1-58023-211-1 **$24.99**

Creating Lively Passover Seders, 2nd Edition: A Sourcebook of Engaging Tales, Texts & Activities By David Arnow, PhD 7 x 9, 464 pp, Quality PB, 978-1-58023-444-3 **$24.99**

Passover, 2nd Edition: The Family Guide to Spiritual Celebration
By Dr. Ron Wolfson with Joel Lurie Grishaver 7 x 9, 416 pp, Quality PB, 978-1-58023-174-9 **$19.95**

The Women's Passover Companion: Women's Reflections on the Festival of Freedom
Edited by Rabbi Sharon Cohen Anisfeld, Tara Mohr and Catherine Spector; Foreword by Paula E. Hyman
6 x 9, 352 pp, Quality PB, 978-1-58023-231-9 **$19.99**; HC, 978-1-58023-128-2 **$24.95**

The Women's Seder Sourcebook: Rituals & Readings for Use at the Passover Seder
Edited by Rabbi Sharon Cohen Anisfeld, Tara Mohr and Catherine Spector
6 x 9, 384 pp, Quality PB, 978-1-58023-232-6 **$19.99**

Life Cycle

Marriage/Parenting/Family/Aging

The New Jewish Baby Album: Creating and Celebrating the Beginning of a Spiritual Life—A Jewish Lights Companion
By the Editors at Jewish Lights; Foreword by Anita Diamant; Preface by Rabbi Sandy Eisenberg Sasso
A spiritual keepsake that will be treasured for generations. More than just a memory book, *shows you how—and why it's important*—to create a Jewish home and a Jewish life. 8 x 10, 64 pp, Deluxe Padded HC, Full-color illus., 978-1-58023-138-1 **$19.95**

The Jewish Pregnancy Book: A Resource for the Soul, Body & Mind during Pregnancy, Birth & the First Three Months *By Sandy Falk, MD, and Rabbi Daniel Judson, with Steven A. Rapp* Medical information, prayers and rituals for each stage of pregnancy. 7 x 10, 208 pp, b/w photos, Quality PB, 978-1-58023-178-7 **$16.95**

Celebrating Your New Jewish Daughter: Creating Jewish Ways to Welcome Baby Girls into the Covenant—New and Traditional Ceremonies *By Debra Nussbaum Cohen; Foreword by Rabbi Sandy Eisenberg Sasso* 6 x 9, 272 pp, Quality PB, 978-1-58023-090-2 **$18.95**

The New Jewish Baby Book, 2nd Edition: Names, Ceremonies & Customs—A Guide for Today's Families *By Anita Diamant* 6 x 9, 320 pp, Quality PB, 978-1-58023-251-7 **$19.99**

Parenting as a Spiritual Journey: Deepening Ordinary and Extraordinary Events into Sacred Occasions *By Rabbi Nancy Fuchs-Kreimer, PhD*
6 x 9, 224 pp, Quality PB, 978-1-58023-016-2 **$17.99**

Parenting Jewish Teens: A Guide for the Perplexed
By Joanne Doades Explores the questions and issues that shape the world in which today's Jewish teenagers live and offers constructive advice to parents.
6 x 9, 176 pp, Quality PB, 978-1-58023-305-7 **$16.99**

Judaism for Two: A Spiritual Guide for Strengthening and Celebrating Your Loving Relationship *By Rabbi Nancy Fuchs-Kreimer, PhD, and Rabbi Nancy H. Wiener, DMin; Foreword by Rabbi Elliot N. Dorff, PhD*
Addresses the ways Jewish teachings can enhance and strengthen committed relationships. 6 x 9, 224 pp, Quality PB, 978-1-58023-254-8 **$16.99**

The Creative Jewish Wedding Book, 2nd Edition: A Hands-On Guide to New & Old Traditions, Ceremonies & Celebrations *By Gabrielle Kaplan-Mayer*
9 x 9, 288 pp, b/w photos, Quality PB, 978-1-58023-398-9 **$19.99**

Divorce Is a Mitzvah: A Practical Guide to Finding Wholeness and Holiness When Your Marriage Dies *By Rabbi Perry Netter; Afterword by Rabbi Laura Geller*
6 x 9, 224 pp, Quality PB, 978-1-58023-172-5 **$16.95**

Embracing the Covenant: Converts to Judaism Talk About Why & How
By Rabbi Allan Berkowitz and Patti Moskovitz 6 x 9, 192 pp, Quality PB, 978-1-879045-50-7 **$16.95**

The Guide to Jewish Interfaith Family Life: An InterfaithFamily.com Handbook
Edited by Ronnie Friedland and Edmund Case
6 x 9, 384 pp, Quality PB, 978-1-58023-153-4 **$18.95**

A Heart of Wisdom: Making the Jewish Journey from Midlife through the Elder Years
Edited by Susan Berrin; Foreword by Rabbi Harold Kushner
6 x 9, 384 pp, Quality PB, 978-1-58023-051-3 **$18.95**

Introducing My Faith and My Community: The Jewish Outreach Institute Guide for the Christian in a Jewish Interfaith Relationship
By Rabbi Kerry M. Olitzky 6 x 9, 176 pp, Quality PB, 978-1-58023-192-3 **$16.99**

Making a Successful Jewish Interfaith Marriage: The Jewish Outreach Institute Guide to Opportunities, Challenges and Resources *By Rabbi Kerry M. Olitzky with Joan Peterson Littman*
6 x 9, 176 pp, Quality PB, 978-1-58023-170-1 **$16.95**

A Man's Responsibility: A Jewish Guide to Being a Son, a Partner in Marriage, a Father and a Community Leader *By Rabbi Joseph B. Meszler*
6 x 9, 192 pp, Quality PB, 978-1-58023-435-1 **$16.99**; HC, 978-1-58023-362-0 **$21.99**

So That Your Values Live On: Ethical Wills and How to Prepare Them
Edited by Rabbi Jack Riemer and Rabbi Nathaniel Stampfer
6 x 9, 272 pp, Quality PB, 978-1-879045-34-7 **$18.99**

Theology/Philosophy/The Way Into... Series

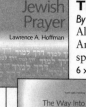

The Way Into... series offers an accessible and highly usable "guided tour" of the Jewish faith, people, history and beliefs—in total, an introduction to Judaism that will enable you to understand and interact with the sacred texts of the Jewish tradition. Each volume is written by a leading contemporary scholar and teacher, and explores one key aspect of Judaism. The Way Into... series enables all readers to achieve a real sense of Jewish cultural literacy through guided study.

The Way Into Encountering God in Judaism
By Rabbi Neil Gillman, PhD
For everyone who wants to understand how Jews have encountered God throughout history and today.
6 x 9, 240 pp, Quality PB, 978-1-58023-199-2 **$18.99**; HC, 978-1-58023-025-4 **$21.95**
Also Available: **The Jewish Approach to God:** A Brief Introduction for Christians
By Rabbi Neil Gillman, PhD
5¼ x 8¼, 192 pp, Quality PB, 978-1-58023-190-9 **$16.95**

The Way Into Jewish Mystical Tradition
By Rabbi Lawrence Kushner
Allows readers to interact directly with the sacred mystical texts of the Jewish tradition. An accessible introduction to the concepts of Jewish mysticism, their religious and spiritual significance, and how they relate to life today.
6 x 9, 224 pp, Quality PB, 978-1-58023-200-5 **$18.99**; HC, 978-1-58023-029-2 **$21.95**

The Way Into Jewish Prayer
By Rabbi Lawrence A. Hoffman, PhD
Opens the door to 3,000 years of Jewish prayer, making anyone feel at home in the Jewish way of communicating with God.
6 x 9, 208 pp, Quality PB, 978-1-58023-201-2 **$18.99**

The Way Into Jewish Prayer Teacher's Guide
By Rabbi Jennifer Ossakow Goldsmith
8½ x 11, 42 pp, PB, 978-1-58023-345-3 **$8.99**
Download a free copy at www.jewishlights.com.

The Way Into Judaism and the Environment
By Jeremy Benstein, PhD
Explores the ways in which Judaism contributes to contemporary social-environmental issues, the extent to which Judaism is part of the problem and how it can be part of the solution.
6 x 9, 288 pp, Quality PB, 978-1-58023-368-2 **$18.99**

The Way Into Tikkun Olam (Repairing the World)
By Rabbi Elliot N. Dorff, PhD
An accessible introduction to the Jewish concept of the individual's responsibility to care for others and repair the world.
6 x 9, 304 pp, Quality PB, 978-1-58023-328-6 **$18.99**

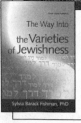

The Way Into Torah
By Rabbi Norman J. Cohen, PhD
Helps guide you in the exploration of the origins and development of Torah, explains why it should be studied and how to do it.
6 x 9, 176 pp, Quality PB, 978-1-58023-198-5 **$16.99**

The Way Into the Varieties of Jewishness
By Sylvia Barack Fishman, PhD
Explores the religious and historical understanding of what it has meant to be Jewish from ancient times to the present controversy over "Who is a Jew?"
6 x 9, 288 pp, Quality PB, 978-1-58023-367-5 **$18.99**; HC, 978-1-58023-030-8 **$24.99**

Theology/Philosophy

The God Who Hates Lies: Confronting and Rethinking Jewish Tradition
By Dr. David Hartman with Charlie Buckholtz
The world's leading Modern Orthodox Jewish theologian probes the deepest questions at the heart of what it means to be a human being and a Jew.
6 x 9, 275 pp (est), HC, 978-1-58023-455-9 **$24.99**

Jewish Theology in Our Time: A New Generation Explores the Foundations and Future of Jewish Belief *Edited by Rabbi Elliot J. Cosgrove, PhD; Foreword by Rabbi David J. Wolpe; Preface by Rabbi Carole B. Balin, PhD*
A powerful and challenging examination of what Jews can believe—by a new generation's most dynamic and innovative thinkers.
6 x 9, 240 pp, HC, 978-1-58023-413-9 **$24.99**

Maimonides, Spinoza and Us: Toward an Intellectually Vibrant Judaism
By Rabbi Marc D. Angel, PhD A challenging look at two great Jewish philosophers and what their thinking means to our understanding of God, truth, revelation and reason. 6 x 9, 224 pp, HC, 978-1-58023-411-5 **$24.99**

The Death of Death: Resurrection and Immortality in Jewish Thought
By Rabbi Neil Gillman, PhD 6 x 9, 336 pp, Quality PB, 978-1-58023-081-0 **$18.95**

Doing Jewish Theology: God, Torah & Israel in Modern Judaism *By Rabbi Neil Gillman, PhD*
6 x 9, 304 pp, Quality PB, 978-1-58023-439-9 **$18.99**

Hasidic Tales: Annotated & Explained *Translation & Annotation by Rabbi Rami Shapiro*
5½ x 8½, 240 pp, Quality PB, 978-1-893361-86-7 **$16.95***

A Heart of Many Rooms: Celebrating the Many Voices within Judaism
By Dr. David Hartman 6 x 9, 352 pp, Quality PB, 978-1-58023-156-5 **$19.95**

The Hebrew Prophets: Selections Annotated & Explained
Translation & Annotation by Rabbi Rami Shapiro; Foreword by Rabbi Zalman M. Schachter-Shalomi
5½ x 8½, 224 pp, Quality PB, 978-1-59473-037-5 **$16.99***

A Jewish Understanding of the New Testament *By Rabbi Samuel Sandmel; Preface by Rabbi David Sandmel* 5½ x 8½, 368 pp, Quality PB, 978-1-59473-048-1 **$19.99***

Jews and Judaism in the 21st Century: Human Responsibility, the Presence of God and the Future of the Covenant *Edited by Rabbi Edward Feinstein; Foreword by Paula E. Hyman*
6 x 9, 192 pp, Quality PB, 978-1-58023-374-3 **$19.99**

A Living Covenant: The Innovative Spirit in Traditional Judaism
By Dr. David Hartman 6 x 9, 368 pp, Quality PB, 978-1-58023-011-7 **$25.00**

Love and Terror in the God Encounter: The Theological Legacy of Rabbi Joseph B. Soloveitchik *By Dr. David Hartman* 6 x 9, 240 pp, Quality PB, 978-1-58023-176-3 **$19.95**

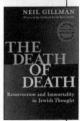

A Touch of the Sacred: A Theologian's Informal Guide to Jewish Belief
By Dr. Eugene B. Borowitz and Frances W. Schwartz
6 x 9, 256 pp, Quality PB, 978-1-58023-416-0 **$16.99**; HC, 978-1-58023-337-8 **$21.99**

Traces of God: Seeing God in Torah, History and Everyday Life *By Rabbi Neil Gillman, PhD*
6 x 9, 240 pp, Quality PB, 978-1-58023-369-9 **$16.99**

Your Word Is Fire: The Hasidic Masters on Contemplative Prayer
Edited and translated by Rabbi Arthur Green, PhD, and Barry W. Holtz
6 x 9, 160 pp, Quality PB, 978-1-879045-25-5 **$15.95**

I Am Jewish

Personal Reflections Inspired by the Last Words of Daniel Pearl

Almost 150 Jews—both famous and not—from all walks of life, from all around the world, write about many aspects of their Judaism.
Edited by Judea and Ruth Pearl 6 x 9, 304 pp, Deluxe PB w/ flaps, 978-1-58023-259-3 **$18.99**
Download a free copy of the *I Am Jewish Teacher's Guide* **at www.jewishlights.com.**

Hannah Senesh: Her Life and Diary, The First Complete Edition
By Hannah Senesh; Foreword by Marge Piercy; Preface by Eitan Senesh; Afterword by Roberta Grossman
6 x 9, 368 pp, b/w photos, Quality PB, 978-1-58023-342-2 **$19.99**

Ecology/Environment

A Wild Faith: Jewish Ways into Wilderness, Wilderness Ways into Judaism
By Rabbi Mike Comins; Foreword by Nigel Savage 6 x 9, 240 pp, Quality PB, 978-1-58023-316-3 **$16.99**

Ecology & the Jewish Spirit: Where Nature & the Sacred Meet
Edited by Ellen Bernstein 6 x 9, 288 pp, Quality PB, 978-1-58023-082-7 **$18.99**

Torah of the Earth: Exploring 4,000 Years of Ecology in Jewish Thought
Vol. 1: Biblical Israel & Rabbinic Judaism; Vol. 2: Zionism & Eco-Judaism
Edited by Rabbi Arthur Waskow Vol. 1: 6 x 9, 272 pp, Quality PB, 978-1-58023-086-5 **$19.95**
Vol. 2: 6 x 9, 336 pp, Quality PB, 978-1-58023-087-2 **$19.95**

The Way Into Judaism and the Environment *By Jeremy Benstein, PhD*
6 x 9, 288 pp, Quality PB, 978-1-58023-368-2 **$18.99**; HC, 978-1-58023-268-5 **$24.99**

Graphic Novels/History

The Adventures of Rabbi Harvey: A Graphic Novel of Jewish Wisdom and Wit in the
Wild West *By Steve Sheinkin* 6 x 9, 144 pp, Full-color illus., Quality PB, 978-1-58023-310-1 **$16.99**

Rabbi Harvey Rides Again: A Graphic Novel of Jewish Folktales Let Loose in the
Wild West *By Steve Sheinkin* 6 x 9, 144 pp, Full-color illus., Quality PB, 978-1-58023-347-7 **$16.99**

Rabbi Harvey vs. the Wisdom Kid: A Graphic Novel of Dueling
Jewish Folktales in the Wild West *By Steve Sheinkin*
Rabbi Harvey's first book-length adventure—and toughest challenge.
6 x 9, 144 pp, Full-color illus., Quality PB, 978-1-58023-422-1 **$16.99**

The Story of the Jews: A 4,000-Year Adventure—A Graphic History Book
By Stan Mack 6 x 9, 288 pp, Illus., Quality PB, 978-1-58023-155-8 **$16.99**

Grief/Healing

Facing Illness, Finding God: How Judaism Can Help You and Caregivers
Cope When Body or Spirit Fails *By Rabbi Joseph B. Meszler*
Will help you find spiritual strength for healing amid the fear, pain and chaos of
illness. 6 x 9, 208 pp, Quality PB, 978-1-58023-423-8 **$16.99**

Midrash & Medicine: Healing Body and Soul in the Jewish Interpretive
Tradition *Edited by Rabbi William Cutter, PhD; Foreword by Michele F. Prince, LCSW, MAJCS*
Explores how midrash can help you see beyond the physical aspects of healing to
tune in to your spiritual source. 6 x 9, 352 pp, HC, 978-1-58023-428-3 **$29.99**

Healing from Despair: Choosing Wholeness in a Broken World
By Rabbi Elie Kaplan Spitz with Erica Shapiro Taylor; Foreword by Abraham J. Twerski, MD
5½ x 8½, 208 pp, Quality PB, 978-1-58023-436-8 **$16.99**

Healing and the Jewish Imagination: Spiritual and Practical Perspectives on
Judaism and Health *Edited by Rabbi William Cutter, PhD*
6 x 9, 240 pp, Quality PB, 978-1-58023-373-6 **$19.99**

Grief in Our Seasons: A Mourner's Kaddish Companion *By Rabbi Kerry M. Olitzky*
4½ x 6½, 448 pp, Quality PB, 978-1-879045-55-2 **$15.95**

Healing of Soul, Healing of Body: Spiritual Leaders Unfold the Strength & Solace
in Psalms *Edited by Rabbi Simkha Y. Weintraub, LCSW*
6 x 9, 128 pp, 2-color illus. text, Quality PB, 978-1-879045-31-6 **$16.99**

Mourning & Mitzvah, 2nd Edition: A Guided Journal for Walking the Mourner's
Path through Grief to Healing *By Rabbi Anne Brener, LCSW*
7½ x 9, 304 pp, Quality PB, 978-1-58023-113-8 **$19.99**

Tears of Sorrow, Seeds of Hope, 2nd Edition: A Jewish Spiritual Companion for
Infertility and Pregnancy Loss *By Rabbi Nina Beth Cardin*
6 x 9, 208 pp, Quality PB, 978-1-58023-233-3 **$18.99**

A Time to Mourn, a Time to Comfort, 2nd Edition: A Guide to Jewish
Bereavement *By Dr. Ron Wolfson; Foreword by Rabbi David J. Wolpe*
7 x 9, 384 pp, Quality PB, 978-1-58023-253-1 **$19.99**

When a Grandparent Dies: A Kid's Own Remembering Workbook for Dealing
with Shiva and the Year Beyond *By Nechama Liss-Levinson, PhD*
8 x 10, 48 pp, 2-color text, HC, 978-1-879045-44-6 **$15.95** *For ages 7–13*

Inspiration

God of Me: Imagining God throughout Your Lifetime
By Rabbi David Lyon Helps you cut through preconceived ideas of God and dogmas that stifle your creativity when thinking about your personal relationship with God. 6 x 9, 176 pp, Quality PB, 978-1-58023-452-8 **$16.99**

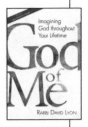

The God Upgrade: Finding Your 21st-Century Spirituality in Judaism's 5,000-Year-Old Tradition *By Rabbi Jamie Korngold; Foreword by Rabbi Harold M. Schulweis*
A provocative look at how our changing God concepts have shaped every aspect of Judaism. 6 x 9, 240 pp (est), Quality PB, 978-1-58023-443-6 **$15.99**

The Seven Questions You're Asked in Heaven: Reviewing and Renewing Your Life on Earth *By Dr. Ron Wolfson* An intriguing and entertaining resource for living a life that matters. 6 x 9, 176 pp, Quality PB, 978-1-58023-407-8 **$16.99**

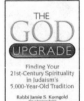

Happiness and the Human Spirit: The Spirituality of Becoming the Best You Can Be *By Rabbi Abraham J. Twerski, MD*
Shows you that true happiness is attainable once you stop looking outside yourself for the source. 6 x 9, 176 pp, Quality PB, 978-1-58023-404-7 **$16.99**; HC, 978-1-58023-343-9 **$19.99**

A Formula for Proper Living: Practical Lessons from Life and Torah
By Rabbi Abraham J. Twerski, MD 6 x 9, 144 pp, HC, 978-1-58023-402-3 **$19.99**

The Bridge to Forgiveness: Stories and Prayers for Finding God and Restoring Wholeness *By Rabbi Karyn D. Kedar* 6 x 9, 176 pp, Quality PB, 978-1-58023-451-1 **$16.99**

The Empty Chair: Finding Hope and Joy—Timeless Wisdom from a Hasidic Master, Rebbe Nachman of Breslov *Adapted by Moshe Mykoff and the Breslov Research Institute*
4 x 6, 128 pp, Deluxe PB w/ flaps, 978-1-879045-67-5 **$9.99**

The Gentle Weapon: Prayers for Everyday and Not-So-Everyday Moments— Timeless Wisdom from the Teachings of the Hasidic Master, Rebbe Nachman of Breslov *Adapted by Moshe Mykoff and S. C. Mizrahi, together with the Breslov Research Institute*
4 x 6, 144 pp, Deluxe PB w/ flaps, 978-1-58023-022-3 **$9.99**

God Whispers: Stories of the Soul, Lessons of the Heart *By Rabbi Karyn D. Kedar*
6 x 9, 176 pp, Quality PB, 978-1-58023-088-9 **$15.95**

God's To-Do List: 103 Ways to Be an Angel and Do God's Work on Earth
By Dr. Ron Wolfson 6 x 9, 144 pp, Quality PB, 978-1-58023-301-9 **$16.99**

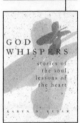

Jewish Stories from Heaven and Earth: Inspiring Tales to Nourish the Heart and Soul *Edited by Rabbi Dov Peretz Elkins* 6 x 9, 304 pp, Quality PB, 978-1-58023-363-7 **$16.99**

Life's Daily Blessings: Inspiring Reflections on Gratitude and Joy for Every Day, Based on Jewish Wisdom *By Rabbi Kerry M. Olitzky* 4½ x 6½, 368 pp, Quality PB, 978-1-58023-396-5 **$16.99**

Restful Reflections: Nighttime Inspiration to Calm the Soul, Based on Jewish Wisdom
By Rabbi Kerry M. Olitzky and Rabbi Lori Forman 4½ x 6½, 448 pp, Quality PB, 978-1-58023-091-9 **$15.95**

Sacred Intentions: Daily Inspiration to Strengthen the Spirit, Based on Jewish Wisdom
By Rabbi Kerry M. Olitzky and Rabbi Lori Forman 4½ x 6½, 448 pp, Quality PB, 978-1-58023-061-2 **$15.95**

Kabbalah/Mysticism

Jewish Mysticism and the Spiritual Life: Classical Texts, Contemporary Reflections *Edited by Dr. Lawrence Fine, Dr. Eitan Fishbane and Rabbi Or N. Rose*
Inspirational and thought-provoking materials for contemplation, discussion and action. 6 x 9, 256 pp, HC, 978-1-58023-434-4 **$24.99**

Ehyeh: A Kabbalah for Tomorrow
By Rabbi Arthur Green, PhD 6 x 9, 224 pp, Quality PB, 978-1-58023-213-5 **$18.99**

The Gift of Kabbalah: Discovering the Secrets of Heaven, Renewing Your Life on Earth
By Tamar Frankiel, PhD 6 x 9, 256 pp, Quality PB, 978-1-58023-141-1 **$16.95**

Seek My Face: A Jewish Mystical Theology *By Rabbi Arthur Green, PhD*
6 x 9, 304 pp, Quality PB, 978-1-58023-130-5 **$19.95**

Zohar: Annotated & Explained *Translation & Annotation by Dr. Daniel C. Matt; Foreword by Andrew Harvey* 5½ x 8½, 176 pp, Quality PB, 978-1-893361-51-5 **$15.99**
(A book from SkyLight Paths, Jewish Lights' sister imprint)

See also *The Way Into Jewish Mystical Tradition* in The Way Into... Series.

Meditation

Jewish Meditation Practices for Everyday Life
Awakening Your Heart, Connecting with God
By Rabbi Jeff Roth
Offers a fresh take on meditation that draws on life experience and living life with greater clarity as opposed to the traditional method of rigorous study.
6 x 9, 224 pp, Quality PB, 978-1-58023-397-2 **$18.99**

The Handbook of Jewish Meditation Practices
A Guide for Enriching the Sabbath and Other Days of Your Life
By Rabbi David A. Cooper Easy-to-learn meditation techniques.
6 x 9, 208 pp, Quality PB, 978-1-58023-102-2 **$16.95**

Discovering Jewish Meditation: Instruction & Guidance for Learning an Ancient Spiritual Practice *By Nan Fink Gefen, PhD* 6 x 9, 208 pp, Quality PB, 978-1-58023-067-4 **$16.95**

Meditation from the Heart of Judaism: Today's Teachers Share Their Practices, Techniques, and Faith *Edited by Avram Davis*
6 x 9, 256 pp, Quality PB, 978-1-58023-049-0 **$16.95**

Ritual/Sacred Practices

The Jewish Dream Book: The Key to Opening the Inner Meaning of Your Dreams *By Vanessa L. Ochs, PhD, with Elizabeth Ochs; Illus. by Kristina Swarner*
Instructions for how modern people can perform ancient Jewish dream practices and dream interpretations drawn from the Jewish wisdom tradition.
8 x 8, 128 pp, Full-color illus., Deluxe PB w/ flaps, 978-1-58023-132-9 **$16.95**

God in Your Body: Kabbalah, Mindfulness and Embodied Spiritual Practice
By Jay Michaelson
The first comprehensive treatment of the body in Jewish spiritual practice and an essential guide to the sacred.
6 x 9, 272 pp, Quality PB, 978-1-58023-304-0 **$18.99**

The Book of Jewish Sacred Practices: CLAL's Guide to Everyday & Holiday Rituals & Blessings *Edited by Rabbi Irwin Kula and Vanessa L. Ochs, PhD*
6 x 9, 368 pp, Quality PB, 978-1-58023-152-7 **$18.95**

Jewish Ritual: A Brief Introduction for Christians
By Rabbi Kerry M. Olitzky and Rabbi Daniel Judson
5½ x 8½, 144 pp, Quality PB, 978-1-58023-210-4 **$14.99**

The Rituals & Practices of a Jewish Life: A Handbook for Personal Spiritual Renewal *Edited by Rabbi Kerry M. Olitzky and Rabbi Daniel Judson*
6 x 9, 272 pp, Illus., Quality PB, 978-1-58023-169-5 **$18.95**

The Sacred Art of Lovingkindness: Preparing to Practice
By Rabbi Rami Shapiro 5½ x 8½, 176 pp, Quality PB, 978-1-59473-151-8 **$16.99**
(A book from SkyLight Paths, Jewish Lights' sister imprint)

Science Fiction/Mystery & Detective Fiction

Criminal Kabbalah: An Intriguing Anthology of Jewish Mystery & Detective Fiction *Edited by Lawrence W. Raphael; Foreword by Laurie R. King*
All-new stories from twelve of today's masters of mystery and detective fiction—sure to delight mystery buffs of all faith traditions.
6 x 9, 256 pp, Quality PB, 978-1-58023-109-1 **$16.95**

Mystery Midrash: An Anthology of Jewish Mystery & Detective Fiction
Edited by Lawrence W. Raphael; Preface by Joel Siegel
6 x 9, 304 pp, Quality PB, 978-1-58023-055-1 **$16.95**

Wandering Stars: An Anthology of Jewish Fantasy & Science Fiction
Edited by Jack Dann; Introduction by Isaac Asimov
6 x 9, 272 pp, Quality PB, 978-1-58023-005-6 **$18.99**

More Wandering Stars: An Anthology of Outstanding Stories of Jewish Fantasy and Science Fiction *Edited by Jack Dann; Introduction by Isaac Asimov*
6 x 9, 192 pp, Quality PB, 978-1-58023-063-6 **$16.95**

Spirituality/Prayer

Making Prayer Real: Leading Jewish Spiritual Voices on Why Prayer Is
Difficult and What to Do about It *By Rabbi Mike Comins*
A new and different response to the challenges of Jewish prayer, with "best prayer
practices" from Jewish spiritual leaders of all denominations.
6 x 9, 320 pp, Quality PB, 978-1-58023-417-7 **$18.99**

Witnesses to the One: The Spiritual History of the *Sh'ma*
By Rabbi Joseph B. Meszler; Foreword by Rabbi Elyse Goldstein
6 x 9, 176 pp, Quality PB, 978-1-58023-400-9 **$16.99**; HC, 978-1-58023-309-5 **$19.99**

My People's Prayer Book Series: Traditional Prayers, Modern
Commentaries *Edited by Rabbi Lawrence A. Hoffman, PhD*
Provides diverse and exciting commentary to the traditional liturgy. Will help you
find new wisdom in Jewish prayer, and bring liturgy into your life. Each book
includes Hebrew text, modern translations and commentaries from all perspectives of the Jewish world.

Vol. 1—The *Sh'ma* and Its Blessings
  7 x 10, 168 pp, HC, 978-1-879045-79-8 **$29.99**
Vol. 2—The *Amidah* 7 x 10, 240 pp, HC, 978-1-879045-80-4 **$24.95**
Vol. 3—*P'sukei D'zimrah* (Morning Psalms)
  7 x 10, 240 pp, HC, 978-1-879045-81-1 **$29.99**

Vol. 4—*Seder K'riat Hatorah* (The Torah Service)
  7 x 10, 264 pp, HC, 978-1-879045-82-8 **$29.99**
Vol. 5—*Birkhot Hashachar* (Morning Blessings)
  7 x 10, 240 pp, HC, 978-1-879045-83-5 **$24.95**
Vol. 6—*Tachanun* and Concluding Prayers
  7 x 10, 240 pp, HC, 978-1-879045-84-2 **$24.95**
Vol. 7—Shabbat at Home 7 x 10, 240 pp, HC, 978-1-879045-85-9 **$24.95**
Vol. 8—*Kabbalat Shabbat* (Welcoming Shabbat in the Synagogue)
  7 x 10, 240 pp, HC, 978-1-58023-121-3 **$24.99**
Vol. 9—Welcoming the Night: *Minchah* and *Ma'ariv* (Afternoon and
  Evening Prayer) 7 x 10, 272 pp, HC, 978-1-58023-262-3 **$24.99**
Vol. 10—Shabbat Morning: *Shacharit* and *Musaf* (Morning and
  Additional Services) 7 x 10, 240 pp, HC, 978-1-58023-240-1 **$29.99**

Spirituality/Lawrence Kushner

I'm God; You're Not: Observations on Organized Religion & Other Disguises of the Ego
  6 x 9, 256 pp, HC, 978-1-58023-441-2 **$21.99**

The Book of Letters: A Mystical Hebrew Alphabet
  Popular HC Edition, 6 x 9, 80 pp, 2-color text, 978-1-879045-00-2 **$24.95**
  Collector's Limited Edition, 9 x 12, 80 pp, gold-foil-embossed pages, w/ limited-edition silkscreened
  print, 978-1-879045-04-0 **$349.00**

The Book of Miracles: A Young Person's Guide to Jewish Spiritual Awareness
  6 x 9, 96 pp, 2-color illus., HC, 978-1-879045-78-1 **$16.95** *For ages 9–13*

The Book of Words: Talking Spiritual Life, Living Spiritual Talk
  6 x 9, 160 pp, Quality PB, 978-1-58023-020-9 **$18.99**

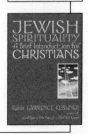

Eyes Remade for Wonder: A Lawrence Kushner Reader *Introduction by Thomas Moore*
  6 x 9, 240 pp, Quality PB, 978-1-58023-042-1 **$18.95**

God Was in This Place & I, i Did Not Know: Finding Self, Spirituality and
Ultimate Meaning 6 x 9, 192 pp, Quality PB, 978-1-879045-33-0 **$16.95**

Honey from the Rock: An Introduction to Jewish Mysticism
  6 x 9, 176 pp, Quality PB, 978-1-58023-073-5 **$16.95**

Invisible Lines of Connection: Sacred Stories of the Ordinary
  5½ x 8½, 160 pp, Quality PB, 978-1-879045-98-9 **$15.95**

Jewish Spirituality: A Brief Introduction for Christians
  5½ x 8½, 112 pp, Quality PB, 978-1-58023-150-3 **$12.95**

The River of Light: Jewish Mystical Awareness
  6 x 9, 192 pp, Quality PB, 978-1-58023-096-4 **$16.95**

The Way Into Jewish Mystical Tradition
  6 x 9, 224 pp, Quality PB, 978-1-58023-200-5 **$18.99**; HC, 978-1-58023-029-2 **$21.95**

Spirituality

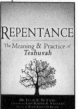

Repentance: The Meaning and Practice of *Teshuvah*
By Dr. Louis E. Newman; Foreword by Rabbi Harold M. Schulweis; Preface by Rabbi Karyn D. Kedar
Examines both the practical and philosophical dimensions of *teshuvah*, Judaism's core religious-moral teaching on repentance, and its value for us—Jews and non-Jews alike—today. 6 x 9, 256 pp, HC, 978-1-58023-426-9 **$24.99**

Tanya, the Masterpiece of Hasidic Wisdom
Selections Annotated & Explained
Translation & Annotation by Rabbi Rami Shapiro; Foreword by Rabbi Zalman M. Schachter-Shalomi
Brings the genius of *Tanya*, one of the most powerful books of Jewish wisdom, to anyone seeking to deepen their understanding of the soul.
5½ x 8½, 240 pp, Quality PB, 978-1-59473-275-1 **$16.99**
(A book from SkyLight Paths, Jewish Lights' sister imprint)

Aleph-Bet Yoga: Embodying the Hebrew Letters for Physical and Spiritual Well-Being
By Steven A. Rapp; Foreword by Tamar Frankiel, PhD, and Judy Greenfeld; Preface by Hart Lazer
7 x 10, 128 pp, b/w photos, Quality PB, Lay-flat binding, 978-1-58023-162-6 **$16.95**

A Book of Life: Embracing Judaism as a Spiritual Practice
By Rabbi Michael Strassfeld 6 x 9, 544 pp, Quality PB, 978-1-58023-247-0 **$19.99**

Bringing the Psalms to Life: How to Understand and Use the Book of Psalms
By Rabbi Daniel F. Polish, PhD 6 x 9, 208 pp, Quality PB, 978-1-58023-157-2 **$16.95**

Does the Soul Survive? A Jewish Journey to Belief in Afterlife, Past Lives & Living with Purpose *By Rabbi Elie Kaplan Spitz; Foreword by Brian L. Weiss, MD*
6 x 9, 288 pp, Quality PB, 978-1-58023-165-7 **$16.99**

First Steps to a New Jewish Spirit: Reb Zalman's Guide to Recapturing the Intimacy & Ecstasy in Your Relationship with God *By Rabbi Zalman M. Schachter-Shalomi with Donald Gropman* 6 x 9, 144 pp, Quality PB, 978-1-58023-182-4 **$16.95**

Foundations of Sephardic Spirituality: The Inner Life of Jews of the Ottoman Empire
By Rabbi Marc D. Angel, PhD 6 x 9, 224 pp, Quality PB, 978-1-58023-341-5 **$18.99**

God & the Big Bang: Discovering Harmony between Science & Spirituality
By Dr. Daniel C. Matt 6 x 9, 216 pp, Quality PB, 978-1-879045-89-7 **$16.99**

God in Our Relationships: Spirituality between People from the Teachings of Martin Buber *By Rabbi Dennis S. Ross* 5½ x 8½, 160 pp, Quality PB, 978-1-58023-147-3 **$16.95**

The Jewish Lights Spirituality Handbook: A Guide to Understanding, Exploring & Living a Spiritual Life *Edited by Stuart M. Matlins*
What exactly is "Jewish" about spirituality? How do I make it a part of my life? Fifty of today's foremost spiritual leaders share their ideas and experience with us.
6 x 9, 456 pp, Quality PB, 978-1-58023-093-3 **$19.99**

Judaism, Physics and God: Searching for Sacred Metaphors in a Post-Einstein World
By Rabbi David W. Nelson 6 x 9, 352 pp, Quality PB, inc. reader's discussion guide,
978-1-58023-306-4 **$18.99**; HC, 352 pp, 978-1-58023-252-4 **$24.99**

Meaning & Mitzvah: Daily Practices for Reclaiming Judaism through Prayer, God, Torah, Hebrew, Mitzvot and Peoplehood *By Rabbi Goldie Milgram*
7 x 9, 336 pp, Quality PB, 978-1-58023-256-2 **$19.99**

Minding the Temple of the Soul: Balancing Body, Mind, and Spirit through Traditional Jewish Prayer, Movement, and Meditation *By Tamar Frankiel, PhD, and Judy Greenfeld*
7 x 10, 184 pp, Illus., Quality PB, 978-1-879045-64-4 **$18.99**

One God Clapping: The Spiritual Path of a Zen Rabbi *By Rabbi Alan Lew with Sherril Jaffe*
5½ x 8½, 336 pp, Quality PB, 978-1-58023-115-2 **$16.95**

The Soul of the Story: Meetings with Remarkable People
By Rabbi David Zeller 6 x 9, 288 pp, HC, 978-1-58023-272-2 **$21.99**

There Is No Messiah ... and You're It: The Stunning Transformation of Judaism's Most Provocative Idea *By Rabbi Robert N. Levine, DD*
6 x 9, 192 pp, Quality PB, 978-1-58023-255-5 **$16.99**

These Are the Words: A Vocabulary of Jewish Spiritual Life
By Rabbi Arthur Green, PhD 6 x 9, 304 pp, Quality PB, 978-1-58023-107-7 **$18.95**

Social Justice

Confronting Scandal
How Jews Can Respond When Jews Do Bad Things
By Dr. Erica Brown
A framework to transform our sense of shame over reports of Jews committing crime into actions that inspire and sustain a moral culture.
6 x 9, 192 pp, HC, 978-1-58023-440-5 **$24.99**

There Shall Be No Needy
Pursuing Social Justice through Jewish Law and Tradition
By Rabbi Jill Jacobs; Foreword by Rabbi Elliot N. Dorff, PhD; Preface by Simon Greer
Confronts the most pressing issues of twenty-first-century America from a deeply Jewish perspective. 6 x 9, 288 pp, Quality PB, 978-1-58023-425-2 **$16.99**
There Shall Be No Needy Teacher's Guide 8½ x 11, 56 pp, PB, 978-1-58023-429-0 **$8.99**

Conscience
The Duty to Obey and the Duty to Disobey
By Rabbi Harold M. Schulweis
Examines the idea of conscience and the role conscience plays in our relationships to government, law, ethics, religion, human nature, God—and to each other.
6 x 9, 160 pp, Quality PB, 978-1-58023-419-1 **$16.99**; HC, 978-1-58023-375-0 **$19.99**

Judaism and Justice
The Jewish Passion to Repair the World
By Rabbi Sidney Schwarz; Foreword by Ruth Messinger
Explores the relationship between Judaism, social justice and the Jewish identity of American Jews. 6 x 9, 352 pp, Quality PB, 978-1-58023-353-8 **$19.99**

Spirituality/Women's Interest

New Jewish Feminism
Probing the Past, Forging the Future
Edited by Rabbi Elyse Goldstein; Foreword by Anita Diamant
Looks at the growth and accomplishments of Jewish feminism and what they mean for Jewish women today and tomorrow.
6 x 9, 480 pp, Quality PB, 978-1-58023-448-1 **$19.99**; HC, 978-1-58023-359-0 **$24.99**

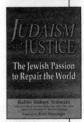

The Divine Feminine in Biblical Wisdom Literature
Selections Annotated & Explained
Translation & Annotation by Rabbi Rami Shapiro
5½ x 8½, 240 pp, Quality PB, 978-1-59473-109-9 **$16.99**
(A book from SkyLight Paths, Jewish Lights' sister imprint)

The Quotable Jewish Woman
Wisdom, Inspiration & Humor from the Mind & Heart
Edited by Elaine Bernstein Partnow
6 x 9, 496 pp, Quality PB, 978-1-58023-236-4 **$19.99**

The Women's Haftarah Commentary
New Insights from Women Rabbis on the 54 Weekly Haftarah Portions, the 5 Megillot & Special Shabbatot
Edited by Rabbi Elyse Goldstein
Illuminates the historical significance of female portrayals in the Haftarah and the Five Megillot. 6 x 9, 560 pp, Quality PB, 978-1-58023-371-2 **$19.99**

The Women's Torah Commentary
New Insights from Women Rabbis on the 54 Weekly Torah Portions
Edited by Rabbi Elyse Goldstein
Over fifty women rabbis offer inspiring insights on the Torah, in a week-by-week format.
6 x 9, 496 pp, Quality PB, 978-1-58023-370-5 **$19.99**; HC, 978-1-58023-076-6 **$34.95**

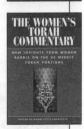

See Passover for *The Women's Passover Companion: Women's Reflections on the Festival of Freedom* and *The Women's Seder Sourcebook: Rituals & Readings for Use at the Passover Seder.*

About Jewish Lights

People of all faiths and backgrounds yearn for books that attract, engage, educate, and spiritually inspire.

Our principal goal is to stimulate thought and help all people learn about who the Jewish People are, where they come from, and what the future can be made to hold. While people of our diverse Jewish heritage are the primary audience, our books speak to people in the Christian world as well and will broaden their understanding of Judaism and the roots of their own faith.

We bring to you authors who are at the forefront of spiritual thought and experience. While each has something different to say, they all say it in a voice that you can hear.

Our books are designed to welcome you and then to engage, stimulate, and inspire. We judge our success not only by whether or not our books are beautiful and commercially successful, but by whether or not they make a difference in your life.

For your information and convenience, at the back of this book we have provided a list of other Jewish Lights books you might find interesting and useful. They cover all the categories of your life:

Bar/Bat Mitzvah	Life Cycle
Bible Study / Midrash	Meditation
Children's Books	Men's Interest
Congregation Resources	Parenting
Current Events / History	Prayer / Ritual / Sacred Practice
Ecology / Environment	Social Justice
Fiction: Mystery, Science Fiction	Spirituality
Grief / Healing	Theology / Philosophy
Holidays / Holy Days	Travel
Inspiration	Twelve Steps
Kabbalah / Mysticism / Enneagram	Women's Interest

Stuart M. Matlins, Publisher